JOHN WEBSTER

THE PERIODS OF HIS WORK AS
DETERMINED BY HIS RELATIONS
TO THE DRAMA OF HIS DAY

════════ BY ════════

ELMER EDGAR STOLL

GORDIAN PRESS, INC.
NEW YORK
1967

Originally Published 1905
Reprinted 1967 by Gordian Press, Inc.

Library of Congress Catalog Card Number: 67-21715
Printed in U.S.A. by
EDWARDS BROTHERS, INC.
Ann Arbor, Michigan

To HARRIET AGERTER STOLL

PREFACE.

THE first three chapters of this book, together with the scheme of the whole, formed my doctor's thesis at Munich in the summer of 1904. Since then, these chapters have been revised, and the remaining ones written. Some headings in the scheme, however, I have had to pass over and reserve for future treatment. They are the very interesting ones of the relationship of Webster's style — *i. e.*, the style of the *White Devil* and *Malfi* — not only to Marston's and Tourneur's, but more especially to John Donne's; and of Webster's relationship as a thinker to tendencies other than dramatic in his day.

It would have been interesting to attempt some investigation of his life. That I renounced at the start: my task was large enough without it, and a long stay in London was out of the question. But I hope that in Chapter I. I have done something in a negative way, by determining that the dramatist was not the John Webster, Clothworker, who made his will and died in 1625, nor a tailor at all.[1]

The book is merely for the Elizabethan scholar. I have not scrupled, in the footnotes, to turn for a moment to this side or to that, in order to clear up a problem in authorship or to settle a date, even though the matter did not concern Webster. I have suffered footnotes, appendices, and index of plays and authors to swell to more than half of the whole. And I have deliberately omitted to give the stories of the plays treated, or summaries of my own argument at the end of chapter or section.

Some of the references, I fear, may prove incorrect. I have verified them, in all possible cases, in the final copy; but many of the works cited were then inaccessible — beyond sea, — and, as for the rest, our old dramatists — even Bullen's — are generally printed so carelessly that one can never be sure of the numbers of act and scene.

My researches upon the source of the *White Devil* are unfinished. I was (and am still) convinced that one special book or Ms. served Webster; the rare *manet alta mente repostum* was my main clew; but, after months of travel and labor, many of the earliest and best accounts of Vittoria still eluded me.[2] The gentleman who alone has dealt with the story of Vittoria like a historian, the Prefect of the Biblioteca Vittorio Emanuele, at Rome, told me he himself had copies of all the contemporary accounts, and offered to put them at my disposal. This he never did; and a very interesting point in the relations of English and Italian literature lies, tantalizingly, still in the dark.

---

[1] There seems to be little hope for Webster. Dyce had investigated pretty thoroughly, and I myself have found no trace of him in the Register of the Merchant Taylors' School (ed. by C. J. Robinson, Lewes, 1882), where one would expect him, as born free of the Company, to have been educated.

[2] See below, p. 84 f.

It remains to mention those I have reason to thank. My wife first and most of all. Then my teachers, — Professor Brandl of Berlin and Professor Schick of Munich for bibliography, and Professors Kittredge and Baker of Harvard for criticism or information. Professor Thorndike of Northwestern University, Professor Sarrazin of Breslau, Dr. Hartmann of Munich, and Dr. Eckhardt of Freiburg i. B. have been so good as to answer the written communications of an utter stranger; and the first-named, Professor Thorndike, as the author of the *Influence of Beaumont and Fletcher on Shakspere* and of *Hamlet and the Elizabethan Revenge Plays* has, besides, shed more light on my path than any other author. The Rev. Mr. Fleay, as author of the histories of the English Drama and Stage, has put me, as every Elizabethan investigator after him, greatly in his debt. And, last of all, let me remember the many kind services of officials, both high and low, at the libraries in Berlin, Munich, Strassburg, Göttingen, Heidelberg, and Vienna, at the many libraries I visited in Italy,[1] at the Bibliothèque Nationale, and most of all at those libraries that are conducted as libraries should be, the British Museum, the Boston Public Library, and Harvard Library. Among these, let me mention only some who have been specially kind or helpful, and whose names I happen to be sure of, — Cav. Fumagalli, Director of the Library of the Brera, Milan, Mr. Kiernan of Harvard, and Mr. Chevalier of Boston; and two rare old gentlemen and scholars of Brescia, one of them Municipal Archivist, whose names I cannot quite recall, but whose courtesy, at least, was memorable.

E. E. S.

CAMBRIDGE, MASSACHUSETTS.
February, 1905.

P. S. It is a matter of pleasure and pride to add that the greater part of the proof has been read by Professor Kittredge. This is only another instance of that signal generosity by which American students of philology, young and old, have long since learned to profit. Much of my indebtedness to Professor Kittredge, being of a purely negative or corrective character, cannot well be indicated; all other indebtedness is.

I add a list of errata for the first sheets, which covers even some annoying slips in punctuation.

——

[1] See below, p. 84.

CONTENTS.

ABBREVIATIONS.

WEBSTER'S PLAYS AND POEMS.

A. & V. Appius and Virginia.

C. C. A Cure for a Cuckold.

D. L. C. The Devil's Law-Case.

Mal. The Duchess of Malfi.

Mon. Col. The Monumental Column.

Mon. Hon. Monuments of Honor.

N. H. Northward Ho.

W. D. The White Devil.

W. H. Westward Ho.

Wyatt. The Famous History of Sir Thomas Wyatt.

OTHER PLAYS AND AUTHORS.

A. & M. Antonio and Mellida.

Ant. Rev. Antonio's Revenge.

Ath. Tr. The Atheist's Tragedy.

B. & F. Beaumont and Fletcher.

Bon. Bonduca.

Bond. The Bondman.

Bussy. Bussy D'Ambois.

Bus. Rev. The Revenge of Bussy D'Ambois.

Candy. The Laws of Candy.

Chall. Beauty. A Challenge for Beauty.

Chap. Chapman.

Contention. First Part of the Contention betwixt the Two Famous Houses of Yorke and Lancaster.

Corinth. The Queen of Corinth.

Cus. Count. The Custom of the Country.

Cup. Rev. Cupid's Revenge.

D. C. The Dutch Courtesan.

Edmonton. The Witch of Edmonton.

Emp. East. The Emperor of the East.

Faith. Fr. The Faithful Friends.

Fair Maid. The Fair Maid of the Inn.

Flet. Fletcher.

Haz. Hazlitt, or Haz.'s Webster.

Hon. Man. Fort. The Honest Man's Fortune.

Hoff. Hoffman.

H. W. The Honest Whore.

Isl. Prin. The Island Princess.

K. Malta. Knight of Malta.

K. N. K. A King and No King.

L. D. Lust's Dominion.

L. F. L. Little French Lawyer.

Lovers' Prog. Lovers' Progress.

Love's Pilg. Love's Pilgrimage.

Loy. Sub. The Loyal Subject.

Love's Mist. Love's Mistress.

Luc. The Rape of Lucrece.

Malta. The Jew of Malta.

Mars. Marston.

Mass. Massinger.

Mass. Paris. The Massacre at Paris.

Match Me. Match Me in London.

M. Tr. The Maid's Tragedy.

Milan. The Duke of Milan.

Mons. Thom. Monsieur Thomas.

M. W. W. Merry Wives of Windsor.

Phil. Philaster.

Pict. The Picture.

Pilg. The Pilgrim.

P. L. The Parliament of Love.

Ren. The Renegado.

Rev. Hon. Revenge for Honor.

Rev. Tr. The Revenger's Tragedy.

Roar. Girl. The Roaring Girl.

Rule Wife. Rule a Wife and Have a Wife.

Sat. Satiromastix.

Sc. L. The Scornful Lady.

Sec. Maid. Tr. The Second Maiden's Tragedy.

Shak. Shakspere.

Shoemaker. The Shoemaker's Holiday.

Soph. Sophonisba.

Sp. Cur. The Spanish Curate.

Sp. Tr. The Spanish Tragedy.

S. R. Stationers' Register.

Thier. & Theod. Thierry and Theodoret.

Thorn. Thorndike.

T. N. K. Two Noble Kinsmen.

Tour. Tourneur.

Trag. of Rich. III. True Tragedie of Richard Third, etc.

Troublesome Raigne. Troublesome Raigne of Iohn, King of England.

True Tragedie. True Tragedie of Richard, Duke of Yorke, etc.

Valent. Valentinian.

Wife Month. A Wife for a Month.

W. or Web. Webster.

Works. Webster's Works, ed. Haz.

Registered (reg.) always means in the Stationers' Register; licensed (lic.), by the Master of the Revels. Ref. to Webster are made generally by the page. Dramatic ref. of 3 figures (e. g., 1, 2, 10) mean always act, scene, and line, except where p. (page) is prefixed to the 3rd fig. Columns are sometimes indicated after page nos. by a, b. In lists of ref. to page nos. the repetition of a number indicates two examples on the page. 2 before a play means Pt. II. Q. & F., Quarto and Folio. — Other ref. are obvious.

WORKS OFTEN CITED.[1]

ARBER, EDWARD. A Transcript of the Stationers' Register, 5 vols., London, 1875–94.

BARTLETT, J. A. A New and Complete Concordance to Shakspere, London, 1894.

BEAUMONT AND FLETCHER. Works, ed. by Darley, 2 vols., London, no date.

CHAPMAN, GEORGE. Works, ed. by R. H. Shepherd, vol. *Plays*, London, 1889.

CHETTLE, HENRY. Patient Grissel, ed. by G. Hübsch, Erlangen, 1893.

    Hoffman, ed. by R. Ackerman, Bamberg, 1894.

CUNLIFFE, J. W. Influence of Seneca on Elizabethan Tragedy, London, 1893.

DEKKER, THOMAS. Dramatic Works, 4 vols., London, 1873.

    Plays, Mermaid Ed.,[2] London, 1894.

DODSLEY, ROBERT. Old English Plays, 4th ed., edited by W. C. Hazlitt, 15 vols., London, 1874.

ECKHARDT, EDUARD. Die Lustige Person im Älteren Engl. Drama, Berlin, 1902.

FLEAY, F. G. Biographical Chronicle of the English Drama, 2 vols., London, 1891.

    History of the Stage, 1 vol., London, 1890.

GARDINER, S. R. History of England from 1603 to 1642, 10 vols., London, 1884.

GNOLI, DOMENICO. Vittoria Accoramboni, Firenze, 1890.[4]

HALLIWELL, JAMES H. Dictionary of Old English Plays, London, 1860.

HENSLOWE, PHILIP. Diary, ed. by J. P. Collier, London, 1845.

    ed. by Walter Greg, Part I, Text, London, 1904.[5]

HEYWOOD, THOMAS. Works, 6 vols., London, 1874.

    Plays,[6] Mermaid Ed., London, 1888.

ISAMBERT, TAILLANDIER, ET DECRUSY. Recueil Général des Anciennes Lois Françaises, 29 tomes, Paris, 1829.

JONSON, BEN. Works, ed. by Gifford, London, no date.

KIESOW, KARL. Die Verschiedenen Bearbeitungen der Novelle von der Herzogin v. Amalfi, Anglia Bd. 17, 198–258.

KOEPPEL, EMIL. Quellenstudien zu den Dramen Jonson's, Marston's, Beaumont's und Fletcher's, Erlangen, 1895.

    Quellenstudien zu den Dramen Chapman's, Massinger's, und Ford's, Strassburg, 1897.

KYD, THOMAS. Works, ed. by Fred. Boas, Oxford, 1901.

LANGBAINE, GERARD. Lives of English Dramatick Poets, London, 1691.

MARLOWE, CHRISTOPHER. Plays, Mermaid Ed., London, 1887.

    Works, ed. by A. H. Bullen, 3 vols., London, 1885.[7]

MASSINGER AND FORD. Works, ed. by Coleridge, London, no date.

MARSTON, JOHN. Works, ed. by A. H. Bullen, 3 vols., London, 1887.

---

[1] Other works used are cited in full in the notes.

[2] Used for all plays contained in it: *Hon. Wh., Shoemaker, Fortunatus, Edmonton.*

[3] Cited ordinarily as "Fleay," with vol. number.

[4] But really of 1867.

[5] This ed. is used unless there is statement to the contrary.

[6] Used for *Lucrece.*

[7] Used when line-numbers are cited.

MARTIN, HENRI. Histoire de France, 16 tomes, Paris, 1844 and 1858.

MEINERS, MARTIN. Metrische Untersuchungen über John Webster, Halle, 1893.

MEYER, EDWARD. Machiavelli and the English Drama, Weimar, 1897.

MICHAUD ET POUJOULAT. Collection de Mémoires, 32 tomes, Paris, 1837.

MIDDLETON, THOMAS. Works, 8 vols., ed. by A. H. Bullen, London, 1885.[1]

PAINTER, WILLIAM. Palace of Pleasure, ed. by Jacobs, 3 vols., London, 1890.

SAMPSON, MARTIN. Webster's White Devil and Duchess of Malfy, Boston, 1904.[2]

SENECAE TRAGOEDIAE. Recens. et emend. Fridericus Leo, Berolini, 1879.

SHAKSPERE, WILLIAM. Works, Globe Ed., London, 1900.

SHAKESPEARE'S LIBRARY, 2nd ed., ed. by W. C. Hazlitt, 6 vols., London, 1875.[3]

SIDNEY, SIR PHILIP. Countess of Pembroke's Arcadia, phot. reprint of 1590 Q., ed. by H. O. Sommer, London, 1891.

SMALL, R. A. Stage-Quarrel of Jonson and the So-called Poetasters, Breslau, 1899.

THORNDIKE, A. H. Influence of Beaumont and Fletcher on Shakspere, Worcester, Mass., 1901.

Hamlet and Elizabethan Revenge Plays, Pub. Mod. Lang. Ass., New Series, vol. X, no. 2, 1902.

TOURNEUR, CYRIL. Plays, Mermaid Ed., London, 1888.[4]

Plays and Poems, ed. by Collins, London, 1878.

WARD, A. W. History of English Dramatic Literature, 3 vols., London, 1899.

WEBSTER, JOHN. Works, ed. by W. C. Hazlitt, 4 vols., London, 1897.[5]

The Duchess of Malfi, Temple Ed., ed. by C. Vaughan, London, 1900.

See *Sampson*, above.

---

[1] Used instead of Dekker for *Roaring Girl.*

[2] This presents the only good texts, but it appeared too late to be used for the citations.

[3] Used for *Contention, True Tragedie of Yorke, True Tragedie of Rich. III, Troublesome Raigne, etc.*

[4] Used for the plays.

[5] Cited as "Works," or "Haz."

CHAPTER I.

CHRONOLOGY, AND THE AUTHORSHIP OF DOUBTFUL PLAYS.

IN order to understand the development of John Webster's art, it is necessary to undertake a rather extensive investigation of the dates of the composition of his plays, and, further, of the authenticity of some of the doubtful ones. Of the eleven plays still preserved to bear his name, two were first published long after Webster and his theatres were silent; and none bears the date of the acting. Of three of these, the authorship has been called in question. One of them, the *Cure for a Cuckold*, I shall seek to prove Webster's own; two, the *Thracian Wonder* and *The Weakest Goeth to the Wall*, spurious.

I. LOST PLAYS.

Of the first plays of Webster, we have the dates and nothing more. These are derived from entries in Henslowe's Diary. The first is as follows :

Lent vnto wm Jube the 3 of novmbr 1601 to bye stamell cllath for a clocke [1] for the Webster
gwisse the some of iij[ll].   P. 149.

This Collier took [2] to be the drama Webster mentions in the dedicatory letter to Sir Thomas Finch, prefixed to his *Devil's Law-Case :*

Some of my other works, as *The White Devil, The Duchess of Malfi, Guise,* and others, you have formerly seen : I present this humbly to kiss your hands and to find your allowance : nor do I much doubt it, knowing the greatest of the Cæsars have cheerfully entertained less poems than this [3] ; etc.

Such a connection as Collier supposes is in itself suspicious. Why should Webster mention the *Guise* with pride, in company with his masterpieces, if it be so early a play as to precede work so crude and colorless as his in partnership with Dekker or his Induction to the *Malcontent?* or if the "Gwisse" be only a recast of Marlowe's

---

[1] This is evidently *cloak,* for the next entry (p. 150) is to " bye fuschen and lynynge for the clockes for the masaker of france."

[2] Footnote to Henslowe (Coll.). pp. 202-3.

[3] Works. vol. III, p. 5.

Massacre at Paris (as Collier also suggests)?[1] But the main objection is in the entry itself. "*Webster*," Collier says, "is interlined, perhaps in a different hand"; but Mr. G. F. Warner says it is *forged*. Even on "internal evidence" the entry is highly suspicious: why, as Mr. Fleay suggests, should the name of the author be added to an entry that has to do with the buying of properties? But it is spurious: "there can be no doubt whatever," says Mr. Warner, "that the name was not written by the same hand as the rest of the entry; and it is equally evident that it is a spurious modern addition."[2] Now it is not cited by Dyce among the other entries in Henslowe at p. v of his introduction to the edition of 1830: it therefore did not then exist.

The "Gwisse," then, is nothing but Marlowe's *Massacre at Paris*, entered eight times[3] in Henslowe, and indifferently as "gves," "Gwies," "gwisse," "gwesse," "masaker," "massaker," "masacer," "masacar," — not Webster's *Guise*. When this last was written no one knows; but it is not improbable, as we shall yet see, that Webster in his words to Finch was writing carefully and chronologically, and that, as in his mention of them *Malfi* rightly follows the *White Devil*, the *Guise* rightly follows *Malfi*, and belongs to the period 1617–22.

Of the remaining lost plays, I have only to record a series of entries[4]:

Lent vnto the company the 22 of maij 1602 to geue vnto antoney monday & mihell drayton webester & the Rest in earneste of a Boocke called sesers ffalle the some of v^{ll}.   P. 166.

Lent vnto Thomas downton the 29 of maye 1602 to paye Thomas dickers drayton mydellton & webester & mondaye in fulle paymente for ther playe called too shapes,[5] the some of iij^{ll}.   P. 167.

Lent vnto Thomas hewode & John webster the 2 of novmbr 1602 in earneste of a playe called cryssmas comes bute once ayeare the some of iij^{ll}.[6]   P. 184.

One more dramatic work, a lost one, completes the list. In Sir Henry Herbert's office-book there is an entry under date of September, 1624:

A new Tragedy, called, *A Late Murther of the Sonn upon the Mother:* Written by Forde, and Webster.[7]

---

[1] Henslowe (Coll. ed.), p. 202, note.

[2] G. F. Warner, *Catalogue of Mss. and Muniments of Alleyn's College of God's Gift at Dulwich*, London, 1881, pp. 161-2. Cf. Greg's Henslowe, pp. xlii-iii.

[3] See the Index to Henslowe (Coll. ed.). But I give Greg's readings, pp. 15, 17, 72, 149, 150, 153, etc., twice with "of France" following, never "at Paris."

[4] Given in Haz., but I take them directly from Henslowe.

[5] Coll. reads 'too harpes.'

[6] There are also two entries recording payments to Dekker and to Chettle on the same play, the 23rd and the 26th of November, p. 185.

[7] See George Chalmers's *Supplemental Apology for Believers in the Shakspeare-Papers*, London, 1799, pp. 218-19.

II. THE MALCONTENT.

In 1604 Marston's *Malcontent* was first published. It appeared in
two editions by the same publisher; the first entirely by Marston,
the second "augmented by Marston, with additions played by the
King's Majesties Servants, written by John Webster." The play
was registered July 5th, 1604. It was in this same year that Webster's part was contributed. Reasons *why* are involved with the
question *how much* he contributed, both of which matters were best
relegated to Chapter II.

Three plays, all first printed in 1607, bear also Dekker's name, —
Sir Thomas Wyatt, Westward Ho, and *Northward Ho*. They are
Dekker's, as we shall see in Chapter II, in substance, style, and spirit;
and nothing in them would suggest that they are also Webster's. But
three title-pages of first editions are too strong to be lightly confuted,
even on evidence of a positive character; and such is wanting.

III. SIR THOMAS WYATT.

Wyatt is the earliest, certainly, of the three. The style is more
primitive (though of course Elizabethan tragedy can not be profitably
compared with comedy in this respect, being far more conventionalized and conservative); and there is earlier external evidence, that
is, in Henslowe :

Lent vnto thomas hewode the 21 of octobr 1602 to paye vnto mr deckers chettell
smythe webester & hewode in fulle payment of ther playe of ladye Jane the some of
v[ll] x[s].   P. 183.

Lent vnto John ducke the 27 of octobr 1602 to geue vnto thomas deckers in earneste
of the 2 pt of Lady Jane the some of v[s].   P. 184.

That the title should here be *Lady Jane* is not surprising : that is Henslowe's way. Marlowe's *Massacre at Paris*, as we have seen, Henslowe
calls indiscriminately "Gwisse" and "Massacre of France," and he
calls the *Spanish Tragedy* "Jeronymo"[1]; hence it is not at all surprising, especially when we remember that, as a rule, these English
historical plays were named after the king or queen at the centre of the
action (cf. Shakspere's Henries and Richards), that Henslowe should
name the play after the occupant of the throne rather than after the partisan, and principal character, Wyatt. As to a Second Part, it is difficult
to conceive of it unless it be in the present play, which contains Jane's
and her husband's death, and the "coronation of Queen Mary, and
the coming in of King Philip "; and Dyce's conjecture [2] that *Wyatt*

---

[1] See Boas, Kyd's Works, Oxford, 1901, p. xli.

[2] See Dyce's *Webster*, ed. 1857, p. xii.

is composed of fragments from the two parts may be correct. Yet the play is over small to be a consolidation of two parts, and the coronation and the "coming in of King Philip" appear only on the title-page, not in the text itself; and loose and fragmentary as the structure is, it is not more so than that of plenty of chronicle-histories. So it is quite as possible that we have here the First Part alone.[1]

IV. THE CITIZEN PLAYS.

The next play in point of time is *Westward Ho*, registered to print March 2nd, 1605. Its probable backward limit is the taking of Ostend, September 24th, 1604 [2]:

> How long will you hold out, think you? not so long as Ostend. *W. H.*, I, 1, p. 71.

> The book of the siege of Ostend, writ by one that dropped in the action, will never sell so well as a report of the siege between this grave, this wicked elder and thyself: an impression of you two would away in a May morning. IV, 2.

The interest of the English in the siege, as history shows,[3] was great, and contemporary allusions in the dramatists are numerous.[4] This first allusion proves that the play was acted at least after the length of the siege of Ostend had become proverbial; and it would fit better, of course,—as insinuating that she could not hold out forever—after Ostend had been taken. The second would seem to indicate the author's own observation, and that the 'book' was out, and the siege over.[5]

---

[1] Mr. Fleay (I, p. 130; II, 269) is of the opinion (without argument) that *Wyatt* was put together from fragments at a date considerably later than 1602. He makes the simple statement, as if the play itself indicated it: "Queen Anne had been crowned, James had come in, and the Cobham plot had been discovered in the meanwhile."—Of all this, there is no shred of evidence.

[2] Mr. Fleay (II, pp. 269–70) settles the very month and day of D.'s and W.'s parts. A story is told in III, 3 (*Just*. I'll tell thee. The term lying at Winchester in Henry the Third's days, etc.), and Mr. Fleay infers that the date of this part was summer, and the summer of 1603! He adds: "In *Northward Ho* we are told that *Westward Ho* was acted 'before Christmas,' but it was only just before." Mr. Fleay does not give a reference to the passage, but it is certainly *N. H.*, I, 2, p. 186: "and for those poor wenches that *before Christmas* fled westward with bag and baggage." It has no possible reference to *W. H.*, but is one of many references to ridding the city proper of harlots. The citizens' wives in *W. H.* were not poor wenches, nor did they flee with bag and baggage: they went on a lark. And "*westward*" by no means equals "*westward ho!*"

[3] Gardiner, *Hist. of Eng. 1603–1642*, vol. I, pp. 102, 214.

[4] Tourneur's *Ath. Tr.*: Chapman, etc.

[5] I am loath to give up what at first seemed to settle the date of *W. H.* definitely, and at the same time shed an interesting light on Dekker's journalistic methods of work,—a coincidence between the name of the Italian merchant Justiniano in the play, and the Venetian ambassador "Justiniano" (Ital. *Giustiniano* and Venet.

The date of *Northward Ho* is somewhat involved with the dates of the two other citizen comedies — *Westward Ho*, and Jonson, Chapman, and Marston's *Eastward Ho*. What was the order of these plays? *Westward Ho, Eastward Ho, Northward Ho*, answers Mr. Fleay, and, I think, rightly. *Westward Ho*, the pioneer, was written by Dekker and Webster for the Children of Paul's [1]; *Eastward Ho* was written by Jonson and the rest, in friendly, interloping rivalry, for the Children of her Majesty's Revels at Blackfriars [2]; and *Northward Ho* was the Paul's [3] rejoinder. For *Eastward Ho* contains in its prologue a reference to *Westward Ho*, not only so precise in character as not to be mistaken, but also so frankly laudatory as evidently to challenge for itself a similar success [4]; and *Northward Ho*, unmentioned

---

Giustinian) mentioned by Mr. Pory in a letter to Sir Robert Cotton, Jan., 1605 (*Court and Times of James I*, London, 1848, I, 44). He tells of the splendor of the presentation of him to the king by the outgoing ambassador, Molino. But the date 1605 is Old Style, actually is 1606 (a date which *Calendar of State Papers, Venetian*, vol. X, art. 544, confirms). Giustiniano was not appointed till Mar. 18, 1605, and did not reach London till Jan., 1606. (Cf. Borazzi e Berchet, Ven., 1863, Ser. IV, *Inghil*. p. 3 f). Yet it seems as if there must be more than chance to explain this coincidence and another, — the name of the character Candido in a drama of this very year (*H. W.*, 1604). A Signor Candido is spoken of by John Chamberlain in a letter dated Mar. 25, 1612 and again, April, 1612, to Sir Dudley Carleton (*ibid.*, pp. 164–6). He seems to be, like Carleton, in Venice, to have to do with the Bishop of Ely, and to have written a panegyric on James I. This Candido *may* have been Vincent Marine Candido, 1573–1637 (Biog. Gén.); — but I make no further progress. Yet there may have been some way for the poet of the *Roaring Girl* (Moll Cutpurse, a character of the day, see Bullen's Middleton, IV, p. 4), of Ravaillac (*If This be not a Good Play*), to learn of these names; and Justiniano may not have been the name of the character at the first performance.

[1] That *W. H.* was from the first written for Paul's — not an acquisition shortly before publication in 1607 — is proved by the registration at the Stationers', Mar. 2, 1604 : "presented by the children of Paul's."

[2] Title-page of 1605 Q.   [3] Title-page.

[4] Noted first by Dyce:

> "Not out of envy, for there's no effect
> Where there's no cause; nor out of imitation,
> For we have evermore been imitated;
> Nor out of our contention to do better
> Than that which is opposed to ours in title,
> For that was good; and better cannot be:
> And for the title, if it seem affected,
> We might as well have called it, "God you good even":
> Only that eastward westwards still exceeds,
> Honor the sun's fair rising, not his setting.
> Nor is our title utterly enforced,
> As by the points we touch at you shall see.
> Bear with our willing pains, if dull or witty,
> We only dedicate it to the city."

in the prologue, contains a satire on Chapman, who was probably the main author of *Eastward Ho*. With this, such dates as are at hand agree. *Westward Ho* was registered, as we have seen, March 2nd, 1605 ; *Eastward Ho* was registered at the Stationers' September 4th, and the authors of it, who were arrested for satire of the Scotch, found themselves in prison at least after May, 1605 [1] ; and *Northward Ho* was not registered till August 6th, 1607.

Northward Ho is, then, the last in the series. In my opinion, it is so late as to fall within the year 1606. [2] It contains (IV 4,) a passage [3] remarkably similar to Marston's *Fawn*, borrowed, I think, from it :

> *Bell.* But what say you to such young gentlemen as they are?
> *Bawd.* Foh ! they, as soon as they come to their lands, get up to London, and like squibs that run upon lines, they keep up a spitting of fire and cracking till they ha' spent all ; and when my squib is out what says his punk? foh, he stinks !
>
> *N. H.*, p. 242.

> *Herod.* . . . What, more fire-works, sir?
> *Page.* There be squibs, sir ; which squibs, running upon lines, like some of our gaudy gallants, sir, keep a smother, sir, with flishing and flashing, and, in the end, sir, they do, sir —
> *Nym.* What, sir?
> *Page.* Stink, sir.   *Fawn*, I, 2, 20 f.

The basis of these two unedifying passages is possibly, as with so many Elizabethan jokes and diatribes, a popular saying ; but there is no question, nevertheless, that in phrasing the one passage is indebted to the other. [4] Which is the original? Certainly, if coherence and continuity of texture are signs of originality (and patchwork of borrowing), it is Marston's. Only in his is the real force of the figure to be felt : it is broken and obscured by the " spent all " in Dekker and Webster. The style of his passage, moreover, is thoroughly his own, — the delight in disgusting images, the " smartness " of expression, the

---

[1] As is proved by Jonson's celebrated letter, dated 1605 (Gifford's *Jonson*, Mem., pp. 40–41). This letter, as Fleay notes, must be subsequent to May 4th, for Cecil was then first created Earl of Salisbury.—That the letter refers to *E. H.*, and is written on occasion of imprisonment for it, no one should doubt ; yet Gifford, Bullen, and Fleay all think this a subsequent imprisonment. There is no space to go into the matter here ; but the only good reason ever offered — J.'s failure to mention Mars. — is absolutely confuted by Jonson's and Chap.'s letters, discovered by Mr. B. Dobell, and pub. in *Athenaeum*, March 30th, 1901. In these complaints to the King, Lord Chamberlain, and others, neither of the authors mentions M.; and Chap. expressly says (to the King), that their offence consists "but in two clawses and both of them not our owne." Marston's, then, who had escaped.

[2] Mr. Fleay (II, 270) dates the play 1605, c. Feb. Yet he holds it the last of the plays !

[3] Pointed out in Bullen's *Marston*, Vol. II, p. 121.

[4] The figure occurs, in other form, phrasing, and application, elsewhere in Dekker, as *H. W.*, p. 219.

real *force* in both rhetorical structure and figure.[1] Yet these same qualities, lacking generally in Webster and Dekker, are perceptible even in the corresponding passage of their play. Now Marston's play was registered March 12, 1606, and published in two editions the same year, while *Northward Ho* was not registered till 1607. When, then, we consider, further, that Marston according to Anthony Wood's account 'was in great renown in 1606 for his wit and ingenuity,' and that Webster himself in his next succeeding work has two quotations from this very play,[2] it seems pretty probable that Webster and Dekker, in order to piece out the rather skimble-skamble stuff of the crazy bawd's speeches, had stolen this impudent saying from Marston.

The *Fawn* first appeared on the boards after January, 1606. It contains a reference to the execution of Sir Edward Digby and his fellows, January 30th, 1606.[3] That the play appeared in print so soon thereafter is only in keeping with what we know of its popularity : two editions appeared that same year, one of them pirated, and in the other the author himself declares, that '' it cannot avoid publishing.'' If, then, the *Fawn* is to be dated after January, 1606, *Northward Ho*

---

[1] It is unprofitable to quote examples, but any one who will read more of the *Fawn* or *D. C.*, or the Erichtho passages in *Sophon.*, will find plenty. In the *Fawn* itself: II, 1, 39-42 ; 1, 94-97 ; 1, 78-81 ; IV, 1, 545-7 ; I, 2, 221 f. Cf. *Malc.*, V, 1, 34, where ' stink-ard ' is used as synonymous with the sort of man Marston here describes.

[2] *Fawn*, IV, 1, 106, and *W. D.*, p. 15 ; *Fawn*, IV, 1, 328, and *W. D.*, p. 22 (this dubious).

[3] *Fawn*, IV, 1, 309 f : '' Nay, heed me, a woman that will thrust in crowds, — a lady, that, being with child, ventures the hope of her womb, — nay, gives two crowns for a room to behold a goodly man three parts alive quartered, his privities hackled off, his belly lanched up.'' — Mr. Bullen (*in loc.*) says it refers to Digby, and cites Stow, ed. 1631, p. 882, which runs thus : '' The next Thursday [Jan. 30th] Sir Edward Digby, Robert Winter, Graunt, and Bates were drawn, hanged, and quartered at the West End of Saint Paul's Church. . . . Friday, the last of January, in the Parliament Yard at Westminster were executed as the former, Thomas Winter, Rookewood, Keyes, and Fawkes . . . their quarters were placed over London gates, and their heads upon the Bridge.'' We must confess that we are dealing here only with probabilities ; executions — hanging and quartering — were not then uncommon. Mr. Fleay, indeed, holds a brief for that of Watson and Clarke, at Winchester, Nov., 1604 (*sic* always, though Gardiner, *Dict. Nat. Biog.*, and Stow himself, pp. 829–31, say 1603), not only in the case of the *Fawn* but also of *Michaelmas Term* (reg. May, 1607) and *Isle of Gulls* (see below). But the point in the *Fawn* and in *Michaelmas* is, that *women* came to see ; that, so great was the crowd, they paid two crowns a room ; that it was in London, and all the audience knew of it, and understood without more words. It is impossible to think that it should have been the execution at Winchester (66 miles away, whither at that day few Londoners would have gone for the show, certainly few women) of two obscure offenders ; rather than that in the heart of London itself, of the reckless devils who startled Eng. from shore to shore. If ever women went, or if ever rooms round Paul's or Parliament Yard sold high, it was at the execution of the Gunpowder Plotters.

(if it be certain that this play draws the passage from the *Fawn*) must come still later.

To reinforce this long and rather too slender thread of argument, let me join to it another. Day's *Isle of Gulls*, printed in 1606, contains, as Mr. Fleay[1] observes, a reference to all three of our plays, in a passage, which, since it deals with the author and his literary identity, cannot possibly be interpreted according to the primary[2] meaning of the phrases. It would say, this author is not any of those popular comic poets you already know : —

Prol. A meere stranger, sir?

3. A stranger! the better welcome: comes hee East-ward, West-ward, or North-ward hoe?

Prol. None of the three waies, I assure you.

1. Prethe where is he?

Prol. Not on his knees in a corner . . . but close in his studie writing hard to get him a handsome suite against Sommer.

This induction was written, very certainly, for the first performance of the play ; for it speaks anxiously of the reception of it, and of the identity, the trying position, and the needs of the author. The play must have been first performed, therefore, after the series of our three plays *Westward Ho*, *Eastward Ho*, and *Northward Ho*, which starts at the close of 1604, and yet enough before ''Sommer '' to give pathos to the author's needs. The dilemma is, whether the summer be that of 1605, or that of publication, 1606.[3] The quotation from the *Fawn*, considered above, should turn the balance in favor of the latter.

V. THE WHITE DEVIL.

The next play is the *White Devil*. It was printed without registering in 1612, and not again till 1631. To the date of the acting there are many clews.[4] One is the reference to Barnaby Rich's *New Description of Ireland*,[5] 1610, long ago pointed out by Reed but hitherto ignored as a means of settling the date :

An Irish gamester that will play himself naked and then wage all downwards at hazard, is not more venturous. *W. D.*, p. 16.

---

[1] *Biog. Chr.*, I, 105.

[2] Haz., I, p. 65: " Eastward Ho and Westward Ho were cries of the Thames Watermen," etc.

[3] That the *Isle of Gulls* should be thought to contain an allusion to an execution (that is, in the quibble of the Induction on " quarter ourselves "), whether Watson and Clarke's or any other, is absurd.

[4] The earliest and most certain are the echoes from *Lear*. See Chap. III. *Lear* was acted on St. Stephen's Day, 1606, and first printed in 1608.

[5] *A new description of Ireland wherein is described the disposition whereunto they are inclined.* Printed for T. Adams, London, 1610.

There is there a certain brotherhood, called by the name of Karrowes, and these be common gamesters, that do only exercise playing at cards, and they will play away their mantels and their shirts from their backs and when they have got nothing left them they will trusse themselves in straw. This is the life they lead, and from this they will not be reclaimed. *New Description*, p. 38.

Another passage, in Brachiano's angry words to Vittoria :

> What! dost weep?
> Procure but ten of thy dissembling trade,
> Ye 'd furnish all the Irish funerals
> With howling past wild Irish

may have been suggested by the description, at p. 12 in the same book, of the demeanor of Irish women at funerals.[1] At all events, this book was registered April 10th, 1610.

Another clew is an echo from the *Atheist's Tragedy* (registered September 14th, 1611) to be found in the celebrated trial-scene:

> *Monticelso :* Away with her,
> Take her hence.
> *Vittoria.* A rape! a rape!
> *Mont.* How?
> *Vit.* Yes, you have ravish'd justice ;
> Forc'd her to do your pleasure. *W. D.*, p. 65.

> *Sebastian.* A rape, a rape, a rape!
> *Belforest.* How now!
> *D'Amville.* What's that?
> *Sebas.* Why what is 't but a rape to force a wench, etc. *Ath.Tr.*, p. 263.

In both cases it is an abrupt cry, unexpected and startling, against unjust force ; in both cases, a tropical expression that has to be explained by the speaker. It is very likely, then, that the one was imitated from the other. That one was Webster's ; for, if borrowed through print, Tourneur's was the earlier ; and if through public rendering, Tourneur's was by far the more prominent and noticeable. The utterance in Webster is without consequence, and is not again alluded to ; that in Tourneur, on the other hand, is the cause of the breach between Sebastian and his father, etc., and is alluded to explicitly twice afterwards.[2] Now the *Atheist's Tragedy* comes later, at least, than *King Lear*, and dates in all probability not long before its publication.[3]

But the most significant evidence is that of the preface and the postscript.[4] Here Webster's mood is evidently like Jonson's in his

---

[1] Neither of these passages could have been suggested by Rich's *Short Survey of Ireland*, 1609 (reg. 1609).

[2] III, 2, p. 293, and II, 3, p. 273.

[3] In 1611. See App. I for the date of this play.

[4] See *Works*, II, p. 143.

prefaces (though more from neglect than from antagonism), and like Jonson he publishes to right himself. He defends himself for taking so much time to write the play, — a rather pointless thing to do if it were already long before this on the stage ; and he alludes to the first performance, twice over, in both preface and postscript, as if it was fresh in his memory. The first time, he assails the ''auditory,'' and the second, he praises and thanks the actors, one of them especially and by name. This he would hardly have done, or cared to do, long after the performance. For why open an old wound? Why recall his own or others' forgotten vexations? Let me quote from the preface and postscript themselves :

In publishing this Tragedy, I doe but challenge to myselfe that liberty which other men have tane before mee ; not that I affect praise by it, for, nos haec nouimus esse nihil, onely, since it was acted in so dull a time of Winter, presented in so open and blacke a theater, that it wanted (that which is the onely grace and setting-out of a tragedy) a full and understanding Auditory ; and since that time I haue noted, most of the people that come to that play-house resemble those ignorant asses (who, visiting stationers' shoppes, their use is not to inquire for good books, but new books), I present it to the generall view with this confidence :

> Nec rhoncos metues maligniorum,
> Nec scombris tunicas dabis molestas.

If it be objected this is no true drammaticke poem, I shall easily confesse it, non potes in nugas dicere plura meas, ipse ego quam dixi ; willingly, and not ignorantly, in this kind haue I faulted : For should a man present to such an auditory, the most sententious tragedy that euer was written, obseruing all the critticall lawes as heighth of stile, and grauity of person, inrich it with the sententious CHORUS, and, as it were, lifen Death, in the passionate and waighty *Nuntius:* yet after all this diuine rapture, O dura messorum Ilia, the breath that comes from the uncapable multitude is able to poison it . . .

To those who report I was a long time in finishing this tragedy, I confesse I do not write with a goose-quill winged with two feathers ; and if they will neede make it my fault, I must answer them with that of Euripides . . .

Detraction is the sworne friend to ignorance : for mine owne part, I haue euer truly cherisht my good opinion of other mens worthy labours, especially of that full and haightned stile of maister CHAPMAN, the labor'd and understanding workes of maister Johnson, the no lesse worthy composures of the both worthily excellent maister Beaumont and maister Fletcher ; and lastly (without wrong last to be named), the right happy and copious industry of m. Shake-speare, m. Decker, and m. Heywood, wishing what I write may be read by their light : protesting that, in the strength of mine owne judgment, I know them so worthy, that though I rest silent in my own worke, yet to most of theirs I dare (without flattery) fix that of Martial,

> — *non norunt Haec monumenta mori.*   *Works*, II, pp. 6-8.

For the action of the Play, 'twas generally well, and I dare affirm, with the joint-testimony of some of their own quality (for the true imitation of life, without striving to make nature a monster) the best that ever became them : whereof as I make a general acknowledgment, so in particular I must remember the well approved industry of my friend Master Perkins, and confess the worth of his action did crown both the beginning and end.   *Ib.*, p. 143.

The nettled spirit and the circumstantiality of these passages seem to me to prove they are not long after the event. Details of phrasing confirm this; for there is evidence that before setting at this his first preface Webster looked round for models. He took, piecemeal, the seventeen-word Latin passage above from Dekker's preface — *Ad Detractorem* — to *Satiromastix*,[1] the final "non norunt haec" from Dekker's preface to his *Knight's Conjuring*,[2] and several phrases and ideas from Jonson's prefaces to *Sejanus* (1605) and to *Catiline* (1611). This last correspondence —

. . . I crave *leave to stand near your light, and by that to be read. Posterity* may pay your benefit the honour and thanks, when it shall know that you dare, in these jig-given times, to countenance a *legitimate poem*.[3] —

might, indeed, be explained away, were it not for the indubitable imitation of the other prefaces, namely, Dekker's, and Jonson's to *Sejanus*.[4]

Finally, at the close of the Epistle Dedicatorie to *If this be not a Good Play*, addressed in this same year of 1612 "to my loving and loved friends and fellowes, the Queenes Maiesties seruants," Dekker says :

I wish a *Faire* and *Fortunate Day* to your *Next New-Play* for the *Makers-sake* and your *Owne*, because such *Braue Triumphes* of *Poesie*, and *Elaborate Industry*, which my *Worthy Friends Muse* hath there set forth, deserue a *Theater* full of very *Muses* themselues to be *Spectators*. To that *Faire Day* I wish a *Full, Free* and *Knowing Auditor*, etc.   *Works*, Vol. III, p. 262.

This play must be the *White Devil*. Fleay, who first noticed the passage (I, p. 134), says the *Devil's Law-Case;* but that play was certainly not written (as I show below) till 1621–3. Anyway, it would not fit. Dekker is interested, it would seem, in a maiden effort. That the *White Devil* is ; and, besides, a " brave Triumph of Poesie," and brought forth by "elaborate Industry," and played, as the title-page of the 1612 Quarto informs us, by the Queen's Servants. Moreover, the fact that Dekker and Webster, after the preceding years of partnership, were now, in 1612, after several changes of company, both writing for the Queen's Men, would argue a great and lasting friend-

---

[1] Non potes in Nugas dicere plura meas,
Ipse ego quam dixi. — Qui se mirantur, in illos
Virus habe : nos haec nouimus esse nihil.

[2] *A Knight's Conjuring* (1607?) ; it is the same, word for word, and, as with W., closes the pref.

[3] Prefatory Letter to Pembroke.

[4] The paragraph beginning "If it be objected," etc., for instance, is fairly a plagiarism of the second paragraph of Jonson's address "To the Reader," prefixed to *Sejanus*.

ship between master and pupil.   With this, Webster's mention of him
by name in the preface is in perfect accord ; and I am even inclined to
think the Latin line appended to Francisco's speech, at the end of the
third act of the *White Devil* (after even the couplet, observe), due,
like the seventeen-word Latin motto from *Satiromastix* and the " non
norunt " from *A Knight's Conjuring*, to their friendly and intimate
relations, and borrowed from the title-page of this very play of
Dekker's.[1]   However that be, it must be the *White Devil* that
Dekker's Epistle Dedicatorie means.[2]

The allusions in the *White Devil* to Barnaby Rich, to the *Atheist's
Tragedy*, and to Jonson's *Catiline*, and the nettled tone of Webster
in his preface, all point, then, to a date shortly preceding its publication, not earlier at any rate than 1611 ; and Dekker's solicitous words
in his Epistle Dedicatorie, still more precisely, to the beginning of
1612.[3]

VI.   THE DUCHESS OF MALFI.

The *Duchess of Malfi* was first printed in 1623.[4]   It must have been
on the stage, as Dyce pointed out, long before, — at least as early as
March 16th, 1619, the date of the death of Richard Burbage, who
appears in the actors' list of the first edition.   Further back than this
both Fleay and Dyce[5] have tried to thrust the date, but without success.

Mr. C. Vaughan, however, in his edition of the play, has offered,
" with great diffidence," a suggestion which leads, in my opinion, to
a definite fixing of the date :

In the opening speeches there is plainly a historical allusion ; and probably to
contemporary events . . . the reference may be to the assassination of Concini,
Maréchal d'Ancre, by order of the young king, Louis XIII.   Concini was bitterly

---

[1] Flectere si nequeo Superos, Acheronta movebo.   In W. it has little connection
with the context : in D. it fits his title. — *If this be not a good Play, the Diuell is
in it.*

[2] The antecedent probability is great.   If D. and W. were still friendly, as their
changes together from Paul's to the Queen's, Web.'s *W. D.* preface, and the borrowings indicate, in whose work should the kindly disposed D. be more interested than
in the first unaided effort of his old protégé?   And who more likely than D. to have
seen the text before the acting?

[3] Fleay says " the cold winter of 1607-8," on the strength of the remark in the
Preface, and of a connection he discovers between the jousting French ambassador
of the play and M. Goterant, who tilted the 24th of March, 1607.

[4] It is not in the S. R.

[5] Dyce sets the date at a venture c. 1616.   Fleay (II, 273) says Dyce is "utterly
wrong : the date of production was c. 1612, when the *White Devil*, with the praise
of the King's men's poets, was published."— What Mr. Fleay means — Mr. Ward
says he does not know what Mr. Fleay means — is the praise Webster bestows upon
the King's Men's poets, Shak., Beau., and Flet., etc., in the preface.   Now *Malfi*, we
know, was acted by the King's Men — *that* is the basis of Mr. Fleay's inference.

hated ; and his murder was skillfully represented as an act of justice against a public enemy and a traitor. Luines, who advised the king in the matter and succeeded to the power of Concini, made a parade of calling the old councillors of Henry IV back to court. . . . If the suggestion be well founded — but it is offered with great diffidence — we should be able to fix the date of the play more closely, to 1617-18.

Temple Ed. of Malfi, p. 146.

This conjecture let me try to base and establish. First of all, consider in the text of the first edition,[1] instead of the very uncertain one of Hazlitt, the two speeches in question :

> *Delio:* How doe you like the French court?
> *Ant:* I admire it,
> In seeking to reduce both State and People
> To a fix'd Order, there iuditious King
> Begins at home : Quits first his Royall Pallace
> Of flattring Sicophants of dissolute,
> And infamous persons which he sweetly termes
> His Master's Master-peece (the worke of Heauen)
> Considring duely, that a Princes Court
> Is like a common Fountaine, whence should flow,
> Pure siluer-droppes in generall : But if 't chance
> Some curs'd example poyson't neere the head,
> " Death, and diseases through the whole land spread.
> And what is 't makes this blessed gouernment,
> But a most prouident Councell, who dare freely
> Informe him the corruption of the times?
> Though some oth' Court hold it presumption
> To instruct Princes what they ought to doe,
> It is a noble duety to informe them
> What they ought to foresee.   *Malfi*, I, 1, first speeches.

There is one clumsy, obscure passage, but it means, no doubt, that the work of cleansing the palace was not his work but that of God through him.

In order to explain the political allusion of the above passage, we have, I suppose, to accept one of four alternatives : the allusion might have been taken from the source of the play itself, Painter's novel ; or it might be an addition of Webster's own, historically in keeping with the story ; or a mere product of the fancy, put in for filling ; or an allusion to contemporary affairs. ·As for the first, Painter contains nothing of this, except the allusion, several times, to Antonio's having been in France ; there is no mention of a French king and court.[2] As to the second, that Webster should have had in mind the French court of Antonio's day, whether that of Lewis XII or Francis I, is out of the question : Webster generally, as the instances of the

---

[1] Brit. Mus. Q.

[2] There are indeed two bare mentions of King Lewis [XII] (Painter, vol. III, pp. 4 and 8) by name : " In the time of King Lewis XII," " returned to King Lewis."

Devil's Law-Case or *Appius and Virginia* show, does not stickle for
chronology, and indeed in this very play, by his truly Elizabethan
handling, has got Bandello's chronology into such a state that it would
be impossible to allude intelligibly, without mentioning them by
name, to any king or court of France historically in keeping.[1] Had
he meant such, moreover, he must certainly have named them for the
audience' sake. As for the third alternative, that it is a purely fanciful and random statement is highly improbable, unlike Webster and
his time. True, there are plays of the pastoral or romantic type
which deal with kings, courts, and people in a land of nowhere, —
not in France, though, but in Pannonia, Dacia, Africa, or Sicilia ; —
but always in full, as the scene of the very improbable action, not, as
here, in a passing allusion, directed *away* from the scene of action.
Passing allusions when without definite names or dates (that is, jokes,
satirical remarks, political judgments, etc.) prove, even in Roman
plays, almost always to be anachronistic, to be directed toward contemporary affairs. For, by the Elizabethan dramaturgy characters,
even ideas, language, customs, and civilization, were generally conceived and represented, not with a historic sense, but — be the time or
scene of action never so far removed — really as coeval, Elizabethan ;
hence, the insertion of allusions to contemporary affairs and events
did not jar. *King Lear*,[2] *Othello*, *Romeo and Juliet*, Heywood's
Rape of Lucrece, Webster's *Appius and Virginia*, ancient stories
though they be, contain such : others would not have been understood. And in the case of *Malfi* (we take up the last alternative) an
allusion to the French king and court, standing at the very beginning
of the play, with nothing in the shape of title, scene of action, or preceding time-references to make the audience think otherwise, could
not, if it fit at all, mean to the audience, or be intended to mean to
it, anything else than the contemporary French king and court.

Does it fit? Let me repeat the story of the D'Ancre affair in brief,
and then consider Webster's words in detail. Mary de' Medici, as
queen regent since the assassination of her consort Henry IV, in

---

[1] It must, according to Bandello, have been King Lewis's court (see footnote,
p. 23) that Antonio saw. Yet in III, 3, 8 Lannoy is spoken of as having taken " the
French king prisoner," which must have been Francis I at Pavia. As Kiesow says
(pp. 243-4), the date of action has been brought down a decade. Moreover, on p. 160,
in his reference to Gaston de Foix's recovery of Naples in 1501, W., through a care-
less treatment of his original, as Sampson (p. 386) observes, is making him take a
city at 12 years old.

[2] The "late eclipses " in *Lear*, I, 2, 112; "hands not hearts " in *Othello*, III, 4, 46;
the earthquake in *R. & J.*, I, 3, 23; countless ones in *Lucrece ;* and some in Corbulo's
and the Lictor's talk — such as "prayer book," "lawyers and term time," "the
suburbs," the oath Appius took as knight, etc., — in *A. & V.*

24

1610, had, through her own incapacity and by the baneful influence of the rapacious, tyrannical Concini and his wife, speedily brought France back into a state of anarchy and misery. The nobles were indignant and disaffected, and the people heavily burdened and in want. The young king, Lewis XIII, moreover, chafed at the condescension and insolence of the Concini, and at the insignificance of his position ; and, incited by his friends, he resolved to assert himself. When all was ready, on the morning of April 14th, 1617,[1] a certain captain of the guard, Baron de Vitri, arrested Concini as he was entering the Louvre ; and, as the official report averred, on a show of resistance, shot him dead. Immediately, a demonstration was made by the King's friends, a proclamation issued announcing the King's assumption of power into his own hands, and a Council summoned of his father's ministers. The Concini faction was either arrested, or expelled from office and the city ; the Queen Mother herself, relegated to Blois. Now the Council sat daily ; virtuous, sober proclamations were issued ; and an Assembly of Notables was called to Rouen, to accomplish what the States-general under Concini had utterly failed to do. Everywhere in Paris and through France the news of the event was heard with joy, and young Lewis was hailed by his people as the Just.[2]

> *In seeking to reduce both State, and People*
> *To a fix'd Order, there iuditious King*
> *Begins at home : Quits first his Royall Pallace*
> *Of flattring Sicophants, etc.*

This is what Louis did : such was the state of his realm. The last States-general rife with dissension and fruitless in outcome,[3] a people everywhere clamorous, an insurrection raging in the south, and a palace swarming with 'sicophants,' 'dissolute,' 'infamous' Italians and Spaniards, — such a spectacle meant neither to French nor to English eyes a 'fix'd order.' And one of the first steps Lewis took to better it was to *purge* the palace, — to imprison Barbin, Mangot,[4] La Place, Oquincourt, Nardy, Concini's wife and some of his confidants[5], and

---

[1] Brockh us, 14th ed., art. *Ancre;* Martin says (ed. 1844), vol. XII, p. 345, the *24th*, and *Biog. Gén.* (ed. 1855), the same. Brock. must be right, for the first entry in the S. R. (see below, p. 29, note) is on the 17th.

[2] Martin, ed. 1858, tome XI, pp. 118–19. Bazin, *France sous Louis XIII*, Paris, 1840, t. II, p. 2 f. There is nothing ambiguous in the attitude of all France. "Chacun vantait le coup d'essai de Louis."

[3] Gardiner, II, p. 315; Martin, ed. 1858, XI, 86; and Louis's own words in his Declaration qui convoque à Rouen une assemblée de Notables, Isambert et Decrusy, Recueil Général, t. XVI, p. 108 f : "n'avaient produit autre fruit sinon que les remonstrances, plaints, et doléances." [4] Martin, ed. 1858, tome XI, pp. 117–18·

[5] *Relation Exacte de Tout ce qui s'est Passé à la Mort du Mareschal D'Ancre* in Michaud et Poujoulat, Série II, t. V, p. 464. Martin says Mangot was *déstitué* only.

to have proclaimed that evening, at the sound of the trumpet, that all those in the service of Concini should leave the city on pain of death. The Spanish Ambassador he directed to refrain from acting further as 'major-domo to the reigning queen.'[1] The Queen herself, one of the worst of the crew, he kept, after the loss of her greatest *sicophant*, under surveillance, and shortly relegated to Blois.[2] And in one of his first proclamations he made known 'that he had besought the queen, his lady and mother, to grant that he himself from now on take in hand the manage of the state, in order that he might rescue it from the straits to which the evil counsels she had followed had reduced it.'[3]

> *Which he sweetly termes*
> *His Master's Master-peece (the worke of Heauen).*

The source of this notion of Webster's is, I think, the French King's *Letter to the Parliament of Rouan*, in 1617 [4]:

A disseigne which they so wrought and effected, that hitherto Wee carried but onely the bare Name of, and title of a King : . . . *Which God of his infinite bountie giving Us the grace at last to discerne, and pointing out unto Us as it were with his omnipotent finger*, the imminent perill that hung over our person and State, through such an insatiable and irregular ambition ; Wee gave testimonie at length of our apprehension at this point, . . . yet were Wee enforced in all our exterior actions, to disguise and cover that, which inwardly in heart Wee determined and resolved upon, while it might please the same *our good God to open us a fit way, and convenient opportunity to apply thereunto some prevalent remedy.* . . . Moved I say, by these just and most weightie considerations and by the *heavenly instinct, that God upon this occasion put into our heart :* Wee resolved to secure Our self of the person of the said Marshall D'Ancre, giving express charge to Sieur de Vitry, Captaine of Our Guards, to apprehend and arrest him within Our Castle of the Louvre. The which Our pleasure hee intending to put into execution, the said Marshall (who according to his accustomed manner had many followers about him) himself with some others of his company made offer to resist : whereupon certain bullets, etc. [5]

---

[1] *Relation Exacte*, p. 470.

[2] See her despicable conduct in Martin above. And see Martin, ed. 1844 (I quote this because ed. 1858 has since become inaccessible to me), XII, 345, note, where account is taken of the popular opinion of illicit relations between her and Concini. In fact, there is quite enough in the fame of the queen and her minions in that day, both in France and in England, to warrant W.'s phrases, "dissolute and infamous persons," "curs 't example."

[3] Martin, ed. 1858, t. XI, p. 119, "les mauvais conseils dont elle s'etait servie."

[4] In the Brit. Mus., marked 8050, bbb. 56, Reg. Apr. 23rd, 1617, — a proof of the popular interest in Eng. — The italics in this passage are mine.

[5] The interpretation thus offered for "Which . . . Heauen" above — that the cleansing of the palace, etc., was God's work through him — seems to me the more certain as I consider other interpretations. Vaughan, who did not take his own suggestion seriously, thinks the antecedent of *which* to be *Pallace!* And Sampson (p. 385) : "possibly 'order,' but probably 'persons,' *i. e.*, man, being the chief work of the creator." That is, this king, whoever he be, "sweetly termes" these "infamous persons" he is chasing away, his Master's Masterpieces! The neatness with

And what is 't makes this blessed gouernment,
But a most prouident Councell, who dare freely
Informe him the corruption of the times?

On his first appearance, immediately after the murder, the King cried, Loué soit Dieu, me voylà Roy: qu'on m'aille querir les vieux serviteurs du feu Roy mon pere, et anciens conseillers de mon conseil d'Estat. C'est par le conseil de ceux-là que je me veux gouverner desormais.[1] He was as good as his word. Villeroi, Jeannin, du Vair, de Silleri and his son were summoned; the Concini faction, except Richelieu, were expelled; and the Council sat daily.[2] The King met with them, and is recorded as having given judicious and worthy opinions.[3] When appealed to by his subjects about important measures, he constantly deferred all promises till he should have deliberated with his council.[4] And on the 4th of October, 1617, he issued an edict[5] convoking an Assembly of Notables at Rouen, of 59 members only, — not a States-general but a '' council,'' rather, — ' a body selected and small enough,' according to his words, ' to be wieldy and practical, which should consider the reformation of the abuses which are to be found in all the orders of the realm' : and he solemnly adjures them all, by the authority God has given him over them, que sans autres respect ni considération quelquonque, crainte ou désir de plaire ou complaire à personne, ils nous donnent en toutes franchise et sincérité les conseils qu'ils jugeront en leurs consciences les plus salutaires et convenables. As for English reports, in *A True Recital of Those Things That Have Been Done in the Court of France since the Death of Marshall D'Ancre*, London, 1617,[6] the King is reported as saying, '' that he would give order to his Councill that the abuses that had crept into his affairs should be remedied by good advice and counsell.''[7] And in *A True Relation of the Deserved Death of the Marquis d'Ancre*, etc., 1617,[8] a full account, quite similar to the French, is given of the summoning of the Council and of the recall of Villeroi.

The allusion fits, then, — fits as well as the vague language addressed to an audience which understands, and describing in a few lines, not events, but mere sober effects and conditions, would permit. Now it

---

which K. Lewis XIII's words fit the passage when we construe it as, to make sense, it must be construed — which referring to the clause '' Quits . . . persons '' — is to my mind cogent argument that W. here had them in mind.

[1] Relation Exacte, Mich. et Pou., V, p. 458.

[2] Relation Exacte, pp. 466, 467, 469, 470, 471, 472 : often two or three times a day.

[3] Relation Exacte, pp. 466, 467.

[4] Relation Exacte, pp. 462 a, 462 b.

[5] In Isambert et Decrusy, t. XVI, p. 108 f.

[6] Registered May 8th.

[7] Pp. 11, 12.

[8] P. 14, Brit. Mus. copy.

could fit no other possible king or court of France, and no other period than shortly after April, 1617. Before that, as far back as the death of Henry IV, in 1610, there was no king in power, and no state of affairs an Englishman would "admire." And by a year after April, 1617, it would have been evident that Lewis XIII had only fallen into the hands of another set of minions.[1] But within the year the court and king of France would seem, especially so far away as in England, as Webster describes them. Lewis was beginning with such promise : he had put an end to the rebellion in the south, and had made peace between Savoy and Spain[2]; himself freed from Spanish control, he was now busied with measures of justice, and schemes of legislation and improvement ; he bore as yet the title of the Just. The allusion can be to no other than him.

But did England feel like France ? What warrant for our finding admiration of Lewis in Webster is there in what we know of the English attitude ? "The cry of exultation which was raised in France," says Mr. Gardiner,[3] "was echoed in all Protestant lands. The Queen-Mother had always been regarded as the chief supporter of the Spanish party. Even James was carried away by the tide, and for once found himself giving expression to opinions in complete accordance with those of Winwood and Raleigh. . . . James wrote to congratulate the young sovereign of France." And the interest of the people is attested by the activity of the press. A dozen or more of pamphlets relating to the affair, bearing the date of 1617, are still preserved in the British Museum[4]; and there are seven entries of books in the Stationers' Register, from the 17th of April to the 3rd of June, 1617, three of which are of books not to be identified with any of those pre-

---

[1] After the abrupt dissolution of the Assemblée at Rouen, in the spring and summer of 1618, when the duplicity, tyranny, and rapacity of Luynes came to light, and the king broke his promises (Martin, ed. 1844, XII, 364-7). Whereas (XII, 353, 359) "Le gouvernement de Louis XIII avait tout propice au début"; "les premiers temps du gouvernement . . . furent cependant assez prospères."

[2] Signed at Pavia, Oct. 9th, 1617. Bazin, *Louis XIII*, t. II, p. 37. Cf. Martin, ed. 1844, XII, p. 359, where the good effect, at home and abroad, of Lewis's conduct in this connection is discussed. [3] Gardiner, III, p. 109.

[4] Ten bound together, marked 8050. bbb. 56. Besides those already cited : 1. *The True Relation of the Deserved Death of that Base and Insolent Tryant, The Marquis d'Ancre, the most unworthie Marshall of France*, etc. 2. *Oration made unto the French King by Deputies of the National Synode of the Reformed Church.* 3. *Last Will and Testament of the Marquis*, etc. 4. *Arraignment of Marquis*, etc. 5. *Funeral Obsequies and Buriall of the Marquis*, etc. 6. *The Ghost of the Marquisse D'Ancre . . . and Mosequin a deluding spirit by whome her husband was misled.* Another, of the same date, is *The Tears of the Marshall D'Ancre's Wife, shed for the death of her husband.* — This "*True Relation*" (the first entered in S. R., see below) gives a very circumstantial account of all events, including the purging of the palace.

28

served. The entries themselves indicate the keenest popular interest, for the first of them are entered only three or four days after the event itself; and the titles betray naively the animus of the writers and of their public.[1] Even the stage responded, for, on June 22nd 1617, the Privy Council wrote to Sir George Buc, Master of the Revels, "to have special care that an enterlude concerning the late Marquis D'Ancre should not be performed."[2]

The evidence, then, is pretty conclusive that *Malfi* alludes to Lewis XIII, at a time not long after the assassination of Concini; and itself, therefore, falls within the year 1617, after April. To this let me add, however, yet one argument.[3] Orazio Busino, chaplain to Pietro Contarini, Venetian Ambassador, left among his manuscripts, now preserved in the Library of St. Mark,[4] one entitled *Anglipotrida*, a miscellaneous collection of notes on his experiences in England. In the 'second appendix' there is this:

Prendono giuoco gli Inglesi della nostra religione come di cosa detestabile, et superstitiosa, ne mai rappresentano qualsivoglia attione pubblica, sia pura Tragisati-ricomica, che non inserischino dentro uitij, et scelleragini di q^{a}lche religioso catol-ico, facendone risate, et molti scherni, con lor gusto, et ramarico de' buoni, fu appunto veduto dai nostri, in una Commedia introdur' un frate franciscano, astuto, et ripieno di varie impietà, così d'avaritia come di libidine; et il tutto poi riuscì in una Tragedia, facendoli mozzar la vista in scena. Un altra volta rappresentarono la grandezza d'un card.^{le} con li habiti formali, et proprij molti belli, et ricchi, con la sua Corte, facendo in scena erger un Altare, dove finse di far orat.^{ne}, ordinando una processione; et poi lo ridussero in pubblico con una Meretrice in seno. Dimostrò di dar il Velleno ad una sua sorella, per interesse d'honore; et d'andar in oltre alla guerra, con deppner prima l'habito cardinalitio sopra l'altare col mezzo de' suoi Cappell.^{ni} con gravità, et finalm.^{nte} si fece cingere la spada, metter la serpa,[5] con tanto garbo, che niente più; et tutto ciò fanno in sprezzo, delle grandezze ecclesiast.^{ice} vili-pese, et odiate a morte in q^{e}sto Regno.   Di Londra a' 7 feb.^{aio} 1618.

---

[1] The first entries are actually Apr. 17th, *A True Relation of the Death of the Marquis D'Ancre*, and Apr. 23rd. The first, on the third day after, indicates a journalistic enterprise almost unbelievable of that day. The entries and pamphlets all of one accord approve the deed.

[2] Fleay, *Hist. Stage*, p. 309. Mr. Fleay adds, "no doubt *Thierry and Theodoret*." There is much doubt, though. Cf. Thorndike's *Influence of B. & F. on Shak.*, p. 75 f. And I would add to his arguments that the name *de Vitri* occurs as that of a character in Chap.'s *Trag. of Byron*, pub. 1608; and that the *Conspiracy of Byron*, pub. at the same time, contains an astrologer and astrology, as do others of Chap.'s plays.

[3] A writer in the *Quarterly Rev.* for 1859, in his review of a translation of Busino's journals and despatches by Rawdon Brown ("not published" then, and so far as I can discover at the Brit. Mus. still not pub.), adds in a note that Busino describes a play in 1618 that must be *Malfi*. Ward repeats this, III, p. 59.

[4] Cl. VII. Cod. M. C. XXII.

[5] *Serpa* it is, very distinctly written. No suitable meaning is to be found in any dictionary that has come to my notice. Nor have Venetians whom I have asked been able to explain it. It must mean *sciarpa*, which is the Italian for *scarf*, *mili-*

Busino does not say he himself saw the play; and if he did, it is not likely that he understood much of it. The movements on the stage are what impressed him and what he describes. With this in mind, nothing could seem to fit Busino's description better than *Malfi*. In Act II, sc. 4, Webster's Cardinal appears with his mistress Julia alone,[1] and very likely with her in his lap: and in Act III, sc. 4, he goes through all the ceremony of laying aside ecclesiastical vestments, with the assistance of 'churchmen,' and of accoutring himself with 'sword,' shield, and spurs. His making show of giving poison to his sister in the interest of her honor (if it means that) might be the banishment of the duchess in dumb-show, in the same scene,[2] as it appeared to an Italian spectator; and the erection of the altar and the prayer might easily be some of the "business" introduced in one of several scenes in the play, as at the beginning of Act II, sc. 2, he himself reappearing immediately after with Julia in his lap. True, the evidence is not conclusive; though *Malfi* fits the description far better than any other known play, the real play may not have come down to us. But the date of that play, at any rate, harmonizes admirably with that which we had already attained for *Malfi* — the latter half of the year 1617.[3]

VII. THE DEVIL'S LAW-CASE.

The *Devil's Law-Case* was published in 1623, again without registering at the Stationers'. Fleay[4] comes at the date 1610 by adding Romelio's 38 years of age to the year of his birth[5] (the year after Lepanto, *i. e.*, 1572); and by drawing conclusions to the same effect from the waiting-woman's asseverations — though she is lying! — as to her remembering two great frosts, three great plagues, and the

---

tary scarf. This in the Venetian dialect takes the form *siarpa* or *sierpa.* See Boerio, *Diz. del dialetto Venez.*, Venezia, 1856. This meaning suits the text admirably. It was suggested by Dr. Hartmann.

[1] Also in V, 2.

[2] This and the investiture, observe, are linked together in Busino's account.

[3] The date of this account (see above) is Feb. 7, 1618. Busino says (see above) *un altra volta*, as if some time ago. The embassy started, according to his *Relazione del Viaggio*, Sept. 2nd, 1617; and his first letter from London he dates Oct. 8th, 1617. — The work of Mr. Sampson on the dates of the plays *W. D.* and *Mal.* seems rather fruitless, particularly in view of his conclusion that the date of the publishing of *W. D.* (1612) may be the date of the composition of *Mal.*, and his doubt whether *Mal.* may not have preceded *W. D.!* (xliv). And think of settling the date of *W. D.* by allusions to Ariosto so uncertain as on p. 187 (cf. xl), or by an allusion to Verton's mulberry-planting, in 1609, which amounts to the word *silkworm* (pp. 188 and xl)!

[4] *Biog. Chr.*, II, 272-3.   [5] *D. L. C.*, IV, 2 (not II, 4, as Fleay says), pp. 87, 93, 95.

taking of Calais. As if the date of the action had to be coincident with that of the first performance ; or as if Webster's audiences, or he himself, sat and counted up time-references !

More to the point is the allusion, found by Dyce, to the Massacre of Amboyna, Feb., 1623 [1]:

> *Sec. Surg.* How? go to the East Indies ! and so many Hollanders gone to fetch sauce for their pickled herrings ! some have been peppered there too lately.
>
> *D. L. C.*, p. 80.

Yet the connection is impossible, for it is now known, as Mr. Fleay [2] points out, that the news of the massacre did not reach England until May, 1624. But Dyce's scent was, as usual, true ; he rightly recognized an allusion to contemporary affairs, and he could have verified it, had he only turned back a little, to the earlier troubles between the English and Dutch in the East Indies. Such verification is to be found, I think, in Gardiner :

> In August [1619] the ' Star ' arrived from England bringing news of the opening of negotiations in London. As no treaty had been signed at the date of its depart-ure, the Dutch seized the vessel, and despatched six ships to Sumatra to look out for English traders. On the coast they found four of the Company's vessels busily engaged in lading *pepper*. The captain of one of these, the ' Bear,' had met Sir Thomas Roe at the Cape on his return from India. It happened that a new Dutch admiral also had been there on his outward voyage, with whom Roe had opened communications, which had ended in an agreement that hostilities should be sus-pended till the result of the negotiations in London could be known. In the sudden-ness of the attack this agreement was either not produced, or was disregarded. One of the English ships, the ' Dragon,' was forced to surrender, after a combat of an hour's duration, and the other three were too much encumbered with their lading even to attempt a defence. The prisoners were treated with the greatest inhumanity, and many of the wounded died from exposure to the rain upon the open deck. Amongst the prizes on board, the Dutch sailors found a handsome knife, which had been sent out as a present from the King to the native sovereign of Acheen. They carried it about the deck in uproarious procession, shouting out at the top of their voices, "Thou hast lost thy dagger, Jemmy." A few days later two other English vessels were taken at Patani, and the captain of one of them was killed.
>
> Vol. III, pp. 180-1.

This, you see, was no insignificant event ; it must have excited public interest ; and the pun on " pepper " [3] would have been, then as now, inevitable. Now the news of Amboyna reached England, as we have seen, after a year and three months ; that of the treaty signed June 2nd, 1619, reached the East Indies on March 8th of the following year [4]: so, allowing the same interval, we may reckon the backward limit of the *Devil's Law-Case* to be the end of 1620.

---

[1] Dyce says wrongly, 1622.   [2] *Biog. Chr.*, II, 272 : cf. Gardiner, vol. V, p. 242.
[3] That the verb " pepper " was then commonly thus used is proved by *1 Hen. IV*, II, 4, 212 ; V, 3, 37 ; *R. & J.*, III, 1. 102 ; *Hoff.*, 1. 1473 ; Mass. *Virg. Mart.*, p. 18 ; *Hum. Lieut.*, p. 238 ; etc.   [4] Gardiner, Vol. III, p. 181.

31

Should the date be rather thrust on, however, nearer the forward limit? Such a question is to be raised in connection with the possible indebtedness of the *Devil's Law-Case* to the *Spanish Curate*,[1] or to the *Fair Maid of the Inn*. The last is entirely to be excluded from consideration by reason of explicit mention of the Massacre of Amboyna,[2] and its having ·been licensed (though written, of course, earlier)[3] only in 1626.[4] And as for the *Spanish Curate* and the *Devil's Law-Case*, they may very well have been produced independently, deriving the law-case story, their only point of contact, the one only from *Gerardo*, and the other from the old play, *Lust's Dominion;* or the *Devil's Law-Case* itself may have influenced the *Spanish Curate*.[5] However that be, it is to be considered improbable that the *Devil's Law-Case* followed the *Spanish Curate*, by reason of two considerations: first, the lack of any reference to Dutch or East India troubles in the *Spanish Curate*, and the presence of so pointed a reference — "lately" — in the *Devil's Law-Case;* second, the nature of the vicissitudes of the Queen's Men. As to the latter point, Webster's play, according to the title-page, was "approvedly well Acted by her Majesties Servants." Now Queen Anne died in March, 1619, and there were no real Queen's Servants again till the time of Henrietta, June, 1625.[6] Still hanging together, however, on the 8th of July, 1622, they obtained a Privy Seal for a new company to be called the "Children of the Revels."[7] In the meantime they had continued to act at the Red Bull[8]; but under what name? Under the old one of Queen's Servants, of course, until they received the patent for the new one.[9] It must have been *before* that, therefore, that they acted the *Devil's Law-Case*.[10] The date of the play must be from the end of 1620 to July, 1622.

---

[1] Lic. by Herbert, Oct. 24, 1622 (Fleay, *Hist.*, p. 301).

[2] B. & F., *Works*, II, p. 374.

[3] Herbert says expressly, "by Fletcher": so, before his death, Aug. 1625. And after Amboyna: so after May, 1624.

[4] In Herbert's Office Book, — Jan. 22nd, 1626.

[5] *I. e.*, *Gerardo the Unfortunate Spaniard, translated by Leonard Digges* (London, 1622), the general source of the *Sp. Cur.* For a discussion of this whole matter see below, Chap. IV.

[6] Fleay's *Hist.*, p. 321.   [7] Though a men's company, Fleay's *Hist.*, p. 270.

[8] Fleay's *Hist.*, p. 272. I know no other authority, yet Fleay must be right. -The *D. L. C.*, as we have seen, must be considerably later than Mar. 2nd, 1619, and yet it was acted by "Her Majesties Servants."

[9] Mr. Fleay seems of the opinion that at Queen Anne's death the Company went on playing without any name. Of the acting of *D. L. C.* he says, simply, "and therefore before 1619." Mr. Sidney Lee repeats this (*Dict. Nat. Biog.*, art. *Webster*).

[10] The company may, of course, have kept the old name popularly, even after the Privy Seal: but not likely, after an official designation was at hand, on the title-

VIII. APPIUS AND VIRGINIA.

Appius and Virginia was first published, so far as is known, in 1654. An *Appius and Virginia* stands last in a list of their own plays, drawn up in August, 1639, by William Beeston, governor of the Cockpit Company [1]; and as the only other *Appius and Virginia* known is antiquated, dull, and childish, a specimen not possibly to be played by a royal company in the day of Massinger and Shirley, this must be Webster's. [2] No other precise data are at hand. But the play is not mentioned in the preface to the *Devil's Law-Case;* and that it was written after that, after 1623, appears from the evidence (to be produced later) [3] that it is indebted to Shakspere, especially to his Roman plays, and in so precise and circumstantial a manner as to indicate the use of the First Folio. A nearer forward limit than that of Beeston's list is unattainable, for the date of Webster's death is unknown. [4] We must content ourselves, therefore, with the date 1623–39. [5]

IX. A CURE FOR A CUCKOLD.

Webster and Rowley's *Cure for a Cuckold* was first published in 1661. It contains an allusion, long recognized, to Middleton and Rowley's *Fair Quarrel:*

> *Pett.* . . . and there falls in league with a wench.
> *Comp.* A Tweak or Bronstrops : I learned that name in a play.   *C. C.*, IV, 1, p. 64.

> *Ush.* What is my sister, centaur?
> *Col's Tr.* I say thy sister is a bronstrops.
> *Ush.* A bronstrops?
> *Chough.* Tutor, tutor, — tell me the English of that; what is a bronstrops, pray ?
> *Col's Tr.* A bronstrops is in English a hippocrene.   *F. Q.*, IV, 1, 105–112.

---

page, especially, I think, as that of the "Queen of Bohemia's players " (*i. e.*, Lady Elizabeth's, so-called after she became such in Nov. 1619) would have made it rather convenient to give up a designation which long had had no meaning, was confusing, and now had no justification. In any case, the Queen's Men existed, even under the new name, only till July or Aug., 1623 (Fleay, *Hist.*, 299, 301),— the absolute forward limit, then, for our play.

[1] Given in Fleay's Hist. Stage, p. 357 ; preserved in the Lord Chamberlain's office.

[2] *Appius and Virginia, Tragi-Comedy*, by R. B., 4to, 1576. — Halliwell (p. 21) thinks it is the old play.

[3] See below, Chap. IV, Sect. III.

[4] See below, pp. 41–43.

[5] Mr. Fleay's work on Webster is, I suppose, on his lowest level. Of *A. & V.* he says: "From its allusion, at the end, to *Lucrece* [Heywood's play of 1608], would seem to date c. 1609. It was undoubtedly a play acted by Queen Anne's men, and passed with the *White Devil* to Queen Henrietta's." This allusion to Hey. amounts to the name " Lucretia "; and there is not a tittle of evidence to show that the play was acted by Queen Anne's.

As the *Fair Quarrel* first appeared in print in 1617, this may be considered a fairly certain backward limit. But there is a nearer. The plot of Webster's portion is in part derived, as we shall yet prove,[1] from Massinger's *Parliament of Love*. This play was licensed for the Cockpit on Nov. 3rd, 1624. The only forward limit, however, of the *Cure for a Cuckold* as of *Appius and Virginia*, is the date of Webster's death, whatever that may be.

X. THE AUTHORSHIP OF THE DOUBTFUL PLAYS.

It remains to consider the authenticity of three plays — the *Cure for a Cuckold*, the *Thracian Wonder*, and *The Weakest Goeth to the Wall*.

The Weakest Goeth to the Wall, registered and published in 1600, is easily disposed of. Neither title-page nor stationers' entry mentions the author. The play itself shows not the slightest trace of Webster's hand, and it was first attributed to him (by Edward Phillips, a nephew of Milton) so late as 1675.[2] "A great mistake," says the judicious Langbaine.[3]

The *Cure for a Cuckold* and the *Thracian Wonder* must be considered, so far as external evidence is concerned, together. Both were first published by Francis Kirkman in 1661. Both, evidently, were sent to press at about the same time, for the title-pages, with the exception of bare title, are, both in phrase and typography, exactly alike.[4] Both bear the names of John Webster and William Rowley. Both have been challenged by most critics of the century; and hardly any one supported the authenticity of either till Mr. Gosse asserted the artistic worth of the main-plot of the *Cure for a Cuckold*, and, on that basis, its authenticity.[5]

---

[1] See below, Chap. IV. Sect. I.

[2] Phillips's *Theatrum Poetarum*, 1675, pp. 116–17, where he assigns to him also the *Noble Stranger, New Trick to Cheat the Devil*, and *Woman will have her Will* (the second probably by association with *D. L. C.*). — Hazlitt wrongly states (vol. I, p. xx) that the attribution rests on the authority of Winstanley, in 1687.

[3] P. 510. He says it of Phillips, in regard not only to the *Weakest* but also the *Noble Stranger, New Trick to Cheat the Devil*, and *Woman will have her Will*.

[4] *A Cure for a Cuckold A Pleasant Comedy As it hath been several times Acted with great Applause. Written by* John Webster *and* William Rowley. *Placere Cupio. London. Printed by Tho. Johnson, and are to be sold by Francis Kirkman, at his Shop at the Sign of John Fletchers Head, over against the Angel-Inne, on the Back side of St. Clements, without Temple Bar 1661. — The Thracian Wonder. A Comical History*, —and the rest identical. See the reproductions of the original title-pages in Haz., vol. IV, pp. 1 and 115. There is no deviation except at *London*.

[5] For Gosse, see below; Ward in his History, Symonds in introd. to Mer. *Webster*, Lee in *Dict. Nat. Biog.*, art. *Webster*, who hesitatingly follow Gosse; Bullen in *Middleton*, footnote to *F. Q.*, IV, 1, 105, 112; Fleay. For Dyce, see below, p. 37.

The attribution, for which Kirkman is responsible, is, indeed, late. But it is unjustifiable to hold, with Fleay and others, that consequently it is worthless[1] (for a late attribution by the first publisher is a very different matter from a late attribution by a mere uncritical critic such as Phillips); or that, if it can be proved wrong in regard to one of the plays, it must therefore be wrong in regard to the other. There could be no *fraud* intended, as there might be in the case of more popular names, such as Shakspere[2] or Fletcher; and there must be some reason other than fraud or caprice for associating with the name of Rowley —not Middleton's, Fletcher's, Ford's, Massinger's, or Dekker's[3] — but Webster's. Very likely, Kirkman had the manuscripts in his hands, and one of the two, at least, avouched this unprecedented partnership. For that he had some basis of fact to go on, is proved by what Mr. Fleay and every one concede—Rowley's unmistakable touch in the *Cure for a Cuckold*.[4]

How did Webster's name get associated with Rowley's? The same story as that of the *Thracian Wonder* as Collier has pointed out,

---

[1] Fleay, II, 273.

[2] As is actually the case with the *Birth of Merlin*, pub. by Kirkman in 1662, and attributed to Shak. and Rowley.

[3] With Middleton's, of course, in many plays; with Fletcher's in the *Maid in the Mill* (Herbert's office book, Chalmers's Supp. Apol., ed. 1799, p. 215); with Dekker's and Ford's in *Edmonton;* with Massinger's in the *The Old Law.*

[4] Fleay, II, p. 99; Ward; Seccombe in the *Dict. Nat. Biog.*, "Rowley"; etc. That is, R. is the author of the under-plot, the story of Compass, his wife, her child, and Frankford. This is altogether apart from the main-plot, not only in subject and style, but also in structure; Frankford's being a brother-in-law of Woodruff is the only link between the two. Mr. Edmund Gosse, the first critic to take a stand for Webster's authorship of the main-plot, separated it from the under-plot—a very simple business of subtraction, — and in his edition of the main-plot, which he calls *Love's Graduate* (Oxford, 1885), takes honor to himself for his discovery. The discovery amounts to Mr. Gosse's oracular reassertion of Kirkman's title-page.

R.'s authorship of the under-plot is indicated by the *tweak* and *bronstrops* passage quoted from his previous play, and by the style in every scene. The extreme, yet laughable, absurdity of Compass's attitude to his "son," of his persisting in spite of all the evidence to the contrary, which he has intellectually accepted, in calling himself "father" (IV, 3, p. 77, "when the father is beyond sea as this was"), is paralleled by the Clown in the *Birth of Merlin*, who can't get over the wonder of it that his sister should be got with child and he not know of it (II, 1, l. 35 f); or (though here with a harder, more cynical touch) by Gnotho, who comes "crowding on afore" with a band of fiddlers, leading his old wife to her grave, and his new-chosen bride to the wedding, and, when the duke plainly tells him the law that the superannuated should die is now abolished, cries in eager hurry, "I'll talk further with your grace when I come back from church: in the meantime you know what to do with the old woman." Of the same stripe are Compass's reasonings before the lawyers (IV, 1).

35

appeared in 1617,[1] with the title, "*The most pleasant and delightful Historie of Curan, Prince of Danske, and the Fayre Princesse Argentile, Daughter and Heyre of Adelbright, sometime King of Northumberland.* This was by one William Webster. Now Kirkman, knowing the story, — for Kirkman, as his advertisements, or addresses to the reader,[2] and his catalogue of Elizabethan plays[3] prove, was a reading man, — might have confused the names of William Webster and John Webster, or put for the unknown the known as a guess. But this is not likely, it seems to me, unless the manuscript of the only other play of John Webster's he ever published, the *Cure for a Cuckold*, which he was publishing, too, as the title-pages show, at this very time, had already John Webster's name attached.

And how, on the other hand, did Rowley's[4] name get on the title-page of the *Thracian Wonder*, which shows not one trace of his hand? This play is already assigned to one author — Webster, — and a second, in a matter of guessing, would be superfluous. Rowley's name, we may rest assured, Kirkman never would have thought of adding to Webster's on the title-page of the *Thracian Wonder*, were it not already connected with Webster's in the only possible instance of such connection, — his manuscript of the *Cure for a Cuckold*.

On either hand, then, external evidence intimates that Kirkman was neither cheating nor blindly guessing — that he erred in the case of the *Thracian Wonder* only through the influence of authority in the case of the *Cure for a Cuckold*. Internal evidence confirms this. The *Thracian Wonder* shows not the slightest trace of either Rowley's or Webster's hand: neither ever wrote in the pastoral-idyllic style; neither ever wrote anything soft and foolish and vulgarly absurd. The ogre of a king belching out destruction in his court, and among the shepherds' cotes meek as any lamb; telling the Sicilian ambas-

---

[1] See Haz., IV, pp. 117–18. Collier and Dyce rest content, however, merely with the theory of the confusion of Wm. with John Webster, and with the assertion that the *T. W.* contains no trace of W.'s hand.

[2] See, for instance, that to the *Cure for a Cuckold* in Haz. Web.

[3] *True and perfect and exact Catalogue of all the the Comedies, Tragedies, and Tragi-comedies*, etc., *that were ever yet printed and published till this present year* 1671 (Brit. Mus.).

[4] Fleay thinks the association of W.'s with R.'s name *prima facie* evidence of error ; " They never worked together." (II, 99.) What that amounts to is, there are no other title-pages bearing their names ! To my mind, on the contrary, the association of Webster's name with Rowley's is presumptive evidence in favor of itself. In the first place, Webster's name could not have got there through being mistaken for any of those names otherwise associated with Rowley, — Middleton, Ford, Massinger, etc., — for the play bears no sign of their hand. In the second, there is no other Rowley-Webster play from which this play could be named by analogy. *Were* there any other, I should be suspicious.

sador on one page he "will lash his king with iron rods," and on the next surrendering to him "in palmer's weeds" [1]; the silly, love-sick shepherds scampering hither and thither and up trees; the chorus blabbing, and Time entering with his hour-glass to "bar" it [2]; and, above all, the very foolish battle wherein the Sicilian prince, injured husband of the ogre-king's daughter, has a mind to fight him at the head of his shepherds, but very suddenly and unreasonably joins with him against his own father of Sicily, yet, in the midst of the fray, leaving his indignant son behind as general, wheels over to the other side, and, after many skirmishes, in which his love-lorn, raving shepherds get the best of him, ends the conflict with a hand-to-hand fight with his son, — when lo, father, son, grandfather, grandson, husband, and wife rush all to a sudden recognition, none the worse for the wear! Such a "Wonder" as this is in a vein foreign to our authors. And the style is equally so. Men come in and fall down dead with the plague:

> *Sec. Lord.*   Mercy, he 's dead!
> *Sophos.*   Bless me! I fear I have taken the infection.
>
> .   .   .   .
>
>   is this a time for music?
> And so it is indeed, for every one
> Is ready to kick up his heels. [*Within.*   Oh! oh! oh!]
>   *T. W.*, II, 1, p. 137-9.
>
> Hail to those sweet eyes,
> That shine celestial wonder;
> From thence do flames arise,
> Burn my poor heart asunder;
> Now it fries.   *T. W.*, II, 4.

Surely, whether on behalf of Webster or of Rowley, there is no reason to accept the *Thracian Wonder*. [3]

It is quite otherwise with the *Cure for a Cuckold*. Dyce long ago suggested that Webster's hand might be traced in it [4]; but of evidence on the subject there has hitherto been none. Yet, viewed in the light of a study of Webster's development and of his relation to his sources, internal evidence declares as decisively for Webster's authorship in the main-plot as for Rowley's in the under-plot. The *Cure for a Cuckold* is really not more unlike Webster's other work than *Appius and Virginia*, which passes unchallenged. The difficulty of critics hitherto lies in a preconceived, vague, romantic notion

---

[1] III, 1, p. 160, and III, 2, p. 163.

[2] I, 3, p. 136.

[3] As Fleay, Dyce, Collier, etc., agree. Mr. Fleay (II, 332) has a very ingenious theory, not proved by his evidence, that the play is Heywood's.

[4] Dyce's *Webster*, 1857, vol. I, p. xv.

of Webster's character and style, derived merely from the *White Devil* and *Malfi*. But nothing is truer than that the Elizabethan dramatists were Protean, enormously susceptible, and that at different periods they followed different tendencies, different fashions. That is what Webster did in *Malfi* and the *White Devil*, — wrote, as we shall see, in the style of a school, — and his whole character is no more to be found in these two sombre tragedies than Shakspere's in *Titus Andronicus* and *Richard III*, or in the *Tempest* and *Winter's Tale*. Now in the *Cure for a Cuckold* he borrowed his plot almost bodily, as we shall yet see, from Massinger's *Parliament of Love*. The presumption, thereby arising, that he should borrow, besides, something of the style and manner, a careful examination confirms ; and not only this play, but the *Devil's Law-Case* and *Appius and Virginia* as well, show traces of the master influence of the day in which they took form — the influence of Massinger and Fletcher. Like Shakspere, like Chapman, Webster followed in their day of honor the lead of more forward and fashionable, though not more knowing, masters.[1]

Yet we need not seem to beg the question — we need not, in order to prove the *Cure for a Cuckold* Webster's, seem to some to rob him of his integrity and make him out a different man. His hand and touch are here, even those of the *Malfi* Webster. Let me bring forward only a few parallels of phrasing to prove this :

1. Four times — in the *White Devil*, the *Devil's Law-Case*, and twice in the *Cure for a Cuckold* — Webster makes a woman cry out at the news of her lover's death (brought, moreover, in three cases by the would-be slayer himself),

> Oh, I am lost forever ![2]

2. On this same occasion, in both the *Devil's Law-Case* and the *Cure for a Cuckold*, she cries to the would-be slayer,

> O, you have struck him dead through my heart ![3]

3. In both the *Cure for a Cuckold* and the *Devil's Law-Case*, the two young men who are about to fight a duel, speak of wearing a "*privy*

---

[1] Shak.: see Thorndike's *Influence of Beaumont and Fletcher*. Web.: see the chapters on *C. C.* and *D. L. C.* Chap.: see App. II.

[2] *C. C.*, IV, 2, p. 69, Clare; III, 3, p. 54, Annabel ; *W. D.*, V, 1, p. 112, Vittoria (here, however, Brachiano is only dying) ; *D. L. C.*, II, 3, p. 46, Leonora.

[3] *C. C.*, IV, 2, p. 69, Clare to Lessingham : *D. L. C.*, III, 3, p. 68, "You have given him the wound you speak of quite through your mother's heart."— In *D. L. C.*, indeed, this speech is uttered not at the same time as "O I am lost," etc., but at the second announcement of Contarino's death, from the mouth of her son, his would-be slayer.— The phrase itself is copied, like so many others in Web., from the *Arcadia*. See below, Chap. III, Sect. I, and *Notes and Queries*, Oct. 15, 1904, p. 304.

coat," — what one in the one play calls his *" heart,"* and one in the other [1] the "justice of his cause." In both cases it is an immaterial, and yet striking, coincidence of phrase and thought, such as would be brought forth only by the same mind under the same circumstances.

4. Compare Clare in this play —

> I am every way lost, and no means to raise me
> But blest repentance! *C. C.*, IV, 2, p. 72.

— and Cornelia to Flamineo, in the *White Devil* —

> To tell how thou shouldst spend the time to come
> *W. D.*, IV, 5, p. 209.

— where the same phrase takes exactly the same position and accent in the metre, a slight matter no imitator would copy.

5. The peculiar curse in the *Cure for a Cuckold*,

> And may my friend's blood, whom you loved so dearly,
> Forever lie imposthumed in your breast,
> And i' th' end choke you! *C. C.*, IV, 2, p. 72.

and in the *White Devil*,

> Die with those pills in your most cursed maw,
> Should bring you health! or while you sit o' th' bench,
> Let your own spittle choke you! *W. D.*, III, 2, p. 65.

6. In *A Cure for a Cuckold*:

> You have ta'en a mass of lead from off my heart
> Forever would have sunk it in despair. IV, 2, p. 70.

In *Malfi*:

> And thou hast ta'en that massy sheet of lead
> That hid thy husband's bones, and folded it
> About my heart. III, 2, pp. 209–10.

7. In *A Cure for a Cuckold*:

> You are to sleep with a sweet bed-fellow
> Would knit the brow at that. IV, 2, p. 74.

In the *White Devil*:

> why, the saints in heaven
> Will knit their brows at that. II, p. 38.

In both cases the expression is used alike figuratively; and in the same place in the metre and the sentence.

8. In *A Cure for a Cuckold* there is a couplet which recalls one that appears in both *Malfi* and the *White Devil* (see note at the end of Chapter II):

> And it were sin
> Not in our age to show what we have bin. I, 1, p. 16.

---

[1] *D. L. C.*, II, 1, pp. 39, 40; *C. C.*, III, 1, pp. 47.

There are yet other parallel passages, but let them pass. Of these quoted, nos. 1, 2, and 3 coincide in wording, dramatic situation, and character; others, as nos. 4 and 8, merely in the expression; but most of them, being colorless and insignificant in themselves, and resembling each other far more in form than in substance, are, like the drawing of ears or little toes in a painter or sculptor, no more the points another would think of copying than he himself of changing.

Another test we might apply to the *Cure for a Cuckold* is the use of the exclamation *ha!*, especially as comprehending a whole speech. This is of extraordinary frequency in Webster. [1] It appears in the *White Devil* 13 times, 6 of them being whole speeches; in *Malfi* 10 times, 2 of them whole speeches; in the *Law-Case* 9 times, 4 of them whole speeches; in *Appius and Virginia* twice; in the main plot of the *Cure for a Cuckold* 7 times, 2 of them whole speeches. In view of the slight extent of Webster's part of the *Cure for a Cuckold* as compared with that of the other plays, and of the frigidity and academic character of the Roman play, *Appius and Virginia*, the statistics for the different plays keep remarkably even, and the *Cure for a Cuckold* seems only to take its place with the others.

There are still other points of similarity, such as cheap, deceptive tricks with words.

> *Less.* Then truth is, he's dangerously wounded.
> *Wood.* But he's not dead, I hope?
> *Less.* No, Sir, not dead:
> Yet sure your daughter may take liberty
> To choose another.
> . . . .
> I told you he was wounded, and 'tis true;
> He is wounded in his reputation.   *C. C.*, V, 1, pp. 86–7.

Compare with this *Appius and Virginia*, I, 1, p. 132, where Appius pretends to go into banishment, but winds up in this fashion:

> Banish'd from all my kindred and my friends;
> Yea, banish'd from myself; for I accept
> This honorable calling.

This is a favorite artifice of Webster's. In the *White Devil*, V, 2, p. 131, Flamineo speaks of his "two case of jewels," which in a moment turn out to be pistols, and Lodovico answers Giovanni's question on whose authority he had committed the massacre, thus:

> *Lod.* By thine.
> *Gio.* Mine!
> *Lod.* Yes; thy uncle, which is a part of thee, enjoined us to 't.
> *W. D.*, V, 2, p. 142.

---

[1] These are the references: *W. D.*, pp. 33, 35, 57, 61, 64, 73, 81, 93, 108, 128, 141, 142; *Malfi*, 177, 190, 190, 211, 232, 241, 249, 267, 273, 276; *D. L. C.*, 25, 59, 62, 62, 65, 68, 69, 70, 116; *C. C.*, 30, 40, 46, 89, 90, 91, 96; *A. & V.*, 152, 214.

In *Appius and Virginia* Virginius surrenders his daughter "into the court — of all the gods"[1]; and in the *Devil's Law-Case* and the *Cure for a Cuckold* this bent of his goes to such lengths as to lose utterly the spectator's confidence and sympathy. See, for instance, Jolenta's letter to Contarino, and Clare's letter (another point of similarity!) to Lessingham.[2]

Another proof is the number of striking parallels in plot between the *Cure for a Cuckold* and Webster's only other independent comedy, the *Devil's Law-Case*, at points where it does not follow the *Parliament of Love*.[3] But enough has been brought forward already, I think, to prove Webster's authorship beyond a cavil.

If, however, the *Cure for a Cuckold* be made to follow the *Parliament of Love*, licensed to play November, 1624, some one well-read in Fleay or the *Dictionary of National Biography* may cry, "But Webster died in 1625." Mr. Fleay says, "He was probably the John Webster, cloth-worker, who made his will the 5th of Aug. 1625, proved 7th Oct."[4]; and Mr. Sidney Lee assents.[5] But, I think, without reason. It was the indefatigable Dyce who first brought forward John Webster, clothworker, and his will of 1625; and Dyce consigns it, as the only shred of evidence there is on the death of any John Webster within a remarkable stretch of time, to a foot-note. To this he adds, for completeness' sake, the will of a John Webster, tallow-chandler.[6]

The abstract of the will furnished Mr. Dyce by the Prerogative Office is as follows :

John Webster, clothworker, of London, made his will on the 5th of August, 1625. He bequeathes to his sister, Jane Cheney, dwelling within seven miles of Norwich 10 l., with remainder, if she died, to her children, and if they died, to his sister Elizabeth Pyssing; to whom he also left 10 l., with remainder to her children. To his father-in-law, William Hattfield, of Whittington, in Derbyshire, 15 l., and to his four children 4 l. each. To his cousin Peter Webster, of Whittington, in Derbyshire, he gives 10 l., and if he died before it was paid, it was to be given to his brother, who was a protestant, "for I hear that one brother of my cousin Peter is a papist." To William Bradbury, of London, shoemaker, 5 l. To Richard Matthew, his (the testator's) son-in-law, 16 l. He mentions his father-in-law, Mr. Thomas Farman. He gives his counsin Edward Curtice, 1 l. 2 s., etc. He leaves the residue of his property to his brothers and sisters in law, by his wife; specially providing that Eliza-

---

[1] *A. & V.*, IV, 1, p. 201.

[2] *D. L. C.*, V, 2, p. 107; cf. III, 3, pp. 62, 63: *C. C.*, I, p. 13; cf. II, 4, p. 38, as to his being mistaken, and the explanations, pp. 38, 54, 69, 74. — And for other deceptive verbal tricks, p. 47 and pp. 48, 49.

[3] Below, Chap. IV, Sect. I, note at end.

[4] *Biog. Chr.*, II, 268.

[5] "He seems to have died," etc., *Dict. Nat. Biog.*, art. *Webster*. Likewise Mr. Gosse, *Jacobean Poets*, London, 1894, p. 166.

[6] Dyce's *Web.*, ed. 1857, p. x.

beth Walker should be one. He constitutes Mr. Robert Aungel, and his cousin, Mr. Francis Ash, citizens, his executors; and his cousins Courtis and Tayler, overseers of his will, — which was proved by his executors on the 7th of October, 1625.

This document is neither written nor signed by the testator; he and three of the witnesses (his cousin Edward Curtis, the fourth, being the only exception) are fain to make their marks.[1] Now it is inconceivable that John Webster, playwright, should not have signed his name unless too weak to hold the pen (which the date of the proving makes unlikely); and it is highly improbable that with friends like Dekker, Munday, Heywood, Ford, and Rowley[2] still living, he should have been abandoned in his last hours to the society of illiterates, or, with so large an estate on his hands, should have bequeathed it only to distant Protestant relatives and a shoemaker. Our Webster, moreover, was not a clothworker. '' Merchant-Taylor '' he designates himself on the title-page of the *Monuments of Honor*, a pageant of '' the Right Worthy and Worshipful Fraternity, the Eminent Merchant Taylors,'' — a thing (as Dyce and Fleay surely knew) very different.[3] And, even as merchant-tailor, he speaks of himself at this same time, in the dedication to Gore, only as of one '' *born* free of your company.''[4] He is, therefore, not any of the three John Websters *made* free[5] of the Company in 1571, 1576, and 1617[6]; still less that one

---

[1] I give this on the authority of Mr. Crofts. See below, p. 43, note.

[2] That these last were also his friends, appears from the partnership with Ford, and his verses addressed to Munday and Heywood.

[3] It is unlikely that in the will of J. W., clothworker, there should have been any such mistake. However loosely and vaguely such three designations as clothworker, merchant-tailor, and draper may be used today, it was otherwise then, when one necessarily understood by each a member of one of the Twelve Great Companies of London (see list in Ashley's *English Econ. Hist.*, 1893, vol. II, p. 133).

[4] See *Works*, III, p. 232; pub. in 1624.

[5] This distinction is important. See Toulmin Smith, *English Gilds* (London, 1870), p. cxxxii: '' the whole household of a Gild-brother belonged to the Gild,'' etc.

[6] *Works*, I, introd., p. vi. — Possibly, on the other hand, he may have been a son of one of the earlier ones. The due-bill dated July 25th, 1591, wherein John Allein and Edward Alleyn acknowledge their indebtedness to '' John Webster, citysen and merchant Tayler of London '' in the sum of 15 shillings, is probably the nearest we come by documentary evidence to John Webster the poet. This may be the poet's father, who may have had dealings with actors and so come to get his son into their society. This would harmonize with our poet's being *born* free of the company. The due-bill is printed in the *Alleyn Papers*, ed. by Collier (who suggests that this Webster may be the father of the poet), London, 1843, p. 14; and is accounted by Warner in his *Catalogue of Dulwich College Mss.* as genuine. — If this be so, the poet can not be the ' nephew John Webster, as near to whom as might be ' John Webster, the tallow-chandler, in his will of Feb. 16th, 1628, wishes to be buried; there could not have been two brothers called John.

assessed 10 shillings on March 15th, 1603 [1]; nor, indeed, is he to be reckoned a craftsman at all. The designation on the title-page is perfunctory, in compliment to the company for which he wrote the pageant; and Webster is no more of a merchant-tailor than any of the other worthies mentioned in this pageant as "free of the company," than that bold soldier of fortune, Sir John Hawkwood, Queen Anne, or the "bad man but good king, Richard the Third." [2]

We may conclude, therefore, without a shadow of doubt, that Webster is not John Webster, clothworker; and since there are no more wills of John Websters at Somerset House, [3] from 1621–35, there is, at any rate, no longer a will and probate in the way [4] of Webster's writing the *Cure for a Cuckold* after Nov. 3rd, 1624.

XI. THE PERIODS OF WEBSTER'S WORK.

Now, at last, we are in a position to tabulate on a secure basis the development of Webster's art. Three periods, of course (according to the hackneyed and inevitable scheme), are to be discerned: Growth, Maturity, and Decay, the point of Maturity being marked by the *White Devil* and *Malfi*. Another principle, however, is to be preferred, — that of the prevalent influences. According to this latter, his work falls into these periods:

1. Period of Apprenticeship and Partnership: mainly under the influence of Dekker.

sesers ffalle	1602
too shapes	1602
Sir Thomas Wyatt (Lady Jane)	1602
cryssmas comes bute once ayeare	1602

---

[1] *I. e.*, toward a pageant for King James. Clode (*Memorials of the Merchant Taylors' Company*, Lon., 1875, p. 596), who takes it as a matter of course that this is the poet himself, admits (p. 601, note) that the records do not show that he ever took up the freedom acquired by birth. Clode seems not to know of the *Alleyn Papers* John Webster, who is probably the man assessed.

[2] *Mon. Hon.*, pp. 238–9. Mischief in this business of the tailor was made by Dyce (blindly followed by Haz.), in quoting wrongly the title-page of the *Mon. Hon.* He says, ed. 1830, vol. I, p. 11, that there W. describes himself as "John Webster Taylor," although in vol. IV, App., he gives the title-page correctly — "Merchant-Taylor," — from the "copy, perhaps *unique*, belonging to the Duke of Devonshire." His calling himself "Taylor" is, of course, a different matter.

[3] What facts I have here given concerning the Clothworker's parchment I owe to the services of Mr. T. Robertson W. Crofts, Highgate. He was not allowed by the authorities to copy it or to have it copied; and after he had furnished me with the above facts, I decided photographing was not necessary.

[4] Excepting always the tallow-chandler's.

Induction to the *Malcontent* [1]	bef. July, 1604
Westward Ho	c. September 1604–1605
Northward Ho	Spring 1605–1606

2. Period of the Revenge Plays : mainly under the influence of Marston.

The White Devil	Winter 1611–1612
The Duchess of Malfi	1617, after April

3. Fletcherian and Academic Period : under the influence not only of Fletcher and Massinger, but of the old-fashioned dramatists, Marlowe, Heywood, and Shakspere.

The Guise	prob. after *Malfi* and before *D. L. C.* [2]
The Devil's Law-Case	end 1620—July 1622
Appius and Virginia	1623–1639
A Cure for a Cuckold	after Nov., 1624

---

[1] This, as I prove in Chap. II, is all Web. wrote.
[2] See below, Chap. IV, Sect. IV, end.

CHAPTER II.

The Period of Apprenticeship and Partnership.

I. SIR THOMAS WYATT.

The Source; Classification of the Play.

The earliest work of Webster's handed down to us is, as we have
seen, the *Famous History of Sir Thomas Wyatt*, by both him and
Dekker. This is an English chronicle-play, or 'history,' like the
English 'histories' of Shakspere and of Marlowe. Like many of
these, it draws its plot from Raphael Holinshed's Chronicle, — in this
special case from Vol. III, p. 1067, to Vol. IV, p. 29, in the edition of
1808. For not only does Holinshed contain all the minor historical
incidents depicted by Dekker and Webster, such as Arundel's lamenting his inability to accompany Northumberland on his march, the
escape and capture of the Treasurer, Northumberland's recreant pro-
claiming of Mary at Cambridge and his arrest by Arundel, the betrayal
and taking of Suffolk, and the later defection of Brett and the Londoners from the royal cause,— but also seems in one case, at least, to
furnish the very wording of a speech. Holinshed reports the Queen's
Master of the Horse as saying,

" Wiat, before thou shalt have thy traitorous demand granted, thou shalt die, and
twentie thousand with thee."   Vol. IV, p. 15.

This was when Wyatt was at Dartford. The incident itself Dekker
and Webster omit, yet make Pembroke from the walls of London say
something quite similar :

> Know that these gates are barred against thy entrance ;
> And it shall cost the lives of twenty thousand
> True subjects to the queen before a traitor enters.   *Wyatt*, p. 47.

And other deviations from the original so slight as this there are of
course. Lady Jane, to add another instance, is made in the play to
die before her husband, instead of after him as in Holinshed ; and
Brett is made to command also under Northumberland. But such discrepancies are probably all intentional — mere dramatic license, — and
do not indicate a different source. [1]

---

[1] *Wyatt*, pp. 21-2. Dekker violates history to save introducing another character.
He cannot be following another source than Holinshed ; for, as a matter of fact,
Brett, had he commanded under the rebel Northumberland, would, in that age,
hardly be available afterward.

As a drama, we have said, Wyatt belongs to the English chronicle-plays, or 'histories.' Of these, previous to Dekker and Webster, there are, one might say, two classes — the popular and the Marlowesque. Both have a fully developed dramaturgical machinery much in common : but the Marlowesque are stately, bloody tragedies, with a towering central character round which the events revolve ; while the popular are loose and rambling in construction, and blend tragedy with low-life and comedy. The one class is represented by such plays as *Edward II*, *Richard II*, and *Richard III;* the other, by the *First Part of the Contention*, the *True Tragedie of Richard Duke of Yorke*, the *True Tragedie of Richard III*, the *Troublesome Raigne of King John*, *Locrine*, and Shakspere's *Henry VI* and *King John*.[1] It is to this latter class that *Wyatt* belongs. It shows no appreciable influence from Marlowe, and contains scenes so popular in character as those between Brett and his soldiers (pp. 20–23, 43–46) and the clown-scene (pp. 29, 30). Much of the machinery and devices common to both classes are to be found in it. Such are the frank Machiavellian villain[2] ; ominous dreams [3]; declamatory ex post facto political prophe-

---

[1] *Edward II*, reg. 1593, pub. 1594 ; *Rich. III*, first 4to known, 1597, but certainly composed earlier ; *The First Part of the Contention betwixt the Two Famous Houses of Yorke and Lancaster*, 1594 ; *The True Tragedie of Richard, Duke of Yorke, and the Death of Good King Henrie the Sixt*, etc., 1595 ; *The True Tragedie of Richard the Third*, etc., 1594 ; *The Troublesome Raigne of Iohn, King of England*, etc., 1591 ; *Locrine*, reg. 1594, pub. 1595 ; Shak.'s *Hen. VI*, Pts. II and III, followed closely upon their originals, the *Contention* and the *True Tragedie*, but were not published till the folio of 1623. Pt. I was acted March 3rd, 1592 (see Sidney Lee's Life of Shak., p. 56). *King John*, first printed in the F., is mentioned by Meres, 1598 ; it is probably several years older. — All of these have low life and comic scenes. *Locrine*, like *Wyatt*, has a clown.

[2] See the account of the Machiavellian villain in Meyer's *Machiavelli and the Eng. Drama*. The Machiavellian villain is a frank lover of evil and enemy of God, whose boast is a program of fraud and violence. — See *Wyatt*, p. 6 :

> What though the king hath left behind
> Two sisters lawful and immediate heirs,
> .   .   .   .   lies it not
> In our powers to contradict it?
> .   .   .   .
> Tut, we stand high in man's opinion, etc.

Such are Shak.'s Rich. III in his avowals ; the Rich. III of *True Tragedie*, and of *Trag. of Rich. III*, as well as Mortimer in *Edward II*, King John to some degree, etc. — Throughout this book I use the term Machiavellian more loosely than Meyer, — for the frank Eliz. villain done after the style of Barabas, Aaron, or Lorenzo (*Sp. Tr.*), whether he actually echo any of the maxims of Machiavelli (or Gentillet) or not.

[3] *Wyatt*, p. 37 — Cf. Clarence's dream in *Rich. III*, I, 4 ; V, 3 ; Duke Humphrey's and his wife's dreams in *Contention*, pp. 421-2 ; *Hen. VI*, Pt. II, I, 2 ; *Sir Thomas More*, Dyce ed., p. 75.

cies which reach beyond the scope of the play itself [1]; forebodings on entering the Tower or some other ill-famed keep [2]; battle-scenes, with wrangling and baiting ; the introduction of foolish, trivial incidents, such as that of the Treasurer's escape, because of their historic character [3]; crude devices, like the starting of a conversation as a character enters by the question "Whither away so fast?"[4]; a stately, even stilted, style ; and a relentless bent for punning in the midst of heroic declamation. [5]

Some of the artifices just recounted are not exclusively peculiar to the histories, but they are peculiar to the dramaturgy of the time when the histories we have been considering arose, 1593-6. Since that and before 1598, appeared plays so free from the old traditional machinery as (in some measure) *Richard II, Edward III*, and above all *Henry IV*.[6] *Wyatt*, then, in 1602, is old-fashioned. Indeed, to the ordinary reader it seems very old-fashioned, more archaic than the histories of 1593-6, for it drops often into rime, which they one and all disdain ; and it often manifests in the tragic portions a puerile ineptitude of language and situation, [7] which, of course, is vastly below the

---

[1] *Wyatt*, p. 59. *True Tragedie*, pp. 84-5, 98, prophecy of the boy Richmond's becoming king, etc. ; Henry's prophecies, *3 Hen. VI*, IV, 6, 68 ; V, 6, 36 ; *Contention*, p. 458, Elinor Cobham's to Humphrey ; *1 Hen. VI*, II, 4, 124, prophecy of the Wars of the Roses ; *Rich. II*, V, 1, 54, etc. ; *Rich. III*, *passim* ; *Troublesome Raigne*, p. 291, prophecy of the doing away with popery in Eng. ; see the ' *history*' *Jul. Cæs.*, III, 1, 111 f, 253 f, Cassius's, Brutus's, and Antony's.

[2] Tower : *Wyatt*, p. 10 ; *Rich. III*, III, 4, 87 f ; III, 1, 142 f ; IV, 1, 98 ; *Sir Thomas More*, p. 90. Pomfret : *Rich. III*, III, 3, 9.

[3] Anecdotal incidents, common in the popular plays. See the incident of Duke Humphrey unmasking the fraud of the would-be blind man in the *Contention* and *2 Hen. VI*, II, 1.

[4] *Wyatt*, p. 6. — Common in Marlowe ; *1 Hen. VI*, III, 2, 104 ; *2 Hen. VI*, III, 2, 367 ; *Rich. III*, II, 3, 1 ; IV, 1, 7 ; *Contention*, p. 479.

[5] *Wyatt*, pp. 6, 56, 60, 62 ; *Contention*, p. 419 ; *Rich. II*, II, 1, 72 f, 82 f, where Gaunt puns on his own name even when dying. *King John :* Pandulph, III, 1, 263-298 ; Arthur, IV, 1, 60-70 ; *Sir Thomas More*, p. 90.

[6] *Rich. II*, pub. 1597 ; *Hen. IV*, Pt. I, reg. Feb., 1598, and Pt. II, 1600 ; *Edward III*, pub. 1596. *Hen. IV*, though so free and unconventionalized, was, with its loose structure, its combination of kingly tragedy and low-life comedy, certainly developed out of the popular type. *Rich. II*, on the other hand, an earlier work, is modelled on Marlowesque lines (though far less closely than *Rich. III*), after *Edward II*. — Since writing this, I have come upon Mr. Felix Schelling's *English Chronicle Play* (New York, 1902), in which some of the distinctions and judgments here arrived at are anticipated.

[7] Such speeches as this :

> O God, O God, that ever I was born !
> This deed hath made me slave to abject scorn.   P. 29.

and such scenes as that of the Treasurer's escape, pp. 14, 15. Cf. the betrayal of Suffolk, with the astounding Judas kiss, p. 28, etc.

level of the Marlowesque class and even generally of the popular. Yet, though crude, *Wyatt* is really not so archaic. Fondness for rime is an idiosyncrasy of Dekker's, we shall see, which follows him throughout his career ; and even *Richard II* and *Edward III*, in 1596–7, have plenty of it. In *Wyatt*, moreover, much of the old Senecan blood-and-thunder machinery, and the motive of revenge, so prominent in most of the histories of both classes of 1593–6, have died out. The Machiavellian villain is atrophied away almost to nothing.[1] There are no ghosts or conjuring or other infernal machinery [2]; no mastiff barons and wolfish ladies, nor baiting of captives ; no chorus of men or women cursing and lamenting ; no poisoning, stabbing, smothering, spilling of blood, nor Machiavellian boasting of such.[3] On the other hand, there is in *Wyatt*, as we shall see, a vein of compassion, soft sentiment, and humanity, foreign to the spirit of those plays of 1593–6, — a development in the hands of Dekker and Webster. Crude, then, on the whole, *Wyatt* is, but only in consideration of its late date and the character of Shakspere's preceding work, specially primitive and old-fashioned.

One of these earlier chronicle-plays of the popular type may have served as model for *Wyatt*, — the *First Part of the Contention betwixt the Two Famous Houses of Yorke and Lancaster, with the notable Rebellion of Jack Cade, London, 1594*, or possibly Shakspere's revision of this, first published, as the *Second Part of Henry VI*, in 1623, but on the stage long before *Wyatt*. In either version there are similar rebel-scenes.[4] Jack Cade, like Captain Brett, is a comic figure — the soul of complacence, an ignorant, unscrupulous demagogue, and a patriotic blatherskite who hates the French as indiscriminately

---

[1] He appears only at pp. 5, 6, 7, and even there he is not ready to commit any crime other than wresting away the kingdom ; later, he gets tame as a lamb.

[2] No ghosts as in *Rich. III, Trag. of Rich. III, Locrine, Contention ;* no conjuring as in *Contention, 2 Hen. VI,* I, 4.

[3] As Queen Margaret in *Contention* (esp. 477), *True Tragedie, Rich. III,* and *Hen. VI ;* Isabella in *Ed. II ;* Barons in *Ed. II* and the York-Lancaster tragedies, esp. Clifford in killing young Rutland, *True Tragedie,* p. 19 f, the Queen and Barons as they bait York and stab him, *ib.,* pp. 24–28, King Edward stabbing Prince Edward, at the end, before his mother's eyes, p. 95. Fierce quarrels in *Ed. II, Contention,* 440–1, 475, *True Trag.,* pp. 7, 8, 24–5, etc. ; boasting, showing of enemies' blood, and throwing down a head as a trophy, *ib.,* p. 4 ; the putting out of Arthur's eyes in *Troublesome Raigne;* smothering of Duke Humphrey in *Contention,* of Edward in *Ed. II,* of the Innocents in the Tower in *Trag. of Rich. III,* etc. ; *all on the stage.* Winchester, of course, and Mary, too, in *Wyatt* are far from agreeable, but they are not of the same stripe as the above. Chorus of cursing and lamenting in *Rich. III,* — Margaret, I, 3, and the women IV, 4 ; *King John,* II, 1 ; III, 1 ; *Troublesome Raigne,* pp. 248, 249, 251–2, 257–8, 261, etc. ; *True Trag.,* p. 50.

[4] *Wyatt,* pp. 43–48 ; *Contention,* pp. 487–506 ; *2 Hen. VI.*

as Brett the Spanish.[1] His speeches, like Brett's, suffer a running comment from his men, which sets off the comic effect. And the rag-tag and bob-tail which follows either, shows the same responsiveness to oratory, the same inconstancy to the cause they have espoused.[2]

WEBSTER'S SHARE.

The consideration of these relations of *Wyatt* to the chronicle-plays leads to the question, how much of the play is Webster's?[3] We should expect it to be mostly Dekker's ; for, according to Henslowe's entries, Part First of *Lady Jane* was by "deckers chettell smythe webester & hewode," and Part Second by Dekker alone.[4] Further to answer the question there is no way but by pointing out what must be Dekker's. For Webster has no independent work with which to compare it ; — what is later shows nothing in common with *Wyatt*, and none of it is contemporary. With Dekker the case is otherwise. Of his unaided work, there are preserved three[5] plays written before *Wyatt* and two shortly after,[6] some of these being his masterpieces, and all thoroughly characteristic of the man.

What features of *Wyatt*, then, are due to Dekker? It is to be remembered, of course, that Dekker is not at home here ; his element is not tragic horror nor heroic verse, but the doings and sayings of a Simon Eyre or an Orlando. Yet even in this play there are characters on which he has left his unmistakable impress. Wyatt, for instance, Brett, and the Clown — the only real characters — are certainly his. Wyatt speaks with an abrupt force, a dogged reiteration, and a breeziness very like Dekker :

> I 'll damn my soul for no man, no, for no man.
> Who at doomsday must answer for my sin?
> Not you, nor you, my lords.

---

[1] *Wyatt*, pp. 44–5 ; *Contention*, 488–90, and for " French," 493–4, etc.

[2] Cf. the defection of the Londoners from the cause of the Queen under the influence of Brett's oratory, and their subsequent sudden desertion of Wyatt, pp. 43–48, with *Contention*, p. 505, where after Clifford's speech Cade's followers call out " A Clifford, A Clifford," and desert Cade, and after Cade's, "A Cade, A Cade," and desert Clifford.

[3] " I think Webster wrote Sc. 1–9, Dekker Sc. 11–17, the change of Dram. Pers. being very marked in Sc. 10 " (Fleay, II. p. 269) ; that is, I suppose, up to p. 36 in the Hazlitt ed. is Webster's. No reasons are vouchsafed.

[4] See Henslowe, p. 183, where "fulle payment" is made to the partners in *Lady Jane;* and p. 184, where, six days later, Dekker is paid 3 pounds in "earneste of the 2 pt. of Lady Jane." Ward notes this. — This holds, however, only if Pt. II is really contained in *Wyatt.* See above, p.

[5] *Shoemaker's Holiday*, reg. July 15, 1599 ; *Old Fortunatus*, reg. Nov. 9, 1599 ; *Satiromastix*, reg. Nov. 11, 1601.

[6] *Honest Whore*, Pt. I, reg. Nov. 9, 1604 ; *Whore of Babylon*, April 20, 1607.

Who nam'd Queen Jane, in noble Henry's days?
Which of you all durst once displace his issue?
My lords, my lords, you whet your knives so sharp
To carve your meat,
That they will cut your fingers.
The strength is weakness that you build upon.
The King is sick, — God mend him, ay, God mend him! —
But were his soul from his pale body free,
Adieu, my lords, the court no court for me.   *Wyatt*, p. 6.

Wyat. He shall pass and repass, juggle the best he can.
Lead him into the city. Norry, set forth,
Set forth thy brazen throat, and call all Rochester
About thee; do thy office; fill
Their light heads with proclamations, do;
Catch fools with lime-twigs dipt with pardons.
But Sir George, and good Sir Harry Isley,
If this gallant open his mouth too wide,
Powder the varlet, pistol him, fire the roof
That 's o'er his mouth.
He craves the law of arms, and he shall ha 't:
Teach him our law, to cut 's throat if he prate.
If louder reach thy proclamation,
The Lord have mercy upon thee!
Norry. Sir Thomas, I must do my office.
Harp. Come, we 'll do ours too.
Wy. Ay, Ay, do, blow thyself hence.
Whoreson, proud herald, because he can
Give arms, he thinks to cut us off by th' elbows.
Masters, and fellow soldiers, say will you leave
Old Tom Wyat?   *Ib.*, pp. 40, 41.

That is certainly not Webster's hand, and certainly is Dekker's.[1]
Parallels in Dekker are abundant; a short search yields these:

Terrill. If she should prooue mankinde, twere rare, fye, fye.
See how I loose myself amongst my thoughts,
Thinking to find my selfe; my oath, my oath.
Sir Quin. I sweare another, let me see, by what,
By my long stocking, and my narrow skirtes,
Not made to sit upon, she shall to Court.
I have a tricke, a charme, that shall lay downe
The spirit of lust, and keep thee undeflowred;
Thy husband's honor sau'd, and the hot King,
Shall haue enough, too. Come, a tricke, a charme.   *Sat.*, p. 225.

Candido. My gown, George, go, my gown. — A happy land,
Where grave men meet each cause to understand.

. . . .

Come, where 's the gown?

. . . .

Good wife, kind wife, it is a needful trouble, but for my gown!
                                            H. W., p. 139.

_____
Cf. also *Wyatt*, p. 50, a similar speech of Wyatt's.

| *George.* Do 't: away, do 't | *Ib.*, p. 135. |
| *Lodovico.* Do, do, bravely. | *Ib.*, p. 222. |

Tucca. Crispinus shal doo 't, thou shalt doo 't, heyre apparent of Helicon, thou shalt doo 't. *Sat.*, p. 201.

Here there is the same liveliness, boisterousness, downrightness of manner, and — what is equally significant — the same style and rhythm.

And Brett is sprung from the author of "Tom Wyatt," and, as I think, of Simon Eyre :

Brett. Right, for he [the Spaniard] carries not the Englishman's yard about him. If you deal with him, look for hard measure; if you give an inch, he 'll take an ell; if he give an ell, he 'll take an inch; therefore, my fine, spruce, dapper, finical fellows, if you are now, as you have always been counted, politic Londoners to fly to the stronger side, leave Arundel, leave Norfolk, and love Brett. . . . Wear your own neat's-leather shoes; scorn Spanish leather; cry, a fig for the Spaniard. Said I well, bullies?   *Wyatt*, pp. 45–6.

In "leave Norfolk and love Brett " Brett uses the same turn as Wyatt in "will you leave old Tom Wyatt?" And he has much the same terms of endearment for his soldiers as Simon Eyre for his workmen : "Stay, my fine knaves, you arms of my trade, you pillars of my profession "[1] ; "Now, my true Trojans, my fine Firk, my dapper Hodge, my honest Hans," etc.[2]

The Clown, too, is Dekker's, for the jokes of his comment on Brett's harangue are in Dekker's broad, hearty style, quite foreign to Webster, and, indeed, are not easily separable from the harangue itself. His speech after the death of Ned Homes contains a sure token of Dekker as opposed to Webster — a phrase in Dutch.[3]

These disposed of, it is hardly possible to speak further of *characters ;* yet, aside from these, there are several who utter phrases and ideas of enough individuality to be Dekker's. Such are :

> *Jane.* A hand as pure from treason, as innocent
> As the white livery
> Worn by th' angels in their Maker's sight![4]
> *North.* O, at the general sessions, when all souls
> Stand at the bar of justice, and hold up
> Their new-immortalized hands, O then
> Let the remembrance of their tragic ends
> Be raz'd out of the bead-roll of my sins !   *Wyatt*, p. 26.

---

[1] *Shoemaker*, p. 30.

[2] *Shoemaker*, p. 45, and there are many other similar ones.

[3] *Wyatt*, p. 30. Cf. the Dutch in the *Shoemaker, passim.* There is none in Web.

[4] *Wyatt*, p. 51. A striking parallel of thought in a different situation is Candido's remark about the *cloth* before him : "O that each soul were but as spotless as this innocent white." *H. W.*, p. 161.

For in these there is a sweet personal tone — one that Webster never shows, and had he ever had, he could hardly have so outlived, — that is altogether like that of the creator of Jane,[1] Bellafront, and Orlando Friscobaldo, — the tender, homely, religious man who just about this time wrote,

> The best of men
> That e'er wore earth about him, was a sufferer,
> A soft, meek, patient, humble, tranquil spirit,
> The first true gentleman that ever breathed.   *H. W.*, p. 190.

And there is a vein of sentiment more simple and commonplace than that, in the mouths of not only gentle Lady Jane and Guildford but of the Machiavellian Northumberland, of Arundel, of Norfolk, of stout Wyatt, and even of the Porter ; a sentiment little varied and of no character, a harping on tears, embracings, love, and compassion, quite unusual in either the popular or the Marlowesque histories, and here pretty certainly to be attributed also to Dekker.[2]

This last point, taken with the others, would go to show the presence of Dekker's hand everywhere in the play ; the metre shows this still more. It bears not the slightest resemblance to any of Webster's — is thoroughly Dekker's. First, in the abundance of rime. All of Shakspere's chronicle-plays, Marlowe's, and nearly all of those since Marlowe, show very little rime ; for the history, like tragedy, had adopted the unrimed five-accent verse. The *First Part of the Contention*, which of all these shows greatest similarity to *Wyatt*, has only 6 couplets in the first 550 lines : *Wyatt* in the first 550 lines has 47, and the *Shoemaker's Holiday*[3] 76. Secondly, in the frequent occurrence of a full pause before either the first or the second rime of the couplet, or of a very short line riming with a long one, — mannerisms which give an emphasis to the rime altogether foreign to Webster's rimed work, as in

> Were this rightly scann'd,
> We scarce should find a king in any land.   P. 9.

> Observe their part,
> Pouring down tears, sent from my swelling heart!   P. 19.

Of this there is abundance in Dekker's other work — in the *Shoemaker's Holiday*, for instance, *Fortunatus*, and even so late as in

---

[1] In *Shoemaker*.

[2] *Wyatt*, pp. 13, 14, 14, 15, 19, 26, 54, 55, etc. ; and the pity and compassion for Lady Jane and Guildford, pp. 60–62. It is hackneyed and commonplace, of the style in which pity and compassion when they do appear in the older histories are clothed, as once in the bloody *True Trag. of Yorke*, p. 27 ; and therefore to be attributed to Dekker also because of his familiarity with this older type. See below.

[3] Date, 1599.

If This be not a Good Play.[1] Thirdly, in the frequent occurrence —
frequent that is, compared to other writers of the day and to Webster,
who has almost none of it, — of rime between two speeches.   This
appears also in the *Shoemaker* and *Fortunatus.*[2] And last of all, in
the general effect of the rhythm, strongly accented and rapid, but
jolting, little varied, and sometimes so rough and crude as to descend
to the level of doggerel :

> I 'll to the dukes at Cambridge, and discharge them all.
> Prosper me, God, in these affairs !
> I loved the father well, I loved the son,
> And for the daughter I through death will run.   *Wyatt*, p. 12.
>
> Then you cried, God speed ;
> Now you come on me, ere you say, take heed.   *Wyatt*, p. 25.
>
> And when thou spendest this ill-got gold,
> Remember how thy master's life was sold ;
> Thy lord that gave thee lordships, made thee great ;
> Yet thou betray'd'st him as he sat at meat.
> On to my grave : 'tis time that I were dead,
> When he that held my heart betrays my head.   *Wyatt*, pp. 28–9.

With this, and with Wyatt's speeches cited above, pp. 49, 50, compare
the following from the *Shoemaker:*

> *Ralph.* I thank you, master, and I thank you all.
> Now, gentle wife, my loving, lovely Jane,
> Rich men, at parting, give their wives rich gifts,
> Jewels and rings, to grace their lily hands.
> Thou know'st our trade makes rings for women's heels :
> Here take this pair of shoes, cut out by Hodge,
> Stitched by my fellow Firk, seamed by myself,
> Made up and pinked with letters for thy name.
> Wear them, my dear Jane, for thy husband's sake,
> And every morning when thou pulls't them on,
> Remember me, and pray for my return.
> Make much of them ; for I have made them so,
> That I can know them from a thousand mo.   *Shoemaker*, p. 15. •
>
> *Ham.* All this, I hope, is but a woman's fray,
> That means : come to me, when she cries : away !
> In earnest, mistress, I do not jest,

---

[1] Of full pause shortly before one of the rimes: *Wyatt:* p. 6 me, p. 8 dead, p. 9
scann'd, p. 13 go, p. 14 stay, p. 15 prove, p. 16 part, p. 19 afraid, p. 21 sense,
p. 21 woe, p. 23 need, p. 26 submit, p. 27 do, etc. *Shoemaker*, p. 10 stay, p. 13
go, p. 15 so, p. 19 can, p. 26 farewell, right, no, stay, gentleman, p. 27 Ford, same,
guest, life, p. 35 grieve, name, p. 36 right, now, brawl, jest, doubt, etc. *If This be not
a Good Play:* p. 266 slave, p. 269 civill, throw, p. 270 beside, p. 272 goe, say, etc. Of
one very short line to a couplet: *Wyatt*, p. 6 stay, p. 7 power, p. 11 be, dead, p. 14 on,
p. 19 part, p. 22 farewell, p. 23 proceed, p. 24 part, p. 25 speed.

[2] *Wyatt:* p. 21 one couplet, p. 39 one, p. 52 three, p. 55 two, p. 60 one ; *Shoemaker*,
great number, as, p. 26, 27, 36, 37, etc. ; *Fortunatus*, p. 359 four, etc.

> A true chaste love hath entered in my breast.
> I love you dearly, as I love my life,
> I love you as a husband loves a wife;
> That, and no other love, my love requires,
> Thy wealth, I know, is little; my desires
> Thirst not for gold. Sweet, beauteous Jane, what's mine
> Shall, if thou make myself thine, all be thine.
> Say, judge, what is thy sentence, life or death?
> Mercy or cruelty lies in thy breath.   *Shoemaker*, p. 52.

Note in both the same persistent, emphatic accent, the endstopt lines and strong endings,[1] and — what is most notable and most Dekker-like — the marked pause in the middle of the line, balancing two rather distinct, and sometimes parallelistic,[2] phrases or clauses.

What real characters there are in *Wyatt*, then, are Dekker's; many scattered ideas and phrases, the sentiment which pervades the play, the metre, and often the cast of the language,[3] seem decidedly of his making; and Dekker's, let me now add, is also the general conduct of the play. For he was already an old hand at the 'history.' Here is a list of his histories, now lost, as recovered from Henslowe's diary :

1598, March 13-25, "the famos wares of henry the fyrste & the prynce of walles."
                                                         P. 85.
March 30, "goodwine and his iij sonnes."   P. 85.
"perce of exstone."   P. 85.
September 29, "syvell wares in fraunce."   Three parts, pp. 96, 98, etc.
1599, September 3, "Robart the second kinge of scottes tragedie."   P. 111.

These were probably all in the 'history' style; and one of them, the third part of "*syvell wares of fraunce*," is given in Henslowe as by Dekker alone.[4] Very likely, then, it was Dekker that laid the plot of *Wyatt*.

There is little left to Webster. One who holds to the opinion that Webster was a haunter of churchyards and always wrote as black as in *Malfi*, might claim for him this meditation :

> *Guild.* The Tower will be a place of ample state:
> Some lodgings in it will, like dead men's sculls,
> Remember us of frailty.
> We are led with pomp to prison.

---

[1] Mr. Swinburne, in his study of Dekker, *Nineteenth Cent.* 1887, speaks of his "abrupt rimes."

[2] As in some of the extracts above, or in these from couplets in *Wyatt :*
     P. 26.   my crime is great, and I must answer it.
     P. 27.   Need bids me eat, need bids me hear thee too.
     P. 20.   If the dukes be cross, we 'll cross their powers.
     P. 36.   To save this country, and this realm defend, etc.
Cf. also *H. W.*, Pt. I, p. 112. We get by many if we lose by one, etc.; p. 60, Hans's second speech.

[3] As in the excerpts quoted from Brett's, Wyatt's, and the Clown's speeches above.

[4] Henslowe, p. 99.

THE

MALCONTENT.

By John Marston.

1 6 0 4.

AT LONDON
Printed by V.S. for William Aspley, and
are to be sold at his shop in Paules
Church-yard.

THE

MALCONTENT.

Augmented by *Marston*.

With the Additions played by the Kings
Maiesties servants.

Written by *Ihon Webster*.

1 6 0 4.

AT LONDON
Printed by V.S. for William Aspley, and
are to be sold at his shop in Paules
Church-yard.

> *Jane.*   O prophetic soul !
> Lo, we ascend into our chairs of state,
> Like funeral coffins in some funeral pomp
> Descending to their graves !   P. 10.

or this :

> Alas ! how small an urn contains a king !   Pp. 8, 9, etc.

But these ten years yet there are no meditations of Webster's to compare with them : and those, as we shall yet see, were written, not out of his own head but strongly under the influence of a school.[1] In Dekker's own work, moreover, there appears, about this very time, a long passage of curious meditation — Hippolito's over Infelice's picture and the skull[2] — more like this before us than is any in Webster. There is no one thing in *Wyatt*, then, that we can claim with any degree of assurance for Webster ; nay, almost all of it we have already ceded to Dekker.

II. THE MALCONTENT.

WEBSTER'S SHARE.

Marston's *Malcontent* was first published in 1604.[3] There were two editions[4] within the year, bearing these title-pages :

The Malcontent. By John Marston. 1604. At London Printed by V. S. for William Aspley, and are to be sold at his shop in Paules Church-yard.

The Malcontent. Augmented by Marston. With the Additions played by the Kings Maiesties servants. Written by Jhon Webster. 1604. At London Printed by V. S. for William Aspley, and are to be sold at his shop in Paules Church-yard.

This second edition is enlarged in two respects : by the addition of an Induction, and by the insertion into the play proper of twelve passages,[5] varying in extent from one line to a scene. The question now arises, how much of this is Webster's ? Criticism has been very supercilious with the question, and has only suffered the penalty for being

---

[1] See below, Chap. III.

[2] *H. W.*, Pt. I, IV, 1, pp. 151-2. — Cf. also I, 1, p. 95, Duke's 4th speech. Cf. also *Sat.*, p. 250 : The breath that purles from thee, is like the Steame of a new-open'd vault.

[3] Reg. July 5, 1604, for William Apsley and Thomas Thorpe. As the second edition was published by the same persons, this entry is probably for the first.

[4] Mr. Bullen (*Marston*, Introd., p. xxviii) says there are really three editions, two unenlarged. But judging from my inspection of the two British Museum copies (enlarged and unenlarged, 1604) and my comparison of them with each other and with Mr. Bullen's lists of variants, I should say there were at least four — two of either class. But these discrepancies within the class, though fairly numerous, are in every case slight — omission·or addition of a word or two words, or the mistaking of one word for another, — and need not here be considered. Nor have I in my list of the inserted passages, p. 57, note, taken account of such minor one- or two-word accretions to the text of the second edition. They are mostly immaterial — form-words, — arising probably from correction of earlier, or from the perpetration of fresh, printer's errors ; not, certainly, derived from any recension by Webster.

[5] See p. 57 for the list.

55

wise above what is written. Relying on its own arithmetic and discernment and holding the title-page to be a stupid blunder, it has answered unhesitatingly, "Induction and inserted passages." [1] Hazlitt alone paid some regard to the title-page, and in the very phrasing of his avowal of ignorance showed that he was on the brink of truth. "It is impossible to determine," he says, "which were Marston's augmentations, which Webster's additions." [2]

It is not impossible. Consider for a moment the title-pages, the titles to the Induction and to the play proper, and a passage in the Induction which explains the appearance of the play. The title-page to the second edition Mr. Bullen calls "curious" — "slovenly wording and vicious punctuation." [3] Not at all, if we will but put ourselves back for an instant into Elizabethan times. Realize that the plays issuing from day to day were printed and set forth like pamphlets — not world-literature, — as appealing only to a momentary interest; and that in this second edition it is taken for granted that the old play of the *Malcontent*, often acted, lately revived, [4] and now a second time printed, was, both it and its author, well known. So, the title-page says only what it means; so, wording and punctuation — the latter with a not uncommon inscriptional use of periods for commas — are natural and clear: *The Malcontent, augmented by Marston. With the Additions played by the Kings Maiesties servants, written by John Webster.* [5] But the slovenly wording gives offence — the redundancy and ambiguity of "augmented" and "additions." The *augmentations* by Marston, as the above reading unquestionably asserts, as Hazlitt seemed on the point of perceiving, and as the facts of the case will shortly prove, consist of the new passages inserted (or rather, replaced) by Marston himself into the text of his own play; and the *additions* by Webster are additions in the strict sense of the term, that is, the prefixed Induction. [6]

------

[1] Mr. Ward, II, 483–4, seems to be of the opinion that here and there in the body of the play proper we have to reckon with the work of Webster. Dyce, ed. 1857, p. xiii, says : " What the additions were we cannot exactly say." Swinburne and others are all of the same opinion. See Bullen and Small below. **[4]** *Induct.*, Haz., IV, p. 109.

[2] Haz., vol. IV, p. 105, after Dyce, ed. 1857, p. 322. **[3]** *Mars.*, introd., p. xxviii. note.

[5] Observe in fac., that the printer lets as much as possible stand, and yet takes pains to insert *augmented*, which, with Small's emended punc. (*inf.*), becomes either superfluous or tautologous.

[6] Dr. Ph. Aronstein in an article on *Marston als Dramatiker, Eng. Stud.*, Bd. 20, at this point, as generally through his article, echoes Mr. Bullen ; finds the wording of the title "sehr sonderbar," but adds, "offenbar auf Mystification berechnet"! Dr. Aronstein simply accepts the common view (cf. p. 382) that W. has made additions to the text of the play proper, without any perceptible attempt to investigate the matter. Since this chapter was finished I have come upon the excellent treatise

THE
INDVCTION TO
THE MALECONTENT, AND
the additions acted by the Kings Ma-
iesties servants.

Written by *Iohn Webster*.

Enter W. Sly, a Tyre-man following him with a stoole.

Tyer-man.

IR, the Gentlemen will be angry if you
sit heare.

Sly Why? we may sit vpon the stage
at the private house: thou doest not take
me for a country gentleman, doest? doest
thinke I feare hissing? Ile holde my life
thou took'st me for one of the plaiers.

Tyre: No sir.

Sly By gods slid if you had, *I* would have given you but six
pence for your stoole: Let them that have stale suites, sit in the
galleries, hisse at mee: he that will be laught out of a Taverne
or an Ordinarie, shall seldome feede well or be drunke in good
company. Where's Harry Cundale, D: Burbidge, and W: Sly,
let me speake with some of them.

Tyre: An't please you to go in sir, you may.

Sly: *I* tell you no; I am one that hath seene this play often, & can
give them intelligence for their action: I have most of the ieasts

THE
MALECONTENT.

ACTVS PRIMVS. SCE. PRIMA.

The vileſt out of tune Muſicke being heard.

Enter Bilioſo *and* Prepaſſo.

Bilioſo.

Hy how now? are ye mad? or drunke? or both?
or what?

Præ: Are ye building *Babilon there?*

Bili: Heere's a noiſe in Court, you thinke you
are in a Tauerne, do you not?

Præ: You thinke you are in a brothell houſe,
do you not? This roome is ill ſented.

Enter one with a perfume.

So, perfume, perfume; ſome vpon me I pray thee: The Duke is
vpon inſtant entrance, ſo, make place there.

SCENA SECVNDA.

Enter the Duke Pietro, Ferrardo, *Count* Equato,
Count Celſo *before, and* Guerrino.

Pie: Where breath's that muſique?

Bilio: The diſcord rather then the Muſique is heard from the
Malecontent *Malenoles* chamber.

Ferrar: Malenole.

Male: * Yaugh, godaman what doſt thou there: Dukes *Cani-* *Out of his
med *Iunoes* iealous of thy long ſtockings: ſhadowe of a woman, *chamber.*
what wouldſt Weeſell? thou lambe a Court: what dooſt thou
bleat for? a you ſmooth chind *Catamite!*

Pie: Come downe thou ragged cur, and ſnarle heere, I giue

The titles of the original quarto of the second edition tell the same story. That to the Induction runs thus: *The Induction to the Malecontent, and the additions acted by the Kings Maiesties servants. Written by John Webster.*[1] Then, after the Induction, in similar large type, as title to the play proper, simply: *The Malecontent. Actus Primus. Sce. Prima.*[1] That is to say, the *Malcontent* now *without* 'additions' acted by the King's Servants (or Induction), written by Webster. A glance at the photographic facsimiles makes this quite plain.

When we take these surprisingly plain and speaking facts, together with the statement of the Induction[2] that this old play had been lost and found again, that it and the *Spanish Tragedy* had belonged to the Blackfriars company and the King's in common, and since the Blackfriars had appropriated the one the King's was about to appropriate the other, the case seems not to need further argument. It was not the augmentations — the twelve passages inserted into the play proper,[3] — the title-page and titles inform us, that were played by the King's Company. Mere talk without action as they are, they would never have been added to a stage-copy. Rather it was an *induction*, which should have a fling at Blackfriars and explain the King's Men's position.

This may seem decisive. If, however, the 'augmentations' should in themselves betray a strange hand (whether evidently Webster's or not), the general impression that it is Webster's would be strengthened. But they do not: they prove unmistakably part and parcel of

---

of Mr. R. A. Small, entitled *The Stage Quarrel of Ben Jonson and the so-called Poet-asters.* "No one acquainted with Elizabethan printing," declares Mr. Small, "would hesitate to alter the punctuation thus: *The Malcontent augmented. By Marston. With the additions played by the Kings Maiesties servants, written by John Webster.*" I, for one, should hesitate: Mr. Small sets at naught both punc. and typog. composition (cf. fac.). And, as he interprets this, he does as much for the phrasing. Content with tautology, he makes no distinction between 'augmentations' and 'additions,' and understands that W. added scenes to the text of the play proper. He even declares that the evidence of style is in favor of W.'s authorship of these, as well as the title-page (p. 115). For the rest of Mr. Small's views on the subject see pp. 59, 60, notes.   [1] As in the Brit. Mus. 1604 quarto.

[2] Induct., *Works,* IV, p. 109: Faith, sir, the book was lost; and because 't was pity so good a play should be lost, we found it, and play it. *Sly.* I wonder you would play it, another company having interest in it. *Con.* Why not Malevole in folio with us, as Jeronimo in decimo sexto with them? They taught us a name for our play; we call it, *One for Another.* — Either Collier or Dyce first interpreted this.

[3] These: I, 1, 146-188, Pietro and Malevole; I, 1, 256-303, Mal. and Bil.; I, 3, Mal. and Pass.; II, 2, 34 Mal.; II, 2, 57-71, Mal. and Bil.; III, 1, 33-156, Bil., Bianca, and Pass.; IV, 2, 123-137, Mal. and Bil.; V, 1 Bil. and Pass.; V, 2, 10-39, Pass.; V, 2, 164-194, Bil. and Mal.; V, 2, 212-226, Mal. and Men.; V, 3, 180-202. — All indicated in Bullen's notes. Small: "M. would not have been employed to add scenes to a play stolen from his own actors" (p. 115). We know nothing of M.'s attitude, but *such* scenes were never added to a stage-copy. They are "cut" passages, restored.

the original text, — before the play was "lost," or, perhaps, before it was ever acted.

For, the peculiar sort of connection subsisting between the 'augmentations' betrays the hand of Marston. Lacking in action or acting qualities,[1] the 'augmentations' lack also connection with the rest of the play; but they are connected, five of them, by direct or implicit references within themselves. The scenes between Bilioso and Malevole, and Bilioso and his wife, are connected by the thread of Bilioso's cuckoldry; and those between Bilioso and Malevole are connected by Malevole's mocking and twitting[2] of Bilioso when the tables are turned. Now this trick of mocking and twitting is far more common in Marston than in any other of the Elizabethan playwrights I know, and is to be found in him elsewhere at least seven times : *Antonio's Revenge*, I, 1, 35–48 ; *Dutch Courtesan*, I, 1, 170, and I, 2, 258 ; IV, 5, 12–15, and V, 3, 127–30 ; III, 2, 7–11, and V, 3, 127–8 ; *Fawn*, IV, 1, 326–330, and V, 1, 110–113 ; IV, 1, 402–3, and IV, 1, 571–2 ; *Sophonisba*, III, 2, 35–38, and V, 3, 64–67. In Webster it appears late and but once,[3] and then in a different form, without the echoing of the very words of the victim, so characteristic of all the cases above.

The matter and style of the 'augmentations,' moreover, are thoroughly Marstonian. The bulk of them have to do with Bilioso; and, these dropped, he would be reduced to nothing in the play. This could not have been the original plan, for Bilioso and his fool Passarello correspond exactly to Balurdo and his page Dildo, and Castilio and his page Catzo, in *Antonio and Mellida*, who appear repeatedly and for long periods, the master airing his vanities and absurdities before his page (or fool), just as Bilioso does before Passarello in *Malcontent*, V, 1, — an 'augmentation.'[4] Likewise the scenes between Malevole and Bilioso (also those between Malevole and Maquerelle, Malevole and Passarello) must be original, for they are meant to provoke Malevole's professional indignation and satire (or his inconsistent ribaldry), just as Balurdo and Castilio do that of Feliche, the malcontent in *Antonio and Mellida*, and Zuccone, Debile-Dosso, and the other scamps and ninnies do that of Faunus, the malcontent[5] in the *Fawn*. Take them

---

[1] Except the one line ! A very Marstonian line, by the way : smart and impudent.

[2] The twitting appears : I, 1, 295–6, and II, 2, 62–3 ; II, 2, 64, and V, 2, 168.

[3] *D. L. C.*, II, 3, and IV, 2 (Ariosto). — *D. L. C.*, pub. 1623, written 1621-23 (see above, Chap. I).

[4] *A. & M.*, III, 2, 25 f ; III, 2, 120 f ; V, 1. Cf. also *Malc.*, III, 1, 33–156. Cf. also with *Malc.*, V, 1, the passage in *A. & M.*, II, 1, 106 f, where Balurdo and Forobosco discuss Balurdo's leg.

[5] Faunus is not gloomy as Malevole and Feliche, but he has just the same part to play — satire, criticism, railing, playing the stops of various forms of vice and

away, and you take away one of the most characteristic features of Marston's comedy, — the witty, foul-mouthed cynic inspecting and manipulating, during lulls of the action, some great fool and ass. And the style of the 'augmentations' itself, — the words chosen,[1] the syntax and rhetorical structure,[2] the impudent, startling, and often outlandish vocabulary and figures, the abrupt and jerky antitheses,[3] the outbursts of railing and satire,[4] the lively, but filthy and hideous, imaginations,[5] — all are of a piece with the rest of the play, and with Marston as a whole. As Mr. Swinburne says, "the passages thus added to that grimmest and most sombre of tragi-comedies are in such exact keeping with the previous text that the keenest scent of the veriest blood-hound among critics could not detect a shade of difference in the savour."[6]

---

affectation before him, and venting ribaldry of his own. For this whole matter of the malcontent as a type in Marston, see below, Chap. III, Sect. II.

[1] There is no need for prolonged comparison of details of style, yet consider the following very Marstonian language, utterly unlike anything in severe and classic Webster: I, 1, 295 f, " mutual, friendly-reciprocal kind of steady-unanimous-heartily-leagued," — and II, 2, 62 f; also II, 2, 66-67, " The serpigo, the strangury, an eternal uneffectual priapism seize thee " (cf. *Fawn*, I, 2, 196, " the hip-gout, the strangury, the fistula in ano," etc.; IV, 1, 434, " Don Zuccone, that dry scaliness, — that sarpigo, — that barren drouth "; *D. C.*, II, 1, 137-8, " a strumpet is a serpigo "). *Strangury, serpigo, priapism* never occur in Webster. So *Catzo*, V, 2, 220, which occurs also in *Malc.*, I, 1, 144, and V, 2, 237 (both ed. I), and, as a proper name, in *A. & M.*, but never in W. The filthy song (which never occurs in W.), V, 2, 34 f, is paralleled in the same scene (l. 1 f) within the text of ed. I. And the harping on revolting olfactory images would of itself be enough to convince one of M.'s authorship. Cf. *Malc.*, pp. 294, 256, 222, etc. See below, Chap. III. But I do not exhaust the material at hand.

[2] The aposiopeses, for instance, of which Marston is at all times fond: and as for syntax, his great bent for using an adjective alone (or with only a personal pronoun) in the vocative, which never occurs in Webster, and seldom in any English outside of a Latin-school crib, as in the "Hence, ye gross jawed, peasantly — out, go!" of the augmentations, II, 2, 63, and V, 2, 168. Cf. with this "Forbear, impure, to blot bright honor's name," *Ant. Rev.*, IV, 1, 126; "Now, thou impudent, if, etc.," l. 139; Thou very poor, why dost not weep," l. 293; " Good honest, leave me," II, 2, 43; " Good, do not weep," II, 2, 118; *A. & M.*, III, 1, 10; etc. It is one of M.'s ear-marks.

[3] See V, 2, 168-193; cf. *Fawn*, IV, 1, 9-12.

[4] See I, 3, 57-9; V, 3, 180 f; I, 1, 287-293; II, 2, 69-71, 64-66, etc.; cf. Feliche's and Faunus's.

[5] I, 1, 170-180, " hideous imagination ! " — It is only a sample of Marston, both in this play and the *Fawn*.

[6] *Nineteenth Century*, June, 1886, art. *Webster;* and 1888, art. *Marston*, to the same effect. Yet, overawed by the usual misunderstanding of that title-page, Mr. Swinburne thinks Webster's hand must be there. — Mr. Small (p. 115) is just as certain, on the other hand, that the evidence of style in these 'augmentations' points to *Webster's* authorship. But he does not offer much discussion in support of his opinion. " Magnificent declamation and smoothness of versification unattained by

But what clinches the matter is the passage in Act I, sc. 3, ll. 18–22 — an augmentation — about the woman's horn,

> . . . and that's the reason the horn of a cuckold is as tender as his eye, or as that growing in the woman's forehead twelve years since, that could not endure to be touched.

read in the light of a pamphlet entitled :

> *A miraculous and monstrous, but yet most true and certayne Discourse of a Woman, now to be seen in London, of the age of threescore yeares or thereabouts, in the midst of whose forehead there groweth out a crooked Horne of four ynches long. Imprinted at London, by Thomas Orwin, and are to be sold by Edward White, dwelling at the little north dore of Paules Church, at the sign of the Gun, 1588.*[1]

Note that these time-references are all exact. That in the augmentation is "twelve years," not "eleven of twelve," nor a round number like "ten" or "a dozen"; and that of the pamphlet-title is, "*now* to be seen." Now Webster himself in 1604 could not have written "twelve years," nor (whether written by Marston or Webster) would the actors in 1604 have spoken it. Marston, without thinking, simply restored to the press-copy this passage as it had stood in the text of 1600.[2]

Marston in 1603." What Mr. Small means I am at a loss to understand. Certainly the augmentations are no way superior in style or verse to the rest of the play. Mostly, they are in prose, and they contain nothing particularly fine such as the address to Night or one meditation of Malevole's (III, 1, 157–170; IV, 2, 139–151), both in the unaugmented text.

[1] Quoted in Bullen's *Marston*, vol. I, p. 233, from Gilchrist.

[2] The importance of the date of the *Malc.* has never been appreciated, not only in its bearings on the addition-augmentation problem, but also on *Hamlet*. *Malc.* III, 1, 250 f,— *Illo, ho, ho, ho, art there old truepenny ?* — present in *both* editions, must be derived from the Old *Hamlet ;* for though the 1603 Q. does not contain the " Art thou there, truepenny ? " (Globe, I, 5, 113, 150), the corrupt state of that very passage argues the leaving of something out. Aronstein sets the date as he pleases at 1603, as that of *What You Will* at 1600 ! But why did Herr Aronstein contribute his chapter on the dates of Marston's plays to a scientific journal? Mr. Small, too (p. 115, 116), allows a date no earlier than 1603 : for, since he conceives the 'augmentations' of the play to be Webster's, the horn passage has for him no import. He bases this judgment on two " unimpeachable references to Shakspere's *Hamlet* " and an " ill-natured allusion to the Scots, which forbid us to date the play earlier than the latter half of 1603." The allusion to the Scots (V, 3, 24 f),

> *Bian.* And is not Signior St. Andrew a gallant fellow now ?

is in the unaugmented text, indeed, but it and the answer,

> *Mar.* By my maidenhead, la, honour and he agree as well together as a satin suit and woollen stockings,

even if necessarily referring to the incoming of the Scots under James, are absolutely separable from the text — not a thread connects them with what stands before or after — and so may have been inserted, long after, for the joke's sake. (Cf. *Biron*, inf. p. 67, and M. would have no more reason than Ch. to cancel it.)

This Induction, the earliest independent work of Webster's, then, that has come down to us, is, as art, of little value. It was meant, indeed, only for the hour. Its purpose, as we have seen, is really no more than to justify the King's Men — perhaps only at the first performance — in reviving this old play; and the parts in it are given (to the confusion indeed of the reader) only in the form of the names of the actors at that performance. It is done in stereotyped style. There is the usual dispute between Tireman and spectators about sitting on the stage, discussion of the character and intent — especially satirical intent — of the play, and quantum of local allusions and Joe Millers. Such, with variations, are the inductions to Marston's *Antonio and Mellida* and *What You Will*, to several of the plays of Jonson,[1] and to Beaumont's *Knight of the Burning Pestle;* and though none of these (or any others I know) that are certainly precedent to Webster's in date can be fixed upon as his model, a model (among the hundreds of plays now lost) he very probably had. And like nearly all such compositions, whether earlier or later, it is, except to the antiquary, exceedingly dull. The conversation is rambling and disjointed, and the characters are wooden or foolish. The jests, when of a more perennial interest than "Blackfriars hath almost spoiled Blackfriars for feathers,"[2] are mouldy: the duodecimo-folio quibble, for instance, is to be found in Chettle[3] and in Middleton,[4] and Sly's "excellent thought" is of the same stamp as one in *Antonio and Mellida.*[5]

As a piece of his independent work, then, the Induction does Webster no credit, and offers no basis to warrant us in claiming much of the partnership work of this Period for him. It is rather the poorest

---

St. Andrew is no person of the drama; like the "Marshall Make-room," Emilia's lover, whom she asks about in the next following speech, it is a name made up for the occasion and on the spur of the moment. And the allusions to *Ham.* are the one discussed above, and another pointed out by Bullen, *Malc.*, I, 1, 350-3. This latter is, to my mind, altogether "impeachable"; and, besides, does not appear in *Ham.* till the 1604 ed. There is everything for, then, and little against, the date 1600. And it is highly probable, too, that Marston, saturated as he was at this time with the very wording of Kyd's two Revenge Plays (see Chap. III), would make Malevole merely echo the *Illo, ho*, etc., of the Old *Hamlet*. — Either this, or Shak.'s *Ham.* in existence in 1600!

[1] *Cynthia's Revels, Every Man out of his Humour, Bartholomew Fair, Staple of News.* [2] Induction, p. 108.

[3] "For thou art a courtier in decimo sexto," *Patient Grissel*, pub. 1603 (ed. Hübsch, 1. 947).

[4] *Father Hubbard's Tale*, Works, Vol. VIII, p. 64.

[5] Induct., p. 111, and *A. & M.*, II, 1, 81-87.

of all the inductions I have mentioned. Yet, when we remember the inferior quality of most inductions and the merely occasional character of this, and when we consider Webster's own native unfitness — to judge from later work — for such a task, we may, at the same time that we bar him from any important part in the work of this Period, whether in comedy or tragedy, nevertheless hold fast to the conviction, that he had, even now, literary powers above the "excellent thought" of Sly.

For, even in this induction there is evidence that Webster's style was forming. There is here something of that terseness and allusiveness — verging on crabbedness and obscurity, — and of that bent for concise, epigrammatic figure, so conspicuous in the *White Devil*.[1]

> Why not Malevole in folio with us, as Jeronimo in decimo sexto with them?[1]

> *Sink.* I durst lay four of mine ears the play is not so well acted as it hath been.
> *Cund.* O, no, Sir, nothing, Ad *Parmenonis suem.*[2]

> No, Sir, such vices as stand not accountable to law should be cured as men heal tetters, by casting ink upon them. Induction, p. 109.

There is weight and point to that phrasing; and in the first two excerpts there is a brevity of allusiveness that has made the commentators, and must have made the audience, scratch their heads.[3]

III. THE CITIZEN COMEDIES.

SOURCES.

There remain in this Period for consideration the two comedies of London life, *Westward Ho* and *Northward Ho*. To *Westward Ho* there is, I suppose, no definite source assignable. The romantic element — the passion of the Earl for Mistress Justiniano, with her feigned death at the critical moment[4] — is, as we shall see, repeated from *Satiromastix*. Further than that, except possibly in regard to the device of the diamond,[5] there need be no source expected : the plot is too exceedingly simple and straightforward, and the incidents and situations too obvious. Three citizens' wives plan for a lark with three gallants; in the midst of it, however, decide to keep within

---

[1] Induction, p. 110. For the interpretation see the footnote, and the footnote in *Marston*, vol. I, p. 203.

[2] Induct., p. 110, note. Cf. footnote in *Marston*, I, p. 204, for the story.

[3] Such is the case with the first two excerpts, and with the phrase "Blackfriars hath spoiled Blackfriars for feathers." Induct., p. 108.

[4] *V. infra*, p. 85.

[5] The diamond which was given by Mrs. Tenterhook to the constable as security for Monopoly, came into Tenterhook's hands, and was to have witnessed against her; but, getting to her through still other hands, witnessed against him instead. It probably is derived from an Italian novella.

bounds; and so face their husbands (who have come in chase of them, as they learn, from the brothel) on the offensive. That is all, and Dekker probably invented all of it.

One incident, however, seems not like Dekker, and bears a strong resemblance to two incidents in Marston's *Sophonisba* (1606). The Earl's discovery of a hideous hag in the muffled figure which passes for the beautiful woman, is like Syphax's finding the black Vangue in his bed, and still more like his recognition of the unspeakable Erichtho [1] as his paramour. The situation may have been borrowed, if *Sophonisba* was already on the stage. [2]

A source for the only part of the plot of *Northward Ho* which cannot easily be accounted Dekker's own invention, was long ago pointed out by Langbaine. The story of the gallants, Greenfield and Featherstone, who pretend not to know the name of the citizen, Maybery, as they meet him at the inn, and pretend to quarrel about a ring of Mrs. Maybery's, which, as they aver, Greenfield had received from her and lost in her company, and Featherstone, another lover, had found and dared to wear, is to be found in Malespini's *Ducento Novelle*, Parte Prima, Novella I. But with two necessary deviations: first, the story to the husband is a lie, intended to make trouble between him and his wife; second, the ring, instead of really belonging to one of the gallants, had been snatched off the woman's hand before her husband's shop door. [3] As, however, there is no edition of Malespini discoverable earlier than 1609, [4] Dekker and Webster's real source remains undetermined. Yet, the story in Malespini being of two Englishmen, John Fletton and Thomas Bampton, [5] retainers of the Cardinal of Winchester, while sojourning at Calais and Gravelines on occasion of 'a meeting of many princes and gentlemen, as well on the side of France as on that of England,' we may presume that the story, unless a pure fiction, was then easily accessible to Englishmen through other channels than an Italian novelist. [6]

---

[1] *Sophonisba*, III, 2, and V, 1.

[2] There is no way of showing this, however. Fleay, indeed, sets a date 1602-3, but without all reason. In the address to the reader in the second ed. of the *Fawn* (both editions 1606) Marston says, "I will present a tragedy to you, which shall boldly abide the most curious perusal." (*Works*, II, p. 113.) This refers, as the marginal note in the 2nd ed. declares, to *Soph.;* but whether as a play already some time on the stage, or just to appear, it is impossible to decide.

[3] A borrowing from *H. W.*, III, 1, p. 134, where Fustigo seizes Viola's ring before the shop.

[4] *Venetia*, MDCIX. See Grässe's *Trésor, Encicl. Ital., Nouv. Biog. Gén.*

[5] "Bamptrone."

[6] It was the occasion of the Field of the Cloth of Gold, in 1520, or, possibly, the occasion of Wolsey's later mission to France. Both times, the English staid several

Further than this (that is, in regard to Webster's part in the author-ship), these two plays had best be discussed together, for they are very like. They have the same theme — the intrigue of gallants with citi-zens' wives, — and are animated with the same spirit of partisanship for the city. They depict the same light-hearted, adventurous, high-flying gallants, the same well-to-do, generous, jealous citizens, the same mirth-loving, coarse-grained citizens' wives. They are infused with the same rough-and-ready morality, liveliness and jollity, and pre-occupation with the stir and whirl of the day. Justiniano, the jealous husband in *Westward Ho*, conducts the plot, so to speak, like May-bery,[1] the jealous husband in *Northward Ho*,— tries, like him, to get even by giving other husbands horns, and exhibits a jealousy of the same conventional type[2]; Mrs. Justiniano, like Mrs. Maybery, has some delicacy, and yet, like her, is coarse-grained enough to ride with her husband to see the fun at Brainford ; and the courtesan, Lucy, in her establishment is like Doll in hers. Both plays, moreover, are largely made up of a series of tricks played on various characters, especially the gallants, explained to the audience beforehand and followed by crowing[3] ; both contain an arrest, and an expedition out of town at the end ; both are written in the same simple, vivacious style, and in prose.[4] For either play, then, the question of authorship is practi-cally the same.

---

weeks in Calais. Oye (' Oia ') and its castle are but a few miles away. — The Cardi-nale di Vincestre is, I think, surely Wolsey. His title as Cardinal was, of course, Roman, of *St. Cecilia trans Tiberim;* but he received the bishopric of Winchester in 1529, after resigning for it in turn Bath and Wells, and Durham. Malespini, who lived 1540 — c. 1580, may have known only of this later bishopric.

[1] With the help of his friend, Bellamont.

[2] Both, like Ford in *M. W. W.*, are settled types of the jealous man. Both express a notion of Othello's, and, very probably, previously to Othello and inde-pendently : " Being certain thou art false, sleep, sleep my brain, For doubt was only that which fed my pain," *W. H.*, p. 72. Cf. Maybery, *N. H.*, 181, 6th speech. This is exactly the point made so much of in *Othello*, as III, 3, 177–192 ; 3, 359–360 ; 364–7 ; 383–7 ; 390. — It is astonishing that this most natural and seemingly unconventional character, Othello, should here (III, 3, 177–192) give a full account of the " humor " of jealousy, as represented by stock figures such as Justiniano and Ford, and then in his own character and subsequent conduct — for all Coleridge and others have said of his passion not being jealousy — literally exemplify it ! — Further, in both *W. H.* and *N. H.* there is a jealous husband discussing comically, before a servant, his wife's treatment of him, — Honeycomb in *W. H.*, p. 83, and Maybery in *N. H.*, pp. 187–8. Both passages very certainly Dekker's.

[3] As *W H.*, 148–9, where the scheme is laid, and 162–3, where the women exult. Cf. the trick played on Bellamont in *N. H.*, 243–6, and his double retort, V, 1.

[4] There is little verse in *W. H.*, still less in *N. H.*

Who, now, had the main hand in these very similar plays? Dekker, again, emphatically. Mr. Fleay, who has a bent for slicing plays up and allotting them by the scene and act to their respective authors, has followed it here unprofitably.[1] The fact is, there are hardly five or six consecutive pages in either play that do not exhibit pretty definite traces of Dekker's lively and facile hand, whether in situation, character, or phrase. All that is striking, all that is above the stereotyped and commonplace — and much that is not — points to him. Any detailed examination of the plays, page by page, is here, to be sure, impossible, and foreign to our purpose : but we can show at least how in the larger elements — construction, pervading spirit, situation, and character — the work bears Dekker's bold stamp.

The quality and spirit of the play are Dekkerian. The bourgeois subject-matter and the spirit of partisanship for the citizens are (as we shall see later, in connection with his obligations to the *Merry Wives of Windsor*) certainly due to him. And his is the satire. For satire there is in *Northward Ho*, though no one seems ever to have taken notice of it but Mr. Fleay. He declares the "hoary poet" Bellamont to be Chapman; and, though his arguments[2] hardly

---

[1] *W. H.* : (*Biog. Chr.*, II, 269-70) " I, II, III, and IV, 2 a are by Webster " ; " the last two acts are nearly all Dekker's." *N. H.*: (*ib.*, p. 270) " Dekker wrote the Doll scenes, I 2, II 1, III 1, IV 1, and Webster, I think, the rest." What does Mr. Fleay make of such Dekker-like repetitions, as " I'll find some idle business in the meantime : I will, I will in truth," *W. H.*, I, 1, p. 72, and " your eyes, your eyes," p. 74, and " hath undone us, hath undone us," p. 75? Or of Moll's naiveté about " gentlemen who come from beyond seas," p. 79 ; or of Honeysuckle as he looks in the glass in the morning and bids the man go tell his mistress to make his night-cap larger—" I can allow her almost an inch ; go, tell her so, very near an inch," p. 83, and so on. If anything in the play is Dekker's, these things are. The same is true of *N. H.* : p. 179, for instance, where Maybery thinks his boots have taken water, and pp. 181-2, where he mutters " I am foolish old Maybery, and yet I can be wise Maybery," — " I am but a foolish tradesman, and yet I'll be a wise tradesman."

[2] What Mr. Fleay says is as follows (*Biog. Chr.*, II, pp. 270-271) : " The Dekker part is personally satirical, Bellamont being, I think, Chapman. He is represented as an ' old ' poet and play-wright. Chapman at this time was forty-eight. In III, 1, Bellamont has made fools of 500 people, *i. e.*, in the last line of *All Fools* addressed to his audience. In IV, 1, he writes of Cæsar and Pompey as Chapman did in his play of that name. The marriage of ' Chatillion, the Admiral of France,' looks like an allusion to *Chabot, Admiral of France*, long after altered and revived by Shirley. The Duke of Biron and his execution surely alludes to Chapman's tragedy, which was prohibited in 1608, after having been acted we know not how long : it is true that the quoted lines are not in the extant version, but that has been expurgated and altered, and these lines are very like Chapman in style. The ' worthy to be one of your privy chamber or laureate ' means worthy to succeed Daniel, now in disgrace for *Eastward Ho* and *Philotas*, but gentleman of the Queen's privy chamber and laureate notwithstanding this. Captain Jenkins, though with far less certainty, I would identify with Drayton."— Mr. Fleay can be, at the same

prove it, and his further identification of the Welsh Captain Jenkins with Drayton is without any shadow of probability, he is in the right.

——The evidence is this. Bellamont is a poet, a dramatic poet associated with one of the companies.[1] He is old, and is repeatedly called white and hoary. He has classical tastes and acquirements, is the author of a *Cæsar and Pompey*,[2] and also is fond of laying his scene in the modern court of France.[3] He writes both comedies and tragedies.[4] He is a respectable and dignified person, with a leaning toward high-flown diction.[5] All this fits Chapman and no one else. Born in 1559,[6] he is the oldest of the well-known dramatists living in 1606, — older far than Shakspere, Jonson, Dekker, or Marston. The emphasis, however, is on grey hairs and respectability, not age; and Chapman, as Wood reports, was a person of "most reverend aspect, religious and temperate, qualities rarely meeting in a poet, and was so highly esteemed by the clergy and academicians," etc.[7] And every one knows Chapman was the classical poet of his day, the translator of Homer[8] as well as the poet of *Cæsar and Pompey;* and he, if anyone deserved the title, was the English poet-laureate of France.

Details agree. In Act IV, 1, 227, Bellamont is ridiculed at length for his predilection for French subjects : he is made to avow his purpose of having his tragedy presented in the French court by French gallants, at the marriage of Orleans and Chatillon, when he will stand behind the Duke of Epernon and be introduced by him to the King as worthy to be his poet-laureate.[9] This must mean Chapman ; for in the case of eight of his plays[10] he laid the scene unmistakably in France, Chatillon appears in one of them as a character, and Epernon

---

time, wonderfully clever and erratic. Some of these errors I confute below. As for "Chatillion," it, certainly, is no reference to the play *Chabot*. See below. This Chatillon, in *Bus. Rev.*, is no less than Coligny, Admiral of France, known in that day as Chatillon. *Chabot* is a late play.

[1] *N. H.*, pp. 177, 188, 225.

[2] *N. H.*, 177, 225, 226, 228.

[3] *N. H.*, 227.

[4] *N. H.*, 177, 226-8.

[5] *N. H.*, 228. Astyanax is meant, perhaps, to be a parody of such monsters of prowess, simplicity, and ranting boastfulness as Bussy, Clermont, and Byron.

[6] Anthony Wood says 1557.

[7] *Athenae Oxonienses*, London, 1815, vol. II, p. 575.

[8] *Seaven Bookes of the Iliades of Homere, Prince of Poets*, etc., London, 1598.

[9] Consequently Chapman is not, as Fleay (*v. supra*, note, p. 65) thinks, candidate for poet-laureateship in Eng. It is the Duke of *Epernon*, introducing him to the king of *France !* Why explain a passage the hardest way?

[10] *Humorous Day's Mirth; Monsieur Olive; Chabot; Bussy d'Ambois; Revenge of Bussy; Conspiracy of Byron; Tragedy of Byron;* and *Fatal Love*, a " French Tragedie by George Chapman," reg. June 29, 1660, but now lost.

— "the only courtier I know there" — in four.[1] "Biron" is the reading for the latter name in the first quarto [2] — a later insertion, as the joke in the Welshman's echo "Peppernoon" proves, — and that must mean Chapman's famous *Conspiracy of Charles, Duke of Byron,* suppressed at the instance of La Boderie.[3] And, further, there is in Doll's speech (III, 1, p. 214) — "See who knocks. Thou shalt see me make a fool of a poet, that hath made five hundred fools." — an allusion to the last line of the Epilogue to Chapman's comedy, *All Fools :*

> We can but bring you meat, and set you stools,
> And to our best cheer say, you all are welcome.[4]

This allusion, detected by the keen-scented Mr. Fleay, seems at first incredible ; one feels inclined to explain "that hath made" in Doll's speech as harking back to "me"[5] for antecedent. But two

---

[1] Chatillon appears in *Bus. Rev.*, p. 212, Epernon in both *Bussys* and both *Byrons*.

[2] Brit. Mus. copy.

[3] *Epernon* is, so far as I can learn, Hazlitt's emendation. Dyce prints *Biron,* so the Brit. Mus. Quarto. It hardly seems possible to read anything but the emendation, for Biron, even pronounced French, could hardly become Peppernoon to the son of Cadwallader. There is here a chance to fix more nearly the date of Chapman's *Byrons,* reg. June 5, 1608. La Boderie (not Beaumont, as Fleay always says), French Ambassador, wrote to Villeroy, April 8, 1608, about the play on Marshal Biron, which he had had forbidden, and which so soon as the court was out of town was played again, until he took further measures against it. (Bib. Nationale, Ms. fr. 15984.) It seems likely that the authors of *N. H.* (mentioned, remember, in the *Isle of Gulls,* 1606) had found it profitable before Aug. 6, 1607, the date of registering, to spoil the joke Epernon-Peppernoon, for the sake of inserting the name of the new drama, then town-talk. This would be at the time of La Boderie's *first* action. Perhaps, too, the passage relating to the execution of a "great man" (*N. H.,* p. 228) refers to the *Tragedy of Byron,* and it also (see below, footnote, p. 69) was inserted at this time. Anyhow, the plays cannot be earlier than 1607.

[4] Between these last two words of the Epilogue there is in the old edition a parenthesized hiatus, thus (—), which, taken in connection with the title of the play, seems to imply a very obvious rime. Another instance of this ingenious device (*i. e.,* of substituting a word which is no rime for an objectionable riming word) will be found in the doggerel lines in *An Humorous Day's Mirth* (p. 44). — Note in Shepherd's Chap., *Plays,* p. 77. Cf. *Ham.,* III, 2, 295, for another ex. (sug. by Prof. Kitt,).

[5] For, the 3rd person, "hath made," makes no great difficulty. Cf. *Wyatt,* p. 48. Why hast thou broke thy promise to thy friend, That for thy sake hath thrust *myself; Wint. Tale,* II, 3, 53, Hear me who professes myself ; IV, 4, 429-30, Thou a sceptre's heir, That thus affects a sheephook ; *Tam. Shrew.,* IV, 1, 104, Thou, it seems that calls for company ; *L. L. L.,* V, 2, 66, To make me proud that jests, etc. See Abbott's *Shak. Gram.,* art. 214 (some of these readings are those of quartos) ; and Franz's *Shak. Grammatik,* Halle, 1900, art. 519. Abbott says, "We are, I think, justified in saying that the relative was often regarded like a noun by nature 3rd per. sing., and therefore uninfluenced by the antecedent." The greater convenience of "*poet*" as an antecedent, and the passage from *Sat.* below, are here decisively on the side of strict grammar. Yet a passage in *H. W.,* II, 1, p. 122 (How many gentlemen hast thou served thus? Nonè but five hundred, besides prentices and servingmen) may outweigh the passage in *Sat. ;* it depends on Roger's meaning.

further considerations are, I think, decisive. *All Fools* was acted at Court, New Year's Night, 1604,[1] and so, with its final stinger, was widely known. And in Dekker's *Satiromastix*, 1602, occurs this passage,

> *Dem.* If you sweare, dam me Faninus, or Crispinus,
> .   .   .   .
> To Poets dam me, or to Players dam me,
> If I brand you, or you, tax you, scourge you :
> I wonder then, that of five hundred, foure
> Should all point with their fingers in one instant
> At one and the same man ?[2]

which proves that with Dekker, at least, the round number five hundred was a common expression for *audience at a play*.

Bellamont, then, is Chapman, and in *Northward Ho* we get a not unexpected retort to the bland plagiarism of *Eastward Ho*.[3] He, the author also of *All Fools*, is made a fool of, and he, the sedate, classical student, and ' poet-laureate to the King of France ' (but who has lately been imprisoned for a seditious play), is represented as paying an obsequious visit at a harlot's house and as penned up among madmen. Why, though, are there no direct references to *Eastward Ho* itself, and no skits at the other partners in that venture, Jonson or Marston ? We must suppose that our authors took the plagiarism not at all ill[4] — indeed, the present satire of Chapman is pitched in a key of the best of good-humor, — and that they were only glad of the opportunity of chaffing Chapman in general. He it was, anyway, that wrote the main part of *Eastward Ho ;* Jonson, as he himself says,[5] imprisoned himself voluntarily, and there are few, if any, traces in the play of either his hand or Marston's. Dekker, moreover, was not ready or disposed to start another war of the theatres ; with Jonson he was now at peace and

---

[1] Halliwell's *Dict. of Old Plays*, sub voc.

[2] *Sat.*, p. 198. Demetrius Faninus (or Dekker) is upbraiding Horace (Jonson), the satirist. — The reader must punctuate for himself anew.

[3] The import of this conclusion is for the history of Chapman's development considerable. *Cæsar and Pompey* (see above, p. 66), for instance, which Chapman declares in his dedicatory letter to the first ed. (1631) never to have touched the stage, must either have been acted before 1606 in another form, or else have been known to our authors as an unsuccessful play ; and see the dating of *Byron*, p. 67, note.

This conclusion affects also, as we have seen, the question of the series of citizen plays — *W. H., E. H.*, and *N. H. That* we found, even on other grounds, to be the probable order, and this tends to confirm it. For there is no other reason known for their satirizing Chapman, whether in this or any other play ; and this is ample. The public would rather expect a retort in *N. H.*, and it gets it. The only difficulty is that *N. H.* has no definite echo from or allusion to the *play E. H.*, except the situation of the man led to betraying, unknown to himself, his own wife to another. (*N. H.*, V ; *E. H.*, III, 2.)

[4] In consideration of the complimentary prologue prefixed to it.

[5] Drummond's *Conversations*, ed. Laing, 1842, p. 20. He there says Marston and Chapman wrote it " between them." And see above, p. 16, note.

with Marston he had always been. Those personages, too, were not to be tampered with, as Dekker knew, even in fun : with the " reverend " figure it was otherwise.

—— For to Dekker, to take up the main thread once more, belongs this satire. Satire, strictly speaking, it is not. It lacks edge and fitness, discrimination and taste ; and it lacks meaning, as satire cannot. Making stately Chapman pay his respects to a whore, and shuting him up in Bedlam for wench-mad, is hardly satire. It is jolly raillery, and the horse-play of raillery, but it does not *hit*. But just such is the satire of Dekker generally. So in *Satiromastix* he poked fun at angry Jonson, without ever hitting his weak places, though here, having himself just been hit, he really tried. Dekker is too loutish and boisterous and good-humored. With Jonson, indeed, he succeeds even less than with Chapman : because he is a little vexed, the ring of his guffaw is spoiled. Yet it is the same man who ' untrusses,' or hazes, Jonson, and makes an ' April fool ' of Chapman. He has Jonson bullied and beaten, tossed in a blanket, and stabbed with a blunt dagger ; haled upon the stage by his satyr's horns, untrussed, and crowned with nettles ; just as he has Chapman bound, struggling and kicking, by the madhouse-keepers. He makes the one hire himself out to sing the praises of hair, and the other treat with a pinchbeck lady about posies for cheese-trenchers. The verses of both are absurd. And what differences there are in Dekker's treatment of the two are to be explained by his personal animus, which makes him in the one case only go to greater lengths. Jonson is made silly, contemptible, affected, cowardly — utterly unrecognizable as Jonson ; Chapman in ridiculous situations remains — not much, indeed, but somewhat — like Chapman. Jonson's verses are keyed to the highest pitch of absurdity ; Chapman's are no more than a parody.[1] But in both cases it is the same method of horse-play raillery and blunt banter. In both cases the ridicule is all outward, without any char-

---

[1] *N. H.*, IV, 1, p. 228 :

> Now the wild people, greedy of their griefs,
> Longing to see that which their thoughts abhorr'd,
> Prevented day, and rode on their own roofs,
> Making all neighboring houses til'd with men.

Mr. Fleay (see above, p. 65, note 2) considers it, indeed, Chapman's own, and from the original *Byron*. I can not think so ; but there can be no question that it is just parody. Oxymora are characteristic of Chapman :

> now our old wars cease
> To wage worse battles with the arms of peace.
> *Byron's Consp.*, I, 1, p. 217.

> The idleness of such security, . . .

The fixed stars waver and the erring stand.	IV, 1, p. 236.
What idle pains have you bestow'd, etc.	IV, 1, p. 234.

acterizing, any hitting-off of foibles and defects, or mimicking of mannerisms, except such obvious ones as Jonson's small-pox and classicism and Chapman's hoariness and French proclivities.   In both cases it is indisputably Dekker's satire.

In the plot, too, of *Westward Ho* and *Northward Ho*, Dekker's hand is everywhere evident.   It is simple, without anything that could be called under-plot ; and it is lively.   The main characteristic, indeed, is liveliness — rather than rapidity or forwardness of movement, — a liveliness which is not inconsistent with abruptness or deviation.   It does not march on steadily and consistently through an intricate complication to a definite resolution, as does that of the *Merchant of Venice*.   There is a goal, indeed, but no considerable complication for the persons of the drama to thread before they reach it, and so they may very well play by the way.   The citizens' wives and their gallants have the lark they had planned with no let or hindrance, and so have time for all sorts of quarrels and pranks.   Such by-play is of two sorts : first, purely unexpected, episodic action, — lively scenes like the mad-scenes, or the hazing of the bawd, lugged in on the spur of the moment ; and second, unmotivated tricks, practical jokes like those on Bellamont and Featherstone in *Northward Ho*, announced beforehand and crowed over at the end.   And as they do go on to the goal, it is often abruptly, by a leap, the knot of the complication, to change the figure, being cut instead of untied, as in the unmotivated, sudden change of mind and heart in the citizens' wives after they have reached Brainford, [1] or the vicissitudes of passion in Doll.   Such is Dekker in his independent plays.   In *Satiromastix*, the *Honest Whore*, and (in less measure) the *Roaring Girl*, the movement is equally lively and abrupt ; the complication is cut by as sudden and arbitrary conversions and adjustments, [2] and the fable, in part at least, is as much a tissue of lively episodes. [3]

Wretched world,
Consisting most of parts that fly each other ;
A firmness breeding all inconstancy — etc.

Byron's Trag., V, 1, p. 271.

[1] In *W. H.   N. H.* is, aside from its tricks and mad-scenes, a more coherent and compact plot.

[2] The conversion of the Honest Whore like that of Mistress Justiniano ; the conversion of William Rufus in *Sat.* like that of the Earl in *W. H.* ; citizens' wives, Gallipot and Openwork, in *Roar. Girl* (IV, 2), wheel about exactly as the wives Honeysuckle, Tenterhook, and Wafer do in *W. H.* (V, 1) : and the Honest Whore suddenly contents herself at the end with a man other than the one she is infatuated with, like Doll.   All these conversions, except that in the *H. W.*, are arbitrary turning-points in the plot, and all are unmotived and sudden.

[3] *Sat..* the slight story of the marriage and William Rufus's intrigue, is bombasted out with the hazing of Horace and Asinius.   The plots of *H. W.*, Pts. I and II,

Turning from construction to *matter* of plot, we find it, too, to be Dekker's, whether borrowed from his earlier plays or itself to be repeated in his later ones.[1] Nothing, indeed, is more characteristic of Dekker than his repeating himself: in style and verse-form, even, he shows not much development and variety, still less in dramatic situations. And this is the case in other plays than our comedies. In the *Shoemaker*, the *Roaring Girl*, and the *Honest Whore* there is a father trying to keep a son or daughter from what he considers an unworthy match, — a slight romantic thread of story, in all cases, to which are loosely attached many picturesque, more or less episodic, low-life and genre scenes. In *Patient Grissel* and the *Honest Whore* there is the same story of a woman angering (or trying to anger) her husband by neglecting or spoiling the feast to which he had already invited people of quality.[2] In *Satiromastix* and *Patient Grissel* a woman is wooed in rivalry, after much the same fashion, by a gentleman and a Welsh knight.[3] In both the *Honest Whore* and *Match me in London* there is the story [4] of a villainous nobleman who hires a doctor to poison a man in his way, the doctor lyingly reporting the deed as committed, and, when he receives nothing for his pains, turning to help the victim. In both the *Honest Whore* and the *Roaring Girl* a gallant pretends to a pliant citizen, at his wife's putting-on and in her presence, to have a claim to her.[5] And in both

---

are largely made up of mere tricks on Candido (avowedly only to try his patience) and others, and of their consequences (such as Fustigo's revenge in *H. W.*, II, 2). Even the closing scenes of the two Parts of *H. W.* — in Bedlam and in Bridewell — contain episodic action.

[1] *I. e.*, in the *Roar. Girl* (see below, p. 72 f), pub. 1611. — Mr. Fleay, indeed (II, p. 132), would have it composed 1604, Dec., for no perceptible reason. The first interest in Moll Cutpurse seems to have arisen 1610–11; there are, at any rate, no dates earlier. Cf. Chamberlain's letter to Carleton (see above pp. 14–15, note), Feb., 1611, and John Day's book on Moll, reg. Aug., 1610. Middleton, IV, pp. 4–6.

In consideration of D.'s and W.'s general proneness to repeat characters, situations, and phrases (shown here in the case of D., and below, end Chap. II, etc, in the case of W.), D.'s repetition of those of *W. H.* and *N. H.* in later plays should be accepted as evidence that they are his own; just as W.'s failure to repeat them should be evidence that they never were part and parcel of his mental life. So, too, with the type of citizen comedy as represented by *W. H.* and *N. H.*, which is exactly repeated in *Roar. Girl* and never appears again in W.

[2] *Grissel*, 1. 1886 f, and *H. W.*, pp. 107–8 (narrated), noted by Bang, *Eng. Stud.*, Bd. 28, p. 223.

[3] Pointed out by Small, p. 122. In *Sat.*, Mistress Minever by Sir Rees ap Vaughan and by Sir Adam Prickshaft; in *Grissel*, Gwenthyan by Sir Owen and Emulo.

[4] *H. W.*, Pt. I, IV, 4. *Match me*, pp. 169–179. In this latter case, the doctor turning without having demanded a reward — suspecting, probably, Don John's villainous intentions on himself.

[5] *H. W.*, Pt. I, I, 2, and III, 1; *Roar. Girl*, III, 2.

Satiromastix and *Match me in London* a citizen's wife [1] is enticed to court by the machinations of a lustful king. In Dekker, then, repetition of dramatic situations is only to be expected.

Nor are we to be disappointed in regard to those in *Westward Ho* and *Northward Ho:* nearly all of them Dekker has used before or uses later:

1. In *Westward Ho*, IV, 2, the scene in the Earl's mansion, where Mistress Justiniano, the object of his lust, is discovered to him dead. Like *Satiromastix*,[2] pp. 251-63. In both, the Earl (or King) had enticed the woman to his house; and now, bidding music sound, enters the room exultantly; but only suddenly to discover her poisoned, dead. In both, the husband avows the deed, and reproaches the libertine; the latter repents; and, the danger over, the woman, having taken only a sleeping potion, awakes. Like this, too, is the first scene in the *Honest Whore*, in which the Duke, seeking to thwart the love of Hippolito for his daughter, gives her out for dead, but, as he is conveying her body through the streets, is forced to set it down that the lover may see her face. She, too, recovers from the potion, and shortly after awakes. Like it, again, are both *Satiromastix* and *Match me in London* in the matter of the seduction of the woman of lower rank to the libertine nobleman's house.

2. In *Westward Ho*, at the beginning of the play, Justiniano feigns to be leaving the country; but really disguises himself as a writing-master, in order in the rest of the play to carry out his plans in secret. So in the *Shoemaker's Holiday*, I, 1, p. 10, and II, 2, Rowland Lacy lets it be reported that he is fighting in France, and really becomes a Dutch shoemaker, in order in the rest of the play to prosecute his love-affair.

3. In *Westward Ho*, I, 2, the gallant, Monopoly, has financial dealings with the citizen, Tenterhook, husband of his friend, somewhat as the gallant, Laxton, in the *Roaring Girl*, III, 2, has with Gallipot, the husband of his friend.

4. In *Westward Ho*, III, 2, there is an arrest of a gallant by a Sergeant Ambush and his yeoman, Clutch; as in *Northward Ho*, I, 2, by two sergeants; as in the *Roaring Girl*, III, 3, by Sergeant Curtleax and Yeoman Hanger. In the *Honest Whore*, Pt. I, IV, 3, moreover, Candido is arrested by officers, and in Pt. II, Candido with others. In the first three instances the sergeants and yeomen are very like in character — important, and stern against evil-doers.

5. In *Westward Ho*, V, 2, Sir Gosling's forcing the bawd to dance and sing is like Tucca's hazing of Horace and Asinius in *Satiromas-*

---

[1] Celestine, by name, in the one, and Tormiella in the other.
[2] Swinburne notices this in the introd. to Shepherd's *Chap.*, p. xxix.

tix.[1] In both, the tyrant is drunk, and the frightened victims plead for mercy. Cf. *Satiromastix*, pp. 230 f, 234 f, 257 f. Similar is Bots's treatment of Candido, *Honest Whore*, Pt. II, IV, 3, and Candido's pleading.

6. In *Westward Ho*, II, 2, a woman — Mrs. Justiniano — turns from her evil way, and, on the next approach of the bawd, curses her. Exactly so in the *Honest Whore*, Pt. I, III, 2, the repentant Bellafront.

7. In the last acts of *Westward Ho* and *Northward Ho* the escapades of citizens' wives and gallants to Brainford and to Ware, husbands following. Like this is the trip to Ware the Roaring Girl pretends to undertake with the impudent gallant who proposed it [2]; and the trip to Brainford which the citizens' wives had agreed to, but suddenly at the last moment refused. [3] Somewhat similar, too, is the expedition out of town at the end of the *Honest Whore*, Pt. I, and even that to Bridewell, at the close of Pt. II. This was evidently a favorite device of Dekker's, in order to bring all the characters of the play together and to make, with ensuing complications, a lively close. So, at least, in *Westward Ho*, *Northward Ho*, and *Honest Whore*, Pt. I.

8. In *Northward Ho*, II, 1 (and after), a fiery Welsh Captain wooes Doll Hornet with something of the jealousy and fervour of rivalry to be found in the wooings of Sir Owen and Sir Vaughan ap Rees; and, again like Sir Owen, he promises her a coach and horses. [4]

9. In *Northward Ho*, III, 1, and IV, 4, the trick of getting the respectable man, Bellamont, into the company of (a) whores and (b) madmen. Like it (a) in *Honest Whore*, Pt. II, IV, 3, and V, 2, is Candido's being inveigled into hobnobbing with the old bawd and Bots, forced to 'drink, dance, and sing bawdy songs,' and lodged among the whores at Bridewell, and (b) in Pt. I, IV, 3, and V, 2, his being carried off, amid protestations like Bellamont's, to Bedlam. In all instances, it is practical joking [5] and horse-play. In connection with this, there are, in both plays, mad-scenes of a like stamp, introduced as a sort of diversion. [6]

10. In *Northward Ho*, III, 1, Bellamont's calling upon Doll becomes the cause, beyond his intention, of her falling in love with him and despising herself and her ways. So in the *Honest Whore*, Pt. I, II, 1, and IV, 1, Hippolito, calling upon Bellafront, converts her and unwittingly causes her to love him. [7]

---

[1] Fleay suggests this. [2] *Roar. Girl*, II, 1, and III, 1. [3] *Ib.*, IV, 2.

[4] See above, p. 71. Last point noted by Bang, *Eng. Stud.*, Bd. 28, p. 221.

[5] Except Candido's imprisonment at Bridewell, which is a mistake.

[6] *N. H.*, 240–4, and *H. W.*, 178–184.

[7] Doll is not exactly converted; but, in her rude way, she is at least disgusted with herself, — " O filthy rogue that I am," — pp. 219, and at p. 232 she is humble

11.   Thereupon, in *Northward Ho*, IV, 1, Doll comes to Bellamont's house, and though he had just forbidden any visitors, forces her way to him, and passionately avows her love, only to be scorned and rejected.   Exactly so in *Honest Whore*, IV, 1, Hippolito forbids callers, yet cannot keep out Bellafront, who avows her love and is rejected.

12.   In *Northward Ho*, V, 1, Doll suddenly contents herself at the end with another, inferior mate, who is entangled into marriage with her, through no fault of hers, by a trick.   Likewise in *Honest Whore*, Pt. I, V, 2, Bellafront and Matheo.[1]

13.   The song at the close of *Westward Ho* is certainly Dekker's; that clear, merry note and lilting rhythm were never Webster's. These qualities are to be found in the First Three Men's Song in the *Shoemaker*, III, 5, and in the Second Three Men's Song, V, 4.

The setting aside of so great an array of situations leaves few remaining to Webster : as little must be left him from the characters. The gallants, citizens and citizens' wives, whores and bawds, Welshmen and Dutchmen, are probably all Dekker's, for they all appear in previous plays, such as the *Shoemaker*, *Satiromastix*, and the *Honest Whore*, as well as in his later ones.[2]   They appear in *none* of Webster's, whether comedy or tragedy.[3]

A few of these types — those that present much individuality — we will examine a little more closely.   The citizens' wives, the bawds, and the whores are done in a striking style, in continuation, perhaps, of Shakspere's types, — the Merry Wives,[4] Mrs. Quickly, and Doll Tearsheet.   Dekker's they are, at all events, through and through, and, as presented both in our comedies and in Dekker's other works, they have much in common.   All three — citizen's wife, whore, and bawd — affect virtue, speak of it freely and complacently, bridle up at any infringement of what they call the proprieties or their own dignity, are coarse, in fair weather good-natured, and naive.   The citizens' wives — Tenterhook, Honeysuckle, and Wafer in *Westward Ho*[5] as well as Gallipot, Tiltyard, and Openwork in the *Roaring Girl*, — the

---

and " will be clean."   In both cases, but more emphatically in that of Doll, love is the cause of the change.

[1] In *H. W.* the trick is Bellafront's ; but she is claiming only her due from Matheo.

[2] They appear, too, somewhat in the same apportionment.   In *W. H.* three citizens, three gallants, three citizens' wives, one whore, and one bawd ; in *N. H.* the same, except that the gallants number two, citizens and wives each one.   In *Roar. Girl* there are again three gallants, three citizens, three wives, one whore.

[3] There are, indeed, gallants in the *C. C.;* but they are of the Fletcher-Massinger type.   See below, Chap. IV, Sect. II.

[4] That is, Mrs. Ford and Mrs. Page.   When I mean the play I use italics.

[5] P. 110.

whores — Doll Hornet[1] in *Northward Ho* as well as Bellafront [2] in the *Honest Whore* — swear by their virtue, and all, even the last named, make much ado at the last moment to defend it. The bawds and whores are incensed when given their titles, and Mrs. Birdlime in *Westward Ho*, like Mistress Horseleech in the *Honest Whore*, considers a bawd not a bawd at all, but an honest, motherly woman.[3] And one and all, not omitting the citizenesses, Mistress Minever in *Satiromastix* and Margery in the *Shoemaker*, are still more insistent on the minor proprieties — will not abide the coarseness and boisterousness of men, as drunkenness,[4] tobacco-smoking and spitting,[5] "swaggering,"[6] "conjuring,"[7] or unseasonable familiarity.[8] A rude and laughable prudishness marks them all, whether of foul name or fair name, both in our comedies and in Dekker's other plays.

The whores, like Doll Hornet and Lucy (to compare Dekker's types with the representatives in our plays), are given to Billingsgate and bravado, to loud anger and to striking.[9] The citizens' wives, like those in *Westward Ho*, are given to naive blundering and Partingtonism,[10] to merriment and larks, to playing the game with a gallant to the last moment and then virtuously and indignantly bilking him. Characteristic, indeed, of both citizens' wives and whores, whether in our comedies or elsewhere in Dekker, is this wheeling about at the end : the citizens' wives undergo a sudden alteration, and help one another to cheat the gallants, as in *Westward Ho* and the *Roaring Girl ;* and the whores (including Mistress Justiniano [11]) fall really in love and by their love are converted, curse the bawd, and take on a new, unworldly tone, as do Doll Hornet and Bellafront.[12] And as for the

---

[1] *N. H.*, 205.   [2] *H. W.*, 119.

[3] *W. H.*, 93 and 154, *H. W.*, 283, the same expression. Cf. Bellafront's indignation, *H. W.*, p. 124 ; Doll Target's, p. 279.

[4] *W. H.*, 143.

[5] *H. W.*, 120 ; *W. H.*, 147 ; *Shoemaker*, 41.

[6] *W. H.*, 143 ; the bawd, 123-4, 133 ; Lucy, 129.

[7] *Sat.*, p. 230, Widow Minever and her dread of "drawing."   [8] *N. H.*, 184-5.

[9] *W. H.*, 127, but Lucy is mild ; *N. H.*, I, 2 ; III, 1 ; pp. 219, 233, etc. ; *H. W.*, Pt. I, II, 1. Cf. also in this scene Bellafront's anger at Roger her servant, with Doll's at the Drawer, *N. H.*, I, 2. And see especially the conduct of the "brave" and scurrilous whores, *H. W.*, Pt. II, last scene.

[10] *Sat.*, 229, 230, Minever's "enamel 'd " for enamoured, misunderstanding of conjuring, and taking Babylon to be in London ; *W. H.*, 145-6 ; *Roar. Girl*.

[11] For she was on the point of becoming one. But, being already married, she does not fall in love.

[12] Cf. the astonishingly new and meek tone of Doll, *N. H.*, 232, and *H. W.*, Pt. I, II, 1, end, after (and in Doll's case before and after) the worst of abuse and ribaldry, and *W. H.*, 97-8. The cursing of the bawd in the case of Mrs. Justiniano and Bellafront, *W. H.*, 98-9, *H. W.*, Pt. I, III, 2.

bawds, they, like Birdlime, are most jealous of their reputations, scandalized at the mere word bawd, ' honest and motherly,' and greatly given to aqua vitæ [1] and tricks of the trade. [2] All these coarse-grained, loud, and jolly women, then, are of one flock, and that is Dekker's.

Manifestly, Dekker's, too, are the Dutch Drawer and Merchant, and the Welsh Captain. [3] A Dutch Hans [4] had already appeared in the *Shoemaker*, as well as a Dutch skipper ; and Captain Jenkins in *Northward Ho* is, in the character of his Cambrian English [5] and blunders, his generosity, the ardor of his suit for a woman's hand, his pugnacity and ready, childlike placability, the counterpart of Sir Vaughan ap Rees in *Satiromastix*.

The rest that may be Dekker's we must pass over — less strongly marked characters, the humor, the phrases and proper names, [6] the structure of the verse, [7] and that anomaly in Dekker, his eruptive, sulphurous style. [8] For enough has been adduced to show the plays — both of them — in character of satire, in plot and situations, in characters, to be thoroughly his.

Yet one thing remains. Who created this type of intrigue between citizens and gallants ? And under what influence ? Dekker, once more, and inspired by the *Merry Wives of Windsor* and by the characters

---

[1] All his bawds use it and speak of it. *W. H.*, 100, 131 ; *H. W.*, 283 ; *N. H.*, 240.

[2] *W. H.*, IV, 1 ; *H. W.*, pp. 143-5. The same trick, spoken of on p. 143, appears in the action of *W. H.*, IV, 1.

[3] Web. never uses dialect, or any foreign tongue except (sparingly) Latin and Italian, and those as quotations (except Lawyer's Latin in *W. D.*).

[4] In *W. H.* and *N. H.*—Lacy is disguised as Shoemaker Hans. The skipper and he both talk broken English and pure Dutch (pp. 21, 32, 33), like Drawer Hans, *W. H.*, 103-104, and Hans Van Belch, *N. H.*, 197-9. They evidently spring from one pen, that of one who knows Dutch fairly well.

[5] See Bang's remarks (*Engl. Stud.*, 28, p. 218) on the similarity of Jenkins' dialect and phrases (*God udge me!* etc.) to Sir Owen's in *Grissel*. Sir Rees ap Vaughan's in *Sat.* is out of the same cloth.

[6] Names like Bellamont (cf. Bellafront in *H. W.*) ; Hans, Doll (*N. H.*, *H. W.*, *Shoemaker*); Moll (*W. H.*, *N. H.*, *Roar. Girl*) ; Birdlime, Fingerlock, Horseleech, Bountinall, etc. ; phrases like Graybeard, goat's pizzle, *N. H.*, 233, *H. W.*, 264, *Sat.*, 200 ; leek having a white beard and green stalk, *N. H.*, 230, and *H. W.*, 202 ; "Baa! lamb" from a woman, *W. H.*, 110, and *H. W.*, 187 ; "Go by, go by Hieronimo," *Shoemaker*, 17, *W. H.*, 100, *Sat.*, 202 ; "pewfellow," references to Ostend, etc., etc. Still others are noted by Bang, *Eng. Stud.*, Bd. 28, in connection with *Grissel*.

[7] The verse in *W. H.* and *N. H.* is in every way like Dekker's. Rimes in *W. H.*, 134, 135, 139.

[8] Extravagant diction at passionate moments :

> *Wife.* Let sulphur drop from heaven, and nail my body
> Dead to this earth ! That slave, that dammed fury,
> Whose whips are in your tongue to torture me, etc.   *N. H.*, 191.

Cf. *N. H.*, 232 ; *H. W.*, 233, 269, Hippolito.

Doll Tearsheet and Quickly in *Henry IV*. For the plot of the *Merry Wives* is very like that of our comedies: a thoroughly bourgeois material and atmosphere, tricks and countertricks all round the program of which is announced beforehand,[1] the main thread of action being the constantly repeated and baffled intrigue of the knight Falstaff with the citizens' wives Mistresses Ford and Page.[2] The Merry Wives are like Dekker's in their free and complacent speaking of their virtue[3]; in their indignation, and their upholding of the honor of their sex[4]; in their merriment, and their fooling of the pursurer to the top of his bent instead of repulsing him; and in the crudeness of their satisfaction.[5] And their husbands are of a piece with the citizens in *Westward Ho* and *Northward Ho*. Ford, like Maybery and Justiniano, is constitutionally jealous, and, like Tenterhook, Honeysuckle, and Wafer, comes down with a company to catch his wife. Mrs. Quickly, the go-between, in her "motherliness and honesty" and her tenderheartedness toward innocence and youth[6] is very like the bawds. Doll Tearsheet in her Billingsgate, in her boisterous anger, in her fullness of affection for a man who will draw for her, is certainly the model for Doll Hornet,[7] as well as for the "brave" and vociferous Doll Target and her sisters in Part II of the *Honest Whore*. Mrs. Quickly's Partingtonism and garrulity,[8] and her own and Doll Tearsheet's aversion to unseemly and boisterous deportment[9] have been inherited by the citizens' wives in *Westward Ho* and by Doll Hornet and Mistress Minever. Finally, for a Captain Jenkins there is a Welsh parson, with similar dialect, blunders, and generous, fiery, yet quickly placable, temper; for the Dutch of Drawer

---

[1] There are, indeed, tricks played on nearly every character in the play; in this respect, and in the constantly *repeated* duping of Falstaff, the *M. W. W.* is more old-fashioned than *W. H.* or *N. H.*, resembling plays like Chapman's *Gentleman Usher, Mons. Olive*, and *All Fools*, rather than an intrigue play such as our comedies or as *A Trick to Catch the Old One*, which, coming later, have shaken off some of the earlier stiffness and monotony.

[2] They are not called citizens' wives, but it is evident that they are of similar rank and station with the wives in Dekker's two comedies.

[3] II, 1, 88; IV, 2, 220–2.

[4] II, 1.

[5] As in last sc., etc.

[6] See her tender care that the boy should know no wickedness (II, 2), and her compassion on Mistress Page. Cf. the Bawd's tenderness toward innocence and youth, *N. H.*, 93–5.

[7] Cf. esp. what she says on this subject to Jenkins (202) with *2 Hen. IV*, II, 4, 232–240.

[8] Cf. the delightful long story of Mistress Tenterhook in *W. H.*, 143–6, much in the manner of Quickly.

[9] See *2 Hen. IV*, II, 4, where Doll will not let swaggering Pistol come up, and Quickly will have no swaggerers, cannot "abide" them.

Hans and Merchant Van Belch, the French of Doctor Gaius ; and for the expedition into the country at the close, where the women meet their gallants and all the characters are brought together, that to Herne's Oak in Windsor Park.

That Dekker drew some of this material from Shakspere directly is made almost indubitable by precise reminiscences — so early as in *Satiromastix* — from *Henry IV* and the *Merry Wives*[1]*;* and so there is nothing left to be accounted for but the partisanship of the city. The Merry Wives, having nothing to do with London, are moved to stand up only for their own sex against the other, not for citizens' wives against gallants. This could easily be added by so loyal a Londoner as Dekker. No dramatist knew the city so well, or had such sympathy and affection for its life and interests.[2] He himself was a citizen, which Webster and even Shakspere never were, to the core. His characters are always bourgeois, or else they are the *citizen's* conception of lord or lady ; his morality is the rough-and-ready, outward morality of the jolly, respectable citizen : and by a thousand picturesque touches of London local color he is always reminding us, even when the scene lies in Milan and Naples, that it is only the life of the city he depicts.[3] And if he loved London, he was the man to take its part, to be its champion, as he is for England and Protestantism in the *Whore of Babylon*. In some of his plays he does.

---

[1] The *M. W. W.* and *Sat.* both appeared in print in *1602*. Mistress Minever's abundant Partingtonism and blunders, her horror at "conjuring" and drawn swords (*Sat.*, 220 and 230) like Mrs. Quickly's at "swaggering" and "naked weapons" (2 *Hen. IV*, II, 4); her affection for Tucca and her determination at the same time not to be conycatched by him (*Sat.*, 231), quite like Quickly's attitude toward Falstaff. Cf. also "we haue Hiren heere " (*Sat.*, 245); "Ma. Justice Shallow " (p. 212); "feed and be fat, my faire Calipolis " (*Sat.*, 230 ; 2 *Hen. IV*, II, 4, 193, though quoted of course from *Alcazar*); the surprising coincidence between *M. W. W.*, II, 1, 50 f, and *Sat.*, p. 205 — "Mistress Minever — you shall be knighted by one of us " (*i. e.*, married to a knight). Cf. also a possible allusion to 1 *Hen. IV*, I, 1, 87-8, in Doll Hornet's " I'm as melancholy as Fleet-street in a long vacation." *W. H.*, 185.

Since writing the above I have come upon Prof. Bang's discussion of the Welsh dialect on the Elizabethan stage (*Engl. Stud.*, 28, esp. 226-7) and of the question which was beforehand in introducing it, Dekker in *Grissel*, or Shakspere in *M. W. W.* The question, as Prof. Bang himself admits, cannot be settled, because the date of the first performance of the *M. W. W.* is not known. It may well be, as Prof. Bang is inclined to think, that Shakspere in this respect imitates Dekker. But even so, that does not affect our position in maintaining, on the definite basis of Dekker's acquaintance with the *M. W. W.* and *Hen. IV*, proved above, that Dekker, in turn, formed the citizen comedy on the type of that play and modeled his characters (aside from the Welsh) after those.

[2] See, besides his plays, his tracts — the *Dead Tearme*, *Gull's Hornbook*, *Bellman of London*, etc.

[3] As in *H. W.*, Pts. I and II, and *Match me*.

In the *Shoemaker*, the Lord Mayor tries to keep his daughter from marrying a gentleman, the Earl tries to keep his nephew from marrying a citizen's daughter, and the whole drift of the play is to celebrate the " gentle craft " of shoemaking; and in the *Honest Whore*, Parts I and II, the gallants who came to taunt and tease a citizen are baffled by him and drubbed by his stout apprentices. Surely, then, it was Dekker who created this type of citizen play, imitating Shakspere in character and general scheme of plot, but adding the specifically citizen spirit[1] and London atmosphere.

As between Dekker and Webster, of course, there is no question : the partisanship of the city, as well as the whole character of the citizen comedy, is none of the latter's. In the rest of Webster's plays we see or hear no more of citizens and their doings, and get not a breath of London air nor an echo from these comedies. Dekker, on the other hand, follows his vein; and in the *Roaring Girl* and the *Second Part of the Honest Whore* he deals again with London, with citizens and gallants, just as in these comedies, the *First Part of the Honest Whore*, the *Shoemaker's Holiday*, and *Satiromastix*.

How little is left in this Period to Webster ! The wooden Induction to the *Malcontent*, and some slight, undetermined part in the more colorless and stereotyped portions of *Wyatt*, *Westward Ho*, and *Northward Ho*, under the shaping and guiding hand of Dekker ! It is a long road from this sort of thing to the *White Devil*. Yet Webster had six years to make it, and there is evidence even in the Induction, as we have seen, that at least his condensed and crabbed style was forming.

IV. DEKKER'S INFLUENCE.

And what of Dekker's influence upon him ? In all but two of the plays of this Period Dekker had been a partner, and in those three which are preserved his hand is uppermost and everywhere. But it never appears again. After *Northward Ho* the *White Devil*, *Malfi*, and the *Devil's Law-Case !* Webster never again enters the field of the chronicle-play or the citizen-comedy, never touches one of the types there developed, and in sentiment or dramaturgy, style or verse, shows hardly a trace of the homely and lively master of his appren-

---

[1] There were citizen plays before this, of course, as *Every Man in his Humour* and *Every Man out of his Humour*, but lacking the spirit of partisanship. — I do not wish to exagerate the partisanship of the city, or of the citizens' wives, in these plays. While Dekker always makes this clear, his method of characterization, inherited from Shakspere, is comic, condescending, and slightly satiric. Their prudishness and touchiness, and their real coarseness !

ticeship. He who in later plays repeats himself in phrase — hardly in situation — as much as Dekker, never reverts to these.[1] This may prove the slightness of Webster's connection with these early plays. It may be proof of his youthfulness at this time, and of the originality, the strong innate bent, of a mind that could develop afterward in so

---

[1] For repetitions in sit. and phrase, see above, pp. 38–40. — Repetitions of phrase Dyce registered long since in his footnotes ; and from these Dr. Vopel (in his generally quite valueless Zür. Diss. and Brem. Prog. on John Webster, 1888), has collected some of the most notable. I subjoin such as are not adduced by him, or by me elsewhere. Many of these, too, are gathered from Dyce. See still others, from *W. D.* and *Mal.* only, in Sampson, pp. xli–xliii.

1. And keep the wolf far thence, that 's foe to men,
   For with his nails he 'll dig them up again.   *W. D.*, 127.

   The wolf shall find her grave, and scrape it up.   *Mal.*, 249.

2. She stains the time past, lights the time to come.
                                       Mal., 165, and *Mon. Col.*, 264.

3.   he 's a mere stick of sugar-candy ;
   You may look quite thorough him.   *Mal.*, 203, and *D. L. C.*, 33.

           go, go, brag
4. How many ladies you have undone like me   *W. D.*, 86.

           Go, go, brag
   You have left me heartless ; mine is in your bosom.   *Mal.*, 176.

           Go, go,
   Complain unto my great lord cardinal.   *W. D.*, 28.

       go, go, complain to the great duke.   *W. D.*, 38.

5. As void of true heat as are all painted fires,
   Or glow-worms in the dark.   *D. L. C.*, 84.

   Cf. Glories like glow-worms, etc.   *W. D.*, 99, and *Mal.*, 242, given by Vopel.

6. Applied to Vittoria :
       No less an ominous fate than blazing stars.   *W. D.*, 65.

   To princes :
       Shall make me like a blazing ominous star.   *Ib.*, 135.

       O, thou hast been a most prodigious comet.   *Ib.*, 139.

7. Man may his fate foresee, but not prevent.   *W. D.*, 137.

   O, most imperfect light of human reason,
   That mak'st us so unhappy to foresee
   What we can least prevent.   *Mal.*, 208.

8. Physicians, that cure poisons, still do work
   With counter-poisons.   *W. D.*, 71.

   As aconitum, a strong poison, brings
   A present cure against all serpents' stings.   *A. & V.*, 186.

9. She 's off o' th' hinges strangely.   *C. C.*, 55.

   Bear with him, sir, he 's strangely off o' th' hinges.   *C. C.*, 91.

different a direction from its master's. But *Malfi* is followed, we remember, by the *Cure for a Cuckold*, just as *Northward Ho* by *Malfi;* the leap in itself is not so great, but it is a greater, perhaps, at such years. Who can say of one so impressionable, or perhaps of

---

10. Compare thy form and my eyes together.
You 'll find my love no such great miracle.   *Mal.*, 262.

Compare her beauty and my youth together,
And you will find the fair effects of love
No miracle at all.   *D. L. C.*, 37.

11.   ere the spider
Make a thin curtain for your epitaphs.   *W. D.*, 136.

Or the flattery in the epitaphs, which shows
More sluttish far than all the spiders' webs
Shall ever grow upon it.   *D. L. C.*, 47.

12. Pray, sir, resolve me, what religion's best
For a man to die in?   *W. D.*, 128.

And let him e'en go whither the religion sends him
That he died in.   *D. L. C.*, 55.

13. It could never have got a sweeter air to fly in
Than your breath.   *D. L. C.*, 14.

Never found prayers, since they convers'd with death,
A sweeter air to fly in than his breath.   *Mon. Col.*, 262.

14. You would look up to heaven, but I think
The devil, that rules i' th' air, stands in your light.   *Mal.*, 182.

The devil that rules i' th' air hangs in their light.   *D. L. C.*, 117.

15. As a dying man's cry :
I go I know not whither.   *Mal.*, 267.

Stay, I do not well know whither I am going.   *D. L. C.*, 118.

16.   O, the cursed devil,
Which doth present us with all other sins
Thrice candied o'er.   *W. D.*, 132.

Thus the devil
Candies all sins o'er ;   *Mal.*, 169.

17. Last cry of the villain :
I do glory yet
That I can call this act mine own.   *W. D.*, 142.

I do glory
That thou, which stood'st like a huge pyramid,   *Mal.*, 280.

18. I have seen children oft eat sweetmeats thus,
As fearful to devour them too soon.
                    Mal., 176, and *A. & V.*, 130.

19. When I have hew'd her to pieces.   *Mal.*, 199.

I 'll have thee hew'd in pieces.   *Ib.*, 267.

81

any Elizabethan dramatist, where character — native bent — begins, and where influence ever ends? What if much that has here been so confidently assigned to Dekker, may have sprung from the youthful imitation and self-effacement of Webster?

———

20.	Sad tales befit my woe :	*Mal.*, 229.
	And, for sad tales suit grief,	*Mon. Col.*, 260.
21.	but no otherwise Than as some curious artist takes in sunder A clock, or watch, when it is out of frame, To bring 't in better order.	*Mal.*, 227.
	Or, like a dial, broke in wheel or screw, That 's ta'en in pieces to be made go true.	*Mon. Col.*, 263.
22.	I discern poison Under your gilded pills.	*W. D.*, 62.
	why dost thou wrap thy poison'd pills In gold and sugar?	*Mal.*, 231.
23.	The office of justice is perverted quite, When one thief hangs another.	*Mal.*, 249, and, verbatim, *A. & V.*, 199.
24.	Did any ceremonial form of law, Doom her to not-being?	*Mal.*, 249.
	Therefore in his not-being imitate His fair example.	*A. & V.*, 222.

Many lesser repetitions, or less verbal ones, as that cited by Ward (III, p. 64), and many strikingly identical details like Flamineo, Bosola, Julio (in *D. L.C.*), Contarino, and Ercole, all being students at Padua (*W. D.*, 27 ; *Mal.*, 220 ; *D. L. C.*, 35, 37), might be added. Of echoes from the partnership plays in Webster's subsequent work, I have found no certain ones. The most probable is the figure of the crystal river being to blame for the man who drowns himself in it (*W. D.*, 62) as borrowed from *Wyatt*, 53,

> Then make the silver Thames as black as Styx
> Because it was constrain'd to bear the barks,

though the phrasing is so different and the figure may have been a common one. Another possible echo is that of the law as a spider's web (*Wyatt*, 54 ; *Mal.*, 164), though the true and exact echo is in Dekker's *If This be not a Good Play*, p. 287. — This utter break between Webster's partnership plays and his independent ones appears all the greater when we consider that both sets repeat within themselves not only situations (as we have seen above) but words and phrases, even the Third Period repeating the Second.

CHAPTER III.

THE REVENGE PLAYS.

We now approach Webster's first independent, and his greatest, work, the revenge plays. In this, as we have seen, he breaks with Dekker and his manner completely, and there is no link between the old and the new. Such a link would have been furnished to hand in the *Malcontent ;* but with that he had nothing to do — merely prefixed an induction for a revival.

I. SOURCES AND PLOTS.

The material of both these revenge plays is drawn, as is the case with those of Marston and Tourneur, from Italian life. The source of the *White Devil* [1] is some chronicle of the historical Vittoria Accoramboni who was murdered at Padua, December 22nd, 1585. Exactly what one

---

[1] The name *white devil* seems to need explanation, esp. since the *New Eng. Dict.* and Sampson omit it. Haz. in his *Bibliog.* of *Old Eng. Lit.* (*sub voc.*) says, "it was a popular name for a wicked woman in Webster's time"; and in his *Man. for a Collector*, "the phrase seems to have grown into use from this source as an expression for a shrew" (p. 251). He is talking at random. In the *Fair Quarrel* (Middleton, vol. IV, p. 220) the phrase occurs applied to the scoundrelly, hypocritical Physician,

What a white devil have I met withal !

and Bullen quotes to explain the phrase (*ib.*) a passage from Hall's *Downfall of Maygames*, ed. 1661, p. 1 : "Lately we were troubled with White Devils, who under pretence of extraordinary sanctity, published open heresy . . . : now we run madding on the other hand, and are like to be troubled with Black Devils, *viz.*, blasphemous drunkards, blasphemous health-drinkers, scorners of piety, Sabbath profaners," etc. This meaning would suit also a passage in *Rev. Tr.* (III, 4, p. 394) where Vendice, on the Duke's saying (several speeches above),

Give me that sin that 's robed in holiness,

cries,

Royal villain ! white devil ;

and an entry in the *S. R.*, April 28, 1613, "a booke called the white divell, or the Hypocrite uncased," — a sermon preached by a Thomas Adams. The phrase must mean, then, simply hypocrite — need not imply anything of Vittoria's sex, or her beauty, or ferocity ; or anything poetic or "mystic," as Mr. Hamilton in his article on *Malfi* in the *Sewanee Rev.*, IX, 415, opines.

of the chronicles it was, my researches have not put me in a position to say.[1] There is a large number of them in various libraries in Italy, mostly still in manuscript and of unsettled date. But one [2] he did use, if we are to judge from the story Count Gnoli has sifted from these, pretty faithfully. The names and characters, the incidents and changes of scene, are all those of history, as well as a lot of details such as insignificant proper names, quotations, and minor circumstances.[3] Knowing, however, my material and data to be so fragmentary, I do not think it worth while to attempt an extended investigation of the relation of the *White Devil* to its source — any more, that is, than is necessary to an understanding of the development of Webster's art.

As in the play, the scene is laid almost entirely in Rome and Padua, and the story is of Paolo Giordano Orsini, Duke of Bracciano,[4] who killed his own wife, and, at the instigation of Vittoria Accoramboni,

------

[1] I visited a dozen or more of the largest libraries in Italy, including all of those at Rome but the Vatican, which was then not accessible, the three at Florence, and those at Bologna, Parma, Venice, Padua, Brescia and Milan, and found nothing that of itself could have served Webster as source. But several of the manuscripts in the Casanatense in Rome were at the time beyond my reach, in an exposition ; and the catalogues to the libraries were so disorderly and the indices of Mss. so incomplete (often not giving titles alphabetically), that one not having months at his disposal could make little progress.

[2] Of accounts certainly early enough to have been used by Webster Ant. Riccobuoni's (1541-1599) in *Opera*, lib. I, *cap.* 12, and Cesare Campana's in *Delle Historie del Mondo*, 1596, pp. 171-4, are too meagre, and the anonymous *Il miserabile e compassionevole caso della morte dell' illustrissima Signora Vittoria Accoramboni, successo nella citta di Padova*, Brescia, 1586, I have vainly sought in all the libraries above mentioned, in most of the large libraries in Germany, and in the Brit. Mus. Another chronicle, that set forth by Federigo Odorici at Milan, 1862, in the *Strenna Italiana* di Ripamonti, entitled *Cronaca del Anonimo del Campidoglio*, may have been early enough, is at any rate according to Gnoli one of the most complete and trustworthy accounts, but seems lost now, either to libraries or the Italian second-hand trade, — even to the large and supposedly complete collections of Odorici's works at Parma and Milan, where he was librarian, and to the collection of his papers in the municipal archives of his birth-place, Brescia. Were all the material accessible, there are clews enough (see below, and p. 87, note) to fix the source. See Pref.

[3] Such as: *sed manet alta mente repostum*, here used by Isabella, *W. D.*, p. 40, but really by Lodovico before his judges, Gnoli, p. 330 ; pirates, *W. D.*, p. 35, Gnoli, p. 136 ; Vitelli, Gnoli, 157 f, 224, etc., which Webster uses, *W. D.*, 64, as the name of Vittoria's family, confusing it in memory, perhaps, with Capelli (v. *infra*) ; house of convertites, *W. D.*, 65, Gnoli, 115 (?) ; the conclave and election ; Flamineo as minion of a cardinal, *W. D.*, 102, Gnoli, 33, 312 ; Camillo in debt to grasping Monticelso, *W. D.*, 60, 63, Gnoli, Chap. II ; Capuchins at the end, *W. D.*, 112 f, and Gnoli, 302 ; summer-house by Tiber, *W. H.*, 62, Gnoli, 102, etc., and in De Rosset's version of Sallustio (Bracciano) and Flaminia (Vittoria), *Histoires tragigues de notre temps*, Lyons, 1621 ; Camillo, Webster's name for Francesco Peretti, Vittoria's husband, from his mother's name, Camilla, Gnoli, 24.

[4] Webster spells it, of course, Brachiano.

84

killed her husband. Though Vittoria is not, as Webster describes her, a courtesan, yet in the eyes of the Medici, the family of Bracciano's murdered wife, she is a low, unworthy match, and in the eyes of Cardinal Montalto,[1] since become Pope Sixtus V,[2] an accomplice in the murder of his nephew, her husband. She is tried and imprisoned, but both she and Bracciano escape to Padua.[3] He dies at Salò (not at Padua), poisoned, according to report, through the intrigue of Francesco de' Medici, duke of Florence.[4] Vittoria thereupon retires to Padua; and there, at the hands of Lodovico Orsini, cousin of Bracciano, and through the machinations of the Medici, she and her brother, Flamineo, are murdered. — To this story Webster has added nothing but Cornelia's and Bracciano's madness and Flamineo's pretended madness; Flamineo's murder of Marcello, his intended murder of Vittoria, and Vittoria's instigation of the murder of the Duchess Isabella; the more active, personal parts of Francisco and Giovanni and the new parts of Zanche and the ghosts.

The characters are made more living and human than history pictures them, but are little changed in type and outward feature. Vittoria is in history, as in the play, fascinating, ambitious, and cruel; bold and artful in prison and under suspicion[5]; but she is a Roman, a poetess, and, in her last days, somewhat given to exercises of piety.[6] Bracciano is in history, as in the play, a man of fierce passions and dark crimes, infatuated with Vittoria. But he is not interesting, as Webster makes him, — is unheroically corpulent, and dependent upon his wife's relatives for money.[7] Lodovico is in history the same fiery, unscrupulous soldier and bravo; — banished Rome for his crimes, employed by the Venetians against the pirates (not turned one himself as Webster has it), and the eager instrument of the Medici against the woman he hates. But his motive is not, as in Webster, revenge

---

[1] Monticelso in Webster.

[2] In Webster (*W. D.*, 93), Paul IV, probably inadvertently by reason of the present reigning Pope's being Paul V. But omitting the great Sixtus V from the story argues lack of historic sense in W.

[3] Not directly, Gnoli, 255.

[4] Gnoli, 299, 300.

[5] Gnoli, 96, 129, 135, 325–6, etc.

[6] See in Gnoli pilgrimage to Loretto, intention to enter a convent (p. 311), rosary, crucifix, and prayers the last night. — Cf. V, 2, " Enter Vittoria with a book in her hand." " What? Are you at your prayers?" Webster is here unconsciously affected in details by his original, even though he represents Vittoria's character differently. — The poetical compositions are given by Gnoli. It is strange Webster suppressed this aspect.— Webster's Vittoria is the "famous Venetian courtesan "; probably (see below) through confusion with Bianca Capello.

[7] W., curiously enough, transfers the corpulence and the power at sea to Francisco, *W. D.*, p. 37.

for the death of the former duchess of Bracciano, whom he had loved : he is related to Bracciano, and revenges the family honor. The Cardinal is in history, as in the play, crafty and revengeful. Francesco de' Medici, however, kept actually away at Florence; and his sister Isabella, Duchess of Bracciano, by no means an innocent woman, was, with the approval of her brother, strangled by her husband before he knew Vittoria.[1] And it was Marcello, not Flamineo, that was Vittoria's bad brother, her pander, and the murderer of her first husband; and Flamineo[2] himself was the upright one. Yet in the main the characters are not changed, only slightly shifted; and for fable and incident Webster depends entirely upon historical report.

The character of Webster's Vittoria, however, may have been affected, especially as regards nationality, by the story of Bianca Capello,[3] the notorious Venetian, who at this same time[4] was mistress of Bracciano's brother-in-law, Francesco de' Medici. She, too, was famous for beauty, wit, and sudden good fortune. Her husband, who came with her to Florence, played the part of wittol somewhat like Webster's Camillo; and her illustrious paramour was thought to have killed his wife, the duchess, at her instigation. The two stories might easily have been confused; but it is more likely that Webster pitched eagerly upon the bolder features of Bianca's story, — the alien beauty coming into Rome and conquering Camillo, Bracciano, Ambassadors, and all, and sweeping out of the way not only her own husband but her paramour's wife!

Was Webster's play known in Italy itself? Count Gnoli thinks it referred to by one of the chroniclers, Paolo Santorio :

> . . . nemo morientium ulilatibus ingemuit, nemo clementer intuitus est. Scio ego apud quosdam actitatum tragediæ argumentum datumque spectantibus in scæna haud suppressis personis nominibusque. Hoc anno ex Senatoribus decessere Nicolaus Caietanus inter primos Senatores, etc.[5]

As there is no paragraphing done here (or elsewhere) in the manuscript, we cannot tell how much of the story just recounted was included in the drama ; but as *immediately* before there are recounted only the events at Padua, one might fairly suppose it was these alone.

---

[1] Gnoli, 61.

[2] There is surely a reminiscence of history in *W. D.*, p. 102 : " Some great cardinal to lug me by th' ears as his endeared minion." Flamineo was the favorite of Cardinal Farnese. Gnoli, p. 33.

[3] Suggested by Gnoli, p. 469. — See here pp. 85 and 87, note 2.

[4] There are letters of Vittoria's to Bianca still preserved. See Gnoli.

[5] Vallicellana Ms., K. 6, entitled *Annales eccles. Greg. XIII, Sixt. V, et cet.*, tom. I, p. 59.

Even were that not the case, the drama must have been Italian ; for, Italy for yet many a day knew nothing of English literature, and little enough of England,[1] and the marvel of an English drama an Italian would not have so lightly passed over. Nor is it likely that Webster imitated the Italian work ; the requirements and conventions of the English stage were so different from those of the Continental that even to a later day the English dramatists chose rather to draw their plots directly from history or romance. Yet it may have attracted his attention to the dramatic possibilities of the story.[2]

The plot of *Malfi* was drawn, as has long been known,[3] from the twenty-third novel of Painter's *Palace of Pleasure*, entitled *The infortunate mariage of a Gentleman, called Antonio Bologna, wyth the Duchesse of Malfi, and the pitifull death of them both.* To this story Webster adds somewhat, but subtracts nothing. In both, the widow Duchess falls in love with the steward of her household, Antonio of Bologna ; declares it to him, has, indeed, to thrust it upon

---

[1] Even yet they know little of it : Gnoli, in 1867, says the *W. D*: is " sconosciuta tra noi," and he himself learns of it " through a friend " (p. 468). And so slight was the intercourse between Italy and Eng. in Web.'s day that only in the last years of Elizabeth, in 1602 (after an interval of forty-four), did the Venetians send to the Court of St. James a secretary (not an ambassador), one Giovanni Scaramelli. At this time there seems to have been no *other* Italian ambassador, to Eng. See *Calendar Venet. State Papers*, vols. 1592-1603, 1603-1607, in the exhaustive indices under *Ambassador*.

[2] The son of " Paulo Giordano Ursini, Duke of Brachiano," (as Webster has it on his title-page) was in 1601, as I have just discovered, special ambassador from the Grand Duke of Florence to Eng. ! And he evidently found favor there, for in 1603 the Pope meditated sending him again, as papal ambassador, to congratulate James, and refrained only on account of Spain and France. See *State Papers, Venet.*, 1592-1603, Art. 982, and 1603-1607, Art. 154, letters of Mocenigo and Badoer to Doge and Senate. In the first letter he is called *Don Virginio Orsini.* and in the second, *Don Virginio Orsini, Duke of Bracciano.* Virginio was Paolo Giordano's son's name (see Gnoli, *passim*), and the fact that Webster changed it to Giovanni (one of the few changes of name in the play), may be indicative of a desire to veil an allusion to a living person. Be that as it may, the visit of Virginio to Eng. makes it probable that the story of his family had become accessible to an Englishman without a visit to Italy or a knowledge of Italian. His mission from the Grand Duke would explain, perhaps, the contamination of the story with that of Bianca Capello. — But all this does not make it more probable — what on the score of his blunders and his own nearness to the events has been suggested by Haz. and Sampson (xxx, xxxi) — that Web. depended on oral tradition. He has too many precise bits of information — *sed manet alta mente repostum, Vitelli,* etc., above, p. 84, note 3, for that. That *sed manet,* indeed, which I have never found outside of Gnoli, would be just the clew. Cf. Preface.

[3] There is a special dissertation upon Webster's relation to his source by Dr. Kiesow. (See above Bibliog.) My discussion rests upon my own comparison ; but I refer the reader to K. for Painter's indebtedness to Belleforest, Belleforest's to Bandello, and the various ramifications of the story, including Lope de Vega.

him in his scruples and faintheartedness; and contracts with him, with her maid as witness, a clandestine marriage. So they live for some time in secret, till several children have been born. This leaks out. The thought that the report should reach her brothers, Duke Ferdinand and the Cardinal, alarms her, and she has Antonio set out to secure a refuge for her at Ancona, whither she, on the pretext of a pilgrimage to Loretto, will follow him. There they meet. But her brothers have meantime heard of the scandal. They rage, and vow revenge; and the Cardinal has both banished from Ancona. Deserted by their train, the Duchess and Antonio think it best to separate. He, taking the eldest boy, escapes to Milan; and she, with the other children, is captured by her brothers' soldiers, and brought back to her castle to prison. There she lingers awhile. One day, she is apprised of her doom, and thereupon, in spite of her indignant protestations, her pleadings for her maid and children, and the struggles of the maid, all of them are strangled. Antonio, meanwhile, sojourns in Milan, anxiously cherishing the fond hope of being reconciled to his brothers-in-law. But he only falls a prey to their revenge at the hands of the mercenary, Bosola.

What Webster adds to the plot is, roughly speaking, the following:

1. The brothers' selfish injunctions, shortly upon her becoming a widow, against a second marriage.

2. The entire Castruccio-Julia-Cardinal by-plot.

3. The entire part of Bosola up to his killing Antonio; including his discovery of the birth of the first child and his report of it, his discovery from the Duchess herself of the name of her husband and of her plans for flight, his torturing of the Duchess, his revenge on her brothers, his killing Antonio only by mistake, etc.

4. The visit of Ferdinand, and his penetrating suddenly to the Duchess's chamber.

5. The prison scenes, and their manifold tortures — the dead hand, wax figures, madmen, etc. Only the bare killing of Duchess, children, and waiting-maid is to be found in the original.

6. The soldier scenes at Rome and Milan.

7. Practically the whole last act of the play: the loss of Antonio's property; the madness of Ferdinand; the intrigues and counter-intrigues of the Cardinal and Bosola; Antonio's visit, the Echo scene, and his death by mistake; and the fate of the Cardinal, Ferdinand, and Bosola, which is left unmentioned by the novelist.

Just as Webster adds more to the plot of *Malfi* than to that of the *White Devil*, so he does to the characters. Those that he found in the original he has drawn somewhat according to hints from the novel. The Duchess is daring and spirited, laments her high estate, and is devoted

to her new husband and her children ; Antonio is gentlemanly and
high-minded, hesitates to permit the Duchess to descend to his level,
and at the end lingers about, brooding instead of acting ; and Duke
Ferdinand and the Cardinal are distinguished after the same scheme
as Painter's, — the Duke ' transported with choler and driven into
deadly fury, the Cardinal grinding his teeth together.' But aside
from these points and a number of minor borrowings of phrase, circumstance, and idea,[1] Webster owes nothing to Painter.[2] Especially
does he do away with the vulgar spirit of the Belleforest-Painter
account, which (though often sympathetic)[3] represents the Duchess
as carried away by her own libidinous passion and uses her fate to
point a moral.

As a source, too, in some measure (though a minor one) we must
henceforth consider Sir Philip Sidney's *Arcadia*. Mr. Charles Crawford has recently shown the great indebtedness of *Malfi* to this work
in phrases and sentiments [4] ; and the indebtedness in incident and
situation, and in conception of character (as Mr. Crawford too sug-

---

[1] Such as : mention of Gaston de Foix, p. 4 (Painter, vol. III), and *Mal.*, p. 160 ; of
Silvio, p. 39, who appears in *Mal.* as a character ; of Castruccio as Cardinal of Siena,
p. 33, the name of whom Web. uses for the cuckold. Also phrases : *Mal.*, p. 176, " I
will remain the constant sanctuary of your good name," and Painter, p. 20 ; Cariola's
foreboding, *Mal.*, 218, and the author's observation, p. 27 ; the jest of the executioner as
he holds the noose to Cariola, *Mal.*, p. 247, " Here 's your wedding ring," and p. 37,
" and instead of a carcanet placed a rope about her neck."

[2] Kiesow, pp. 208, 233, thinks Web. follows the act-divisions given by Belleforest
and Painter, — " hat die schon bei Belle-Painter vorhandene einteilung benützt."
But comparison of the act-divisions in Belle. and Web. has little point. K. himself
says that Web. has divided acts I and II differently, and I have already shown acts
IV and V to be almost entirely Web.'s contribution.

[3] See Sampson, pp. xxxvi, xxxvii.

[4] In *Notes and Queries* (1904, Sept. 17th to Nov. 12th), Mr. C. points out dozens of
parallels, or rather borrowings, some of them even to the length of 9 lines, word for
word (Sept 17th, p. 222, an example) ; and I myself have collected, without sys-
tematically seeking them, almost as many more. This is of a piece with his
borrowing Latin mottoes from Dekker (see above, pp. 21–2), with his borrowing of a
" ditty " for Act III, sc. 4 (margin — ' the author disclaims it to be his '), and of
the many saws and apothegms (many of them marked with quotation marks in the
old editions) in this play and *W. D.* Mr. C. thinks Web. made elaborate notes from
Sidney : he may have had him, and the others, by heart. If the one be true, he
pieced his plays together very laboriously ; if the other, he shows much memory,
little spontaneous invention. Shak., B. & F., etc., did not reproduce exactly. How
different Shak.'s reminiscences, whether in general or from the *Arcadia* itself !
See Eliza West's *Shak. Parallelisms coll. from Sidney's Arcadia*, priv. printed, 1865.
(Many of these, indeed, are imaginary.) At most, when he has a certain author,
as Plutarch or Holinshed, before him to dramatize, some fragments of phrase will
adhere to the subject-matter : there is never accurate, extensive repetition and
piecing together as in the examples below, pp. 90–1, and in Crawford, *passim*.

gests) is not inconsiderable.　This appears undoubtedly in the prison scenes, and, as I am inclined to think, in the Echo scene.[1]

The situation of the Duchess in prison is modelled after that of four personages imprisoned in the *Arcadia* — the Queen Erona, who, like the Duchess, had married one of mean birth, and the Princesses Pamela and Philoclea and the Amazon Zelmane, who were imprisoned at the same time and place.　Queen Erona, whom we will consider first, bears most likeness to the Duchess, whether in fortune, character, or utterances ;

> But *Erona* sadde in-deede, yet like one rather used, then new fallen to sadness (as who had the ioyes of her hart alreadie broken　seemed rather to welcome then to shunne　that ende　of　miserie, speaking　little, but what　she　spake　was　for Antiphilus . . . But her witte endeared by her youth, her affliction by her birth, and her sadnesse by her beautie, made this noble prince *Plangus* . . . to perceyue the shape of louelinesse more perfectly　in　wo, then in ioyfulnesse . . . So borne by the hastie tide of short leysure, he did hastily deliuer together his affection, and affectionate　care.　But　she (as　if he　had　spoken　of　a　small　matter, when he mencioned　her　life, to which she had not leisure to attend) desired him if he loued her, to show it, in finding some way to saue Antiphilus. For her, she found the world but a wearisom stage unto her, where she played a part against her will : and therefore besought him　not to cast his loue in so unfruitfull a place, as could not loue itselfe.　　　　　　　　　　　　　　　　　　Q. 1590, Lib. II, f. 229v.–230.

And after she learns of Antiphilus's death :

> ——glorying in affliction and shunning all comforte, she seemed to haue no delight, but in making herselfe the picture of miserie.　　　　　　　　　　　Lib. II, f. 240 r.[2]

> > She's sad, as one long us'd to 't, and she seems
> > Rather to welcome the end of misery,
> > Than shun it ; a behaviour so noble
> > As gives a majesty to adversity [3] :
> > You may discern the shape of loveliness
> > More perfect in her tears than in her smiles :
> > She will muse for hours together ; and her silence,
> > Methinks, expresseth more than if she spake.　　　　　*Mal.*, p. 230.

> > *Duch.*　I account this world a tedious theatre,
> > For I do play a part in 't 'gainst my will.
> > *Bos.*　Come, be of comfort ; I will save your life.
> > *Duch.*　Indeed I have not leisure to tend so small a business.

Mr. C. infers (Sept. 17th, Oct. 14th) from the greater number of the reminiscences in *Mal.* and *Mon. Col.* (1613) a date c. 1613 for *Mal.*　But dates are not settled after that fashion.

[1] It is a little difficult to draw the line between what should be held a mere quotation and what should be considered here, under the head of source. For instance, Julia's pleading for the Cardinal's confidence, *Mal.*, 265, an explicit reminiscence of Philoclea's pleading for Pamela's (Crawford, p. 262), but not similar in situation.

[2] By an error, there are two leaves numbered 240 ; this is the first, after 231.

[3] This sentence from another part of *Arcadia*, Lib. I, f. 9 r : "A behaviour so noble, as gave a maiestie to adversitie."

```
Bos.  Now, by my life, I pity you.
Duch.  Thou art a fool then,
To waste thy pity on a thing so wretched
As cannot pity itself.                                    Mal., p. 234.
```

```
Duch.  Whom do I look like now?
Car.  Like to your picture in the gallery,
A deal of life in show, but none in practice[1] ;
Or rather like some reverend monument
Whose ruins are even pitied.
Duch.  Very proper.                                       Mal., 238.
```

The borrowings are literal, indubitable; but the more interesting thing to us here is that the Duchess, in a like situation, shows the same beauty in sadness, the same desperation, the same self-conscious glorying in affliction, as Queen Erona.

In the case of the other three, Webster imitates mainly in the matter of their tortures. Their ogress of an aunt, Cecropia, plagues them as Ferdinand does his sister, to bring them to despair. Like him she would "give them terrors, sometimes with suddaine frightings in the night, when the solitary darkness thereof might easier astonish the disarmed senses."[2] And like him she frightened with sham shows of horror. Her victims are imprisoned separately, yet so that all, without seeing each other, might look out into one hall. The curtains of these windows are twice suddenly withdrawn: the one time Pamela is beheaded, the other, Philoclea's head exposed in a bason.[3] Even the effect wrought is the same as in *Malfi*. On beholding her sister's head Pamela grows desperate, and resolves like the Duchess to starve herself[4]; and Zelmane tries to brain herself. At this juncture occurs the same interesting incident as in *Malfi*:

. . . he[5] heard one stirre in his chamber, by the motion of garments; and he with an angry voice asked, Who was there? A poore Gentlewoman (answered the partie) that wish long life unto you. And I soone death to you (said he) for the horrible curse you haue giuen me.   Lib. III, f. 337 r.

Enter Servant.

```
Duch.  What are you?
Serv.  One that wishes you long life.
Duch.  I would thou wert hanged for the horrible curse
Thou hast given me:                                       Mal., 234.
```

---

[1] This, again, from another part of *Arcadia*, Lib. I, f. 61 r. — " I stood like a well wrought image. with some life in show, but none in practise."

[2] *Arc.*, f. 326 v. Cf. *Mal.*, IV, 2, p. 236 : " What hideous noise was that? *Car.* 'Tis the wild consort of madmen," etc. Later on, these madmen come before her. And much, if not all, this torturing is done in darkness.

[3] *Arc.*, Lib. III, ff. 330 v.–335. Comp. the dead hand given the Duchess, and *behind a traverse artificial figures of Antonio and his children, appearing as if they were dead.* *Mal.*, 232.

[4] *Arc.*, Lib. III, f. 339 ; *Mal.*, p. 233.

[5] That is, Pyrocles. alias Zelmane, disguised as an Amazon.

Finally, from the *Arcadia* Webster seems to have taken the notion of the Echo scene.[1] Sidney was no pioneer in this species of dialogue: it appears in Gascoigne's Masque at Kenilworth in 1575, and it appears in real drama several times, from Lodge's *Wounds of Civil War* on, before Webster.[2] With some one or other of these Webster very probably was acquainted, but in view of the astonishingly minute and literal intimacy with the *Arcadia* evinced in *Malfi* — not with certain portions but with every book, almost every chapter,[3] — and, further, of the melancholy character of Sidney's Echo, quite unlike in this regard Jonson's and the rest, it seems altogether likely that it was the *Arcadia* that suggested the device here.[4]

The relations of the two plays to their sources it is interesting to view as a whole. For one thing, in both plays Webster deals with his sources after the old-fashioned chronicle-play style; takes over an epic story covering a long period of time quite whole, instead of thoroughly reworking it or weaving two or more together, like Beaumont and Fletcher or Massinger.[5] This, like much else in them, makes them old-fashioned. Common to both of them, too, are incoherence and lack of motivation. What has the papal election or Lodovico's banishment to do with the dramatic movement of the *White Devil*, or what are the motives of Vittoria's, Flamineo's, or Bosola's villainy? The sources of both plays lacking in business and minor incident, moreover, Webster contributed of this to both, but far more abundantly to *Malfi*, and in less episodic fashion. Page upon page in the *White Devil*, nothing happens, as in the trial scene and the frequent baiting-scenes; while to *Malfi* Webster contributed the intrigues of Bosola, the visit of Ferdinand, and the whole action of the com-

---

[1] *Arc.*, Lib. II, f. 243.

[2] Nichols's *Prog. of Q. Eliz.*, Lond., 1823, I, p. 485 (Echo, p. 494); *Wounds of Civil War*, pub. 1594 (Dods., VII, p. 148); Dekker's *Old Fortunatus*, pub. 1600 (Act I, sc. 1); *Return from Parnassus*, pub. 1606 (Dods., IX. Act. II, sc. 2); *Cynthia's Revels*, I, 1; *Hog hath lost his Pearl*, acted 1613 (Dods., XI. pp. 477–8).

Lodge's Echo scene is certainly influenced by Sidney's: there may have been earlier scenes of the sort in the drama, but the connection here is unmistakable. It has seven echoes in common with Sidney's, all but three of the simpler of which are not to be found in any other Echo scene I have noticed, and none of them in Gascoigne. Hence *Wounds* was not acted in 1587, as Fleay holds (II, p. 49), not before 1590.

[3] As the 4th and 5th books, not contained in the Q., but in the F. of 1593 and after.

[4] Prof. B. Wendell (*Temper of Seventeenth Century*, N. Y., 1904, p. 90) says Web. is imitating *Cynthia's Revels*. By no means. Web.'s Echo scene resembles almost any of the others more than Jonson's.

[5] See an account of this so far as B. & F. and Shak. are concerned in Thorndike's *Inf. of B. & F. on Shak.* And see below.

92

paratively rapid fifth act. Webster has gained somewhat, then, in constructive independence and skill.

Further, in both plays there is a marked tendency to make the story more terrible and horrible, to make the guilty more deeply guilty and the victims more anguish-stricken, as Vittoria and the Duchess. Webster doubles or triples the murders,[1] and all the elaborate paraphernalia of torture and terror, all the heavy atmosphere of gloom and dissolution, are his own addition. And the supernatural element — the madness, ghosts, visions, unearthly echoes, conjuring, forebodings, and omens — likewise. This is interesting as determining with emphasis Webster's adherence to the Kyd-Senecan school[2] : the two main notes of it — wanton bloodshed and torture, and the active part played by the supernatural — he adds on his own account. Nay, in the *White Devil*, the more conservative, old-fashioned revenge play, he even replaces the historical motive — revenge for injured honor — with the Senecan one of blood for blood, by making Francisco and Lodovico revenge Isabella.

Lastly, in both plot and characters the two plays are very similarly handled and arranged. Quite apart from the notable similarity of the original stories — revenge at the hands of relatives for offended honor — both plays alike contain torture-scenes, unnecessary blood-shed and murders, mad-scenes, baiting-scenes, dumb-shows, tales and fables, dirges, presentiments and omens, and a scene of supernatural foreshadowing just before the catastrophe.[3] But the main correspondence between the two is in the characters. These pair off as follows : Francisco and the Cardinal, the revengers in the *White Devil*[4]— Duke Ferdinand and the Cardinal ; Giovanni, the Duchess's son — the young Duke, and (as the good person who pronounces the closing speech) Delio ; Flamineo as a meditative tool-villain — Bosola ; Lodovico as the nobler revenging-villain — Bosola ; Zanche — Julia, as the in-

---

[1] Flamineo's murder of Marcello, the murder of an innocent instead of a guilty Isabella, the murder of Zanche, in the *W. D.* ; and in *Malfi* the useless murder of Julia and of the servant (p. 278), not to mention the wholesale killing in the last scene (demanded, indeed, by dramatic justice, but not furnished in the source) of the Cardinal, Ferdinand, and Bosola.

[2] See next chapter for these matters.

[3] Brachiano's ghost appearing to Flamineo with a skull, and casting dirt upon him, and the Echo scene in *Mal.*, V, 3, where Antonio is warned by the Echo, and has a vision of the Duchess's face folded in sorrow.

[4] A few of these correspondences, of course, are due to the similarity of the original stories. Such are those of the two pairs of revengers (both in the original and in the *W. D.*, Montalto, having become in the meantime pope, really does not wreak revenge), and of Giovanni and the Duchess's Son ; but of none of the others mentioned above.

triguing women who betray secrets and bring about the catastrophe at the end; Antonelli and Gasparo — Grisolan and Roderigo, as characterless " stage-furniture "; Camillo — Castruccio, as ass and cuckold. And the repetitions of figure and phrase are, as we have already seen, as marked.[1]

II. A SKETCH OF THE DEVELOPMENT OF THE REVENGE TYPE.

To whom does Webster owe the type of revenge play he here handles, and what does he himself contribute to the development of it?

About 1590 [2] there arose on the London stage, not soon to leave it, two species of the Tragedy of Blood, one created by Marlowe and the other by Thomas Kyd. To the one class belong the *Jew of Malta*, the *Massacre of Paris*, *Titus Andronicus*,[3] Dekker's *Lust's Dominion*,[4] and Chapman's late dramas, *Alphonsus* and *Revenge for Honour*[5]; to the other, Kyd's *Spanish Tragedy* and *Hamlet*,[6] Marston's *Antonio's Revenge*, Chettle's *Hoffman*, Chapman's *Revenge of Bussy D'Ambois*, Tourneur's *Revenger's Tragedy*, and

---

[1] See, above, note at end of Chap. II.

[2] The date of the *Spanish Tragedy* is very probably before 1589, because of Nash's allusions to it in that year. See Boas's Kyd, pp. xxviii, xxix. The *Jew of Malta*, reg. May 17, 1594, certainly is, as Fleay suggests, subsequent to Dec. 23, 1588, because of the mention of the Guise's death in the prologue. This last applies also to the *Massacre at Paris*, only it must be still later. The earliest entry for it in Henslowe is Jan. 30, 1593, and that for *Malta* is Feb. 26, 1591. See Fleay, II, 61, 63 ; Henslowe, pp. 13, 15. It is probable that Kyd's play antedates both of Marlowe's. See Thorndike's review of Boas's Kyd, *Mod. Lang. Notes*, 1902. Bang (*Eng. Stud.*, Bd. 28, p. 229 f) upholds a date 1589–90.

[3] " the 23 of Jeneway 1593 " [*i. e.*, 1594]. Henslowe, p. 16.

[4] Published 1657, but very certainly to be identified with the *Spanish Moor's Tragedy* of Henslowe, Feb. 13, 1599 [*i. e.*, 1600]. See Fleay, I, 272 ; Henslowe, p. 118 ; and below, Chap. IV, Sect. I, in conn. with *D. L. C.*

[5] Both in 1654, but, of course, much earlier than that. For date of *Rev. Hon.* see App. II.

[6] I take for granted without any discussion what, as most critics agree, has been proved beyond a doubt, that Kyd was the author of the Old *Hamlet*, and probably by 1588. See the argument, and summary of former argument, in Boas's Kyd, Introd., Sec. IV. But the question of the authorship of the Old *Hamlet* is not essential to my discussion ; I am dealing with the Kydian type of revenge play, and to that, *Hamlet*, even in its 1623 form, as has long been recognized, unquestionably belongs. — See on this, and on the whole subject so far as *Hamlet* is concerned, the excellent essay of Mr. A. H. Thorndike on the *Relations of Hamlet to Elizabethan Revenge Plays*, in which he discusses *Sp. Trag.*, *Ant. Rev.*, *Ath. Trag.*, and *Hoffman*, as well as the first parts of *Ant. Rev.* (*Antonio and Mellida*) and of *Sp. Trag.* (*Jeronimo*), which, as being only *first parts* and not revenge plays, I consider but slightly. Where I am indebted to him I shall try to indicate in the footnotes,

Atheist's Tragedy, the *Second Maiden's Tragedy*, and Webster's *White Devil* and *Duchess of Malfi*. The two species had, indeed, something in common ; and in the process of development sometimes influenced each other.[1] Both were full of revenge, intrigue and childish stratagems, rant, blood, melo-dramatic devices and setting. Yet they keep remarkably distinct.

THE KYDIAN TRAGEDY OF BLOOD.

The Kydian [2] Tragedy of Blood is distinguished above all by its Senecan character. Before Kyd's time, indeed, Seneca had influenced the English drama in many direct and indirect ways : it was he who stood sponsor for those firstlings of Elizabethan tragic genius, *Gorboduc*, *Tancred and Gismunda*, and the *Misfortunes of Arthur*. But Kyd came into contact with him directly and anew, and Kyd was the first to put genius into his imitation — to take and to give generously. From Seneca he took the motive and convention of revenge,[3] — revenge not of the merely personal and voluntary sort such as in the *Jew of Malta* or *Lust's Dominion*, but as a sacred duty, for murder of a relative or corruption of a wife or mother, revenge, too, inherited, and associated with supernatural incentives and sympathies.[4] The revenge of Atreus and the revenge of Ægisthus are altogether

---

though it is sometimes difficult to show where I begin and he leaves off. Naturally, my purpose is different from his, — to distinguish the two types, Senecan and Marlowesque, and to show the relation and contribution of Webster to the one.

[1] As in *Hoffman* and *Titus Andronicus*. See below.

[2] It is necessary to coin the word ; it is no worse than Keatsian.

[3] As in the *Thyestes*, where Atreus revenges himself for his wife's dishonor, and where the word and notion revenge is harped on almost as much as in Kyd or Marston. The convention of revenge as a moral obligation, in a sense in which it is not used in Marlowe's plays (though here a convention, too, appears, in the phrase. '' sweet revenge ''), appears also in Seneca, but not in so intense a form. *E. g.*, l. 176,

> Ignave, iners, enervis et (quod maximum
> probrum tyranno rebus in summis reor)
> inulte, post tot scelera, post fratris dolos,
> fasque omne ruptum, questibus vanis agis
> iratus Atreus?

— In this brief discussion I must use the word Seneca or Senecan somewhat loosely, without stopping to inquire at each point whether the influence be derived from him direct, or through English, or French, or Italian, channels. That Kyd did draw from Seneca directly is not to be doubted. (See list of quotations in Cunliffe, *Infl. of Sen.*, p. 127.) Here, however, I am concerned only with the differentiation of the Kydian type from the Marlowesque.

[4] See the Furia in *Thyestes*, and Thyestis Umbra and Tantali Umbra in the prologues of the *Thyestes* and *Agamemnon*, and compare the portents at the killing of the children in *Thyestes*. Cf. ghosts arising from Limbo in *Sp. Trag.* and *Ham.*, and the Fury *Revenge* in the former.

different from the revenge for indignities and contempt, blent with ambition and wanton murderousness, which characterizes Barabas, Aaron, Eleazar, and Abrahen,[1] and is very like that of Marston's Antonio, Tourneur's Vendice, or Webster's Francisco. He took, too, the revengeful ghosts, the presentiments,[2] the fatalism, something of the Stoic philosophy and of the Stoic demeanor[3] of heroes before pain and death, meditations on Fate, Fortune,[4] Justice, etc., physical horrors on the stage,[5] and many tricks of the tumid Senecan style,[6] — all of which but the last two are lacking in the Marlowesque variety.

To this Kyd added much else, some of which is handed down even to Webster : — madness such as Hieronimo's or feigned madness such as Hamlet's, an idyllic love-story such as that of Belimperia and Horatio and of Hamlet and Ophelia, an incestuous relation[7] such as that of Claudius and Gertrude, and various stratagems and intrigues to bring about the ends of villain and revenger, 'the most characteristic and effective of which is the play within a play,' found in both the *Spanish Tragedy* and *Hamlet*. He created (or borrowed) a princely villain of decidedly Machiavellian stamp, and a hireling tool-villain whom the master despatches betimes by a trick.[8] He pushed the revenge motive to further extremes, so as not merely to reach to the victim's kin but even to his soul in the other world. And he set this round about with more than Senecan sound and fury, with curses, lamentations, and dirges, with a melodramatic environment of night, with mutilation

---

[1] The Machiavellian villain, or hero, of Chapman's *Rev. Hon.*; Eleazar in *L. D.*

[2] Presentiments are frequent in Seneca. See Cunliffe, p. 77 ; *Sp. Tr.*, II, 4, 6 (7, 15, 46), and the presentiments in *Hamlet*.

[3] See Hieronimo's indifference at the end and Isabella's boldness. See III, 1, 32–34, for philosophy.

[4] *Sp. Trag.*, III, 1, first speech, etc. ; Seneca's choruses.

[5] Such as the slaying of Thyestes's children and serving up their limbs, reproduced in Marston's *Ant. Rev.* But Seneca outstrips even him : Thyestes unwittingly *eats*. And he and Atreus harp on it: si natos pater humare et igni tradere extremo volo, ego sum cremandus. *Thyestes*, 1090–2, etc. — This incident in *Tit. And.*

[6] Such as a series of rhetorical questions, *Thyestes*, 1–12 ; aphorisms and sententious expressions, *Thyestes*, 86 f, 207 f, 295 ; antitheses, *Thyestes*, 200 f, 1030 ; anaphora and epiphora, *Thyestes*, 290–3 ; noisy apostrophes, 623 f ; and addressing one's self by one's own name or as " heart " or " soul," *Thyestes*, 180, 270, 283, 423. Cf. *Sp. Tr.*, II, 2, 19–23 ; III, 2, 37, etc. Stichomytheia, *Thyestes*, 303, 310, etc., *Sp. Tr.*, I, 2, 155 f ; 3, 43 f, etc. Some of these tricks had been transplanted into Eng. tragic style from Seneca previously ; some of them, but sparingly, adopted also by Marlowe. For passages borrowed from Seneca, see, further, Cunliffe, and Boas's Kyd, index *sub* Seneca.

[7] This latter to be found, of course, in Seneca.

[8] Lorenzo and the comic tool-villain Pedringano. Cf. the play *Jeronimo*, in which Lorenzo holds the distinguished Lazzarotto in fee, I, 1, 114 f, and I, 3. — Whether this play too is Kyd's, or is a foolish imitation of him, is a debated question. See Boas's Introd., Sect. III.

and murder, with properties like ropes, daggers, gallowses, and even trees for hanging.

But the most signal innovation of Kyd is his taking of the ghost out of the induction where he had hitherto stood,[1] and making him, instead of an environing influence, one of the dramatis personæ, nay, the inciting force, the heart and soul, of the drama. This he first accomplished with the ghost in *Hamlet*, — that ghost which "cried so miserally at the Theator like an oister-wife," according to Lodge's report in 1596, "Hamlet, revenge," and so must have been, even in Kyd's version, promoted above a prologue,[2] — and it, not the old-fashioned, more Senecan *Spanish Tragedy*, served as the model for all the ensuing plays of the Kydian tradition. The ghost, then, is always an actor, and thereby the convention of revenge as duty is made visible, personal, theatrically forcible. This introduction of a direct mandate from the other world probably only accentuated a feature already noticeable in the *Spanish Tragedy* — the unmotived delay in executing the project of revenge. This feature, due, very likely to a great paucity of incident and intrigue in the sources[3] Kyd drew from, to Kyd's own inability to construct of himself a consecutive intrigue tending to the execution of the project, and his inclination to "bombast out" a tragedy with introspective, declamatory mood-scenes such as he could imitate from Seneca, was too great a blemish to stand before the eye of Shakspere. By him the delay was grounded in Hamlet's indecision of character.[4] But this stroke was not further developed or imitated[5]; the Kydian play-wrights were after more

---

[1] Both in Seneca (for, whether called so or not, the first speeches of Furia and Tantali Umbra in *Thyestes*, and the introductory speech of Thyestis Umbra in *Agamemnon*, are equivalent to prologues) and in such *early* Eng. Senecan work as the *Misfortunes of Arthur* and the *Sp. Tr.* — This improvement in structure (which must have been present in Old *Hamlet*, as well as in the Shaksperean, as is proved by its presence in the *Bestrafte Brudermord*, the Ger. version of Old *Hamlet*) is interesting comfirmation of other evidence pointing to a *later* date for it than that of the *Sp. Tr.* The earlier play would naturally be that with less innovations, the more Senecan. And Old *Hamlet* "must date before Aug. 23, 1589, when Greene's *Menaphon* was reg. Nash's prefatory epistle contains a reference to ' whole Hamlets.' (Thorn., p. 129.) Bang, *Eng. St.*, 28, pp. 229-234, sets *Sp. Tr.* after *Menaphon* and *Ham*.

[2] In *Wits Miserie*. Quoted in Boas, p. xlvii. Shak.'s version, of course, was not in existence at this time.

[3] The source of the *Sp. Tr.* is unknown ; but every one knows how little intrigue and incident there was to take in Saxo Grammaticus's or Belleforest's version of the story of Hamlet.

[4] Boas calls attention to this.

[5] This is one reason (taken with the evidence of the *Sp. Tr.*) why we must think Kyd could not have anticipated Shak. in motivating Hamlet's delay. It is Kyd's *Hamlet*, as we shall see, not Shak.'s, that influenced further development.

tangible, telling things than psychology; and even Hieronimo's hesitation, his hectoring himself for his remissness, and his search for further proof fail to appear again. After *Hamlet*, the revenger delays, indeed, yet only as one biding his time, like Antonio, or bustling about on other business, like Vendice.

Of all this there is, of course, nothing in the Marlowesque plays. In them the revenge is, as we have seen, not an obligatory, social, or sacred matter, but a matter of personal resentment and retaliation, and is altogether subordinate to ambition, lust, and wanton murderousness, as in Barabas, or Eleazar, or Alphonsus. Nor are there supernatural elements — ghosts, portents, omens, or presentiments, — Senecan fatalism, or Stoic philosophy. Instead of the solemn, half-mad, shrinking Revenger, who strikes only at the end, there is a burly Machiavellian villain for hero, an atheist, murderer, and poisoner by principle,[1] who has not one but many revenges, and brushes away human beings like flies. His energy and self-confidence take the place of fatalism; and schemes of fraud and violence, poison and murder — the Machiavellian program — that of reflections on fortune, sacred duty, suicide, and the Stoic philosophy. True, there are instances in the Marlowesque drama of a more Senecan spirit of revenge, as in the *Alphonsus*, in which a minor villain[2] is seeking revenge for his father, and in *Titus Andronicus*, which, though swayed mainly by the spirit of Marlowe, had come also into direct contact with both Seneca and Kyd.[3] On the whole, however, the types keep surprisingly apart.

MARSTON.

The Old *Hamlet* is the model of the succeeding plays, and of none so markedly as Marston's *Antonio's Revenge*.[4] This absorbs nearly everything at hand in the *Spanish Tragedy* as well; but its

---

[1] See below, and Dr. Meyer's *Machiavelli*.

[2] Alexander.

[3] The character of Aaron is at numberless points — such as professional villainy, blasphemy, paganism (or rather pure devilishness), cursing at death, lust, ambition, and racial resentment and antipathies, — at one with Barabas and Eleazar; and there are frequent echoes and imitations of Marlowe's style and rhythm. But the counter-play shows decided evidences of the influence of Kyd (see Boas, introd., lxxix, lxxx). It lacks, indeed, almost *all* supernatural features; but the Thyestean banquet is, of course, Senecan, and there is revenge for a murdered son, madness and crafty madness, appeals to Heaven, and strongly objective presentiments (II, 3, 195 & 211), Latin quotations from Seneca (Cunliffe, p. 128). In short, *T. A.* is a cross betwixt the two.

[4] Date 1600. See pp. 99, 100, note. Consequently anterior to Shak.'s *Ham.*, which internal evidence, here given, confirms. Cf. Thorndike.

model is the Old *Hamlet*. There is a main revenger, Antonio, who, like Hamlet, revenges his father's death, is, like Hamlet, a "gentle boy," a meditator, and, like Hieronimo and Hamlet, a scholar [1] ; and an ancillary one, Pandulpho, who, like Hieronimo, revenges his son's death ; and a revenger's mother, the Duchess, who is sought in marriage by the murderer, and who joins her son in revenge, like the Queen in Old *Hamlet* [2]; and a maiden, Mellida, imprisoned, like Belimperia, for her love of the "gentle boy," to keep her silent. And there is a ghost as mainspring of the action. This is the father, not, as in the *Spanish Tragedy*, the friend, of the lover ; he cries, like Hamlet's father, "remember me," [3] and, as in Old *Hamlet*, "revenge" [4]; and appears at night to him alone, and in his mother's chamber to them both to rebuke her. He himself is bloodthirsty, and (after the deed) exultant, [5] like the ghost of Andrea in the *Spanish Tragedy*, and (very certainly) that in Old *Hamlet;* and though his son does not expressly avow a yearning to kill both body and soul, yet, like Hieronimo, he stretches his revenge even to the innocent and friendly members of the murderer's family. [6] Here, too, are to be found a villain, Piero, still more deeply dyed in Machiavellism, and his tool-villain, Strotzo, of whom Piero, like Lorenzo, rids himself by a merry trick ; real madness in Pandulfo, on and off again as suddenly as a convulsive fit, like Hieronimo's, [7] and pretended madness in

---

[1] Thorn. notices the last points. As to the phrase, "gentle boy" — really a rough characterization, I think, of the type of sensitive, reflective, high-minded youth in love with a maiden and devoted to his father, whom Marston in Antonio, and Kyd in Horatio and his Hamlet, try to represent, — it is to be found in *Ant. Rev.*, III, 1, 36, and *Sp. Tr.*, III, 13, 138, addressed by their fathers to Antonio and Horatio. It probably stood in the ghost's speech in Old *Ham.* (Like the "Antonio [Hamlet] revenge!" and "remember me.")

[2] Like Belimperia, too, in *Sp. Trag.*, and Lucibella in *Hoff.* — This passage is actually in *Ham.*, Q. I (as Thorndike points out), in the latter, less changed part, III, 4, pp. 46-7.

[3] Andrugio says, indeed, "remember *this* " (*Ant. Rev.*, III, 1, 50). It comes at the end of the speech and line, as in *Ham.*, Q. I and II and F. I.

[4] "Antonio, revenge," *Ant. Rev.*, III, 1, 34, which corresponds exactly to the oister-wife cry of the ghost cited above, and is lacking in both Qq. and the F. of *Ham.*

[5] Andrea, *Sp. Tr.*, IV, 5, 12 and 30 f ; *Ant. Rev.*, V, 1, dumb-show and speech, and sc. 2, 53, 54.

[6] In killing innocent little Julio, as Hieronimo in killing the father of Lorenzo at the end.

[7] *Ant. Rev.*, I, 2, 263 f, and recovers completely, 312 to end. This, when we consider the remarkable literalness of Marston's imitation, especially in phrases and devices (as above, and in the "dirge to be said, not sung," below), is rather strong evidence that the corresponding madness of Hieronimo, *Sp. Tr.*, II, 5, 45–(99), (an addition of the 1602 Q., which contains according to its title-page "additions "), stood in that text when Marston set to work. This last must have been not later than 1600, for

Antonio [1] for intrigue's sake, like Hieronimo's and Hamlet's; and instead of the stratagem of a play within a play, or the final duel, a masque (already used for other purposes in the *Spanish Tragedy*), this also not without surprises and treachery. [2]

So saturated is Marston with his master's melodramatic art that not the slightest trick of it escapes him; — not the running upon the stage, [3] the conspirators digging with daggers, [4] the hanging up of the body, cries from the cellarage, stuttering, [5] the dirge which " must be said not sung," [6] the revenger appearing in black, book in hand, to meditate, and falling down in the midst of his meditation [7]; not the presentiments, dreams, and night-scenes, apostrophes to Heaven and to Nature, [8] Latin and even Italian for curses, dark threats, or moments

---

both Parts of *Antonio and Mellida* were registered Oct. 24, 1601, and both Parts must have been done some time before that, for the style of the *Malcontent* (which belongs to 1600, see above) is a great change and advance. — The evident connection between *A. & M.* (date 1599, see V, 1, 8, " Anno Domini 1599 "), V, 1, the Painter episode, and the " Painter's part," *Sp. Tr.*, III. 12 A, points the same way; for I cannot think with Small (*Stage Quarrel*) and Thorndike that this absurd parody *precedes* that highly tragic scene; least of all, if a man like Ben Jonson wrote it. Likewise, Jonson's reference to *Jeronimo* in Induction to *Cynthia's Revels* (reg. May 23, 1601) " as 't was first acted." For this date of registration makes it probable that the *Sp. Tr.* had been changed, and by himself, some considerable time *before* those records of payment to him in Henslowe — the main basis hitherto for the late date of the additions — Sept. 25, 1601, and June 22, 1602 (Henslowe, pp. 149, 168). I therefore would suggest that the language of the title-pages of the enlarged editions (in Boas's Kyd, introd., pp. lxxxv-vi, all are given) — " and enlarged with new additions of the Painter's part, and others " — may fairly be interpreted to mean *new* additions to the Painter's parts, not such as Marston here parodies. Be that as it may, Marston must, I think, be parodying, and B. J. cannot, in all seriousness, be echoing his enemy's balderdash.

[1] Antonio's pretended madness is really disguise as a fool. But he, too, as Thorn. remarks, is driven by his meditations and the appearance of the ghost to the verge of real madness, like Hieronimo, and like Hamlet even in the Shaksperean version — the " wild and whirling words."

[2] Act V, sc. 2. Comp. Hieronimo's treachery, *Sp. Tr.*, IV, 4, in his entertainment.

[3] *I. e.*, for no reason, unlike Alberto's, IV, 1. Cf. Pandulfo's running, V, 1, with Hieronimo's *Sp. Tr.*, III, 13, and IV, 4, where there is reason for it in Hieronimo's madness. Another instance of Marston's undiscriminating effort after boisterousness. — Thorn. notes some of these details.

[4] *Sp. Tr.*, III, 12, 71; *Ant. Rev.*, IV, 2, 87, stage-dir.

[5] From the first part — *Jeronimo*. Whether the play be Kyd's or not we need not here concern ourselves: it is sufficient that it was connected always with the *Sp. Tr.* Piero's stuttering, *A. & M.*, III, 2, p. 57.

[6] *Sp. Tr.*, II, 5, 66 f, and *Ant. Rev.*, IV, 2, 88-96.

[7] Thorn. — *Sp. Tr.*, III, 13; I, 3; *Ant. Rev.*, II; 2, IV, 2.

[8] There is constant mention of sky, sun, and night, and their changes, and now and then addresses to them, in Mars. and Tour. Of appeals in *Ant. Rev.* (except to " heaven," " heavens "), such as on pp. 104, 134, 156. For the religious element in *Ant. Rev.*, see ref. below, p. 103.

too violent for English,[1] the revenger's cry *Vindicta*,[2] and frequent references to "tragedy."[3] And his language, though far more bombastic and boisterous, more archaistic and sophisticated, constantly echoes (however it may have been with the lost *Hamlet*) at least the *Spanish Tragedy;* shows the same rhetorical figures in exaggerated form — anaphoras, epiphoras, prodigious antistrophes,[4] and passionate apostrophes,[5] — as well as a considerable number[6] of borrowed phrases.[7]

For all that, Marston made several contributions to the development of the type, some of which continue down to Webster. He greatly enlivened the dialogue; he kept the meditative soliloquy of Kyd, but cut down long speeches and mere mood-scenes; and he decidedly increased the stage business. He lifted the villain into a more important rôle, — a Machiavellian with a program of ambitious schemes,[8] active consecutively in a way that Lorenzo, whose activity after the crime is made up of isolated efforts to escape detection and punish-

---

[1] Hieronimo's Latin dirge; Antonio's speech on recovering utterance after the ghost's appearance (III, 1), last lines of his address to ghost and of ghost's speech, and Ant.'s thanks to Heaven on feeling Julio's little limbs in his clutch (ll. 148–9). Italian : *Sp. Tr.*, pp. 48, 80 ; *A. & M.*, 59, 61.

[2] Thorn. — *Sp. Tr.*, III, 13, 1 ; *Ant. Rev.*, V, 1, 57.

[3] This is frequent in revenge plays after Kyd : *Sp. Tr.*, pp. 7, 53, 99 (not counting the use of the word in the play within the play). *Ant. Rev.*, pp. 120, 140, 174 ; Tour., see below.

[4] Anaphoras and epiphoras are to be found in other dramatists of the time — Chapman and Marlowe — but antistrophe is very rare. The most astounding is Piero's, *A. & M.*, III, 2, 272–3. Cf. *Sp. Tr.*, I, 4, 35–7, etc.

[5] *Passim* in *Sp. Tr.* in soliloquies, as III, 7, 45. See below, under Tourneur.

[6] Lines and situations such as : *Sp. Tr.*, I, 1, 91 — *Ant. Rev.*, I, 2, 301 ; *Sp. Tr.*, IV, 1, 159–60 — *Ant. Rev.*, II, 2, 220 ; etc. See notes to Bullen's *Ant. Rev.*

[7] I have insisted above upon the Old *Ham.'s* being the main model of the succeeding revenge plays, and have shown it to be the case in the main matters of structure. And though I find no evidence of any reminiscence of Shaksperean language or of, possibly, Shaksperean incident (just as the dates would lead us to expect), there are the following striking minor reminiscences (besides those adduced above, and the many adduced by Thorn., pp. 155–168) of the Hamlet story, and of the Old *Ham.* language as quoted by Dekker and Web. For brevity I cite merely the page numbers in Bullen's *Marston:*

1. Dekker and Web. in *W. H.*, p. 159, " Let these husbands play mad Hamlet, and cry revenge." Ham. himself does not cry that in Shak. Antonio does (pp. 179, 181), twice over in Latin — *Vindicta !*

2. P. 146. Antonio's vow, like Hamlet's, esp. in the line " if my brain Digest a thought but of dire vengeance." Cf. *Ham.*, I, 5, 98–105 (in Q. I).

3. Maria enters, announces and describes the death of Mellida, just as the Queen does in both Q.'s of *Ham.* (Thorn.) — In this she reports Mellida as saying (p. 170), " the world is too subtle for honest creatures." Cf. Ophelia's " tricks in the world," *Ham.*, IV, 5, 4, 5.

[8] Enounced several times : *Ant. Rev.*, IV, 1, 260–8, etc.

ment, was not.[1] As a consequence, his play is not so slow as the *Spanish Tragedy*, though its acceleration is due, not to the revenger's, but to the villain's intrigue. He added, further, the important device of disguise (not merely in the masque) for the revenger's safety; and (an addition of still more important consequences) the *torture-scene*, with its mutilation, its taunting and triumphing of the revenger over the villain, which appears in the *Spanish Tragedy* only in the germ.[2] He greatly developed the melodramatic setting — night-scenes as appropriate to horrors,[3] appeals to Nature and represen-tations of her as sympathetic with tragic events[4]; — increased and varied the horrors of bloodshed and mutilation generally[5]; and added to the presentiments quite objective omens and portents.[6] And he introduced a new moral element. The stereotyped and colorless brooding and lamentation of Kyd on fate and fortune, death and the course of this world, give way to satire. This is not altogether "free" (to use a mineralogical figure), but generally takes dramatic form: on the one hand, there is a special mouth-piece provided for criticism and censure, which we for convenience may call the malcontent,[7] and

---

[1] But the stratagems of Piero are little less childish and transparent than Lorenzo's. Cf. his murder of Feliche and Andrugio, or his imprisonment of Mellida and his preposterous report of it, or his fatal jest with Strotzo, with Lorenzo's way of getting truth out of Pedringano, his bearing him in hand while in jail and on the scaffold, his imprisoning Belimperia so that she may not tell, and his " shooing " Hieronimo away from court.

[2] The last scene, where the maskers mutilate and taunt Piero, prompted probably by Seneca also. See *Thyestes*, 1020 to end, the tauntings of Atreus. That Marston had *Thyestes* before him in this play is proved by Piero's banquet and by prolonged quotations such as III, 1, 166 f. — *Sp. Tr.*, last scene, where Hieronimo, after he is caught, is threatened with torture. In both cases the tongue is cut out. But that in *Sp. Tr.* is really not a torture-scene, for Hieronimo, though caught, is still the only one who is active — bites out his own tongue and kills the Duke by craft.

[3] See *Ant. Rev.*, III, 1, throughout for Marston's use of night for its melodramatic fitness, esp. l. 1 f, 184 f; I, 1, 3-7; IV, 2, 107 f. — To III, 1, 184 f, above, there is a strik-ing parallel in drift, situation, and wording in *Ham.*, III, 2, 405. This last is not, indeed, in Q. I, but it must have been in the Old *Ham.*; it is so much in the style of the Kydian melodrama that it could hardly have been Shak.'s addition.

[4] *Ant. Rev.*, I, 2, 155; I, 2, 118 f; I, 1, 19-21. These descriptions of and addresses to Nature almost supersede such passionate appeals to Nature as Hieronimo's, *Sp. Tr.*, II, 5, 26-7.

[5] Murder of Julio, exhibition of Feliche's corpse and of Julio's limbs.

[6] And the objective omens and portents, which from now on are peculiar to Kydian tragedy (unless, like those in *Jul. Cæs.*, or in *Mac.* [the horses, the falcon, and the owl], contained in the source), are inspired, at least the portents, by Seneca. *Thyestes*, 776 ff, 985 f. See *Ant. Rev.*, I, 2, the ominous dream, comet, blazing heaven, and the nose-bleed. See Chettle, Chapman's, and Tour.'s pat thunder and lightning.

[7] Feliche in *A. & M.*, Malevole in *Malc.* (see as to the *Malc.* being in the revenge tradition, p. 110, note 6).

on the other, there are subjects furnished him on the boards. The malcontent plays with and rails at the various forms of affectation and rascality about him, or these themselves evoke, or imply, satire through their extravagant, ridiculous deportment.[1] But the *malcontent* goes further : he rails at parasites and flatterers, whoremongers and intelligencers, at courts, at great men and princes whether they be on the stage or off, and at mankind as a whole. He takes on even a prophetic cast — in keeping with that cosmical, religious point of view [2] which prevails here as in Kyd, Seneca, and the type generally, — presumes to speak to God and even for him, and from "the height of contemplation " contemns, and (as he terms it) pities, the "feeble joints men totter on." [3] This last, rather declamatory, element, to be found in *Antonio and Mellida*, gives place in *Antonio's Revenge* (through the death of the malcontent, Feliche) to Antonio's conversational and more dramatic meditations, which are of an ironic, bitter, but no longer quite prophetic cast [4]; but it reappears in Malevole.

CHETTLE AND CHAPMAN.

The further development of the type proceeds from Marston directly, through Tourneur and the *Second Maiden's Tragedy*, to Webster. Yet two other off-shoots [5] from Kyd himself — Chettle's *Hoffman* and Chapman's *Revenge of Bussy* — demand a word. *Hoffman*, composed probably a little later [6] than *Antonio's Revenge*, is, like it, inspired by both the *Spanish Tragedy* and the Old *Hamlet*, mainly by the latter. The story itself is Danish, and is of a son who revenges his father's death. Lodowick, like Horatio, is slain by the

---

[1] Balurdo, Forobosco, Castilio, Balthazar, in *A. & M.* and *Ant. Rev.* They make satire necessary often. See Feliche with them, *A. & M.*, II, 1, and III, 2. Cf. *Ant. Rev.*, I, 2 ; II, 1 ; III, 2, where a malcontent is lacking.

[2] This, which appears in Tour. too, in imitation, is rather remarkable : see passages in note 3 and the following pages in Bullen. *Ant. Rev.* : 151, 149, 171-2, 178, 180, 190, 147 ; and in connection with revenge, sanctifying it : 149, 151, etc. The striking thing is, that as the drama loses in ethical purity, from Kyd through Tourneur, it gains in prophetic and religious parade.

[3] *A. & M.*, Feliche, pp. 19, 50, 51. Cf. Andrugio's splendid railing, III, 1, and Antonio's, III, 2, 203-12.

[4] *Ant. Rev.*, IV, 1, 1-60, esp. "there is no essence mortal That I can envy, but a plump-cheek'd fool." — Of Kyd's irony of dialogue — understatement, and the statement of the *contrary*, for retort's sake and for safety's sake — there is some here, too. *Ant. Rev.*, III, 1, 91-6, " for the good, good prince, most dear, dear lord," etc. ; Pandulfo with Piero, II, 1.

[5] But *Hoff.* influences Tourneur. See p. 105, note.

[6] Hens., p. 173, " 29 of desembr 1602." It is likely, as Thorn. thinks, that Chettle is influenced only by the *Sp. Tr.* and Old *Ham.* There is nothing to prove contact with Shak. Chettle does not affect Web., so I refer the reader to Thorn. for a fuller discussion of the relation of his play to *Ham*.

side of his sweetheart on a flowery bank in the moonlight [1]; Lucibella, like Ophelia, goes mad, wanders through the country, adorns herself with flowers, sings like songs, and, like Belimperia, discovers the murderer; the Duchess, like Maria, is wooed by the murderer, and joins the conspiracy against him; and the villain has a comic tool-villain, Lorrick by name, like Lazzarotto, Pedringano, and Strotzo, whom he uses until he has done, and then by craft despatches. And there is Latin, childish stratagems and intrigues, poison and slaughter, and the swearing of the conspirators. [2] One change there is, though, and that a great one : — the revenger and hero is now the villain. By the murder of Otho, Hoffman's vendetta was really accomplished at the beginning of the play, but he works on nevertheless, from sleight to sleight and murder to murder, against his enemy's kin. Really, he is a Machiavellian villain instead of a revenger — generally jocular and galliard in his murders instead of solemn and passionate, eager to inveigle others into doing them for him instead of performing a revenger's duty with his own hand, and more engaged, toward the end, in schemes of lust and ambition than in revenge; — a Piero, in short, turned revenger. This degeneration, made general by doing away with the ghosts, [3] is, however, too early to be more than sporadic ; there is life in the convention yet.

The only play of Chapman's we have at all to consider is the *Revenge of Bussy*. The late dramas *Alphonsus* and *Revenge for Honour*, [4] — too late to have influenced Webster, — though containing some traces of the Kydian type, show by the Machiavellian sweeping cruelty, fraud and hypocrisy, atheism and valedictory cursing, ambition and lust, of their heroes or main characters, and the absence of the supernatural, or of revenge as a simple motive, that they belong to the type of the *Jew of Malta* and *Lust's Dominion*. The *Revenge of Bussy*, however (though, like all the Bussy and Byron plays, strongly under the influence of the author of *Tamburlaine*), approaches, as the conception indicated by the title makes unavoidable, the Kydian type. Much, indeed, is merely Senecan, not Kydian, whether derived directly, as the Nuntius, the Umbra, [5] the exuberance of Senecan philosophy and

---

[1] To Thorn. this scene seems more like the familiar one in *Mid. Night's Dream*. To me it seems far more like that in *Sp. Tr.*, and that it was influenced by this the other points of contact with that play would tend to prove.

[2] L,l. 2088-2102. Cf. *Ant. Rev.*, end Act IV, and the swearing of his friends by Ham.

[3] The ghost is, in a way, replaced by the body of his father, hanging there at hand to witness revenge and be addressed by his son. And see below, p. 105, note.

[4] Pub. 1654. See App. II, for date.

[5] *Bus. Rev.*, V, 1, first speech, certainly Senecan at first hand. See first speeches in *Agamem.* and *Thyes.*, — those of Thyestis Umbra and Tantali Umbra.

moralizing, the epic similes and stichomythia, or through the earlier English drama, as the conjuring and necromancy.[1] But from the Kydian drama — probably Marston's — was derived the devices of a Second Part to be entitled *The Revenge*, and of the ghost who demands revenge, "stands close" in the last act, and celebrates the fulfillment of his longings.[2] Yet Chapman ranges widely from the Kydian spirit and practice. With him the ghost is no longer the mainspring of the action, and appears in the last act only ; and this one and Chapman's other ghosts, — the dancing-party of them at the last of the play,[3] and the Umbra of the Friar in *Bussy* — are treated rather as convenient constructive features, conveying news, directing movements, prophesying, and serving for ill omens. Of other foreshadowings, indeed, than oracles, or the prophecies and warnings from ghosts and spirits and the omen of their sheer appearance, Chapman has few, — no portents or presentiments.[4] And the old Kydian passion for revenge is quite absent. Clermont, the revenger, deprecates revenge, and the ghost of Bussy enounces it, as in a philosophical view of its cosmical relations, only a form of justice.

TOURNEUR.

It is Tourneur who continues the direct Kydian revenge tradition, and that, in the two tragedies which have descended to us, — the *Revenger's Tragedy*, published in 1607, and the *Atheist's Tragedy* in 1611. In both, a son revenges, or refrains from revenging, a murdered father. In the one, his father's ghost does not appear, but he has at least the skull of his poisoned sweetheart, whom he is also revenging, to remind him[5] ; in the other, the ghost of the father appears to

[1] The last appears only in the first pt. of *Bussy* — the invocation of the spirit Behemoth (IV, 1) and the use of him to reveal by dumb-show what is taking place at the same time elsewhere, and to prophesy. A device used by Web. See below. Possibly derived from *Faustus* or from such plays as *2 Hen. VI*, I, 4, or its original, *The First Part of the Contention;* or from Greene's *Friar Bacon and Friar Bungay.*

[2] Cf. Andrugio's Ghost in *Ant. Rev.*, introducing (like this) Act V with a long speech, "standing close" thereafter, "between the music-houses," to view the action and gloat. [3] Chap., Vol. *Plays*, p. 212.

[4] An "aversation," p. 196 ; bare mention of an ominous dream, p. 208 ; and a wooden set of "ostents," p. 256. Aside from these, nothing but prophecies or warnings by oracles or "messengers." — In the cases of Chettle and Chap. above, I have purposely omitted citations, except at points where they influence the later development of the Type.

[5] As in *Hoff.*, it takes the place of a ghost. And the first speech of the *Rev. Tr.*, as Churton Collins points out, is modelled upon the first of *Hoff.* Another point of contact with Chettle is the use of thunder and lightning as a sign from Heaven. *Hoff.*, l. 11 f ; *Rev. Tr.*, pp. 411, 428, and *Ath. Tr.*, p. 279; still another, the cave as a scene of horror.

hinder his revenge. In the one, the revenger yearns to "stick the soul with ulcers [1] " : in the other, he is warned to leave revenge to the King of Kings. In both, the son has a sweetheart — in the *Revenger's Tragedy*, dead, and, like Meilida, to be revenged; in the *Atheist's Tragedy*, separated from him, as usual, by a villainous father. In the one, there is a masque at the end with treachery, two torture and taunting scenes,[2] and startling portents; in the other, church[3] and churchyard[4] scenes, the appearance of the ghost to the watch,[5] and numerous presentiments.[6] Common to both are violent deaths in horrible melodramatic surroundings, and the usual unmotived delay, or pointless activity, of the revenger.[7]

Both plays are unmistakably under the shadow of Marston. In mental and moral quality and bent Tourneur and Marston are more alike than any two other dramatists of the Elizabethan age; and, for the best of reasons, they are like in matters of form. The discipleship of Tourneur began early, with satirical writing, and it affected every fibre of his poetic and dramatic art, even his language and verse.[8] Tourneur cultivates Marston's lively dialogue, his more complicated intrigue with its startling and horrible reversals,[9] and his satirical characterization. He reproduces the preconcerted feigning of the villain and tool-villain,[10] the disguise of the revenger (only pushed to even greater extremes of improbability [11]) without the "antic disposi-

---

[1] *Rev. Tr.*, III, 4, p. 395.

[2] At the killing of the Duke, III, 4, and Lussurioso, V, 3.

[3] As in *Ant. Rev.*

[4] As in *Ham.*

[5] As in *Ham.*

[6] See below, p. 112.

[7] The intrigue of the *Rev. Tr.* being conducted more than usual by the revenger, but much of it not to the purpose; and the intrigue of the *Ath. Tr.* being conducted by the villain.

[8] Cf. the style of M.'s early poems and satires with T.'s *Transformed Metamorphosis* (1600) for cloudy rhetoric and outlandish vocabulary imitated undoubtedly from the former. (See Collins's introd. to his ed.) T.'s metrical obligations to M. are equally great. See App. I.

[9] Cf. *Rev. Tr.*, III, 4, where the Duke gets a horrible surprise, with *Ant. Rev.*, I, 2, 190 f, where Antonio expects, at the removing of the curtain, to see Mellida at the window, and instead sees Feliche's corpse. Cf. further *Rev. Tr.*, III, 5, p. 400, where Ambitioso and Supervacuo receive, instead of Lussurioso's head, their own brother's; *Soph.*, III, 1, 184, where Syphax discovers Vangue; V, 1, Erichtho; *Ath. Tr.*, p. 314.

[10] *Ath. Tr.*, II, 1, D'Amville and Borachio, and their forged tale. Cf. Piero and Strotzo, *Ant. Rev.*, I, 2, and IV, 1.

[11] M. and T. use disguise more freely and more unplausibly than any of the dramatists of the day. Just a change of suit, and you are safe with your father or mother or patron, who spoke with you a moment before! See the escape of Ant. and Mell. in disguise from under Piero's nose, and their failure to recognize even each other (*A. & M.*, IV, 1) ; Ant.'s impenetrable disguise in *Ant. Rev.*, Malevole's in *Malc.*, Hercules's in *Fawn*, Freevill's and Cocledemoy's still more audacious ones

tion " of Antonio or Hamlet,[1] the treacherous masque at the close, and the revenger's frisky, anticipatory glee.[2] He carries forward the same religious point of view, and develops further the Marstonian omens and portents. He adopts Marston's exclamatory manner — his appeals to Heaven,[3] personifications and apostrophes.[4] Nay, he copies such details as the Marstonian self-conscious references to rhetorical matters[5] and to tragedy.[6]

But it was not Marston's revenge play alone that influenced him : he abandoned the traditional Kydian plot which Marston had reproduced in *Antonio's Revenge*, invented his plots, as Marston did in the *Malcontent* and others,[7] and modelled them, especially the *Revenger's Tragedy*, much after these.[8] Dondolo, the fool in the *Atheist's Tragedy*, is taken — name and character — from the *Fawn*[9]; Levi-

---

in the *D. C.;* Vendice's disguise which, after a few hours, effectually conceals him from both mother and sister, and the change to his true form, which permits him, as a complete stranger, to take service with his offended patron anew. Chap. in *May Day*, II, 4, p. 285, has surely Marston in mind as he inveighs against this " stale device " ; — an opinion in which I am confirmed by Mr. Fleay's detection (I, p. 57) of ridicule of Marston in some quotations from him here, though Mr. Fleay makes something very different out of the " disguises."

[1] Vendice disguises himself for safety as he takes service with Lussurioso, as Ant. takes the fool's costume in *Ant. Rev.*, IV, 1.

[2] *Rev. Tr.*, III, 4, pp. 389–90; V, 1, pp. 419–20, with corresponding vexation at the thought of losing the chance. This has all the " smartness," the dancing for glee, of Ant. on clutching little Julio, *Ant. Rev.*, III, 1, 152 f, and on the point of murdering Piero, V, 2, 47 f. It is a characteristic of M. See *Malc.*, III, 1. 286–9.

[3] " Angels," p. 372; " Heaven," p. 372; " O suffering Heaven," p. 368; " is there no thunder," p. 411 ; " Dost know thy cue," p. 428; " Heaven! is 't my fate," etc., p. 272; " Prithee tell me," " Nature," p. 275.

[4] Apostrophe to Vengeance, Vend.'s first speech ; to Impudence, p. 355 ; to Liberty, 385 ; to Night, 377 (cf. Marston's *Malc.*, III, 1, p. 260–1); to love, 272 ; to sorrow, 293 ; as well as plenty of personification of abstract qualities without apos. : Advancement, 368 ; opportunity, 283 ; love and courage, 260. (Cf. *Ant. Rev.*, 124, hate, sweet wrongs, etc.) Besides much personification of inanimate objects and addressing them, as " O hour," 357 ; " that twelve, the Judas of the hours," 357 : " heaven " and " earth," 372.

[5] P. 405, " you fetch about well "; 419, " I could vary it not so little as thrice over again," etc. ; 378, " you flow well," etc. Cf. *Ant. Rev.*, 112, " retort and obtuse, good words," etc. ; pp. 113–14, " simile " ; 116, " nay, leave hyperboles, and thou canst not form hyperboles " ; 125, " endear, and intimate; good," etc. ; 140, " Look, here 's a trope " ; 153, " a very pretty word." Part of this, however, belongs to Balurdo's character. But it is to be found, both in this play and in others that served as models, quite *out* of character : as *A. & M.*, pp. 24, 27, 39 ; *Malc.*, 226, 254 ; *Fawn*, etc.

[6] P. 392, " tragic business," " useless property " ; 396, " then is the tragedy good " ; 344, " tenant to tragedy "; 429, " heaven likes the tragedy "; 429, " a piteous tragedy " ; 337, " their deservèd tragedies."

[7] See Koeppel's *J. M., B. & F.*, on M.'s plots.   [8] See p. 110, note.

[9] Pub. 1606, and (see above, pp. 17, 18) very probably written the same year : hence a pretty secure clew to the backward limit of the date of *Rev. Tr.* See App. I.

dulcia is imitated from the *Insatiate Countess* [1]; Vendice, as revenger, tool-villain, and malcontent critic, all in one, from the *Malcontent*. Marston's *Malcontent*, indeed, is the main model. [2]   There is the same tissue of lust and unspeakable crime for a plot, the same "humorous" [3] method of character-drawing with the tell-tale Italian adjectives for names, the same baboonish creatures drawn, [4] the same intolerable atmosphere of corruption, ghoulish humor, [5] prurient railing, and satiric characterization, [6] and much the same vein of sombre, curious meditation.

These meditations of the malcontent, though in the mouth of a revenger, have, both in Marston's *Malcontent* and in Tourneur, nothing to do with revenge ; and deserve further consideration, both in themselves, as surviving in Webster, and also as affording an explanation of the satiric and cynical bent of these writers.   Those of Malevole are sombre broodings, somewhat like those of Solomon in Ecclesiastes, more like those of Hamlet in the churchyard (by which, however, they were not inspired [7]), and the sum of them is, *all is alike, all is vanity and filth :*

Think this : — this earth is the only grave and Golgotha wherein all things that live must rot ; 'tis but the draught wherein the heavenly bodies discharge their corruption ; the very muck-hill on which the sublunary orbs cast their excrements : man is the slime of this dung-pit, and princes are the governors of these men ; for, for our souls, they are as free as emperors, all of one piece ; there goes but a pair of shears betwixt an emperor and the son of a bag-piper ; only the dying, dressing, pressing, glossing, makes the difference.   *Malc.*, IV, 2, 140-151.

I ha' seen a sumptuous steeple turned to a stinking [8] privy ; more beastly, the

---

[1] Suggested by Collins.   [2] See below, p. 110, note.
[3] In the Eliz. sense of "humor," as in *Every Man in his Humour*.
[4] Such as Ambitioso, Spurio, Supervacuo, Lussurioso : cf. Don Zuccone and Sir Amoroso Debile Dosso in *Fawn*, Bilioso, Maquerelle, and Passarello, etc., in *Malc.* — Don Zuccone ("cuckold") as jealous man, Sir Amoroso as the weakling lover, are done similarly (though not so revoltingly) to Spurio, Lussurioso, etc.   The same "humorous" method appears also in Malevole, Vendice, etc.   They are settled types, as even their names indicate.   See below, pp. 124-7.
[5] I mean such jests as : *Fawn*, IV, 1, 546, and *Rev. Tr.*, I, 3, p. 356, "bonesetter." Such ingenious, ghastly gaiety as Vendice's over the skull, 391-3 ; D'Amville's, 312 ; or Snuffe's mistake, 314, like Syphax's discovery of Vangue, and later of Erichtho.
[6] See above, on Mars., p. 103.   Satirical characterization had appeared in *A. & M.* and *Ant. Rev.*, railing (Feliche's) in *A. & M.*, but prurient railing and prurient satiric characterization appear first in *Malc.*, *D. C.*, and *Fawn*.
[7] That Hamlet's broodings are not the original is proved absolutely by the date of the *Malc.*, 1600.   But other things show it.   Ham.'s broodings are dramatically formed, not of this professional, "humorous" cast (see below, p. 133).   They are a freer, more human development, such as could arise from these.
[8] He has a great predilection for the words *dirt* and *stink*.   He has passages such as these : *Malc.*, p. 222, "Did your signorship ne 'er see a pigeon house, that was

sacredest place made a dog's kennel, nay, most inhuman, the stoned coffins of long-dead Christians burst up, and made hogs' troughs: *hic finis Priami*.

II, 3, 195–200.[1]

or, as Hamlet says,

> O that that earth, which kept the world in awe,
> Should patch a wall to expell the winter's flaw!

Now this pessimistic brooding, which bores down to dirt and decay, if cherished, would furnish sombre, uncanny imagery for illustration of common discourse; if carried into the moral region, would lead to obscenest cynicism. This is the case with Marston, not merely in the character of malcontent, but generally: his main fund of imagery is from death and dirt, he is penetratingly cynical, and his humor is not only filthy, but often inventively, morbidly filthy. Satire and railing are a luxury to him: he knows how to lay things so bare; he can be so prurient in his righteous indignation.

Such is the case with Tourneur, too, and worse.[2] His malcontent, Vendice, meditates and broods in the same spirit as Malevole, but only on the darkest themes. He utters the same disgust with the day as Malevole,[3] but always on lust and nameless crimes. His main aim in his brooding and burrowing, indeed, is to throw up the dust and ashes under fleshly passion; and he broods and dilates ingeniously, with a curious, Donne-like fancy, on slight things as if they were beings in themselves, as the once worshipped eye or lip of the woman's skull before him, or the "minute"[4] of pleasure. The transitoriness of these all[5]! And this ingenuity and pointed force — worse than Marston's impudence — produces, when disposed to gaiety, a humor of the most unsightly sort.[6] These traits permeate all the fibre

---

smooth, round, and white without, and full of holes and stink within?" Cf. *A. & M.*, II, 1, p. 35, "Egyptian louse," "maggot," etc.

[1] Other such passages are *Malc.*, IV, 2, 25–30; I, 1, 290–300; III, 1, 274–79.

[2] I give the pages where Vendice's more considerable meditations occur: 406–7, 356–7, (Charlemont's) 307–8, 391–2, 377 (on night and what it hides, as Feliche in *A. & M.*, p. 49, and Tourneur's quality and contribution appear on comparison of the two).

[3] Continual allusion to this "luxurious day," "age," etc. See pp. 247, 355, 358, 360, 367, 368, etc.   [4] *Rev. Tr.*, 362.

[5] See ref. in note 2. As in this mild and unobjectionable instance of his brooding, p. 344. He addresses the skull of his sweetheart:

> O thou terror to fat folks,
> To have their costly three-piled flesh worn off
> As bare as this; for banquets, ease, and laughter
> Can make great men, as greatness goes by clay; etc.

[6] See ref. above, note 2, esp. that to pp. 391–3.

of Tourneur's thought, and color his imagery.[1] As with Marston, moreover, this prurient cynicism breaks out in the malcontent often in the form of satire, of indignant railing, even delivered, *infandum!*, from that " height of contemplation "[2] assumed by Marston on other occasions,— " that eternal eye, that sees through flesh and all" [3] !

As for the particular type of the malcontent himself — Vendice, — he, like Malevole and no other, and unlike the first, simple malcontent, Feliche,[4] is not only malcontent — cynical critic and sombre meditator — but also revenger and tool-villain,[5] all in one. A chaos of psychology and morals! But it is worse in Tourneur. In Malevole many of the jars arise still, as in Feliche — therefore within the limits of the character of malcontent proper, — from his language, from the inconsistency of his foul talk with his pretentions as righteous critic and meditator ; and as tool-villain in tempting his own wife, he does not go to work with such needless alacrity and thoroughness as Vendice.[6] But in both, the three 'parts are morally — *humanly* — at

---

[1] To choose unobjectionable and very forcible ones : " stick thy soul with ulcers," p. 395 ; "had he been taken from me like a piece o' dead flesh," 276. He uses : "ague, " 356 ; " tetter," 293 ; various revolting imagery, 302-3 ; " damps that rise from bodies half rotten in their graves, " 312, etc. Two very characteristic images, very common in Marston and Tourneur, borrowed, probably, by the latter : "Paint a rotten post, " 329 ; cf. Marston, *Satire*, X, "paint not a rotten post with colours rich " ; " bound to the dead carcass of a man," 313 ; cf. *D. C.*, p. 27, " a carcass three months dead " (and *Fawn*, p. 128, " thou didst bind the living and dead bodies together, and forced them so to pine and rot "). — This subject, in conn. with Web., is reserved to further discussion. See Pref.

[2] See above p. 103, note.   [3] See *Rev. Tr.*, p. 357, for an instance.

[4] In *A. & M.*   First, that is, in revenge dramas.

[5] Malevole as tool-villain to the villain Mendoza ; Vendice to Lussurioso. Both in disguise, and for their own ends, but going needless, shameful lengths in obedience.

[6] Marston's *Malc.*, though called a comedy, has much of the technique of a revenge play — has even the revenge-play treacherous masque at the end to bring about the (bloodless) catastrophe. At all events, Malevole is certainly the model to Vendice in his triple character : is the malcontent critic *par excellence*, becomes in his disguise the tool of Mendoza the principal villain, takes money from him (*Malc.*, III, 1, 283, and *Rev. Tr.*, I, 3, pp. 355-7, 408), when receiving the villain's commission to commit murder and to tempt his own wife, just as Vendice when receiving his to kill Piato and to tempt his own mother and sister (*Malc.*, V, 2). Besides, so far as may be in a comedy, he is a revenger. He undertakes by his machinations to spoil the other villain's (Pietro's) peace of mind, and his revenge, which he speaks of often, " the dear soul kills " (I, 1, 195-210). Vendice, then, is modelled on Malevole ; and when we consider this fact along with the further revenge-element, — the Machiavellian villain Mendoza, who is hypocritical, exults in evil (p. 267), usurps, schemes to marry the wife of the old duke, expresses a hypocritical affection for his tools, and tries to despatch them with poison in the conventionally crafty way, following the Machiavellian axiom of " nails to drive out one another " (IV, 1, 240-1 ; V, 2, 236), and orders (after the revenge-play style) his own fatal masque (p. 306) ; con-

variance, without a qualm or scruple to make them plausible, — nothing but the factotum disguise. This throws light on Marston's and Tourneur's morals, but more, as we shall see, on their dramaturgic art.[1]

Finally, what more formal contribution has Tourneur made to the Kydian type, play by play? In the *Revenger's Tragedy* the main thing, of course, is the break, heralded by the *Malcontent*, with the old stereotyped plot (consisting of revenge, idyllic love-story, love between villain and revenger's mother, with madness and feigned madness, ghosts, ranting mood-scenes and soliloquies, dirges and the rest), and the adoption of a new story, in which revenge yields place, in a measure, to more piquant motives, such as seduction and pandering. One of the most striking elements of this is the consolidation of malcontent, revenger, and (by playing a part in disguise) of tool-villain, as in Vendice; — of itself a sign of the decay of the revenge motive. Another is the development of the portents. This convention, though quite as unreal as those of revenge and ghosts, had its course yet to run; and the comet which foretells the death of princes actually blazes on the stage, and the voice of God answers Vendice's appeal in thunder.[2] In Marston the portents were only reported on the stage, but here they are represented immediately, as a result of patent effort after intenser melodramatic effect. These, together with a condensed, often crabbed, but pointed and brilliant style, after Marston's fashion boldly figurative, and an increasing amount of railing at princes, intelligencers, and whoremongers at large, and a further development of the melodramatic setting in the shape of the dark cave and the painted skull at the scene of torture,[3] are the main contributions from this play to the type.

The *Revenger's Tragedy* stands unmistakably under the shadow of Marston; the *Atheist's Tragedy*, as echoes from *Macbeth*, *Lear*, *Othello*, and other plays,[4] and borrowings from *Hamlet*, indicate,

---

sider, further, the break made in this play with the old Kydian story (followed so faithfully in *Ant. Rev.*) and the substitution of an intrigue of lust, "humorous" characterization (in some measure), with Italian tell-tale names, we cannot but conclude, I think, that the *Malc.* is imitated by the *Rev. Tr.*, is, though a tragi-comedy, the real innovator in the development of the type, and is the connecting link between *Rev. Tr.* and *Ant. Rev.*   [1] See below, p. 124 f.

[2] See pp. 411, 427, 428-9, and one in *Ath. Tr.*, 279: comet and thunder, the latter three times in answer to appeals to God and once in denial of a blasphemous statement. See above, p. 105, note. In Tour. portents play the part of the supernatural left vacant by the ghosts.

[3] See similar development in *Ath Tr.*; the cave (probably derived from *Hoff.*), the gravel-pit, the skulls in the churchyard, the gallows (appears in *Sp. Tr.*).

[4] The name Borachio probably derived from *Much Ado:* p. 251, "And I am of a confident belief That even the time, place, manner of our deaths Do follow Fate

somewhat under that of Shakspere. The echoes, which serve (some of them) as corroborative evidence, may be relegated to the foot-notes; but the borrowings from *Hamlet* demand further consideration. As in *Hamlet*, there is a man killed by his brother through treachery, whose ghost appears to his son at night to admonish him, is bid by the sentinel to stand, and (instead of being struck at with a partisan) is fired at. As in *Hamlet*, the ghost appears later, but to remind the hero of the duty of patience instead of revenge. And as in *Hamlet*, there is a churchyard scene, with curious meditations on man's end from the lips of the hero (not a malcontent) more like Shakspere's Hamlet's than any others I have found,— suggested directly by the situation, and that a like one, and freed of the set humorousness of Vendice's or Malevole's. There is an idyllic love-story, moreover, of the old *Spanish Tragedy* and *Hamlet* sort, — the son of the murdered man separated, again, by the villain from his daughter by force and craft. Now the distinctly Marstonian elements of the Kydian type, so evident in the *Revenger's Tragedy*, are all gone [1] : the portents, [2] the masque with its treachery, the malcontent with his railing and his gruesome meditations, and the torture scene. So, even though some of the features of the *Hamlet* story adduced above may have been taken from the Old *Hamlet*, or from *Antonio's Revenge*, it is likelier that they come from a new source, the same as that of the verbal borrowings, — Shakspere. [3]

---

with that necessity," etc., probably from *Ham.*, V, 2, 230 f; p. 287, "Our boyling fantasies Like troubled waters falsify the shapes of things retained in them," etc., *Mac.*, I, 3, 79; p. 294, "so you'll put money i' my purse," *Othello*, I, sc. 3, 345, 347, 349, 351, 353, 359; p. 299, Castabella's account of mercy, possibly imitated from Portia's; pp. 307-8, Charlemont's meditations in the churchyard and Ham.'s; p. 322, "The sea wants water enough to wash away the foulness of my name," perhaps (though the notion is to be found even in Greek), from *Mac.*, II, 2, 60-2 (these three pointed out by Collins) ; and D'Amville's raving, p. 332, "I would find out by his anatomy What thing there is in Nature," from *Lear*, III, 6, 80, 81; and p. 333, "I will find out The efficient cause of a contented mind," *Lear*, III, 6, 81-2. These from *Lear*, as well as Charlemont's meditations, are pretty clear cases. For the latter, see below, and for the former, see *App.* I. The rest, except that from *Othello*, are dubious ; — but *nothing* of the sort appears in *Rev. Tr.*

[1] I mean just this much and no more : M.'s spirit still rules T. in many noticeable ways; for instance — the further development of the melodramatic setting, the treatment of the horrors of the gravel-pit, and of the churchyard by night amid the skulls, and the very Marstonian trick on Snuffe.

[2] There is one left, II, 4, p. 279, — the pat thunder and lightning.

[3] Thorn. finds nothing of Shak.'s influence (though, of course, that of Old *Ham.*), for he is led astray by his chronology. — Whether Charlemont be modelled upon Ham. or not, he certainly has interesting points of resemblance. Thorn. notes that he has Hieronimo's and Ham.'s bent for meditation, his eagerness to die and be rid of life's burden. But *that* the "gentle boys" (*v.* p. 99), all but Horatio, likewise have,

This is the first trace of Shakspere's influence that we have found. He hardly could plume himself much upon it, for the play is inferior to its predecessor in artistic worth, and is one of the rawest, most unpalatable existent. Yet really of influence, aside from direct borrowings of phrase and situation, there is little. Traces of such may be found in the abundant presentiments, which supplant the Marstonian portents of the *Revenger's Tragedy*, the emancipation from the blood-thirstiness of the *Revenger's Tragedy*, and, not improbably, the innovations in metre.[1]

The two great innovations of the *Atheist's Tragedy*, however, are sprung from Tourneur's own brain. The one is the introduction of a reflective element which is continuous,[2] is connected with the course of the story, and is led by it to a final upshot or moral. This last is double : — that there is a providence that rules the world, and that the honest man's revenge is patience. How different from the disjointed meditations of the earlier revenge plays, without any didactic issue[3]! The second innovation is the repudiation of the revenge-motive by means of revenge machinery, so as to sound, without seeking it at all, like a parody.[4] This reactionary cry shows that the convention of revenge, as motive of the hero at least, had about run its course.

THE SECOND MAIDEN'S TRAGEDY.

The next revenge play following the *Atheist's Tragedy*, and the last before Webster, is the *Second Maiden's Tragedy*, licensed to act by Sir George Buc, October 31st, 1611. The name of the author is unknown,[5] but it is a fact that Tourneur, whether author or not,

---

and in a form that the raging Marshal has it not. Here, as in the points adduced p. 99, note, Hamlet, Antonio (*Ant. Rev.,* p. 143), and Charlemont are very like, and very different from revengers contaminated with malcontent and tool-villain like Malevole and Vendice.

[1] The advent, in considerable number, of light and weak endings; the abandonment of rime, Marstonian riming-methods and rhythm. See App. I.

[2] Thorn. notices this. — The rise of it can be traced, I think, from the sophistical speculations in the *Rev. Tr.* and in such of Marston's plays as the *D. C.*

[3] This double moral is enounced by those concerned in it : that against atheism by the atheist D'Amville, p. 336, and that against revenge by the revenger who does not revenge, Charlemont, *ib.* — Yet another moral there is, in my opinion, but one less conspicuous, — against lust. Levidulcia is emphatically the adulteress, as D'Amville the atheist: like him she seeks to defend her position philosophically (pp. 261, 320, etc.), and like him she sees the error of her way, and, at her end, points the moral, p. 322.

[4] The ghost, for instance, bolting in and out as of old, crying for forbearance instead of revenge.

[5] Both author and title : "This Second Maiden's Tragedy (for it hath no name inscribed) may, with the reformations, bee acted publickly, 31 October, 1611, G. Buc."

greatly influenced the play. Helvetius's temptation of his daughter to yield to his master and Votarius's temptation of the wife of his friend Anselmus at his instigation, together contain all the elements of Vendice's temptation of his mother and sister [1]; and the conversion of Helvetius through his children is very like that of Gratiana through hers. The painting and poisoning of the face and lips of the woman as a means of revenge on her ravisher is identical with Vendice's expedient in the *Revenger's Tragedy*, even to the preposterous disguise of the poisoner. [2] The bloody, bustling intrigue of the under-plot [3] resembles that in the *Atheist's Tragedy;* and the ending, with the death of the villain and the prosperous survival of the hero, that of the same play. Minor correspondences, too, are not lacking — a church and tomb scene with a sentimental visit of the lover, [4] the villain's supercilious conception of court-life as above virtue, [5] and the pangs of the husband at hearing, amid the throes of death, that he is a cuckold. But what is most like Tourneur and what most interests our study, now that the *form* of the Kydian type is nearly dissolved, is the spirit and tone of the play. As in the *Atheist's Tragedy*, though not quite so completely, the revenge-motive has died down : the ghost says nothing of it, and the motive of the revenger is more to recover the ravished lady than to revenge. [6] The sentiment of the loves of Charlemont and Castabella reappears in the sentiment between

Haz. *Dods.*, vol. X, p. 383. Both Massinger's and Tourneur's names have been suggested as authors, the latter by Fleay. There is nothing in favor of Mass. except the poisoning sc. in the *Duke of Milan*, and the presence of a play of his in the list of those destroyed by Warburton's cook, with the title *The Tyrant*, which would fit this play very well. But the poisoning sc. points equally well to Tour., as well as much other evidence cited above. — We cannot, of course, be quite sure of our chron. Possibly the *W. D.* precedes *S. M. Tr.* But see above (pp. 21, 22, Dekker's Epistle, etc.), and below, p. 118, note.

[1] The vow urging him, in the second case.

[2] The king had seen him so recently and known him so thoroughly !

[3] I mean the story of Anselmus, his wife Votarius, Leonella the waiting maid, and Bellarius her lover, little less closely connected with the main issue of this play than the story of Levidulcia, Belforest her husband, Sebastian her lover, Snuffe and Soquette, etc., is with that of the *Ath. Tr.* Under-plots are novelties in the Kydian Revenge play, though there is something of one in the *Rev. Tr.*

[4] As in *Ath. Tr.*, III, 1.

[5] This is strikingly like Lussurioso's in *Rev. Tr.* See *Sec. Maid. Tr.* in *Dods.*, X, pp. 447, 463. Cf. *Rev. Tr.*, p. 406, " should we name God in a salutation, 'twould ne'er be stood on " ; p. 369, " the better sort cannot abide it " [charity]; p. 371, " you 'd scorn to think o' the devil, an you were there once " [at court]. — This is a sort of satire peculiar to T.

[6] The word " revenge " is used at pp. 461, 464 ; but pp. 451-3 and the last sc. show how little of that feeling there really is, and how the thing really insisted on is that the body shall be reinterred, that it may have rest. The conversation of Govianus and the ghost is mostly exchange of endearments.

Govianus and his Lady. And, most significant of all, the peculiar diseased moral tone reappears in the ghoulish humor and ghastly gaiety [1] at the disinterment, and in the horrible conception of the Tyrant's passion for the dead. [2]

Many elements of the play, however, had other sources. Some belong still to the revenge tradition. From Kyd or from Marston come the appearance of the hero in black, book in hand, to meditate [3]; from Marston alone, the visit of the hero by night to the church, the address to the departed spirit, and the rise of the ghost from the tomb [4]; possibly from Marston, too, the reappearance of the ghost at the end. [5] Other elements, still of seeming Marstonian stamp, are without the pale of the revenge tradition. Such are the points of contact with *Sophonisba :* the classical (but not Roman) atmosphere, [6] the killing of the wife to save her, [7] the crowning of her at the end, and the old, classical motive of the ghost's complaint at being denied burial. [8] Such, too, are those with the *Malcontent:* — a deposed, righteous ruler in disguise and a usurping tyrant, the righteous ruler coming again at the last to his own.

What is the contribution made by this play to the type? The revenge action, first of all, starts, not at the beginning of the play, but near the end; and then not at the death of the lady, but only after her ghost informs the hero of the theft of her body. Secondly, the revenge-motive is weakened down to little more than recovery of one's rights. Thirdly, the ghost is a woman, the revenger's wife. Fourthly, a soft, sentimental tone appears, especially in the two tender songs, in the treatment of the relations of Govianus and his lady, and (most conspicuously for a revenge play) in the words of the ghost. Fifthly (still further betraying a sentimental bent), a new stagecraft is employed, which aims at the *sensations* — the harmless scares — and the spectacular effects of Beaumont and Fletcher. [9] Such are : the final happy outcome for Govianus ; Govianus's charging upon his wife, sword in hand, only to swoon at the last step, [10] and his felling his father-in-law by a pistol-shot without injuring him [11]; the spectacular resurrection of the ghost from the tomb in "a great light

---

[1] See pp. 448, 463, 464.
[2] See p. 452 and last sc.
[5] As in *Ant. Rev.*, last act.
[6] The Latinish names. Definite sc. of action there is none.
[7] Really, she has to kill herself, which is also a classical motive, p. 432.
[8] As in Asdrubal's ghost, who appears to Syphax. None of these, of course, *need* to have been taken from Marston.
[9] How far this is actually influenced by B. and F. is a problem in chronology not here to be solved. We can only note similarities. See further below, p. 118 and note.
[10] P. 432.

[3] P. 450.
[4] Pp. 450-1.
[11] P. 411.

. . . all in white, stuck with jewels, and a great crucifix on her breast '' [1]; and the operatic finale, with the crowning of the body, the gentle ghost itself standing by. — All this is much changed, observe, from the simple old story of Hieronimo and his son, or of Hamlet and his father ; more changed, in plot and treatment alike, than any play we have examined, even the *Atheist's Tragedy ;* for the only vestiges of *Hamlet* or the *Spanish Tragedy* remaining are the ghost, [2] the revenger in black with a book in his hand, and the bare *name* of revenge.

III. THE WHITE DEVIL AND MALFI AS REVENGE PLAYS.

We now approach the last and, with one immortal exception, greatest of revenge plays — Webster's. Yet, before that, one glance back at the development of the type up to him. Kyd started it, as we have seen, with a simple, melodramatic, and bloody plot, built on the motive of revenge for father or for son under sanction of supernatural incentives, with a Senecan technique of mood-scenes, long speeches, and soliloquies on justice, death, fate, fortune, suicide, and revenge, of an induction or chorus, ghosts and presentiments, crude stratagems and stage effects, [3] and a tumid, artificial style. This plot and technique have, but for vestiges, disappeared, or have been replaced by their more modern melodramatic equivalents. The revenge motive has weakened in force, and has had to yield a place by its side to other motives — of lustful intrigue, ambition, satire, etc., — still melodramatically and bloodily treated. New rôles and devices have arisen, such as the malcontent, the ridiculous affected person, the masque as a stratagem, the torture-scene, the poisoning-scene, portents, the revenger's disguise, songs, spectacles, and the like. In these, two tendencies prevail : first, an inclination to enrich the melodramatic setting — to accumulate night-scenes, torturings, properties like the skull and dark cave, to exploit the supernatural as a spectacle, [4] and to develop in sympathy with this a figurative, picturesque style ; and second, a bent for cynical, imaginative reflection and meditation. These tendencies, together with the new technique and the remnants of the old, pass over to Webster.

Both of Webster's tragedies are, we learned on p. 93, emphatically and by choice, Senecan and Kydian. The bare motive revenge was practically all this sort of thing he could draw from his sources,

---

[1] P. 451.

[2] Both omens and presentiments are quite lacking here.

[3] Cf. Thorndike.

[4] As in the portents, and spectacles such as that of the ghost's first appearance in *Sec. Maid. Trag.*

and the supernatural, the tortures, the abundant bloodshed, and the melodramatic accessories and setting were almost altogether his own addition.

THE WHITE DEVIL.

The *White Devil*, the earlier, is also the more old-fashioned. The revenge is for murder. The revenger holds an old-style soliloquy to spur himself on to the deed,[1] and the ghost of his dead sister appears to him. There is a villain (not the revenger), and a tool-villain and malcontent combined.[2] There is a scene of poisoning, two torture-scenes [3] in which the revengers are disguised and yearn to kill both body and soul,[4] two reminiscences of the treacherous revels,[5] madness in the villain and feigned madness,[6] omens for presentiments,[7] cynical meditations, a highly imaginative and picturesque style, menaces in Latin,[8] and even allusions to "tragedy."[9] With this, there is more novel matter. One ghost is a woman. There are spectacles (but without sentiment) as in the *Second Maiden's Tragedy*, dumb-shows and conjuring after Chapman's style,[10] Cornelia's ravings and her dirge,[11] and Isabella's and Brachiano's ghosts. Spectacles I call them, for neither of the ghosts speaks; the one is frankly nothing more than mental image of his sister,[12] and the other, with his pot of lily-flowers

---

[1] As in *Ham.* and *Sp. Tr.*; *W. D.*, III, 3, pp. 78–80.

[2] The villain Brachiano; the malcontent tool-villain Flamineo, according to his own account (pp. 119, 130) cheated, as were Strotzo, Pedringano, Lorrick, Lazzarotto, but not, as they, with death.

[3] As the revengers, disguised as Capuchins, bait Brachiano; and as they at the end bait Vittoria and Flamineo.

[4] This last often: *W. D.*, pp. 100, 101, 110, 117, 118.

[5] ' Our duchess' revels,' the occasion which the conspirators take to work their revenge. See p. 100, where Brachiano, by inviting them, invents, as Gasparo says, his own ruin; this last an ironic trick sometimes added in connection with the masque, as in the *Sp. Tr.*, where the play is proposed by the unwitting victim Lorenzo; in *Ant. Rev.*, where Piero orders his masque (IV, 1, 314 f). — See further *W. D.*, p. 110, "now to the barriers," and 111, Flamineo's cry, "Here's unfortunate revels!" Also p. 137, "we have brought you a masque," etc.

[6] Brachiano's and Cornelia's madness; Flamineo's feigned madness for safety's sake, *W. D.*, pp. 67, 68.

[7] The only thing resembling a presentiment is Marcello's remark (p. 107) about Flamineo's breaking the crucifix. To my mind, it is completely objective, — not a presentiment.

[8] As well as much other Latin: pp. 40, 62, 80, 117.   [9] *W. D.*, p. 79.

[10] *W. D.*, pp. 47, 48. See below.

[11] *W. D.*, p. 126, Frankly introduced as a spectacle: " They are behind the traverse; I'll discover their superstitious howling."

[12] *W. D.*, p. 79: And in a melancholic thought I'll frame

> *Enter Isabella's ghost.*

Her figure 'fore me. Now I ha't — how strong
Imagination works! etc.

and skull, casting earth on Flamineo, is little more than a symbol of death, a slightly operatic omen of evil.[1] And there are stagey elements, possibly drawn from the *Second Maiden's Tragedy*, — Cornelia's rushing at Flamineo with her knife drawn and stopping short of him, and Vittoria's shooting Flamineo down with a blank charge.[2]

THE DUCHESS OF MALFI.

Malfi, last of Kydian revenge-plays, is a long step ahead, both in the discarding of worn-out conventionalities, and in the harmonious development, after the stern Kydian spirit, of sombre, melodramatic setting, meditation, and style. It has no ghost, no poisoning-scene, no conjuring, no revenger's soliloquy or feigned madness, no killing of the soul, or blood-curdling Latin. A revenger there is, a villain and a malcontent tool-villain, who is, as of old, ill-served[3] ; a multiplicity of omens and a prolonged torture-scene, — but all are newly treated. The convention of revenge as prime motive, long a-dying, is now dead; it no longer drew the sympathy of the audience to the hero; and, whereas in the *White Devil*, villains and hero had to be villains, in *Malfi* the place of the victim, hitherto held by the villain, is taken by the hero,[4] and the revenger, as the now prevailing moral and esthetic canons require, is represented as he *is* — a villain.[5] The tool-villain, on the other hand, who, like Flamineo and unlike Malevole and Vendice, is tool-villain in his own character and not as a disguise, chooses, after being cheated, the better part, and avenges his victim.[6] And the torture-scene — the torture of the heroine now, not of the villain — is made the centre of interest and plot.[7] Many old, specially Marstonian devices, also, are used anew. The tool-villain as torturer is disguised; omens, presentiments, and gloomy natural phenomena are introduced, not as with Tourneur for momentary, astounding effect, but, somewhat as with Marston, to infuse a

---

[1] *W. D.*, pp. 128–9. So Flamineo himself interprets it

[2] *W. D.*, pp. 109, 135. See above, p. 115. And both of these tricks appear in B. & F.'s *Hon. Mqn. Fort.*, "plaide in the yeare 1613," acc. to the superscription of Dyce's Ms. As each of the three plays contains both of the tricks, it would seem as if they were directly related. The earliest ascertainable date is that of *Sec. Maid. Trag.*, Oct. 31, 1611. Yet I cannot help thinking B. & F. the likelier source: such tricks are more in keeping with their sensational art. See below, Chap. IV. *W. D.* is very unlikely, both on account of date (see above, p. 22) and of W.'s great dependence (esp. in *W. D.*) as a dramaturgist.

[3] Bosola cheated by Ferdinand, as was Flamineo by Brachiano, *Mal.*, p. 250.

[4] That is, heroine, the Duchess.

[5] Ferdinand, and less actively, the Cardinal.

[6] Bosola, end of Act IV, p. 251, and on.

[7] Engrossing, as it does, an entire act (IV), and containing Web.'s most elaborate art and noblest poetry.

vague, onward-looking fear and dread [1]; and meditations far more in the vein of Malevole than of Vendice, ethical and stoic ideas recalling Marston's, and satirical characterization are further developed. Spectacular and lyrical tendencies, moreover, in form somewhat like those of the *Second Maiden's Tragedy*, but of a sterner, more melancholy spirit, here come to their climax. There are the "noble ceremonies" of the cardinal's investiture as a warrior and of the banishment of the duchess, and the dumb-show of the wax figures of her dead husband and children; a dirge,[2] two songs, a dance of madmen, and a weird Echo-scene. These, together with the brooding weight of omens and presentiments, a style encrusted with highly-wrought, sombre imagery, a setting of night and gloom, and a paraphernalia of torture and uncanny properties beyond example, give an effect of tragic environment and atmosphere more varied and complete than any hitherto on the melodramatic stage.

IV. WEBSTER'S CONTRIBUTION TO THE REVENGE TYPE.
THE REVENGE MOTIVE.

In completing the development of the Kydian revenge-play, what did Webster contribute to it? The revenge motive, first of all, loses with him its conventional character as a duty, and has to fall back upon Nature as its basis, upon the moral sentiment of the day; it can be no longer, therefore, the part for a hero, but must fall to the villain. This return to Nature — the inevitable lot of conventions — was brought about, as I think, by three causes: the rapid degeneration of the convention in the hands of the Kydian authors, the widely divergent moral and esthetic taste of the day, and Webster's own character. Marston and Tourneur, as we have seen, united revenger, malcontent, and tool-villain — incompatible elements — and by the intolerable chaos in character and morals thus resulting from the attempt to rep-present sympathetically one who professes a sacred duty and severe, high-flown notions of morality, and himself on the flimsiest of pre-texts not only talks and acts disgracefully, but even plays tool-villain and pander, made it necessary that the next revenger, Govianus, should have that quality only in name, that the following one, Francisco[3] in the *White Devil*, should be one of the villains, and the next, Ferdinand, the villain *par excellence*. As to the second, taste in the day of the *White Devil* and *Malfi* was ruled (or represented, if

---

[1] See below (as in the case also of the other statements) the fuller discussion.

[2] Dirge, pp. 243-4; songs, 222-3 and 239.

[3] Francisco shows scarcely any honorable or attractive traits: he has his murder-ing done by proxy and by poison, and at the end is called by his nephew Giovanni (p. 142) a murderer.

119

you please) by the spirit of Beaumont and Fletcher and the dramatic romance ; few, even among villains, died now in a fashionable play, and bloodthirstiness in a hero [1] was impossible ; and though revenge-plays (and the Kydian circle) had long been out of the fore-front of fashion — probably since *Hamlet* [2] — they too, in the hands of so impressionable a poet as Webster, must succumb to the reigning influence. Side by side with them, moreover, and for long, revenge had been treated with little conventionality, as in the Marlowesque Tragedy of Blood, or with none at all, as in *Othello*. [3] And as for the last cause, Webster himself was enough to kill the old convention. Not that he would have done so while it was yet in its heyday : the style of his later period — that of the *Devil's Law-Case* and the *Cure for a Cuckold* [4] — proves Webster was not, any more than Shakspere, aloof from the influences and tastes of his time. But he was not like Heywood a caterer to them ; and his was too skeptical and clearsighted a mind to try to revamp so crude and false a convention as the religiousness of revenge.

THE SUPERNATURAL.

Along with the Kydian convention of the religious nature of revenge went, as having no further office, the Kydian ghosts and portents. The forms remain, but applied to a new purpose, in keeping with Webster's skeptical attitude and the more artistic spirit of his melodramatic art. They contribute to the tragic atmosphere. The ghosts are neither of the old sort, real and lively as flesh and blood, which appeared to the revenger and started the revenge a-going, hectored their relicts at night about it, and gloated over it when done ; nor of the subjective, Shaksperean sort, which appeared only to the murderer himself, as a retribution, an embodiment of conscience and disordered imagination. [5] One ghost, indeed, that of Isabella, is in so far like

---

[1] That is, *genuine* bloodthirstiness. See Chap. IV, for B. & F.'s pretences and hoaxes.

[2] *I. e.*, Shak.'s. — Unfashionable, for after *Ham.* there is no revenge-play by an important author till Web. The fashionable B. & F. wrote none.

[3] Iago's revenge for Othello's familiarity with his wife, and for the slight of promoting Cassio above him.

[4] See above, pp. 37–8, and below, Chap. IV.

[5] As in *Rich. III*, V, 3, before the battle ; *J. Cæs.*, IV, 3, Cæsar's ghost to Brutus ; *Mac.*, Banquo's ghost. In all these cases the ghost appears to his murderer (in the revenge-play never), and is hardly to be considered objective. Those in *Rich. III* speak, it is true, but only in a dream ; and, as for Cæsar's ghost, he, too, comes when the lights burn dim, and speaks barely what Plutarch reports. The ghost in *Ham.*, belonging to the Kydian tradition, is, on the contrary, purely objective. — Of ghosts as mere omens there are none in Shak. ; — nothing remotely like it but the spectacular " vision " in *Hen. VIII*, IV, 2, 82 f, and there there are no ghosts. See below.

the Shaksperean, that it is doubted by the beholder,[1] and passes for an hallucination, the effect of "meditation" and "melancholy." The other, however, is unmistakably objective, an omen, a poetic use of the popular superstition of the fatefulness of the appearance of ghosts, but, like the first, without any notion of retribution.[2] Both have none of the old hard realism. They are no longer dramatis personæ. They do not speak; they are seen by no second party; they appear in solemn, lonely places, and have not to stand fire or blows, or to do odd jobs of stage-work such as Andrugio's when he closes the curtains of Maria's bed, or to run errands like the Umbra of the Friar.[3] They are kept aloof, unreal, intangible, enough to serve for atmosphere, to suggest supernatural distance and majesty without a jar. They are no dramatis personæ, but—ghosts and Echo[4] alike—a vague, environing influence, and an atmosphere of fate. So, too, with Webster's omens; they lack the prodigiousness and the downrightness of such signs as the comet, or the fiery sky, or God's voice in thunder.[5] They are such more natural occurrences as the nose-bleed and the drowning of the letters of one's name in blood,[6] the owls cry,[7] the laurel withering,[8] the hair tangling,[9] the premonitory Echo,[10] dying men's mention of one's name,[11] unreasoning aversions to a sinister figure,[12] and dreams,[13] all of which, unlike the portents, and like his own abundant presentiments, depend for their force more upon the context and the

---

[1] Francisco's explanation, *W. D.*, p. 79.

[2] *W. D.*, p. 129. The first ghost appears to the revenger; the second appears to his tool-villain. The Shaksperean notion of retribution, Nemesis, in the mere appearance of the ghosts, so prominent in Banquo's visitation and (in less degree) in Cæsar's, is not to be found in the whole Kydian tradition. Up to Web. the Kydians have no mind to psychology or symbols.

[3] In *Bussy*, p. 172 f. Cf. the management and interpretation of the plot in *Bussy's Rev.* by the Umbra of Bussy, Act V.

[4] That the Echo (*Mal.*, V, 3) takes exactly the place of Brachianos' ghost (*W. D.*, V, 1, p. 128) is shown: 1. By the same foreshowing of the person's fate to whom they address themselves. 2. By the exactly similar position—at the close, just before the catastrophe. 3. By the same effect on the person himself,—defiance of his fate and rushing into it, *W. D.*, p. 129, *Mal.*, p. 272. Indeed, the stage-direction (in the oldest copies) *from the Duchess' grave*, and Antonio's remark and the Echo's reply—"'T is very like my wife's voice," "*Ay, wife's voice*"—would give us to understand that the Echo is but the ghost of the Duchess. This ghost, then, is a parallel of Brachiano's—a friendly, warning ghost, an omen of death, not the retributive ghost of Shak.

[5] See note on Tour. above, p. 111.

[6] *Mal.*, II., 3, ll. 42–6, in Samp., who alone has the true reading. Cf. his note.

[7] *Mal.*, p. 190.

[8] *Ib.*, p. 228.

[9] *Ib.*, p. 207.

[10] *Ib.*, pp. 270, 271.

[11] *W. D.*, pp. 116, 117.

[12] See Antonio's instinctive fear of Bosola, II, 3.

[13] *Mal.*, 225.

varying mood of the characters, are often, indeed, called in question,[1] are not insistently unambiguous, not, like Tourneur's, too unambiguous for art.

Now equally unambiguous in Tourneur (less in Marston) is the connection between portent (or presentiment) and the particular event it foreshadows; it comes pat on the minute, and its effect is rather to startle and astound, than to awe with a hint or dim intimation of a distant, approaching fate. Webster's omens, on the other hand, singly hardly noticeable, are repeated and multiplied, and placed far from the events they point to, so as to cast their shadow throughout the drama. So they, too, contribute to the tragic atmosphere, and are of constructive value in that they impart to the play unity of tone. Particularly so is Webster's subtle faculty of arousing in the hero early in the play, by the accumulation of dubious omens and presentiments,[1] a vague dread, as if he felt fate brooding and weighing on him from the beginning.[2]

THE TORTURE SCENE.

The torture scene, too, is treated in a new way, in a similar spirit of subtler art. Marston and Tourneur had sought tragic effect by the direct and crude means of the revenger's menaces and taunts, the tortures applied, and the sheer agonies of the victims, and (Tourneur at least) also by stage effects. This, of course, is not tragic, but revolting; and in the *White Devil*[3] even Webster has something of it. In *Malfi*,[4] however, Webster depends for effect, above all, upon the utterances of the victim — the Duchess's intense, imaginative speeches, as of a soul in Tartarus, — and upon the ironical, searching meditations and "unanswerable questions" of Bosola. Yet the more material and physical side is by no means neglected: rather, the tortures are increased, and the physical horror heightened; but this is done far more ingeniously, and made to appeal, while still physical, to the imagination. As in Tourneur, the scene is laid in darkness and loneliness[5]; but instead of the poison in the old duke's veins and the knife at his throat and deadly taunts in his ear, there are the figures of the duchess's murdered children before her, the madmen's songs, the coffin which she herself shall fill, her tomb-maker, the horror of

---

[1] See *Mal.*, pp. 189, 190, 191, 192.

[2] See p. 136. As in Antonio (*Mal.*, II, 3), who has the nose-bleed, finds two letters of his name drowned in blood, and fears blankly before he has an object; the Duchess's and Cariola's fears and forebodings, pp. 172, 178, esp. p. 211, where, after the startling visit, the knock of Bosola rouses great dread, though the tragic occurrences are yet long in coming.

[3] V, 1, pp. 117–119.   [5] The torture-sc., *Rev. Tr.*, 394–7.

[4] Act IV, practically.

her waiting-maid's cries, Bosola's "whispering,"[1] her own dirge sung out to her before her death. These give the spectator something to think about, as they come one after another — they reach beyond the senses to the imagination. And even at the point where Webster is nearest to Marston and Tourneur, — where Vendice's victim kisses the lips of the woman who turns out a painted, poisoned skull, and Antonio uncovers to Piero, as the cates he had ordered, Julio's limbs, and the Duchess receives in the darkness the hand which seems her husband's and turns out a severed one,[2] — into the dead chill of the horrible common to all these situations Webster, in his case, has contrived to infuse a little more tragic, less brutal effect than the others.

STYLE.

The same is true of style. Webster's, like Marston's and Tourneur's, serves melodramatic ends, the ends of gloom and horror; but theirs works by direct appeal, Webster's deviously. Theirs, compared to his, is not highly figurative; they deal with revolting and harrowing notions, phrased as vividly and realistically as possible, at first hand, or by metaphor and brief simile. Webster's is nothing if not imaginative; he, too, deals with revolting things,[3] but preferably from the decent distance of imagination, by similes subtle and elaborate. And even their metaphors and similes harrow and startle, have little beauty; Webster's metaphors, and above all his similes, touch one lightly, like real art. So Webster's imagery is fit to make a tragic atmosphere. Mournful, wild, uncanny, yet subdued, subtle, picturesque, it serves, whether scattered through the play or accumulated in dreams, fables, mad-scenes,[4] vivid descriptions of scenes on the stage,[5] or dirges, to allay the crudities of the Kydian Convention and make it plausible.

Generally, however, his style is more meditative than dramatic, and it is something new in the drama. The condensed, concise utterance, the figures so abundant and so curiously and elaborately wrought, the moral 'sentences' and apothegms of a new sort sown up and down the play, and, more especially, the fables,[6] are undramatic in effect,

---

[1] *Mal.*, IV, 2, p. 245.   [2] *Mal.*, p. 232.

[3] Like them, with corruption and decay, with human anatomy, with diseases and medical notions — ague, tetter, lupus, etc., but, of course, less with stinks, filth, maggots, etc. Yet see *Mal.*, 180, 181, etc.

[4] Vittoria's celebrated dream, p. 24, with its splendid imagery, the Duchess's dream, p. 225. The fables, a peculiarity of Web.'s reflective art, are numerous. *Mal.*, 210, 215, 229; *W. D.*, 44, 90, 123, 124. The mad-scenes: Cornelia's (twice), Brachiano's, Ferdinand's (twice); the madmen at the torture of the Duchess.

[5] See below, pp. 127–8.

[6] Fables were used by the epic poet, Chapman. See below. Rarely by others.

are borrowed, in fact, from the technique of contemporary prose and non-dramatic poetry. The conciseness of expression, and the imagery are modelled upon Donne, the fables are after the fashion of those in Burton's *Anatomy of Melancholy*, and the ' sentences ' and apothegms are, many of them, taken bodily from Donne, Bacon, Sidney,[1] and probably others. Now of this Marston and Tourneur had none : they made plays first of all, not poetry ; they flung them off with a free, large hand ; and their work reads still with a lilt. Webster's, on the contrary, reads, as it was done, slowly and hard. His style is, for dramatic dialogue, surcharged ; or it is abrupt, uncontinuous, like a mosaic of precious stones as compared to a picture in oils ; or it subserves purely reflective interest, as in the fables, instead of dramatic. In short, it is the style of the literary artist — like Donne — in the day when impulse is spent, and high, severe notions of style prevail ; and it is the style of a mind as much elegiac and gnomic in bent as dramatic.

CHARACTERIZATION.

In characterization Webster follows, in his way, the Kydian tradition. Marston and Tourneur treat character, as I have said, "humorously" ; not in the Jonsonian style at all, yet as conventional types, loosely enough marked and distinguished, ticketed with Italian names, and kept to one definite place in the dramaturgic mechanism, such as that of malcontent, malcontent's butt, villain, tool-villain, or the like. It is this part they play that is the character : personality and humanity, consistency in morals or psychology, motivation, even, have little to do with it. Malevole and Vendice the malcontent meditators, Spurio and Supervacuo the baboonish princes, Bilioso and Castruccio [2] the cuckoldy asses, are mere parts, rôles, not in any sense characters.

This explains Webster's treatment of Flamineo and Bosola. They are not characters at all, but direct descendants of Malevole and Vendice ; and like them they represent two [3] incongruous, incompatible rôles, — malcontent and tool-villain. As with these, now one rôle is uppermost, now the other, now villain, now moralist, without any ethical or psychological coherence between the two, without even an effort for such coherence in the shape of a contention of motives.

For, motives they, as conventional figures, have none. As tool-villains it is their part, for all their fine ideas, implicitly to obey their

---

[1] For the borrowings from Sid. and Bacon see Mr. Crawford's article, cited above, p. 89. The other matters there is no space here to discuss. See Pref.

[2] In *Mal.;* the rest in Tour. and Mars.

[3] M. and V. each represent *three* parts — also the revenger.

master; as malcontents, to meditate gloomily and rail and flout: they are but cog-wheels in the machinery. Malevole, like the others, speaks of himself as the malcontent, as if there were no help [1]; the "humor," or professional rôle, of Vendice,[2] of Bosola,[3] and of Flamineo [4] is discussed as a definite and known thing, but with never a hint at the cause of this condition of mind or at its human bearings. There is no personal grief latent in Malevole's, or Flamineo's, or Bosola's meditations, nor do these come to any head or purpose; they are merely observations on life in general kept to one note and key, of which he is the mouth-piece, and are nowise actuated by motives or made alive with personality as are Edmund's, for example, in *King Lear.*[5] They themselves are not men, but malcontents and tool-villains, just as they might have been prologues or epilogues.

Yet in Bosola Webster tried, perhaps, to connect the two alien rôles, to intimate by Bosola's scruples — once at hiring out to Ferdinand and once in the middle of his work,[6] — and by his later repentance and

[1] *Malc.*, pp. 210, 211, 218, 220, 261. The malcontent is, of course, only a feigned part in Malevole; but this, like all Marston's and Tourneur's feigned parts, or parts in disguise, is represented really as genuine. Altofronto, Duke of Genoa, has no character at all except as Malevole, the Malcontent; and throughout the play we forget that he is anything else. The same is true of Vendice as malcontent or as tool-villain: he plays the parts he takes upon him thoroughly and absolutely, with no reserve of another, real nature (except, slightly, when tempting relatives). Another striking indication of the unreality, the mechanical "humorousness" of Marston's and Tourneur's characterization. The persons of their dramas take on new parts just as they put on the Marstonian disguise (*v.* p. 106, note 11), and are forthwith, inside as well as outside, new men.

[2] *Rev. Tr.*, pp. 403, 405–8, where Vendice's "humor" is discussed and exhibited.

[3] *Mal.*, pp. 158, 160, "this foul melancholy," "black malcontents"; p. 182, "now, sir, in your contemplation," etc., "this out-of-fashion melancholy, leave it, leave it"; p. 180, "observe my meditation now"; p. 169, "keep your old garb of melancholy."

[4] He is not, indeed, spoken of as having a "humor," but he himself makes his part as professional meditator conspicuous: addressing the audience and explaining to it, p. 91; addressing the audience with moral observations out of dramatic keeping, p. 136 ("O men," — and there are none on the stage); general observations much to the detriment of dramatic propriety, p. 141, etc.

[5] That the malcontent was a stock part long before Marston's play is made probable by Marston's own frequent use of the word without explanation as a known thing (*Malc.*, I, 1, 24); by "Marquess Malcontent" as nickname in *Bussy's Rev.*, p. 192. Cf. "wreathe your arms like a malcontent," *T. G. V.*, II, 1, 20; "thou art the Mars of Malcontents," *M. W. W.*, I, 3, 113, etc. Jaques is a malcontent; he explains self-consciously enough the composition of his melancholy — "a most humourous sadness." — See p. , note, where the set and "humorous" character of the speeches is further shown. — That Marston's malcontent, Malevole, is not meant as a character, but as a "humor," as a sort of rare and admirable monster, is shown plainly by the first sc. (ll. 1–70), where they fetch him out like a beast from the cage, and he, as the stage-direction indicates, "*howles again.*" [6] *Mal.*, pp. 235–6.

vengeance, the contention of two natures within him. But that is mere plastering and patchwork. Only at these moments does Webster deal with the motives of Bosola ; and it would take a more subtle network of them than even Robert Browning ever wove to bridge the gulf between Bosola the malcontent-meditator and Bosola the tool-villain, as engaged together in the torture-scene [1]: — the one brooding and subtilizing, and calling the soul in the body a "lark in a cage," the other going roundly to his work of torture and slaughter with no more qualms or faltering than a Sultan's mute. Really, he is like the Messengers, the Prologues or Epilogues, or the person last on the stage at the end of the scene, who has to drag the bodies off, — a dramaturgic puppet, a fine sort of stage-property. Flamineo, on the other hand, Webster makes no such attempt to unify ; being, like the whole play of the *White Devil*, less immediately under the Marston-Tourneur influence, he needs it less. Yet he, as well as Bosola, Vendice, and the rest, is a "discontented gentleman" who has no way to live but by cutting throats by hire, and in the end is cheated [2]; he, too, gives up

---

[1] In the torture-sc. B. shrinks at nothing, and wastes not a thought upon his devilish work. In fact, he goes into it, like Vendice at the tempting of his mother and sister, with a thoroughness far exceeding what is required by fidelity to his master, just because melodramatic effect demands it. See *Mal.*, pp. 243-5. And yet, after killing the woman by inches, and her children and maid, and having hunted her down in the first place, all without the slightest motive of passion — nothing but the traditional "gold," though he himself seems never to think of it, — after all that, comes the tender language and tears of p. 251 ! With so mechanical and ready a villain, moreover, such meditations as his do not fit. Such things as p. 242 :

> this world
> Is like her little turf of grass, and the heaven o'er our heads,
> Like her looking glass, only gives us a miserable knowledge,
> Of the small compass of our prison.

or p. 281, "O this gloomy world !" etc. These meditations, indeed, have a unity of tone in themselves — Bosola the meditator has a character ; — but Bosola the meditator and Bosola the tool-villain have little in common.

[2] Symonds in *Shak.'s Predecessors* (London, 1900, p. 393) first pointed out that Lazzarotto, as described in *Jeronimo* (I, 1, 113-119), is the precursor of Vendice and Bosola. This is the case only so far as concerns the "discontented gentleman" and his working for gold — two points not touched on in the characterization of Pedringano in the *Sp. Tr.*, Strotzo in *Ant. Rev.*, and Lorrick in *Hoff.*, who are nevertheless dependants of exactly the same function as Lazzarotto, and are cheated in the same way by their masters; but reappearing in Vendice (*Rev. Tr.*, pp. 403, 407) ; in Bosola (*Mal.*, p. 158) where B. claims reward of the Card. ; 167, where Ferdinand hires him ; 160, where the pity of his neglect is mentioned as likely to make him worse ; p. 249, where he is bilked by Ferd. ; and see above the references as to his melancholy (p. 125, note 3); and in Flamineo (*W. D.*, p. 27, where he declares poverty to be the cause of his villainy, shows he had been a gentleman, etc.). But Flamineo, though "discontented," lacks the usual melancholy. The tools Ped., Lor., and Strotzo, then, belong together (esp. Ped. and Lor. in their comic element); and Laz., Ven., Bos.,

his spare time to the part of meditator and malcontent.[1] His medita--
tions, it is true, are of a more flippant[2] tone, more in keeping with the
part of stage-villain; but he himself is, perhaps, even more of a
puppet than Bosola. ' Motives or personal passions *never* appear: his
murders never enter his meditations, and are done and over before we
can catch breath[3]; and though he has at the very last some twinges
of conscience and touches of humanity such as Webster's ethical spirit
would insist upon,[4] even then he keeps up a running fire of comment
at the audience, altogether undramatic and out of character, but
within his professional rôle.' These two figures, then, for all the
wisdom and poetry put into them, the greater harmony of tone
brought about in them between their dual natures, remain, like their
prototypes, unmotived, ununified.

Inheriting, then, as a part of the Kydian tradition, a conventional
and "humorous" method of dealing with character, Webster, when
not following it, is left to his own resources. Yet he finds methods,
handseled by the preceding Kydian dramatists, or merely hinted at
by them, which are in keeping with his and their melodramatic art
and bent for concrete phrasing. Symonds long since noted that his
most characteristic way of presenting them is by many separate
touches, which give features rather than the whole.[5] No one, I
think, has observed, more narrowly, that this is done in at least two
ways: first, by brief, vivid, and picturesque description of the outward
appearance or facial expression of characters, or of action going on at
the same moment upon the stage; and, secondly, by isolated, highly-
charged, utterances of the character himself in moments of passion.

---

and Flam. But the last three descend in more essential matters (as I have shown
above in regard to Vendice) from Malevole: *i. e.*, as malcontent-critic, as revenger,
as taking service by means of disguise with his main enemy, and Flamineo, perhaps,
as playing pander to his sister. — Both Flam. and Bos. are represented as poor
scholars from Padua. This is in keeping with their character as malcontent and
curious meditator; and is, perhaps, an attempt to make the rôle more human and
plausible.

[1] See *W. D.*. 91, "It may appear," etc. (to the audience), and his comments at
unreasonable times, cited above, *W. D.*, pp. 136, 140, 141.

[2] He inherits the gruesome gaiety and loose cynicism of Malevole and Vendice.
There is less of this in Bosola — none of the Marstonian liveliness, friskiness, and
impudent familiarity.

[3] See p. 108, the killing of Marcello without a moment's wait, yet not in a burst
of anger; and that of Camillo, p. 48, spoken of by him once before the deed and
never after.

[4] The "maze of conscience," the "something called compassion," etc., the
"infinite vexation of man's own thoughts"; but they belong to the brilliant meditator, not to the callous cutthroat.

[5] Mer. ed. of Webster and Tourneur, introd.

The picturesque description of persons, which is imitated and developed from Marston, is discussed further on ; of the descriptions of scenes — an amplification of the former — there is a fine example in *Malfi*.

Pes. Mark Prince Ferdinand :
A very salamander lives in 's eye,
To mock the eager violence of fire.
Sil. That Cardinal hath made more bad faces with his oppression than ever Michael Angelo made good ones : he lifts up 's nose like a foul porpoise before a storm.
Pes. The Lord Ferdinand laughs.
Delio. Like a deadly canon
That lightens ere it smokes.
Pes. These are your true pangs of death,
The pangs of life, that struggle with great statesmen.
Delio. In such a deformed silence, witches whisper their charms.[1] *Mal.*, III, 3.

There is no analysis, observe ; rather, the method is pictorial ; and by it Webster contrives to give such a picture of the characters of the Cardinal and Duke Ferdinand as our pre-raphaelite novelists, Pater and Hewlett, paint, also without analysis, with their subtly discriminated descriptions of gestures, tones of voice, lines and shades of color in the face, and poise of body. The second method works from the inside rather than the outside, but again only for moments :

Cover her face ; mine eyes dazzle: she died young.	*Mal.*, p. 248.
Tis welcome !	*Mal.*, p. 208.
I would have my ruin Be sudden.	*Mal.*, p. 228.
I 'll have thee hew'd in pieces.	*Mal.*, p. 267.
If they would bind me to that lifeless trunk, And let me freeze to death.	*Mal.*, p. 233.
I am Duchess of Malfi still.	*Mal.*, p. 242.
Now what you please : What death ?	*Mal.* p. 244.

And even this method is concrete. How suggestive of poise, gesture, and tone ! Each passage is a vignette of a dramatic instant.

HUMAN NATURE AND MORALITY IN CHARACTERIZATION.

The greatest contribution of Webster to characterization, however, is a stern, true moral sense. From the beginning it was an evil in the Kydian drama that it rested on a convention at variance with morality, a revengeful, bloodthirsty hero ; but the bloodthirstiness and murderousness of the otherwise blameless Hieronimo was forerunner

---

[1] There are no other contemporaneous descriptions of long scenes, but these of short ones : *Mal.*, p. 238, and see below, pp. 134-5.

to far more unseemly breaches between art and morals. Tourneur represents his hero Vendice, — partly, no doubt, as a result of the "humorous" and mechanical method of characterization, — as a most revolting villain and hypocrite: as living on close terms with his Maker and fired with a hatred of sin, yet as interested in the most morbid matters, engaged in the most scandalous undertakings, and inclined to the vilest of merriment, with never a pang or a scruple to hinder. A mechanical combination of the incompatible, and in themselves sufficiently unpleasant, individuals — malcontent, revenger, and tool-villain, — he is too chaotic to be either a character or a moral entity. Up and down his plays, moreover, Tourneur scatters a great quantity of puerile and revolting casuistry at large. Now this is not true of Tourneur alone. This same combination in a hero of specious piety (or noble pretences) with the most shameful conduct, and this casuistry at large, appear, too (though, as we have seen, in less revolting form), in Marston, and, in spite of all his parade of piety, in Chapman.[1]

Webster, on the other hand, sweeps this false piety and sophistry — this fungus growth of hypocritical corruption, which had sprung up and clustered about the unnatural and bloody convention of Kyd — quite away[2]; and his heroes and villains are what they are. By this clearing-up he is put into a position as a dramatist really to deal justice. Of justice, of nemesis in a true sense, there is none, and could

---

[1] For Vendice's hypocritical familiarity with Heaven see *Rev. Tr.*, pp. 357, 368, 372, 376, 392, 411, 428-9, and *ante;* for Faunus's noble pretences see *Fawn*, pp. 133-4, and 158-9. — Vendice glozes over his tempting of his mother and sister, and the *Ath. Tr.* is full of casuistry and sophistry on the part of D'Amville, Snuffe, and Levidulcia, pp. 261, 311, 320, etc.

Mars. has still more casuistry, and much like Tour.'s, on " Custom " and "Nature " in the *D. C.*, pp. 20, 21, 25, 27, 39, 73, 89 ; *Sophon.*, p. 255. Chap. presents Tamyra in *Bussy* with evident sympathy, and yet at the moment she seems to be discouraging, and really is encouraging, Bussy's adulterous proposals, she reminds him of " One that wakes above, whose eye no sleep can bind, who sees through doors," etc. (II, 1, p. 153). Quite similar is the Friar, Tamyra's tender, solicitous confessor and Bussy's true friend, who really is no better than a bawd, even after he is become an *Umbra*. Like the Friar, Bussy's brother Cleremont is saturated with sage Senecan morals, and seems far above all human passion ; yet has no very becoming relation to the Countess of Cambray (*Bus. Rev.*, IV, 1). Of casuistry and sophistry Chapman has no end ; —defences of treason, of foreswearing, of Bartholomew's Eve, of treachery, etc. (Vol. *Plays*, pp. 219, 227, 190, 199), and (what resembles the Mars.-Tour. sort) of lust (p. 154). These authors, to be sure, are not the originators of all this. Chap.'s commixture of piety and adultery (like Marston's impervious disguises) is to be found in the old romances (as that of Tristram and Isolt) and the novelle.

[2] Except in his attempt to plaster over the cleft in Bosola's character, as *Mal.*, pp. 168-9, " O, that to avoid ingratitude . . . I must do all the ill man can invent," etc., and in the inappropriate tears and emotions, pp. 235, 251.

be none, in the revenge-plays of Marston and Tourneur, of Kyd, of Chettle, and of Chapman,[1] since they have within them no moral order and direct our sympathy or judgment in no consistent manner. There, heroes and villains alike suffer or die for no perceivable tragic fault, and they themselves are far from recognizing any. Suffer and die they generally do, and deserve it ; but by a slip or through caprice, instead of by necessity, and for melodramatic effect. Webster, however, is stern and clear of mind, and is able (especially in *Malfi*) to hold our sympathies — for all our shrinking — to the retribution he pours down upon both villains and heroes. Some killing he has still for plot's sake, and some for blood's sake alone[2] ; but most of his victims have themselves to acknowledge,[3] at the last, that they have pulled their fate down upon their own heads.

What Webster did for the heroes he did for the villains — substituted humanity and morality again for a religious, or rather mythological,[4] convention. He took away from the Machiavellian villain — the type of Piero, Lussurioso,[5] and D'Amville — his atheism, his diabolic boasting and exultation, his large-letter program of poison, craft, and slaughter, knowing that man is not at all so frank and crude a creature; and though he does not by a consistent and thorough motivation make him vital as Edmund or Macbeth, he models him nevertheless

---

[1] Think of Bussy, the Friar, and Tamyra demanding our sympathy in their enterprise : or, on the other hand, of Montsurry and Monsieur, the scoundrels, in theirs. And there is the same chaos of morals in the late *Rev.Hon.*, — in the presentment of Abilqualit and Caropia, the disgusting adulterous hero and heroine. In *Hoff.*, the hero is an unmitigated monster. In *Rev. Tr.*, the hero, Vendice, and his brother earn every penny of their wages of death. But why, according to the dramatist? The new duke says, because they might murder *him;* Vendice says, for blabbing (431-2): at all events, they die, for all their detestable career, conscience-clear ! In *Ant. Rev.*, the questionable hero, Antonio, receives no retribution whatever.

[2] Bosola's killing of the servant in the last sc. to keep him from bringing help. And for blood's sake, the strangling of the children and Cariola in Act IV, the killing of Marcello in *W. D.*

[3] Bosola, Ferdinand, the Cardinal, Flamineo actually do so : the rest, generally, should do so, either for their crimes or for their rashness and irresolution, the last being the fault of the Duchess and Antonio.

[4] The Elizabethan Machiavellian — poisoner and hypocrite, lover of evil and implacable hater of God and all good, who boasts of his exploits — is a sort of incarnate devil, a creation of popular mythopœic fancy.

[5] For Piero's atheism, see above. For his conventional Machiavellian exultation in evil and craft, *Ant. Rev.*, pp. 104, 106," is 't not rare? " ; 124, 136," laugh Strotzo, laugh." — D'Amville's atheism, of course, *passim.* His conventional exultation in evil; his and Borachio's merriment and laughter over the death of his brother, p. 277. — Lussurioso's atheism and exultation in evil, pp. 358, 373 — " cozen her of all grace," " hast thou beguiled her of her salvation? " This general unmitigated and revolting villainy, and his Machiavellian principle, p. 403, of using men as " nails to drive out one another."

more after their original — human nature. His are villains who have
better moments, when they 'feel the strange thing called compassion,'[1] or start back at the beauty of a murdered sister's face; or
who are subtle and adroit like Vittoria and the Cardinal; or proud,
triumphant in blood, like Lodovico and Bosola[2]; all of them being
more or less poetically treated, with a sense of the artistic aspects of
the villain, and no longer painted diabolical and cunning in the black-
and-red of a pedlar's print. And though his villains are still atheistical,
they are so, not in the old Machiavellian sense of hatred and enmity
toward God, but in our modern, broader one of skepticism or spirit-
ual darkness. The Cardinal, on the one hand, is ready to die for good
and all and ne'er be thought of, and Vittoria, on the other, cries out in
blank fear amid the storm of death.[3]

The same service of humanizing, finally, is done the malcontent's
meditations. These have, indeed (though less marked), the old
"humorous," professional rather than dramatic, character,[4] the old
main theme of 'all is alike and all is vanity,' the old cynical preoccu-
pation with corruption and decay, and more than the old brilliant
phrasing and striking imagery. But the high-flying is gone — the
haughty, hypocritical piety and railing and indignation. The malcontent no longer looks on men as on grasshoppers before him, but
numbers himself among them; and, leaving the old cocksure heights
of censure, he has come down into the mystery and pathos, the paradoxes and irony, of human inquiry and endeavor.[5] For, skeptical
Webster is through and through[6]; but his cynicism, arising out of

---

[1] Flamineo's words, *W. D.*, p. 128.

[2] Both "glory" at the end, *W. D.*, p. 142, *Mal.*, p. 280.

[3] Bosola's, the Cardinal's, Flamineo's, Vittoria's, Julia's, last words all convey the
notion of despair and blindness: Flam.'s "a long silence," "in a mist," pp. 138, 140,
141; Vittoria's "I know not whither," p. 140; Julia's "I go, I know not whither,"
p. 267; Cardinal's "let me Be laid by and ne'er be thought of," p. 281; Bosola's "in a
mist," etc., "mine is *another* voyage," p. 281; Flam.'s "the maze of conscience,"
p. 128; "while we look up to heaven, we confound knowledge with knowledge,"
p. 141; Bosola's words to the Cardinal, p. 280, "a kind of nothing." Cf. even in
D. L. C., p. 70, Lenora's last words as she falls in a swoon,

> Let me ink where neither man
> Nor memory may ever find me.

and Romelio's, p. 118: "Stay, I do not well know whither I am going."

[4] See below, p. 133, note.

[5] Reserved for future discussion, in conn. with Donne. *V.* Pref.

[6] See above, note 3. See Bosola's most pregnant observations, as IV, 2, pp. 241-2,
"the heaven o'er our heads only gives us a miserable knowledge of the small
compass of our prison"; the frequency of paradox, and of the figure "mist" as
applied to life. See ref. above, and *Mal.*, 244, "a general mist of error," "mist,"
141, *A. & V.*, 184.

skepticism, is of a far humaner and sincerer sort than that which, like Marston's and Tourneur's, arises out of a dogmatic, hypocritical spirit. Gone, too, are the erotic themes, the filthiness and prurience, so common in these : dignity and moral cleanliness, indeed, are as conspicuous a contribution as the more sympathetic human tone.

V. WEBSTER'S DEBT TO PARTICULAR REVENGE DRAMATISTS.

Of those playwrights we have been considering, none influenced Webster discernibly but Marston, Tourneur, and Chapman. Marston, above all ; on his style, as Dyce long ago remarked, our author seems to have formed his own.[1]

To Marston.

That Webster was well acquainted with the text of Marston is proved by the familiarity with the *Malcontent* evinced by him in his Induction[2] to that play (the play which, as we have seen, influenced both Tourneur and Webster most), and by various borrowings of phrase scattered through the revenge plays. Of these I bring forward only the more probable[3] :

---

[1] Introd. to ed. of Webster, 1830.

[2] There are allusions to the jests, the "bitterness" of the play. Anyhow, it is unthinkable that Webster should not have both heard and read the play proper.

[3] The less certain ones I give below :

a. Fear in this kind, my lord, doth sweeten love. *Insat. Countess*, III, 2, 8.
    Love mixt with fear is sweetest.   *Mal.*, III, 2, p. 207.

b. The galley-slave, that all the toilsome day
    Tugs at his oar against the stubborn wave.   *Malc.*, III, 1, 162-3.
    I am acquainted with sad misery,
    As the tann'd galley-slave is with his oar,   *Mal.*, IV, 2, p. 237.

c. *Fer.* Who dost think to be the best linguist of our age?
    Mal. Phew ! the devil.   *Malc.*, I, 1, 69, 70.
    To hide his cloven foot. I 'll dispute with him ;
    He 's a rare linguist.   *W. D.*, V, 1, p. 115.

d. Through rotten'st dung best plants both sprout and live ;
    By blood vines grow.   *Soph.*, II, 3, 35-6.
    As in cold countries husbandmen plant vines,
    And with warm blood manure them.   *W. D.*, III, 2, p. 62.

e. And as you see a snow-ball being roll'd,
    At first a handful, yet, long bowl'd about,
    Insensibly acquires a mighty globe, —
    So his cold grief, etc.   *Soph.*, V, 4, 13-16.
    Ay, ay, your good heart gathers like a snow-ball,
    Now your affection 's cold.   *W. D.*, IV, 2, p. 89.

This imagery (in *e*) is in Marston's and Webster's day unusual; yet, like most of the Elizabethan imagery, it, too, may have been common property. (*a*) and (*c*) are probably adages, yet W. may have drawn them from M.

Fie on this satiety ! — 'tis a dull, blunt, weary, and drowsy passion.

> *Fawn*, IV, 1, 106–7.

whereas satiety is a blunt, weary, and drowsy passion.　*W. D.*, I, 2, p. 15.

ride at the ring till the fin of his eyes look as blue as the welkin.

> *Malc.*, I, 1, 102–3.

The fins of her eyelids look most teeming blue.　　*Mal.*, II, 1, p. 181.

These, together with a joke borrowed from the *Fawn* for *Malfi*,[1] are proofs clear and conclusive.

But it is influence that is at issue. In the meditations of the malcontent, first of all, especially Bosola's, Webster follows Marston and not Tourneur. They have a brooding mournfulness which has little to do with the business in hand, like Malevole's, with the same theme of all is alike and all is at last vanity and corruption (only the very last of which is prominent in Tourneur),[2] and have none of Tourneur's prurience, or his ghastly gaiety, or his fanciful dwelling on points. Indeed, it is a peculiarity which distinguishes them from Hamlet's also, not only that they do not dwell on particularities like the skeleton or lip, or the hour twelve, or the like, but also that they are almost without dramatic connection or occasion, are couched in general or universal terms, are, in short, nothing but the set speeches of a malcontent's "humor."[3] Compare the following passages,

> Say you were lineally descended from King Pepin, or he himself, what of this? Search the heads of the greatest rivers in the world, you shall find them but bubbles of water. Some would think the souls of princes were brought forth by some more weighty cause than those of meaner persons: they are deceived, there's the same hand to them; the like passions sway them; the same reason that makes a vicar to go to law for a tithe-pig, and undo his neighbours, makes them spoil a whole province and batter down goodly cities with the cannon.　　*Mal.*, II, 1, pp. 182–3.[4]

---

[1] *Fawn*, II, 1, 39–42, and *Mal.*, II, 1, p. 185.

[2] In the *Ath. Tr.*, 307–8, indeed, appear more of the other qualities, but the passage is imitated from *Ham.*

[3] Bosola's meditations are delivered in great wads, complete in themselves and separable, instead of being broken, and connected with the main current of speech in the scene; and their separable, as well as professional and "humorous," character is further indicated by the prefatory phrase, "*Think this*" (*Malc.*, IV, 2, 141) — "*Observe my meditation now*," (*Mal.*, 180). Cf. Romelio, who as villain and meditator corresponds, even in comedy, to the malcontents, Bosola and Flamineo: (*D. L. C.*, 47), "I have a certain meditation. I'll say it to you." Whereupon he *says* it. It is these and the rest of Bosola's speculations that make Mr. Gosse in his essay on Web. (*Seventeenth Cent. Stud.*, 1883) ask, "Did the clerk of St. Andrews, Holborn, talk so among his contemporaries, and mystify them, we wonder?" betraying himself a naive ignorance of the import of literary convention. Shall we wonder whether Marlowe in his private walk ranted like Tamburlaine, or Shakspere like Titus Andronicus?　　[4] Quoted, however, from Vaughan's ed., as prose.

> But in our own flesh, though we bear diseases,
> Which have their true names only ta'en from beasts,
> As the most ulcerous wolf and swinish measle,
> Though we are eaten up of lice and worms,
> And though continually we bear about us
> A rotten and dead body, we delight
> To hide it in rich tissue, etc.   *Mal.*, II, 1, p. 181.

with those cited from the *Malcontent* on page 108. They have the same theme, and in style they resemble those, not Tourneur's.[1]

The same may be said of Webster's style and imagery. Though in this regard it is Tourneur that resembles Marston most, and though he stands between Marston and Webster in point of time, still Webster owes more to Marston than to anybody else, and must have drawn directly from him. He has not Marston's daring and energy, or his boisterousness and flippancy, or his filth; he has not his metaphors, personifications, or apostrophes; he has not his outlandish figures of antistrophe, reiteration, and the like, and his far-fetched, absurd vocabulary, — all of which, at one time or another, Tourneur drew from Marston before him. For Webster evidently came into contact with Marston in his later and meeker period,[2] that of the *Malcontent* and the *Fawn;* and (what is more to the point) he himself brought into play a more reflective, artistic, spirit. Consequently he imitated him, not in his boisterousness and extravagance, but in his calmer and more classic qualities; not in metaphor, apostrophe, and personification, but in the colder simile. And that not the more old-fashioned Virgilian simile, either, such as, especially under old-world influences and Chapman's example,[3] Marston parades in *Sophonisba;* but the shorter simile, cast in prose rather than in verse, highly original and inventive, concrete and picturesque, applied to the description of persons [4]:

---

[1] Of the same stripe exactly are Francisco's meditations, *W. D.*, pp. 102, 103, " What difference is between the Duke and I? no more than between two bricks, all made of one clay," etc. The "humorous," professional theme, the same as Malevole's above, p. 108. Fran., indeed, in the quality of malcontent (even to the heralding of his humor before his entrance, *W. D.*, 99; cf. *Malc., Mal., Rev. Tr.*), and of revenger in disguise, appearing at the revels at the close of the play, is a distinct reminiscence of Malevole or Vendice.

[2] Tour. was influenced also by Marston's earliest work, his Satires.

[3] There is no question that Chap. influenced *Soph.*, that this is not Marston's own style. Space does not permit of anything but an enumeration of a few points: the conjuring, pp. 292-4 (Bullen, Vol. II), as proved by the quotation from *Bussy* on p. 292 (cf. footnote); the very Chapman-like ghost whose function is prophecy; the Nuntius; the false maid-servant Zanthia, just like Pero in *Bussy;* the convenient vault, — the sign-manual, one might say, of Chap. (though it goes back as far as to *Tancred and Gismunda*); epic similes; long speeches, few broken ones.

[4] See above, p. 128.

> He is made like a tilting staff ; and looks
> For all the world like an o'er-roasted pig :
> A great tobacco-taker too, that 's flat ;
> For his eyes look as if they had been hung
> In the smoke of his nose.   *A. & M.*, I, 1, 123–7.

> When thou dost girn, thy rusty face doth look
> Like the head of a roasted rabbit.   *Ant. Rev.*, I, 2, 77, 78.

She has three hairs on her scalp and four teeth in her head ; a brow wrinkled and puckered like old parchment half burnt — . . . Her breasts hang like cobwebs.
Fawn, IV, 1, 537.

She were an excellent lady, but that her face peeleth like Muscovy glass.
Malc., I, 3, 42–3.

The red upon the white showed as if her cheeks should have been served in for two dishes of bar-berries in stewed broth, and the flesh to them a woodcock.
Malc., III, 1, 143–6.

Of the same stamp are Webster's :

He carries his face in 's ruff, as I have seen a serving-man carry glasses in a cypress hatband, monstrous steady, for fear of breaking ; he looks like the claw of a blackbird, first salted, and then broiled in a candle.   *W. D.*, III, 2, p. 53.

Look, his eye 's bloodshed, like a needle a chirurgeon stitcheth a wound with.
W. D., II, 1, p. 42.

> Mark her, I prithee, she simpers like the suds
> A collier hath been wash'd in.   *W. D.*, V, 1, p. 122.

. . . when he wears white satin, one would take him by his black muzzle to be no other creature than a maggot.   *W. D.*, I, 2, p. 20.

. . . he shewed like a pewter candlestick fashioned like a man in armour, holding a tilting staff in his hand, little bigger than a candle of twelve i' th' pound.
W. D., III, 2, p. 53.

> And whereas before she looked like a nutmeg-grater,
> After she resembled an abortive hedge-hog.   *Mal.*, II, 1, p. 180.

> *Pes.* The Lord Ferdinand laughs.
> *Del.* Like a deadly cannon,
> That lightens ere it smokes.   *Mal.*, III, 3, p. 221.

> I do not think but sorrow makes her look
> Like to an oft-dy'd garment.   *Mal.*, V, 2, p. 260.

In both cases, observe, the imagery is brand-new, ingenious, and striking ; not, as is so commonly the case in even the better Elizabethan plays, the old metal recast, but evidently virgin ore ; imagery, moreover, decidedly pictorial in effect, and serving the same function of satiric description.

Again, Webster has many little tricks of the art from Marston. Some are to be found also in other dramatists : — as addresses to the audience, Latin for threats and dark sayings, the plot-device of a lost paper that betrays the secret,[1] remarks about " tragedy," and Stoic

---

[1] Antonio's paper containing the horoscope of the infant, which is found by Bosola, *Mal.*, II, 3 ; almost as crude a device as Antonio's note found by Piero, *A. & M.*, IV, 2.

maxims. Others are almost unmistakably derived from him : — the placing of the bodies of Antonio and his children behind a traverse, imitated, as a means of torture, from Piero's exhibition of Feliche's body [1] ; the omen of the nose-bleed, [2] and Forobosco as name for a character, repeated from *Antonio's Revenge;* the use of omens generally, and the art of inspiring by means of them a vague dread. This last matter is important. In Tourneur, as we have seen, the foreshadowings and omens are all portents ; and in Chapman there are none. They must, then, be inherited by Webster, as the case of the nose-bleed indicates, directly from Marston. Along with them, he derived the faculty for rousing in the hero (and audience) a vague feeling of dread by the accumulation of presentiments, omens, and the terror of Nature and stage-setting, before it can yet have an object. Much the same in this respect is the treatment of Antonio's feelings in *Malfi*, Act II, scene 3, as that of Antonio's in *Antonio's Revenge*, Act I, sc. 2. [3]

Finally, the satiric element in Webster was influenced by Marston. Satire proper, as distinguished from satiric characterization, has in Webster, as we have seen, much abated ; there is no railing at all, no satirical remarks even (except, as below, where an object of satire is on the stage [4]), for all the old railing at large has lost its particular and pointed quality, and is shrunk and generalized into an object of meditation — to illustrate the paradox between the shows and realities of life. [5] Satire there is, however, in the part of the malcontent in

---

[1] *Mal.*, IV, 1, p. 232, and *Ant. Rev.*, I, 2, 195 f. In both it is introduced suddenly and as a terrible surprise. — Mars., I suppose, is here W.'s dramatic model ; but W.'s source is rather the *Arcadia*. See above, p. 91.

[2] *Mal.*, II, 3, p. 192, and *Ant. Rev.*, I, 2. 125. It must be rare as an omen. In my reading of Eliz. dram. lit., I have not found it elsewhere.

[3] In the omen of nose-bleed and the accumulation of omens, the blank presentiment of unknown danger and evil, the effect of nature (the night in both cases, though, in *Ant. Rev.*, in restrospect, for it is now dawn), the "silence and unmoved calm " in *Ant. Rev.*, and the slight noises in the dead of night in *Mal.* (the woman's shriek, or " maybe 't was the melancholy bird, Best friend of silence and of solitariness," or "else I dreamed "). Cf. end of *Mal.*, II, 2. See for same method, *Mal.*, p. 211, where at the knock the Duchess ' feels as if a mine beneath my feet were ready to blow up.' — But in M. the evil forboded is never far off. *V. sup.*

[4] As when Castruccio, the Old Lady, or Malateste, is on the stage, in *Mal.*

[5] The skits and flings at court, great men, politicians, rascality, and affectation of all sorts, I mean, have lost in W.'s hands all their *railing* qualities, all the incisive or prurient detail they had in Tour., and are reduced to axioms, moral sentences, material for imagery. See *W. D.*, 112, Fails you as oft as great men's needy friends ; *W. D.*, 128, like some great men That only walk like shadows up and down ; *W. D.*, 113, To see what solitariness is about dying princes ; flatterers are but the shadows of princes' bodies, etc. : *Mal.*, 245, heaven-gates are not so highly arched As princes' palaces ; *Mal.*, 242, Thou art some great woman sure, for riot Begins to sit on thy forehead ; *Mal.*, 216, I would sooner swim to the Bermoothes on Two politicians'

connection with satiric characterization, the malcontent putting the asinine parasite or cuckold through his paces just as in Marston. Bosola plays with the egregious fool and cuckold Castruccio, without his understanding it, and Flamineo does with just such another, Camillo, quite as Malevole does with still another, Bilioso. [1] And Bosola makes fun of a painted, affected Old Lady, with less vigor, indeed, and with more brooding, but still after the general fashion of Malevole, Feliche, and Faunus with their victims. [2] Besides this, there is one instance of satiric characterization carried through — still like Marston — without the presence of malcontent or any critic: Castruccio, the arrant ass and unwitting cuckold (exactly the counterpart of Marston's Bilioso, both at these points and in silliness, stupidity, and importance), playing before his lord, as does Bilioso, still another part, that of sycophant. [3] — All this must be from Marston; for Tourneur has nothing of it, and Chapman nothing but the ass of a gentleman-usher, such as Prepasso in the *Malcontent,* a different type. [4]

By the borrowing, then, of phrases and of details of dramatic device, by the imitation of meditation, of imagery, of dramatic device, of satire and satiric characterization, Webster's revenge plays, particularly *Malfi,* [5] are indebted to Marston. [6]

rotten bladders, tied Together with an intelligencer's heart string Than depend, etc. Cf. further, *W. D.*: 26 funerals, 31 wretched, 49 great men, 73 great men, politician, 97 great men, 106 ambassadors; *Mal.*: 175 great men, 183 princes, 203 princes', 215 princes, 220 foxes, 168, 215, 218, 225, etc., etc. There are, of course, passages where something of the old satire appears, as in *W. D.*, 97, greatness; but generally this old satiric material is either used in aphorism or else turned into imagery to illustrate Webster's favorite theme — the hollowness of the shows of life. This is all in keeping with Web.'s general meditative bent, his fondness for fables, etc.

[1] *Mal.*, II, 1; *W. D.*, I, 2; and for Bilioso, *Malc.* I, 1, 255 f; IV, 2, 107 f. There is no doubt that Castruccio and Camillo are formed on Bilioso. They all have young wives. And see below.

[2] *Mal.*, II, 1: cf. Fel. with Flavia, *A. & M.*, II, 1, esp. l. 251 f; III, 2; Mal. with women, *Malc.*, II, 2; V, 2, etc. — The brooding is in Malevole's vein. *V. supra.* — Somewhat the same situation, Bosola with the "gentlemen of the woodyard." *Mal.*, II, 2.

[3] Castruccio with Ferdinand, *Mal.*, I, 2, pp. 161-3. — Bilioso is kept almost out of his lord's presence on the boards; yet once (V, 3, end) he plays the part with him, and very often with others, as pp. 241, 288-9, 302-3, 308. The same trait is exploited abundantly in *A. & M.*, as in Forobosco.

[4] Prepasso is of this profession, but has no pronounced traits. — Bassiola in the *Gentleman Usher*, Argus in *Widow's Tears*, all of the type of Shak.'s Malvolio, Olivia's Steward.

[5] The references to *Mal.* in the above discussion sufficiently indicate this: Bosola's meditations; Castruccio as cuckold, sycophant, and ass; the madness in the torture-scene and Ferdinand's madness, more like Pandulfo's in *Ant. Rev.* than that in *W. D.*, which imitates Shak. (*v. infra*); the torture-scene, the properties of torture

To Tourneur, Webster is far less indebted ; like pupils of one master generally, they themselves have much less in common.   That he knew Tourneur's work is made probable by the echo in the *White Devil* from the *Atheist's Tragedy* already cited, [1] and by an unsavory joke in

---

(hand, counterfeits of bodies of husband and children, like Feliche's body), the omens and dread, Stoicism (III, 2, p. 216; V, 3, p. 272), and the religious element in the Duchess (III, 5) and in the torture-scenes.

[6] Two other points of contact, not so certain, which I relegate to fine print :

a. A peculiar sort of abrupt, prancing dialogue, which, by the way, appears often also in the baiting-scenes (see for them below, p. 141, note 2), is to be found in *W. D.*, 72 :

> *Lod.* Shalt thou and I join housekeeping ?
> *Flam.* Yes. Content:
> Let 's be unsociably sociable.
> *Lod.* Sit some three days together, and discourse ?
> *Flam.* Only with making faces ;
> Lie in our clothes.
> *Lod.* With faggots for our pillows.
> *Flam.* And be lousy,
> *Lod.* In taffeta linings, that 's genteel melancholy ;
> Sleep all day.
> *Flam.* Yes: etc. —

Cf. *Ant. Rev.*, II, 2, 193 f :

> *Strotzo.* I 'll weep.
> *Piero.* Ay, ay, fall on thy face and cry, "why suffer you
> So lewd a slave as Strotzo is to breathe ? "
> *Stro.* I 'll beg a strangling, grow importunate —
> *Piero.* As if thy life were loathsome to thee, etc.
> *Stro.* Applaud my agonies and penitence, etc., etc.

See the same trick in *Fawn*, II, 1, 470 f ; III 1, 57 f. Generally, the lively, abrupt, dialogue of the *W. D.* shows, I think, distinct traces of Marston's influence ; but that is too detailed a matter to deal with here.

b. The latter half of *W. D.*, p. 42 (" *He will shoot pills* " to " *scruples* "), one would almost take, in my opinion, for Marston's. The joke about the Irish is altogether in his vein (it occurs, indeed, several times, as in *Malc.*, III, 1, 261), as W.'s few filthy jokes generally are ; and the portion,

Let me embrace thee, toad, and love thee, O thou abominable, loathsome gargarism, that will fetch up lungs, lights, heart, and liver by scruples ;

with its insistence upon revolting physical things, unrelieved by a touch of the imagination, is also like Mars. This tone of flippant familiarity with scamps and scoundrels is common in M.'s malcontent. See *Malc.*, I, 1, 62 f : " And how does my little Ferrard? Ah, ye lecherous animal! my little ferret, he goes sucking," etc. ; *Malc.*, II, 3, 172, " Ah, you treacherous, damnable monster, how dost? how dost, thou treacherous rogue? Let 's be once drunk together, and so invite a most virtuously-strengthened friendship," etc. ; *Malc.*, III, 1, 250, " Art there, old true-penny? I see flattery in thine eyes and damnation in thy soul. Ha, ye huge rascal," etc. This trick Tour. copies exactly (and it is an illustration of his greater nearness to Mars.), *Rev. Tr.*, 356, " how dost, sweet musk-cat? "

[1] See p. 19, above. But see Addenda.

Malfi, possibly imitated from the *Revenger's Tragedy*.[1] But of influence unmistakably derived from it he shows almost none. It is rather historically, as to a link in the development of the type of the revenge-play, as we have seen it expounded through the ten years back from the *White Devil* to Marston's *Malcontent* and *Antonio's Revenge*, that Webster can be shown to bear much relation to him. The gap between the half-emancipated *White Devil*, on the one hand, and the absolute revenge tragedy *Antonio's Revenge* and the revenge tragi-comedy *The Malcontent*, on the other, Tourneur, so far as revenge-plays have descended to us, is the only one left to bridge [2]; and he does bridge it, as we have seen, by taking up the Malevole type, by breaking down the revenge motive through extreme handling of it in his one play and inveighing against it by means of revenge-play machinery in his other, by doing away with the old stereotyped revenge plot of Kyd, Chettle, and Marston, by introducing an erotic intrigue, and by developing further the melodramatic setting. But there may have been still other plays, now lost, that did much the same thing, and influenced Webster more directly. True, there are points that suggest Webster's direct imitation of Tourneur. The poisoning and torture scene, with the poisoning of the face; the taunting of the victim, the disclosure of the poisoner's own identity as an additional torment, and the endangering outcry of the victim [3]; Bosola's hiring out to his villain master and, with like comment, receiving gold from him [4]; the conflict suggested in Bosola between conscience and obedience to his master [5]; and the condensed, pointed, sombre style and imagery [6]; — all these may have been imitated from Tourneur, but possibly from others.

---

[1] *Rev. Tr.*, 409, and *Mal.*, I, 2, p. 171. It is only a chance. — The notion of binding a living to a dead body, found in both Mars. and Tour. (see p. 110, note), appears also in *Mal.*, IV, 1, p. 233. Drawn orig. (by Mars.) from the story of Mezentius, but very probably taken by T. and W. from Mars.

[2] Excepting always the *Malc.*, comedy though it be. See above, p. 110.

[3] *W. D.*, pp. 110, 116–19; *Rev. Tr.*, 393–7. But the elements are all to be found elsewhere. In the *Sec. Maid. Tr.* the manner of poisoning is as like that in *W. D.* The disclosure of the torturer's identity is common — to be found in some form or other in all cases, as in *Ant. Rev.* (V, 2, 62 f), *Sec. Maid. Tr.* (V, 2, pp. 464–5), as well as in the last act of *Rev. Tr.* (V, 3, p. 430), the second torture-scene. (Here again the outcry of the victim, *Rev. Tr.*, 429.) The *Sec. Maid. Tr.*, as we have seen (pp. 117–18), probably influenced the *W. D.* in yet other respects.

[4] *Mal.*, I, 2, p. 167, and *Rev. Tr.*, I, 3, p. 357. — But (see above, p. 110) Malevole does the same.

[5] *Rev. Tr.*, 374, 376; *Mal.*, I, 2, pp. 168–9, and IV, 1, end. There is no resemblance except in the slight attempt to smooth over the contradictions of character, — an attempt in both cases unplausible and hypocritical enough.

[6] There is an increase of the imagery of decay in Tour. over Mars.

To Chapman.

Still less does Webster owe Chapman; for Chapman, being off the main line of development, has far less than Tourneur of what *could* have influenced him. Undoubtedly his work was known to Webster, for Chapman, alone of revenge-play writers, is mentioned in the long list of contemporaries in the preface to the *White Devil* — not only mentioned but especially praised; and in the *Monumental Column*, of 1613,[1] he is mentioned again, and with reverence and tenderness. Yet, strange to say, though there is not a word about Marston and Tourneur, and only a passing mention of Shakspere, Dekker, and Heywood,[2] to all of whom Webster is manifestly indebted, to Chapman, whom he praised and loved, he is indebted least of all.[3]

Of borrowings in phrase or situation there is none at all probable[4] but one in *Alphonsus Emperor of Germany*, where the atrocious Duke of Saxon, on dashing out his grandchild's brains when Prince Edward refuses to acknowledge it as his offspring, cries,

> There, murderer! take his head and breathless limbs,
> There's flesh enough, bury it in thy bowels,
> Eat that, or die for hunger;   *Alph.*, IV, 3, p. 408.

somewhat as Virginius cries to Appius on slaying his own daughter,

> And if thy lust with this act be not fed,
> Bury her in thy bowels now she's dead.   *A. & V.*, IV, 1, p. 201.

Of influence, properly speaking, there are, probably, traces in the conjuring of the dumb-shows. In no other revenge plays than *Bussy's Revenge* and the *White Devil* does this appear; and in both these cases events occurring in one place are represented, by black-art, contemporaneously in another.[5] Further than this, nothing is certain.

---

[1] *Works*, vol. III, p. 264.

[2] See below on the indebtedness of Web. to Heywood's *Lucrece*. See also his verses to H., and the entries from Henslowe (Chap. I) which prove he had worked with him.

[3] So, too, with Jonson, to whom, with Chap., is given the place of honor in the pref. to *W. D.*, but whose influence I fail to find. See Prof. Wendell's assertion, p. 92, note. But Mr. Crawford (see above, pp. 89 ff) has found one unquestionable case of borrowing in the *Mon. Col., Notes and Queries*, x, vol. 2, pp. 381–2.

[4] Other faint possibilities are: *a*, the joke, certainly old, a "matchless eye" — "true, her eyes be not matches," *May Day*, 275, and *A. & V.*, 172; *b*, *Byron's Tr.*, p. 263 b, and *A. & V.*, 190, the notion of the soldier's fear of the lawyer's gown; *c*, *Byr. Tr.*, 245 b, and *Mal.*, 218, quilted anvil and politics; *d*, "that toad-pool that stands in thy complexion," *Bussy*, 161, and "the spring in his face is the engendering of toads," *Mal.*, 164 (the same general conception as in *Mer. of Ven.*, I, 1, 88–9).

[5] *Bussy*, IV, 1, pp. 166–7; *W.D.*, III, 1, pp. 47–8. Web.'s resembles this rather than conjuring-scenes such as *2 Hen. VI*, I, 4, in that this aims at revealing a contemporaneous action. The same device appears (forming a part, however, of the very essence

What in the function of the ghosts as omens is common to both Webster and Chapman is no more than the popular superstition of their appearance to the fey. Tales are common in Chapman and fables are to be found, but both are to be found in others [1] ; and of baiting there is no end, but it is not of Webster's variety. [2]

Of revenge-plays, none, then, influenced Webster's but Marston's, Tourneur's, and (as we have already seen) the *Second Maiden's Tragedy* [3] ; and Marston's influence, not only in his one revenge tragedy, *Antonio*, but also in his other work, is the predominant one. [4]

---

of the fable, not being, as here, a sheer dramaturgic device) in Greene's *Bacon and Bungay* (Dyce ed., 1861, p. 175), where Bacon lets two scholars see by means of his glass what their fathers are doing. But the fact that no other revenge-play has this element, together with Web.'s praise of Chap. in the pref. to this play, makes him the likelier source. Cf. above, p. 134, note, Marston's borrowing of this very thing from Chap. in *Sophon.*

[1] Of short illustrative tales, pp. 188, 189, 192, 193, 195, 197, 223, 247-8, 266, 376; and of fables : pp. 185, 189, 249. — Cf. Web.'s above, p. 123, note; And further, *Mon. Col.*, p. 260, *A. & V.*, 199, etc. The fable of the Belly and the Members is told in *Coriolanus*. It is likely, however, that Web. was influenced in this respect by Chap.

[2] The baiting-scenes (as I call them) are scenes in which a character is rated or taunted soundly. They are characteristic of the *W. D.*, — padding rarer in the more artistic *Mal.* Examples : Antonelli and Gasparo seem not unfriendly to Lodovico (I, 1), and yet their discussion of his life in his presence is couched in the terms of an onslaught; the baiting of Brachiano (II, 1) by Monticelso and Francisco, esp. pp. 31 and 32, and of Isabella, p. 36; the baiting of Vittoria by the Cardinal and Francisco in the trial-scene (III, 2), esp. pp. 58-9, where the two vie with each other in hitting : Flamineo and Lodovico (III, 2, pp. 73-4) : Brachiano and Flamineo (IV, 1, p. 82) ; Marcello and Flamineo (IV, 4, p. 105) : the torture-scenes above all (V, 1, pp. 117-18, and V, 2, pp. 138-41). In these, or in isolated speeches like them, they try to stab with mere words ; as, p. 66,

> *Brach.* Now you and I are friends, sir, we 'll shake hands
> In a friend's grave together.

— a hyena-like exultation over the murder of his wife, Francisco's sister; or, p. 96,

> Dost thou imagine, thou canst slide on blood,

or the taunts of the Cardinal, III, 2.

Chap.'s baiting is formal : *a*, A mutual set-to to see who can hit hardest, as pp. 161-2 (Monsieur and Bussy) ; *b*, A preconcerted abuse of one to try his "humor" of Senecan stoicism, pp. 182-3 (Monsieur and Clermont, see purpose avowed, foot of p. 181). And it inclines to long speeches, has not W.'s short, sharp phrases. On the whole, it seems quite as likely that W.'s baiting is derived from the taunts of Mars, ton's and Tourneur's torture-scenes.

[3] See above, p. 118, note. — For the influence of *Ham.* on Cornelia's madness, see below.

[4] The above discussions include all W.'s indebtedness to these authors, whether in the revenge-plays or not. The account of his relation to Shak., on the other hand, which follows, is limited to Web.'s revenge-plays. Further relations to him are pointed out in connection with *A. & V.* Even with these added, however, my investigation is incomplete : I have not read Shak. through with an eye to Web.

VI. THE INDEBTEDNESS OF WEBSTER IN HIS REVENGE PLAYS TO SHAKSPERE.

Of another revenge-play, *Hamlet*, we have seen the influence, in the earlier development of the type, only in Marston and Chettle; and that most certainly not the *Hamlet* of Shakspere, but of Kyd. Subsequently, there is nothing to prove the direct influence of either Kyd's or Shakspere's *Hamlet*, up to the *Atheist's Tragedy*, which is influenced evidently by the latter. The *Second Maiden's Tragedy*, on the other hand, seems related to *Hamlet* in neither form; and Webster, in his two plays, shows no sign of the direct influence of *Hamlet*, except in so far as in his study of Shakspere's representation of madness he imitates, as well as the madness of Lear and that of Lady Macbeth,[1] that of Ophelia. A rather surprising result!

MADNESS.

Of representations of madness in the *White Devil* and *Malfi* there are four: Cornelia's and Brachiano's madness in the one, and Ferdinand's madness and the Bedlam-let-loose of the torture-scene in the other. The last named is one of those purely episodic mad-scenes such as often appeared on the Elizabethan stage (as in the *Honest Whore* and *Northward Ho*[2]), which, bringing forward as mad, characters which had not previously appeared, lacked all psychological and dramatic interest, and were interesting, even to Elizabethans, only for the extravagant grotesque of their utterance and demeanor. The first three, on the other hand, like Shakspere's and those of the best Elizabethans,[3] depict the madness of characters already well known to us, and hark back to their former disposition, vocation, or experience, in a truly pathetic and terrible manner. In each of these representations reminiscences of Shakspere are manifest. Cornelia[4]

---

[1] The sleep-walking may be classed as madness.

[2] This may be a vestige of the Dekker period: one of the few possible ones.

[3] Such as, in some measure, Hieronimo's in Jonson's Additions.

[4] They are the following, (b) and (e) being already noted in Dyce:

   a. O you abuse me, you abuse me, you abuse me!   *W. D.*, p. 108.

That is, in the sense of *deceive*, as in Lear:

   Do not abuse me.   *Lear*, IV, 7, 77.

   I am mightily abused.   IV, 7, 53.

   b. Of the dead Marcello before her, just as Lear of Cordelia:

Give me him as he is; if *he be turned to earth*, let me but give him one hearty kiss, and you shall put us both into one coffin. *Fetch a looking-glass:* see if his *breath will not stain it;* or pull out some *feathers* from my pillow, and lay them to his lips.
                                                    W. D., pp. 108–9.

142

uses phrases belonging unmistakably to Lear, to Ophelia, and, in one case (perhaps), to Lady Macbeth; Brachiano and Ferdinand[1] use

------

> I know when one is dead and when one lives :
> *She 's dead as earth.   Lend me a looking-glass ;*
> If that *her breath will mist or stain the stone,*
> Why, then she lives.
> This *feather* stirs ; she lives !   *Lear*, V, 3, 260-5.

c. When I am dead and rotten.   *W. D.*, 126.
    he 's dead and rotten.   *Lear*, V, 3, 285.

d. Cowslip-water is good for the memory :
    Pray, buy me three ounces of 't.   *W. D.*, 127.

Give me an ounce of civet, good apothecary, to sweeten my imagination.
                                                       Lear, IV, 6, 132.

In all these cases the words are Lear's own when *mad*.   The similarity of situation is what makes the echoes so unmistakable.

e. From Ophelia's mad talk :

> There 's rosemary for you, and rue for you, [*To Flamineo*]
> Heart's-ease for you ; I pray make much of it,
> I have left more for myself.   *W. D.*, p. 126.

There 's rosemary, that's for remembrance. . . .   There 's fennel for you, and columbines : there 's rue for you ; and here 's some for me : we may call it herb-grace o' Sundays : O, you must wear your rue with a difference.   *Ham.*, IV, 5, 175 f.

In which the play on "rue" as addressed by the mad woman to the guilty man present, is in both cases identical.

f. And at exit :

Bless you all, good people.   *W. D.*, p. 128.

And of all Christian souls, I pray God.   God be wi' ye.   *Ham.*, IV, 5, 200.

g.   here 's a white hand :
    Can blood so soon be wash'd out?   *W. D.*, 127.

Possibly suggested by the words and conduct of Lady Macbeth.

Aside from this, there are the following passages (all noted by Dyce) probably from Shak., though (a) at least is proverbial :

a. Forward lap-wing !
    He flies with the shell on's head.   *W. D.*, p. 34, and *Ham.*, V, 2, 193.

b. Whose death God pardon !
    Whose death God revenge.   *W. D.*, 85, and *Rich. III*, I, 3, 136-7.

c. Yet stay, heaven-gates are not so highly arched
    As princes' palaces : etc.   *Mal.*, 245, and *Cymb.*, III, 3, 2 f.

d.   physicians thus
    With their hands full of money, use to give o'er
    Their patients.   *Mal.*, 224, and *Tim. of Ath.*, III, 3, 11.

[1] Here Web. does not so much borrow Shak.'s phrases as imitate the method of characterization and reproduce ideas.   Yet there is the same "abuse" again :

phrases and notions of Lear's; there is definite evidence, in short, that Webster copied the very situations, phrases, and turns of Shakspere's mad-scenes. But he emulates them, as well. Sometimes, indeed, as in the startling suddenness[1] of Cornelia's outburst into lunacy, he follows (quite in keeping with his own melodramatic neglect of motivation) a more primitive style,—that of Hieronimo in the enlarged *Spanish Tragedy* and of Pandulfo[2] in *Antonio's Revenge*. But the madness of Ferdinand he developed more gradually[3]; and, with a sense of psychological fitness, he makes him, the man of fierce and fiery passions,—not the crafty Cardinal—go mad. And he makes him, Brachiano, and even Cornelia, run upon long-past experiences connected with their main vocations,—money-raising, hunting, the cares of government,[4] the turmoil of battle,[5] on the one hand, or household affairs, on the other[6];—makes the passion or crime at the root of their madness show itself—

> that perilous stuff
> Which weighs upon the heart

---

    a. Away, you have abus'd me.   *W. D.*, 114.
    b. Use me well, you were best.   *Mal.*, 257.

Said as they lay hold of him, just as Lear, in the same situation, says:

                    Use me well:
    You shall have ransom.   *Lear*, IV, 6, 195.

    c. Ferd.'s objection to his doctor's personal appearance, like Lear's:

    Let me have his beard sawed off, and his eyebrows filed more civil.
                                      Mal., 258.

You, sir, I entertain for one of my hundred; only I do not like the fashion of your garments: you will say they are Persian attire; but let them be changed.
                                       Lear, III, 6, 83.

    d. I am studying the art of patience.   *Mal.*, 257.

    No, I will be the pattern of all patience.   *Lear*, III, 2, 37.

    Thou must be patient.   *Lear*, IV, 6, 182.

    We must be patient: but I cannot choose but weep, etc.
                            Ham., IV, 5, 69 (Ophelia).

    e. And Brachiano harps upon coining, the oppression of the poor, and Ferdinand upon battle, flattery, and lechery, much as Lear does.

[1] See *W. D.*, 108. — As also in her notions that her son is not dead.

[2] *V. supra*, p. 99, note.

[3] As IV, 2. After seeing the duchess's face,—after the whirling words "Cover her face," etc.,—"the wolf shall find her grave and scrape it up"; which precede the final, already distracted, words, "I'll go hunt the badger by owl-light" (p. 250), and the full madness of Act V, sc. 2.

[4] Brachiano, *W. D.*, 115.

[5] Ferd., *Mal.*, 279. These all—hunting and hawking, battle and army life, cares of government and justice,—appear over and over again in Lear's ravings.

[6] *W. D.*, 126—This sheet I have kept this twenty year, etc.

with which Macbeth and his Lady were acquainted,—as in Brachiano's ravings on his acomplice Flamineo and the devil,[1] and in Ferdinand's refusal to confess[2] ; and makes them ponder philosophical and general satirical themes, such as the hollow shows of life they had been used to — hypocrisy, flattery, and what is called justice.[3] All this is characteristic of Lear, some of it of Lady Macbeth, and of the mad folk of no other Elizabethan dramatist whose work remains to us.[4]

VII. DOUBTFUL INFLUENCES, POSSIBLY SHAKSPEREAN.
BOYHOOD.

Another point at which Webster may be indebted to Shakspere is the portrayal of the boy. Shakspere learned the art from Marlowe,[5] and amplified it ; Webster, in his Giovanni, follows in Shakspere's steps.

---

[1] *W. D.*, 115–16.

[2] *Mal.*, 257.—Just as the murder breaks out in Lady Macbeth's speeches, and the grief and repentance of Lear at his folly, in his.

[3] Brachiano's ravings about Flamineo, money-bags and the gaping lawyer, and Vittoria's powdering, pp. 115–16; and Ferdinand's upon "flattery and lechery," p. 259, are like Lear's upon the hypocrisy and hidden lechery of judge, beadle, and virtuous-seeming lady, and upon flattery and injustice. And L. remembers his fault, as they their crimes.

[4] Other points of Shak.'s influence are marked by Mr. Sampson (pp. xviii–xxi), none of which —except the two from *Mac.* (*Mal.*, 190–1, 211), which, I suppose, occur to everybody, though without the best of reasons, — seems to me probable. Bosola's echoing of Mercutio (instead of Malevole, *v. sup.* p. 137), Julia's of Brutus' Portia (instead of Sidney's Philoclea, *v.* p. 90, note 1), Antonio's of Ant. in *Mer. Ven.*, etc., would deserve a moment's consideration, only on the supposition that Shak. was the great, overshadowing influence of the day. *W. D.*, p. 98, however, contains a likely allusion to Othello.

[5] That the Prince Edward in Marlowe's *Ed. II* served Shak. as model for the Prince Edward in *3 Hen. VI* (*i. e.*, in revising Marlowe's play of the *True Tragedie*) and for the Prince Edward in *Rich. III* (both plays being elsewhere charged with Marlowe's spirit), is beyond doubt. The dates permit of it, for the *True Tragedie*, original of *3 Hen. VI*, which contains the Rutland speeches all but one line, and the Prince Edward part substantially the same, appeared in 1595, and *Rich. III* in 1597, while *Ed. II* was reg. July 6, 1593. The Prince Edward of *Ed. II* has the same fond affection and reverence for father, mother, and uncle, uttered (as also in these plays) in a far sturdier, less pathetic manner than that in *Tit. And.* and *K. John*. See IV, 2, 21 f; V, 4. He has the same precocity and incisiveness of judgment and advice as Prince Edward in *3 Hen. VI* (see IV, 2, 4–8 and 68 ; 5, 41; and *3 Hen. VI*, II, 2, 78 f, 131 f : III, 3, 78; 169, etc.); the same boldness and vows for the future, as IV, 2, 21–5. And though a little stouter in his pleading with Mortimer and the Queen for Kent's life, he is not unlike Rutland in *3 Hen. VI*, and Arthur in *King John*, pleading for their own.

Whether Shak. was influenced also by other, popular traditions, as represented by the sources of *K. J.* and *Rich. III* — the *Troublesome Raigne*, Pts. I and II, and *Trag. Rich. III: Wherein is showne the death of Edward the fourth, with the smothering of the two yoong Princes*, etc. ; or whether these too were drawn from Mar., I cannot say. Certain it is that though they present children in just the same situa-

Both poets take the man's point of view, not at all the child's. The boy's ambitions, his eagerness to carry a pike and whip the French, they portray admirably, because here the boy most approaches the man. And they fail with the boy's pathos and wit only because they, as men, stand aloof: remembering roughly that a boy is "cute" and tender, they make his wit pert and sophisticated, and his sentiment and pathos drooping and effeminate. No more striking contrast and inconsistency could be imagined than that between the burly assertiveness of Young Lucius and Giovanni when talking of fighting and revenge, and their self-conscious languor when uttering their affections or their longing for death. Here, they are boys through and through; there, weak-eyed girls.

All this appears, as we consider Webster's adoption of the Marlowe-Shaksperean convention piece by piece:

1. Intrepidity, eagerness to fight the French or to revenge his own or his family's wrongs; the vows prefaced generally by an *if I live*, which, in the bloody early plays, is ironic: see *White Devil*, pp. 34 and 35, especially,

> If I live
>
> I 'll charge the French foe in the very front
> Of all my troops, the foremost man.

> I say, my lord, that if I were a man,
> Their mother's bed-chamber should not be safe
> For these bad bondmen to the yoke of Rome.   *Tit. And.*, IV, 1, 107 f.

> Ay, uncle, so will I, an if I live.   *Ib.*, IV, 1, 112.

> Ay, with my dagger in their bosoms, grandsire.   *Ib.*, IV, 1, 118.

> An if I live until I be a man,
> I 'll win our ancient right in France again,
> Or die a soldier, as I lived a king.   *Rich. III*, III, 1, 91.

Compare also the intrepidity of Macduff's son, *Macbeth*, IV, 2, and of Prince Edward in *3 Henry VI*, passim; the more childish stoutness of Young Marcius,

> 'A shall not tread on me:
> I 'll run away till I am bigger, but then I 'll fight.   *Cor.*, V, 3, 127-8.

---

tions as Shak., they have left few traces — whether originally Marlowe's or not — on his characterization. Yet these few, wooden as they are, are objective, unmistakable. *Troub. Raigne:* Shak. Libr., Pt. II, Vol. I, p. 238, Arthur's pride in Eng. character; p. 249, wishes his Grandam would pull forth his heart (see below, p. 147) if that would 'appease the broyles'; p. 259, "For I am king of Eng., though thou weare the diadem." *Trag. of Rich. III*, Shak. Libr., Pt. II, Vol. 1, p. 70, "Farewell good unckle, ah gods, if *I do live* my father's yeares as God forbid but I may, I will so roote out this malice," etc. — However we explain it, these all, and a touch of Prince Henry's impulsive revengefulness not reproduced by Shak. in *K. John* (*Troub. Raigne*, pp. 317-18, "Sweet Uncle . . . let not a stone of Swinsted Abbey stand") are very like Marlowe in *Ed. II* and *True Tragedie*.

and of Mamilius in *Winter's Tale*, I, 2, 162; and the revengefulness of Clarence's children, *Richard III*, II, 2, 11–16.

2.   The interest of the boy in weapons and his begging for them : — a horse and armor of his uncle, *White Devil*, 29; a pike, *White Devil*, 34.   Compare York's begging dagger and sword of his uncle, *Richard III*, III, 1, 109 f.

3.   The boy's love for his mother, uncle (with whom he most often appears), and others who have charge of him, uttered, like his wish for death (see below), in a thin and plaintive pathos, and often with a self-conscious account of his feelings :

> *Giov.*   My sweet mother
> Is —
> *Fran.*   How? where?
> *Giov.*   Is there; no, yonder : indeed, sir, I 'll not tell you,
> For I shall make you weep.
> *Fran.*   Is dead?
> *Giov.*   Do not blame me now,
> I did not tell you so.
> . . . .
> *Giov.*   What do the dead do, uncle? do they eat,
> Hear music, go a hunting, and be merry,
> As we that live?
> *Fran.*   No, coz; they sleep.
> *Giov.*   Lord, lord that I were dead !
> I have not slept these six nights. When do they wake ?
> *Fran.*   When God shall please.
> *Giov.*   Good God, let her sleep ever !
> For I have known her wake an hundred nights,
> When all the pillow where she laid her head
> Was brine-wet with her tears. I am to complain to you, sir;
> I 'll tell you how they have used her now she 's dead :
> They wrapp'd her in a cruel fold of lead,
> And would not let me kiss her.   *W. D.*, 67–8.
>
> O this will make my mother die with grief.   *King John*, III, 3, 5.
>
> Although, my lord, I know my noble aunt
> Loves me as dear as e'er my mother did,
> And would not, but in fury, fright my youth.   *Tit. And.*, IV, 1, 22.
>
> O grandsire, grandsire ! even with all my heart
> Would I were dead, so you did live again !
> O Lord, I can not speak to him for weeping ;
> My tears will choke me, if I ope my mouth.   *Ib.*, V, 3, 172 f.

Compare also Arthur's love for Hubert, *King John*, IV, 1, and Lucius's for his father and aunt.

4.   The boy's wish for death :

> Lord, lord that I were dead !
> I have not slept these six nights.   *W. D.*, p. 68.
>
> O grandsire, grandsire ! even with all my heart
> Would I were dead, so you did live again !   *Tit. And.*, V, 3, 172 f.

> Good my mother, peace!
> I would that I were low laid in my grave:
> I am not worth this coil that 's made for me.   *King John*, II, 1, 163 f.

5. Wit — jest and repartee — so knowing as almost to give the effect of cynicism:

> *Fran.* Ha! Without their ransom!
> How then will you reward your soldiers,
> That took those prisoners for you?
> *Giov.* I 'll marry them to all the wealthy widows
> That fall that year.
> *Fran.* Why then, the next year following,
> You 'll have no men to go with you to war.
> *Giov.* Why then, I 'll press the women to the war,
> And then the men will follow.   *W. D.*, p. 35.

> *Son.* Who must hang them?
> *L. Mac.* Why, the honest men.
> *Son.* Then the liars and swearers are fools, for there are liars and swearers enow to beat the honest men and hang up them.
> *L. Mac.* . . . But how wilt thou do for a father?
> *Son.* If he were dead, you 'ld weep for him: if you would not, it were a good sign that I should quickly have a new father.   *Mac.*, IV, 2, 52 f.

Compare York in *Rich. III*, II, 4, 26 f, and III, 1, 107 f.

6. A common device is the use of *I have heard* or *I have read* to make plausible some opinion or piece of information beyond the child's years. See *W. D.*, pp. 34, 68; *Tit. And.*, IV, 1, 18, 20.

Webster's treatment of boyhood, then, is along the conventional lines of Shakspere, with the old contrast between stout ambition and revengefulness, and weak-kneed pathos and sentiment. But greater. In none of Shakspere's children is the pathos so long drawn-out and brooding, so self-conscious and indirect, as that of Giovanni's prattling about his mother and death. He points mutely to the earth, checks himself and points to heaven, to answer the question where his mother is; and thinks he must do so, and say not a word, lest his uncle weep. And when asked whether he loved her, he makes such an answer as this:

> I have often heard her say she gave me suck,
> And it should seem by that she dearly lov'd me,
> Since princes seldom do it.

With this self-consciousness there is of course much beauty in single passages, as in

> I 'll tell you how they have us'd her now she 's dead:
> They wrapped her in a cruel fold of lead,
> And would not let me kiss her.

but, as a whole, the part is unnatural, more self-conscious than innocent, — a beautiful, sickly out-growth from the self-conscious innocence of Arthur and Lucius.

148

To whom is this later development due? Either to Webster, or to Fletcher in *Bonduca*. Hengo, like Giovanni, only continues the Shaksperean tradition of pluck, of hatred of his country's enemies,[1] of desire for revenge of his father's wrongs,[2] and of valiant vows for the future.[3] And in matters of sentiment, like Giovanni again, he exceeds it. He weeps copiously,[4] wishes himself dead,[5] and has a very un-childlike premonition of death's approach[6]; he dwells on his brother's death as Giovanni on his mother's,[7] and asks his uncle like pathetic questions about heaven, its inhabitants, and its occupations[8]; and he expresses an affection for his uncle much more plaintive and profuse than that of Giovanni himself.[9] In short, for all his brave deeds and promises, Hengo is a quavering milk-sop, and, though a little more stagey, strikingly like Webster's boy.

Now the probabilities are all for Fletcher. He and Beaumont are pioneers in so many forms of sentimentality (even at this period, as we shall see, Webster is their follower[10]), and this sentiment and pathos are so like that of their 'pretty, sad talking'[11] boys, or girl-pages, Euphrasia[12] and Veramour,[13] that the case seems theirs on the spot. But the date forbids a judgment. Of it we know no more than the broad conclusion of Messrs. Fleay and Thorndike: *Bonduca* may be as early as 1611 or as late as 1616."[14] If the earlier limit be the date, then, unhesitatingly, we may have Webster influenced by Fletcher. If not, we can do no more than conclude that Webster felt the atmosphere of that day of which Fletcher was the main exponent — the main factor, — an atmosphere of sentimentality and decadence.

By the influence of Fletcher the supposition of Shakspere's influ-ence would be made unnecessary. Even without Fletcher it is unnec-essary: there may have been many plays, now lost, that cultivated the same Marlowe-Shakspercan tradition. But there *are* no such plays;

---

[1] *Bon.*, 49 a, 62 b.
[2] *Ib.*, 71 b.
[3] *Ib.*, 49 a, 62 b.
[4] *Ib.*, 68 a.
[5] *Ib.*, 67 b and 62 b.
[6] *Ib.*, 71 b.
[7] *Ib.*, 62 b.
[8] *Bon.*, 62 b, 72 a.
[9] It appears in the irritating harping in falsetto on " uncle," " uncle " (pp. 62, 71, 72) ; in questions whether he shall see his uncle in heaven, etc.
[10] See below, p. 151.
[11] See *Philaster*, p. 34, for the phrase.
[12] *I. e.*, disguised as the boy Bellario, in *Phil.* (dated c. 1608, Thorn.), who has a similar self-consciously innocent manner and affection for his master ; wishes for death (pp. 40, 43), considers, like Hengo, his life but a piece of childhood thrown away (*Phil.*, 45 a ; *Bon.*, 72 a). See, too, the elaborate, sentimental description of B. by his master, p. 31.
[13] In *Hon. Man. Fort.* (" plaide in the yeare 1613," Dyce Ms. copy), Veramour's devotion toward Montague, his master, has something of the same piping tone (pp. 489–90), and he ' thinks in conscience he shall die for him.'
[14] Thorndike, *Inf. of B. & F.*, p. 91.

149

Heywood's (to cite one of the few who treat children at all) follow another fashion.[1] And to Shakspere, as we have seen, Webster at this time was looking as to a model. If he turned to him as the master-hand at madness, he might well turn to him as the master-hand at childhood. In default of Fletcher's, then, we may conclude Shakspere's influence to be probable.

THE LYRICAL, SPECTACULAR AND SYMBOLICAL.

Due possibly in some measure to Shakspere, but more probably to the atmosphere of the day, are some tendencies working in Webster in conjunction — tendencies lyrical, spectacular, and symbolical. The lyrical and the spectacular had reached Webster, indeed, through the *Second Maiden's Tragedy* (a play which he must have known), but with results little similar. In the *Second Maiden's Tragedy* there are two songs of regret, the elaborate spectacle of the Lady's rising from the tomb, and the ceremony, at the end, of the crowning of her body in the presence of her ghost. In the *White Devil* there are the spectacles of the two ghosts, and a dirge; and in *Malfi*, the ceremony of the Cardinal's investiture accompanied with song and music, the song and dance of the madmen, and a dirge. But there is no more to be made of it.

There is a little more likeness, on the other hand, to Shakspere's romances. They show all of these tendencies, under the influence of the masque elements in the romances of Beaumont and Fletcher,[2] perhaps, or merely of the masque itself. So far, indeed, as Webster shows anything of the masque, as in the anti-masque[3] of madmen in

---

[1] Hey. has two boys, one in the *Late Lancashire Witches* (date *1634*), *Works*, IV, p. 196f, who is nowise similar; and in *2 Ed. IV* (pub. 1600, reg. Aug. 28, 1599), Princes Ed. and Rich., who appear in vol. I, pp. 147–9, 153–5. The sc. before the Tower is in evident imitation of the one in *Rich. III*, but the characterization is unlike. — Jonson and Dekker have no children; B. & F. none not mentioned here except Ascanio, in *Sp. Cur.*, who is rather to be classed as a sentimental youth; and Mass. has only 'pert pages.'

[2] Cf. Thorn., *Inf. of B. & F.*, pp. 130–2.

[3] *Mal.*, IV, 2. — The antimasque, the comic, grotesque foil to the stately masque, presented the lower classes — country-men, milk-maids, savages, or the like, or monsters such as satyrs and monkeys; antics, grimaces, and wild leaps instead of graceful dances; and a dialogue lively and full of jests, instead of high and poetical. All this fits the masque of madmen in Web. Introduced to furnish "some sport," it contains a song, an outlandish dialogue, and a dance to music at the end. As here, song and prose together are found in the antimasques of Jonson's masques, *Christmas*, *News from the New World*, and the *Irish Masque*. — Soergel, in his *Engl. Maskenspiele* (Halle, 1882), fails to mention this in *Malfi*, at pp. 86–92, where he considers the occurrence of masques in the dramatists, incl. Web. — The antimasque is represented, as Thorn. points out in *Inf. of B. & F.*, in *Triumph of Time* by a troop of Indians, in *Wint. Tale*, IV, 4, by the dance of satyrs, in *Tempest*, III, 3, by strange shapes, etc.

Malfi, he is as near to Beaumont and Fletcher[1] as to Shakspere; but (except in the matter of spectacles with music) not otherwise. He has nothing of the masque proper—its stately, decorous dances, its mythological, allegorical, or courtly personages, introduced for a show;—and he has dirges, solemn symbolism, splendid pageants with music, somewhat like Shakspere's.

Merely to show a general likeness, I repeat, not any indebtedness, let us consider these points for a moment. There were dirges in the old Kydian plays, as in the *Spanish Tragedy* and *Antonio's Revenge*, but in Latin (one of them), and 'said, not sung.' Since these, there are none till Webster; and his

> Call the robin red-breast and the wren

and (in less measure)

> Hark, now everything is still

are no longer in any sense hoarse and Senecan, but things of clear imagination and lyric sweetness, more like the dirges in *Cymbeline* and the *Tempest*[2] than anything else, and shedding, like them, a pensive atmosphere through the play. Again, the ghost in the Kydian plays was, as we have seen, a hard, material thing. But Brachiano's silent ghost, bearing a lily-pot and skull in one hand and casting dirt on Flamineo with the other, is attenuated and subdued into a symbol, an allegory of death; and in this character it approaches the allegorical *Vision* of Queen Katharine. So, too, in *Malfi*, with the "noble ceremony" the pilgrims at Ancona linger to behold, where, in dumb-show, the Cardinal lays aside his vestments, girds himself for war, and banishes his sister, to the ditty of the churchmen. It is such a combination of song and elaborate spectacle as is not to be found in any previous revenge-play, but to be paralleled in the *Two Noble Kinsmen* and *Henry VIII.*[3] Here, then, as often in the course of our investigation, Webster, though not in the forefront of fashion, does not scorn to follow in its wake.

---

[1] There is no evidence that Web. drew any of his masque elements from B. & F. The question whether in this Period he was otherwise influenced by them depends on the settlement of the matter (broached above, p. 118, note) of the dates of *Hon. Man. Fort.*, *Sec. Maid. Tr.*, and *W. D.* I myself am of the opinion, moreover, that the construction of *Malfi* shows B. & F. influence: *a*, first two scenes of *Malfi* (*one* sc. in Vaughan's text) infl. by the first sc. of the immensely popular *Phil.*, where Antonio and Delio describe and discuss the characters as they come on the stage and while they act upon it, as do Dion and his friends; *b*, the rather complicated and quickly-moving last scenes seem to show the influence of B. & F. Contrast *W. D.*

[2] Cf., too, the song 'Come away, come away, death,' *T. N.*, II, 4.

[3] See the elaborate ceremonies and pageants prescribed by the stage-directions in *Hen. VIII;* and the combination of song, music, and spectacle in *T. N. K.*, I, 1, and I, 5.

151

VIII. THE PERIOD AS A WHOLE.

When we hear Webster's name, it is the *White Devil* and *Malfi* that we think of; and not without reason. In his first period — in *Wyatt* and the citizen comedies — Webster is, if anything, a sheer mimic of Dekker. In his last period he is no very stalwart student and imitator of Fletcher and Massinger. Only in his middle period does he rise above his models and his mediocrity, and get on his feet and use his own voice. It is but natural, then, that with the world at large these two gloomy, terrible tragedies should stand for the man.

But when we go farther, and conceive of Webster as if the author only of these, as the 'terrible Webster' of Dyce, as the clerk of St. Andrews, Holborn, of Mr. Gosse, 'talking like Bosola among his contemporaries, and mystifying them,' as the haunter of churchyards and charnel houses of a score of essayists and belletristic triflers, we go sadly astray. We have to remember that this cannot be if the *Cure for a Cuckold* and *Appius and Virginia* are yet to follow. Above all have we to remember that at almost every point in the art of his two great tragedies Webster is dominated by the art and thought of his day. The revenge tragedy in its essential make-up — motives, dramatic and scenic machinery, types of character, prevailing tone of gloom and horror — comes to him, as we have seen, straight from Marston, Tourneur, and the *Second Maiden's Tragedy.* And even many of those finer elements, which seem to be Webster's original contribution, his more human and poetic treatment of revenge, madness, and villains, and, as must some day be shown, his skepticism, his turn for paradox, and the quality of his melancholy and of his imagery, are by no means his unique possession. There is hardly a spot in these plays where we can lay our finger, and say, with assurance, This is Webster.

Yet he is here. An intangible element — Webster's subtle and powerful spirit in the background — distinguishes this Period from either of the others as creative and original. The work bears a likeness to this and to that; but it is a new product, and often a finer one. It carries his own stamp; it is not stereotyped like his later work, nor counterfeit like the earlier. The material (and even the fashions in which it is moulded) might be borrowed: but the fire of the imagination which fused the harsh and stubborn stuff of the traditional revenge-play and transmuted it to poetry, could not be. Whatever Webster's indebtedness in this Period (and it is great, we have seen), far greater and richer was his benefaction — that sternness of morals, that breadth and sadness of intellectual candor, and all the various humanity there is in true poetry, in sublimity, pathos, irony, sombre beauty of image and phrase.

152

CHAPTER IV·

THE FLETCHERIAN AND ECLECTIC PERIOD.

The remaining dramas are not to be classified so neatly and precisely as the preceding. They show distinct traces of four or more influences — at least those of Fletcher and Massinger, of Marlowe, of Shakspere, and of Heywood, — and each of them two or more of the four. We therefore gather all these plays into one chapter, — discuss first their sources, then the influences in order, then the characteristics of this Period as a whole in the light of the preceding Period.

I. THE SOURCES.
THE DEVIL'S LAW-CASE.

The source of that part of the fable which deals with Romelio's beneficent revenge is undoubtedly to be found in Goulart's *Histoires Admirables*, Genève, tome i, p. 251, whether of the edition of 1610 or 1620.[1]

Un certain Italien ayant eu querelle contre quelque autre, tomba malade si griefuement, qu'on n'y attendoit plus de vie. Son ennemi sachant cela vient au logis : s'enquiert du seruiteur & lui demande, ou est ton maistre ? Le seruiteur respond, il est aux traits de la mort, & ne passera pas ce jour. L'autre grondant à basse voix, replique, il mourra par mes mains. Quoy dit, il entre en la chambre du malade, lui donne quelque coups de poignard, et se sauue. On adoube les playes de ce pauvre malade, qui par le moyen d'une si extraordinaire saignée reuint en convalescence. Ainsi recouura-il santé et vie par les mains de celui qui ne demandoit que sa mort. — *R. Solenander au 5 liur de ses conseils quinziesme cons. neufiesme sect.*

The physician, Reinerus Solenander,[2] whom Goulart here cites, he does no more than freely translate. Valerius Maximus,[3] as Langbaine

---

[1] Langbaine, ed. 1691 : " An accident like that of Romelio's stabbing Contarino . . . is (if I mistake not) in Skenkius his observations : At least I am sure, the like happened to Pheræus Jason, as you may see in V. Maximus, lib. I, cap. 8. The like story is related in Goulart's *Histoires Admirables*, I, p. 178." — The paging in Goulart seems to be uniform in all editions, and consequently editors and critics have hitherto tried hard to make the story on p. 178 (which will never do) fit. Dyce thought Lang. hardly worth quoting ; Haz. searched Goulart for another in vain. The 1702 ed. of Lang. reads *p. 27*, which does no better. — In Skenkius's (*i. e.*, Schenkius) *Observ. Medicae*, the three oldest editions in the Brit. Mus., I have not been able to find it.

[2] *Consil. Med.*, Hanov., 1609, sect. v, cons. 15, cap. ix.

[3] Ed. Kempf., Lips., 1888, lib. i, cap. viii, extr. 6.

points out, tells the same story, though in a simpler form. But Webster's source was Goulart. For that he was acquainted with the Genevese theologian's collection so far back as in the day of *Malfi* is proved by the passage on the loup-garou,[1] cited by Dyce. It is unlikely, moreover, that a story to be found in one of the great collections of *novelle* in a vulgar tongue, should reach an Elizabethan play-wright through the Latin, from an obscure writer on medicine or the old Roman epitomist.[2]

Another part of the fable — the *devil's law-case* — is a problem not so easy to solve. A similar story appears in Dekker, Houghton, and Day's *Lust's Dominion*,[3] in the *Spanish Curate*,[4] and in the *Fair Maid of an Inn*.[5] The first, because both of the likeness of its story and of the convenience of its date, must be taken to be the source.

In *Lust's Dominion* there are these points of contact. A widow revenges upon her son injuries done the man she loves by spreading abroad a report that he, though her own son, is a bastard. By this she hopes to injure his fame and deprive him of his inheritance. On the pretense of scruples of conscience she goes into a public assembly to avow it,[6] giving all the particulars of proof in the most shameless way, and naming the father. All this is pure invention, and is denied by the father named.[7]

---

[1] *Mal.*, V. 2. Dyce's note in Vaughan's *Mal.*, p. 152. It is indubitable:

> And he howled fearfully:
> Said he was a wolf, only the difference
> Was, a wolf's skin was hairy on the outside,
> His on the inside.

> Il asseura fermement qu'il estoit loup et qui'il n'y auoit autre difference si non que les loups ordinairement estoyent velus dehors et lui l'estoit entre cuir et chair.

Prof. Sampson has found (at the Brit. Mus., doubtless) an Eng. Goulart, by E. Grimeston, Lon., 1607, which may have served Web. here, as well as above for the source of the *D. L. C.*

[2] Mr. Ward (III, 61) calls attention to a similar story in Fletcher's *Wife for a Month* (lic. May 27, 1624). Poison, said to be furnished by a Jew physician, works a cure (IV, 1, and V, 1). But the story, quite apart from matters of date, could not have been Web.'s source.

[3] Pub. 1657, but see below, p. 156.   [4] Lic. 1622; see below.

[5] Lic. 1626, Jan. 22. Both it and *Sp. Cur.* were first published in the 1647 folio of B. & F. — Mr. Swinburne, in an essay on Web. in *Nineteenth Cent.*, June, 1886, p. 864, observes that the plot of *D. L. C.* is derived from the *F. M. I.* He surely means only the *devil's law-case* proper; — further than this there is nothing except the proper name, Prospero (the only other instance of it I know out of the *Tempest*); and we show below, p. 155, that even that cannot be.

[6] *L. D.*, IV, 4, and IV, 5.

[7] *L. D.*, V, 1. — She avows it in public repeatedly.

In the *Spanish Curate* the situation itself is not so like, but there is an actual court-scene. Lord Henrique, in order to keep his estate from his younger brother, Jamie, resolves to acknowledge an heir, who, as he himself admits, will shame him, — a son by a woman with whom he had lived long since, but whom he had deserted for his present wife. So far, there is no close likeness. But there is, as in Webster, a trial to which the victim is summoned in ignorance of the question at issue ; in which the scheme of Henrique, kept like Leonora's from the audience till now, is unfolded, and the client justified, on the score of conscience, by the greedy, pettifogging, pompous lawyer in his harangue. Yet, as the plaintiff is a brother instead of mother, and avows what is true instead of what is false, and has no motive of thwarted love inciting him to revenge, there is nothing notable here for Webster to borrow except the combination of shameless intrigue with a law-suit.

The *Fair Maid of the Inn* has, so far as outward details are concerned, a more similar story. A mother has her son summoned, in all ignorance of the cause, to trial, in order to prove (to her shame, as she admits) his birth mistaken, and so disinherit him. But her motive is to save her son's life, not to revenge herself on him ; her shame is for deceiving her husband, not for any infidelity to him ; and in the trial there is no lawyer.

The presumption is strong that at this time, when not only Webster but the whole Jacobean stage was imitating Fletcher's manner and technique, Webster should borrow also of the substance of his fables. But the *Spanish Curate* was licensed by Herbert only on October 24th, 1622. This leaves just one year for the slow writer, Webster, to write his play and get it acted and printed ; it makes his allusion to the peppering in the East Indies pretty much belated and pointless [1] ; and seems to run counter to what we learn of Queen's Companies in these years.[2] The thing is not impossible, but very improbable. And the claims of the *Fair Maid of the Inn*, as we have seen, are absolutely to be ruled out by reason of the explicit reference to Amboyna, impossible in 1623.[3]

Possibly, I say, the *Spanish Curate* may have influenced Webster in the more general matter of shameless intrigue and law-case. Yet Webster might very well be indebted to no source but *Lust's Dominion*. The law-case, the pompous, pettifogging lawyer, etc., were for him not far to seek : he had used them all in the *White Devil*, and he

---

[1] "Some have been peppered there *too lately*." See above, p. 31. It would make the illusion come at least two full years after the news of the "pepper," etc.

[2] See above, p. 32.   [3] See above, p. 32.

used them again in *Appius and Virginia*. And though *Lust's Domin-ion* did not appear in print till 1657, it very probably is the *Spanish Moor's Tragedy* [1] of 1600. It shows at all events the hand of Dekker, and must have been known to his old pupil and friend, whether in manuscript or on the boards.

Indeed, in spite of similarities, all three plays in question—Fletcher's and Webster's — could have influenced each other only in the most general way, as appears when we look to their sources. The *Spanish Curate* drew its story entire, even to the matter of the law-case, from Leonard Digges's translation (just issued) of *Gerardo, the Unfortunate Spaniard* [2]; and it need not be further considered. The *Fair Maid* and the *Law-Case* drew originally, indeed, from one source, yet independently, like twigs on different boughs. Of the story of the *Fair Maid*, Langbaine long ago remarked that it was to be found in Nathaniel Wanley's *Wonders of this Little World, or General History of Man*, [3] transcribed from Nicolas Caussin's [4] *Holy Court*. From the latter I quote at length :

Manuscriptum P. Sirmundi. *Joannes Magnus, & Laurentius Venetus.*,

Pursuing the maxims I will recount an admirable passage, which he used among others, to make his justice remarkable. A *Roman* Lady left widow by the death of her husband, had lost a son born of this marriage, who was secretly stolen from her, and in servitude bred up in another Province. This child grown up a young man, received notice from a good hand, that he was of free extraction, and son of a Ladie, whose name was given him, her aboad, and all circumstances, which caused him to undertake a voyage to *Rome* with intention to make himself known unto her. He came directly to his mother, who was much perplexed with certain love-affairs, having betrothed herself to a man, who often promised her marriage, yet never accomplished it. This lover then absent, and detained by urgent affairs very far from *Rome*, the Ladie had the space of about thirtie days free, wherein she kept this young man in her house, acknowledging him, and particularly avowing him for her son, thoroughly convinced by evident tokens, so that then her charitie was so great towards him, that she ceased not to weep for joy, in the recovery of her loss.

---

[1] Henslowe, p. 118 : "Layd owt for the company the 13 of febrearye 1599 [*i. e.*, 1600] for a boocke called the spaneshe mores tragedie unto thomas Deckers wm. barton John daye," etc.—This Collier identified with *Lust's Dominion* because of the Spanish Moor—Eleazar—a sort of Aaron, the central character. Bullen (*Dict. Nat. Biog.*, art. *Dekker*) rejects this without discussion ; Sidney Lee (*ib.*, art. *Marlowe*) accepts it as likely ; Fleay (I, p. 272) as certain. It must be so. Dekker's hand is unmistakably present (see Haz.'s *Dods.*, XIV, pp. 131, 133, 157, 174, for "do, do, do" and other abrupt language and rhythm of Dekker's, unlike anything in the models of this play—*Malta* or *Tit. And.* The metre, too, suits a date 1600.
[2] *Gerardo the Unfortunate Spaniard, of Gonzalo de Cespides*, transl. by Leonard Digges, reg. Mar. 11, 1622, and pub. the same year. Only seven months, and the *Sp. Cur.* was licensed ! Both main-plot and under-plot are drawn from it. And the main-plot, with which we have here to do, is to be found at p. 231 f, the law-suit at p. 234. There is nothing to show that Web. had known this book.
[3] Lon., 1678, p. 185. Wanley uses, not the French version of *Sainte Cour*, but the one quoted here, by Sir Thomas Hawkins.
[4] Confessor of Louis XIII. B. 1583, d. 1651.

The thirtie days expired, the Lover returned, and seeing this guest newly come to her house, demandeth of the Lady what man he was, and from whence he came. She freely answered, he was her son. He, whether moved by jealousie, thinking this might be but a colour, or that pretending the marriage of the widow, he would not have a charge of children, plainly told her, if she sent not away this found child from her lodging, never should she have any share in his affection. The unhappy creature surprized with love, to serve his passion, renounceth her own entrals, and readily banisheth from her house this son, over whom she had so many tears. The young man seeing himself as between the hammer and the anvil, in so great a necessitie of his affairs, hasteneth to require justice of the King, who most willingly heard him, and commanded the Lady should be brought before him to be confronted by him. She stoutly denied all the pretensions of the young man, saying : *He was an impostor and ungrateful, who not contenting himself to have received the charities of a poor creature in her house, needs would challenge the inheritance of children.* The son on the other side wept bitterly, and gave assurance, she had acknowledged him for her own, very lively representing all the proofs which passion and interest put into his mouth.

The King sounded all passages to enter into the heart of the Lady, and asked her whether she were not resolved to marry again. She answered, *if she met with a man suitable to her, she would do what God should inspire her.* The King replied, *Behold him here, since you have lodged this guest thirtie days in your house, and have acknowledged him so freely, what is the cause why you may not marry him?* The Lady answered : *He had not any means, which ever is necessary for household expence. And to what may your state truly amount,* saith the King? The Lady replied, *She was very well worth a thousand crowns, which was a great riches in that time. Well,* (*saith Theodorick*) *I will give as much to this young man for his marriage, on this condition that you shall marry him.* She much amazed, began to wax pale, blush, tremble, and to shew all the countenances of a perplexed woman, who sought to excuse herself, but faltered in her speech. The King yet to affright her more, swore deeply she should marry him presently, or tell lawfull causes of impediment. The poor woman condemned by the voice of nature which cried in her heart, and having horrour of the crime proposed unto her, cast her self at the feet of the King, with much profusion of tears, confessing her loves dissimulation, and mishap. Then this great Prince taking the word from her : *Are not you a miserable woman* (saith he) *to renounce your own bloud for a villain who hath deceived you, get you to your house, forsake these fond affections, and live in the conditions of a good widow, taking unto you such support from your son as he by nature ought to afford you.*

Caussin's *Holy Court*, tran. by Sir T. H.,[1] London, 1650, p. 285.

In the margin the reader will note Caussin's authorities. Of these, Joannes Magnus, the famous archbishop of Upsala, whose history appeared in 1554,[2] drew directly, as he admits, and almost word for word, from a 'Iustinanus Venetus,' the same as the 'Laurentius' of

---

[1] *I. e.*, Sir Thomas Hawkins. A French ed. is, so far as I can discover, not to be found in America.

[2] Magnus, b. 1488, d. 1544. — *De omnibus Gothorum Sveonumque Regibus qui unquam ab initio nationis extitere, eorumque memorabilibus bellis, operà Olaı Magni Gothi Fratris in lucem edita.* Romæ, 1554, lib. ix, cap. 29, pp. 333-4. Reprinted, Basil., 1558, Stock., 1620. A book widely known in the 17th cent. (Kittredge).

Caussin, or, in the vulgar, Bernardo Giustiniani.[1] The latter, a Venetian senator, of the same illustrious family we have already learned to know, inserted this story into his history *De Origine Urbis Gestisque Venetorum*, first published in 1492.[2]

. . . sed ut ad Theodericum revertamur, justitiam in primis mirifice coluit. Haec duo feruntur exempla. Fures adeo acribus paenis est insectatus, ut liceret per omnem fere Italiam apertis januis speculisque dies & noctes agere. Alterum autem quod cum mulier defuncto viro secundas nuptias amatori sponpondisset, & conditionem addidisset filium domo ejecturam, questus est filius de matre apud Theodoricum. Negabat constanter mulier suum esse filium, suppositum dicebat[3] cum eniteretur, multis hinc atque hinc argumentis contendebatur. Rex ingenio sagax ut veritatem erueret: *Atqui* inquit o *mulier potes, si me audis faciliter ista te molestia liberare: Quin tu juvenem istum qui filium tuum se facit, maritum accipe : minor est aetate & facile** *liberalior.*[4] Mulier animo commota, primum substitit quid responderet, cum aliquantum se collegisset multis cavillationibus eam rem subterfugere, neque sibi ipsi constare caepit, sed omnia ambagibus involvere. Theodorico major orta suspicio est. Itaque finxit se paenam addere, nisi consentiret. Tum adacta mulier sceleris horrore suum esse filium confessa est. Usus praeterea liberalitate est erga Patavinam urbem, etc.

* *forte*, facie.

De Origine Urbis Gestisque Venetorum Historia. ap. Graevii
Thesaur. Antiq., Lugdun. Batav., 1725, t. v., p. i., p. 51.

This, the oldest record, the only other one I have been able to discover, is certainly, I think, not Caussin's source. In the margin above he cites first a manuscript of a Pater Sirmundus (or Pére Jacques Sirmond, his friend, like him a Jesuit, and like him a man of wide reading and author of many books).[5] *This* was his source — some old, popular tale. For that the additions and variations of their version were made by either of these stiff-minded Jesuits of the seventeenth century is unthinkable; and Giustiniani's version, on the other hand, seems to have been taken, not from ancient history, but from the exemplum or novella which Caussin used, and to have been shorn of its human graces and circumstantiality only to serve as a grave, historical proof of Theodorick's virtues as a judge. However this last be, the story in both versions but especially in Caussin's, with its simple humanity and pathos, its Byzantine motive of the finding of relatives, its Oriental one of the shrewd judgment of the king, and its identification of that king with one of the late Roman sovereigns, is unmistakably medieval, and takes its place among the tales of a collection

---

[1] B. 1408, d. 1489. That Laurentius and Bern. Justinianus are the same appears from one of the *Elogia* prefixed to the latter's work, a letter headed *Benedictus Brognolus Laurentio Justiniano Sal. Pl. D.*   [2] *Nouvelle Biog. Univ.*

[3] Magnus reads *dicebat. Cum*, etc. He evidently does not understand eniteretur in the sense of *being in travail.*   [4] M. reads *facie liberaliore.*

[5] *Nouv. Biog. Univ.* — B. 1559, d. 1651. He succeeded C. as confessor to the king in 1637.

like the *Gesta Romanorum*,[1] or, better, among the French or Italian novelle. Like most such stories, it may have been widely disseminated.

Either version, Caussin's or Giustiniani's, would serve for the *Fair Maid of the Inn*. The *substitution* of the child in the latter version would make it fit better ; but that was something at that day easily to be added ; and we may suppose that Fletcher got his material from either Joannes Magnus or a contemporary compendium. But it is highly probable that he used Caussin himself. The story of Gerardo, we have already seen, he took wet from the press. The *Sainte Cour* appeared at Paris so early as 1624, the second edition in 1625, and when we consider the immediate and wide-spread popularity of the work — the eighth edition appeared in 1629,[2] — together with the fact that the *Fair Maid* could not possibly have been written before May, 1624,[3] it seems every way likely that the wide-awake Fletcher had, even in England, seen the book and used it.

Webster, on the other hand, drew directly from neither version, but through Dekker [4]; and he from Magnus, or some compendium going at his day. Curiously enough, Dekker took the first half of the old story, as Fletcher in the *Fair Maid* took the latter. Dekker reproduced only the scandalous conduct of the widow, intensifying it by reading bastardy for substitution ; Fletcher, only the king's judgment, making her motives, in the sequel, just and good. To this, Dekker adds the widow's intent for conscience sake to dishonor and impoverish her son, her naming of the father, and the rest. And Webster goes a step

---

[1] I have searched for it in the old authors that deal with Theodorick, as Procopius, Jornandes, Isidorus Hispalensis, etc., in vain. But it certainly is only a medieval tale like that — so popular in the Middle Ages — of the judgment of Solomon, to be paralleled by the judgment on the Jew in the *Pecorone* (and in *Percy Soc. Pub.*, viii, p. 114, De milite conventionem faciente), reproduced in the *Mer. of Ven.*, and one in the Latin tale *De muliere conquerente de violentiâ* (*Percy Soc.*, viii. 22) — attached to Theodorick's great name. Common to all three of these judgments, as to Solomon's is the yielding at the outset to the claim of the unrighteous plaintiff. All these are unmistakably Oriental. See Gladwin's *Persian Moonshee* (Calcutta, 1801), Pt. II, which contains (stories i–xvi) a multitude of similar judgments, including the same as that of Solomon and De muliere. See particularly story x, wherein the Cazy declares he will believe the woman if she will stand naked before him. The innocent refuses, the guilty acquiesces.

[2] These facts in the *Bibliothèque de la Comp. de Jésus*, Paris, 1891, *Bibliog.*, t. II, *sub. voc.* — "The work had an immense circulation." See Bayle's *Dict.* for the number of editions (17), and of the languages into which it was translated. Prof. Köppel dismisses this subject summarily. See *J., M., B., & F.*, p. 118, where he asserts that Caussin's *Cour Sainte* was first pub. in 1632, and, conseq., the source is *unbestimmt*. Here, as in the case of *P. L.*, below, Prof. Köppel betrays no acquaintance with the plots of W.

[3] Because of Amboyna. See above, p. 32. [4] *I. e.*, him and his associates.

159

farther, — puts the motive revenge for a dead [1] lover in the place of desire to profit a living one, [2] and (if this be not, indeed, a step backward) adds an actual law-suit.

The plot of the *Law-Case* is Webster's first attempt at free invention. His earlier plots, those of the *White Devil* and *Malfi*, he borrowed as wholes — the story of *Malfi* is but the story of Bandello — but here he weaves several old strands, with some of his making, into a web quite his own. For it is altogether probable that there is no source for the rest of the play. Some of the remaining motives and situations, no doubt, are old and time-worn ; some are odds and ends picked up from history and general curious information : but surely no two or more of them were ever before together. [3] For the first time he makes a plot, instead of cutting up a novel into acts and scenes.

APPIUS AND VIRGINIA.

The final source of *Appius and Virginia* is, of course, Livy. [4] Whether Webster went to him directly, or through the medium of some of the later versions of his tale, is a question Dr. Lauschke has

---

[1] *I. e.*, as she believes.

[2] *I. e.*, in the *L. D.*, to give the crown to Eleazar.

[3] Led astray by Web.'s method in previous plays, and by two curious bits of information in the remainder of his story, such as are likely to be left standing from some old Italian novella, I thought at first there must be one source for this all. The one is a reference to the cloister of the Bathanites, as a customary place of pilgrimage before engaging in mortal combat (p. 106). This seemed like a vestige from an old story ; but research reveals no such order anywhere in Christendom. Curiously enough, however, one in Islam. "Bateniti, o Bataniti : setta particolare che si formò fra i mussulmani e che si componeva di uomini del populo " — *Encic. Ital.*, III, p. 45. Consequently, a slip of Web'.s, and merely his own contribution.

The other is a story (p. 51) told by Ercole, of Contarino's hereditary exemption from punishment, by virtue of his father's services to Charles V in carrying his answer to the French king's challenge, when he was engaged to fight upon a frontier arm of the sea in a flat-bottomed boat. This story of the kings and their challenge seems of itself a legend ; and, as for the use made of it, it seems one of those stopgaps frequently left standing from Italian tales. But it is strict history. Charles in 1528 uttered imputations against the honor of Francis I : the latter challenged him to single combat, and the former, in reply, named as the field "la rivière [de la Bidassoa] qui passe entre Fontarabye et Andaya." The herald, Borgona, who carried this cartel, was forced to undergo the greatest delays, privations, and indignities, before he was permitted to deliver it ; but whether he was finally thus rewarded, I cannot discover. — *Papiers d' État du Cardinal de Granville*, Paris, 1841, t. i, p. 405. Mignet's *Rivalité* (1875), II, p. 401 f. And this incident has been blent with another,— Charles's challenge of Francis in a full consistory of Pope and Cardinals, at Rome, in 1536, to "combatre en une isle, ou sur un pont ou batteau en quelque rivière . . . et quant aux armes . . . que luy de sa part les trouverait toutes bonnes, fust-ce de l'espée ou du poignard, en chemise." — Pettitot, *Collect. Compl. Mém.* (Paris, 1821), t. xviii, pp. 343-4. Sandoval, *Historia de Carlos V*, Pamplona, 1614, t. ii, p. 304.

[4] Lib. III, cap. 43 seqq.

attempted to solve in his Leipzig dissertation.[1] He concludes that
Webster did both ; and that Webster used not only Livy but his paraphraser William Painter, and not only Dionysius of Halicarnassus [2]
but his paraphraser Giovanni Fiorentino.[3]

To these conclusions we cannot altogether assent ; nor, when we do
assent, do Dr. Lauschke's reasons always seem sufficient. On Painter,
indeed, he lays no stress, but merely thinks it very probable that it
was the version of the famous *Palace of Pleasure* that led Webster to
turn to the original, Livy ; and, as a conjecture, we may let this pass.
But when we turn to his arguments for Livy himself, we immediately
ask, Why Livy, and not Painter alone ? All [4] the supposed word-for-
word translations out of Livy may well enough come from Painter
instead. One point only, and that not advanced by Dr. Lauschke,
turns the balance for the great Paduan, — the name Minutius for the
general at Algidum, which does not occur in Painter, Giovanni, or
Dionysius, and does in Livy just before the story of Virginia.[5]

Nor do we agree with Dr. Lauschke as to Webster's having used
the *Pecorone*, and so, of course, not with his precipitate corollary —
Webster's Kenntnis der italienischen Sprache.[6] Nothing can be said
for the *Pecorone* that must not also be said for Dionysius, except
matters of no moment,[7] such as a very Websterian discrepancy between
"Numitorius" and "Icilius" as sender of the message to Virginius,
and — what could very well be suggested by Livy, Painter, or Heywood's *Lucrece* — the association of Virginia's name with that of
Lucretia as having given Rome liberty through her death. It may
well be, but there is no proof.[8]

---

[1] *J. W.'s Trag. A. & V., Eine Quellenstudie*, Potsdam, 1899.

[2] *Antiq. rom.*, lib. xi, cap. 28 seqq. [3] *Il Pecorone*, sec. novel of twent. day.

[4] Except the "disguised in dust and sweat"—*sordidatus*—lacking in Painter.
But this can have little weight.

[5] Lib. III, cap. 41.—In Dionysius the commander is several times named
Antonius. Only far back in lib. x is Minutius mentioned.

[6] Lauschke, p. 32.   [7] *Ib.*, 31-2.

[8]   Two fair, but ladies most unfortunate,
       Have in their ruins rais'd declining Rome.
       Lucretia and Virginia, both renown'd
       For chastity.   *A. & V.*, p. 224.

E così, come la morte di Lucrezia fu cagione di liberare la città dalla tirannide di
Tarquinio superbo, così la morte di Verginia diede occasione di liberare la patria da
quei dieci tiranni.   *Il Pecorone*, Lauschke, p. 32.

Sequitur aliud in urbe nefas ab libidine ortum haud minus foedo eventu quam
quod per stuprum caedemque Lucretiae urbe regnoque Tarquinios expulerat, ut non
finis solum idem decemviris qui regibus, sed causa etiam eadem imperii amittendi
esset.   *Liv.*, Lib. III, 43, ed. Hertz.

. . . who committed no lesse filthy facte, then was done by Tarquinius, for the
rape of Lucreece.   Painter, Vol. I, p. 35.

Dionysius, on the other hand, was used. He represents Appius as feigning to refuse the magistracy offered, just as in Webster, and inveighing, too (as there), against public life as aeque negotiosa atque invidiosa.[1] And he makes the defense raise the same questions as in Webster — why Marcus had let the matter of Virginia's birth lie for fifteen years unmooted, and why Virginius's wife had not chosen to cheer her lord by palming off on him a boy instead of a girl.[2] These striking similarities are, as Dr. Lauschke holds, real proof of Webster's acquaintance with the version of the Ionian rhetorician.

How far Webster follows the version of Dionysius, how far that of Livy, is, for our purposes, a question hardly worth inquiry : the stories are almost the same, and, as they do not abound in incident, Webster seizes on all in either. That of Dionysius furnishes most. From it Webster takes Appius's tempting of Virginia clandestinely with large promises, the deceptive part Virginius's wife is accused of playing, the injured appeal of Marcus for justice, the throng of witnesses, and the bond-woman's oath.[3] And from Livy he takes some of Virginius's speeches to the army[4] and the suicide of Appius. A better question is, what are Webster's contributions[5]? Such are Virginius's mission to the senate on account of the famine, the mutiny on his return which he alone can quell, his quarrel with Icilius, his relentings toward Appius at the end and Icilius's medicine for them, the plot to coerce Virginia by plunging her father into pecuniary straits, the death of Marcus, the parts of the clown Corbulo and of the Advocate, and the raising of Virginius and Icilius to the consulate at the end.

A Cure for a Cuckold.

A source of Webster's part of the *Cure for a Cuckold* is, as I have already said, Massinger's *Parliament of Love*. Not *the* source, for this comedy, like the preceding one, is woven out of several materials ; and the *Parliament of Love* has furnished only the story of the lover commanded by his mistress to kill his dearest friend, else never enjoy her love ; of the search for the friend under show of search for a Second in a duel ; of finding him, at last, on the eve of his marriage-night (or of a meeting with his mistress) ; of the disclosure of the truth in a long speech, sword in hand ; of the agreement to deceive

---

[1] Cf. Appius's conduct, *A. & V.*, 129–32. — Dionysius : Ille primum ficte recusabat, missionem petens ab administratione aeque negotiosa, etc. Contr. Livy, who represents Appius as seeking the office by hook or by crook. — Lauschke, pp. 24–5.

[2] Lauschke, pp. 29 and 37.   [4] *Ib.*, p. 42.

[3] *Ib.*, pp. 26, 29, 32, 35, 37.   [5] For all these see Lauschke, pp. 47–52.

the woman by reporting the friend dead; and of marriage as the happy outcome.[1] It has furnished some of the details, as well. In both plays the hero despairs of finding such a friend, and yet is but "miserably blest"[2] when he finds him; the friend renounces the joy of meeting with his sweetheart (which the hero himself urges[3]), and is for taking horse forthwith; the field is far away, and Second is to fight as well as Principal[4]: the friend, in ignorance, congratulates the hero on their being first on the field,[5] and later doubts the goodness of the quarrel[6]; the hero reveals the truth in a startling way, before (or at the end of) a long declamatory speech, then turns bitter and relentless, and there is fiery eloquence on both sides[7]; and the woman goes unpunished, is married, indeed, by the indignant hero. All this, surely, is enough to prove that the plots of the two plays are closely related, whether it be that Webster's is derived from Massinger's, or Massinger's from Webster's, or both from a common source.

The merits of these alternatives (the last two of which have already been advocated)[8] can be settled only after a separate examination of the treatment of the story in the two versions and in their common source.

The common source of the two versions is Marston's *Dutch Courtesan*.[9] This story is of a courtesan who accepts a second lover only on

---

[1] This part of the plot of *P. L.* is to be found in Act II, 2; III, 2; IV, 2, and the final sc.

[2] *P. L.*, 130, 131, and 132 a, "To have the greatest blessing . . . the greatest curse," etc. *C. C.*, p. 24.   [3] *P. L.*, 131 b, "such a mistress too." *C. C.*, 23.

[4] In *P. L.* throughout that is taken for granted (see esp. 131 b), and so in *L. F. L.* (see below, p. 170). But Web. remarks upon the strangeness of the require-ment (pp. 19, 20), and so gives, perhaps, an incidental proof that he is adopting an already finished story. To have done away with the *fighting* of the Seconds would, of course, have knocked a great hole in the plot. Yet instances of the fighting of Seconds are to be found in other plays of B. & F. (*Hon. Man's Fort.*, p. 486; *Lovers' Prog.*) and in the judicial combat at end of Web.'s own *D. L. C.*— For clearness sake, I capitalize *second* and *principal* throughout.

[5] *P. L.*, 134 b; *C. C.*, 44.   [6] *P. L.*, 135 a; *C. C.*, 44, 47.

[7] *P. L.*, 134 b, 135 a; *C. C.*, 45–48. Much more eloquence, of course, in Mass., but Lessingham's long speech (p. 45) strikes a key of declamatory eloquence found nowhere else in Web. See below, p. 189.

[8] Genest (in *Hist. of English Stage*, quoted in Haz., IV, p. 4) was the first to point out that it was the same story in both plays. He himself thought they might have drawn from a common source independently. Mr. Edmund Gosse in his *Love's Graduate* (see above, p. 35), p. v, thinks Mass. saw Web.'s play; Mr. Swinburne (quoted in same introd.), "I cannot but think that the two poets must have gone to a common source." Neither offers reasons. Prof. Koeppel ignores W. every time he discusses the Marstonian story and its derivates.

[9] It may be that some more recent version, such as the latter part (final sc.) of the Violante-Jamie-Henrique story in the *Sp. Cur.* (lic. Oct., 1622) attracted Mass.'s

condition that he first kill the former (his friend, as she knows), who had deserted her. These agree to feign fulfillment of the command in order to circumvent and cheat her. She, however, lays a counter-mine, and has the second lover up for murder. But at the right moment the seemingly murdered one appears, and the woman is sent to prison.[1]

At one point this story may seem nearer to Webster's than to Massinger's. Here jealousy is the motive, and one particular friend is meant. Now in Massinger the motive is cruelty and offended modesty,[2] and the command — to kill the dearest friend — is meant only as a penalty on the lover himself.[3] In Webster, on the other hand, the motive at the start is evidently jealousy of Bonvile, later discovered to be Lessingham's "dearest friend":—Clare sulks at the marriage, and later avows to him and to Lessingham that she had loved him, and had tried through Lessingham to kill him.[4] Yet often (such is the obscurity and confusion in the motivation of this play) Clare's motive seems, like Leonora's,[5] not to regard a third party: she herself declares several times that Lessingham had mistaken it, and once that she had meant by "dearest friend" herself[6]; and Lessingham interprets it, like Cleremond in the *Parliament of Love*, only as "malice" and "loathing" for himself.[7] There is no point in Webster's version, moreover, so precisely like the original as that in Massinger's of the woman's haling her lover before a court of justice on a charge of murder.[8] Neither version, then, is demonstrably enough nearer the original than the other to be taken on that ground alone for an intermediate step; and that such an intermediate step is necessary — that the two versions did not draw from the original independently, but one from the other — is proved by the

attention (and Web.'s, possibly) to the story. But that this could not of itself be the source is clear. Violante offers herself instead of being sought, and Jamie does not report Henrique's death. That *D. C.* is the source was pointed out by Gifford. See Koep., *Ch. M. F.*, p. 106.

[1] The source accepted for Marston's story is Painter's (Bandello's) tale of the *Countess of Celant* (Koeppel *in loc.*). But to this M. owes nothing but the matter of a courtesan setting one lover on to kill another, his friend, and his promising, and failing, to do so; no other circumstances, no motives or incidents.

[2] *P. L.*, 127 a. [4] *C. C.*, 70, 74, 75.
[3] *P. L.*, 127 b. [5] The heroine in *P. L.*

[6] Because, of course, of her misery for love and jealousy of Bonvile. The obscurity and confusion is so great that half the time it is impossible to tell whether by "friend" is meant Bonvile or Clare herself. See p. 71, l. 6, where "that friend" seems for the moment just after the explanation to mean her; but farther down the page evidently means Bonvile. See pp. 74, 75, where "your friend" and "his friend" seem certainly to mean Bonvile: but on p. 69 again are explained as Clare.

[7] Expressly, pp. 46-7; but implicitly, *passim*. [8] *P. L.*, 140.

great number of the points, not to be found in the original, at which they meet.[1]

Which was the intermediate step? Webster's, on the mere face of the matter, it could hardly be. For, in the first place, in the technique of no play of Webster's is the influence of Massinger and Fletcher so paramount as in this very one : characters, stage-effects, and structure, — all show, as we shall shortly see, their unmistakable impress, which stands out in strong relief against Webster's previous, more old-fashioned style in the *Devil's Law-Case*. Study and imitation of technique, it is but natural to suppose, would lead to (or ensue upon) borrowing of subject-matter. In the second place, Webster's invention would never have been equal, unaided, to the thrilling, yet well-ordered and continuous, succession of effective situations, attained not only in Massinger but in his own version. Witness the clumsy and jerky movement of the *Devil's Law-Case*, and the great measure of confusion and blunting he has managed, as we have seen, to bring into the motivation and drift of the play now in question. In the third place, Webster's version shows internal evidence of derivation rather than of originality — of blundering contamination of two plots and of sophistication in the handling. Confusion, obscurity, we have already seen, prevailed in the motiving. This was due, as I think, to Webster's taking over bodily into his ground-plot of jealous love — Clare sulking at the wedding and the hitherto unrequited Lessingham offering marriage — the command sprung from offended modesty and virtuous, virago hate, with all the chain of incidents connected with it, the story, in short, of the *Parliament of Love*. Clare, when wooed, cries, not, as Webster had intended, like the Dutch Courtesan, "kill Bonvile,"[2] but like Leonora,

> Prove all thy friends, find out the best and nearest,
> Kill for my sake that friend that loves thee dearest.[3]

Nothing, as Clare's own previous and subsequent conduct proves, could be more unnatural or unintelligible, for not the slightest cause has been given her or us to suspect that Bonvile, the object of her jealous hate, will be the man. Lessingham himself understands the command only as sprung from malice and loathing toward himself, not another. This, then, inserted into the ground-plan, and put side by side with Clare's later positive protestations that she had meant one particular friend, Bonvile, — even meant herself, — proves to be nothing but blind borrowing from an already elaborated and finished fable, a borrowing which does not fit. Lastly, Webster's version is

---

[1] See above, p. 163.   [2] *D. C.*, II, 2, 176.   [3] *C. C.*, p. 13.

too sophisticated, turns too much on word-play and lawyer-like tricks of phrase, to be the earlier. Webster's resolution of the complication "kill thy friend" by Bonvile's words,

> And thou may 'st brag thou 'st done 't; for here for ever
> All friendship dies between us.[1]

is much farther removed than Massinger's from the original, in which the two friends simply come to an agreement to feign death and cheat the woman. How unthinkable, moreover, that the same mind that first wrought out the later, intensely dramatic story (such even in Webster), with its two moments of suspense — the miserably-blest discovery of a friend to slay and the bitter disclosure to him of the truth on the field,— objective as it is and stage-fit through and through, should have been the one to solve complications with hair-splitting and word-play, or should have been capable of breaking the back, so to speak, of the whole action by interpreting "dearest friend" as the woman herself. Surely, then, if any sort of case can be made out for Massinger, the award must be to him.

To this case we turn. Some of the elements foreign to Marston's, and common to both Webster's and Massinger's version, bear Massinger's impress. The thrilling combat between friend and friend, in a lonely place, entered upon with a reluctant eagerness, together with the fiery, eloquent speeches on either side, full of startling disclosures, is like nothing so much as that 'unnatural combat' between father and son of an earlier play [2]: and the likeness is greater (as we should expect, if it was Massinger that conceived both) between this and his version of our story in the *Parliament of Love*. Such far-sought, complicated situations, and thrilling conflicts of feeling, moreover, are not rare in Massinger, appeal to him, indeed, above all other dramatists of the day, as opportunities for the play of his bent for subtle, dramatic eloquence, and for swinging passion like a pendulum from one extreme to the other. Such another situation is that in the *Fatal Dowry*, where stern, fond Rochfort judges and condemns to death his own daughter, or that in the *Roman Actor*, where Domitian reluctantly condemns, at his own suit, the favorite, the really guiltless Paris.[3] Now this sort of thing is not to be found in Webster. Even a bare conflict of feelings, of which Massinger makes so effective and frequent use, is to be found nowhere outside of this

---

[1] *C. C.*, p. 48. — See the further solving of complications by hair-splitting on p. 49:

> It would show
> Beastly to do wrong to the dead : etc.

[2] *Unnat. Combat*, c. 1621 (Fleay). It must be early.   [3] See below, p. 167.

166

play [1] ; and in this how greatly it is reduced, nothing shows so strikingly as a comparison of the philosophic, parabolic treatment of Lessingham's search for a friend in *A Cure for a Cuckold* with the thoroughly dramatic, palpitating-reluctant search of Cleremond. [2]

Massinger, moreover, was the only one of the two, in fact the only man living, [3] who could have constructed the story. He, as is well known, was the greatest dramatic architect since Jonson and Beaumont. No one now could hold and vary the interest in a tragic action as did he in the *Bondman* or the *Roman Actor*. And with him invention — pure invention, after the example of Beaumont and Fletcher — played a great part, a thing it never did or could do with Webster. In the *Bondman*, or the *Maid of Honor*, or the *Picture* (to take only the certain cases), how little he owes [4] ! And for how many plays, like the *Unnatural Combat* or the *Fatal Dowry*, no satisfactory or definite source has been found, or, perhaps, ever can be ! In no case, moreover, does he take the borrowed story in the lump for the plot of his play, as does Webster generally. He always makes it over, and adds far more of his own, for dramatic needs : it is only a germinal idea that he borrows, and he grows, so to speak, his own play. And the result always is, as in this part of the *Parliament of Love*, an intelligible unity, terse and stage-fit to the end, — what Webster's two experiments in this kind, the *Devil's Law-Case* and *A Cure for a Cuckold*, by no means are.

That Massinger actually did construct his story independently (and if he independently of Webster, Webster, remember, dependently on

---

[1] W.'s situations are all extremely simple and outward — the Duchess being tortured, or Vittoria a-baiting like a bear at the stake. There where it would seem that a conflict of feeling is forced upon him, where Virginius should be torn with love for his daughter's honor and for her life, there is nothing of the sort, V. gives some fine outcries of grief and tenderness, but not a sign of a struggle, or even of a purpose ; and we, except for our Livy, are as astounded as Appius or the People when he kills her. And where Isabella, out of love for her brutal husband, publicly divorces herself from him (*W. D.*, 39–41), she plays the part (like Marston's characters) *completely*, as if a different person, a thorough virago. Web., in short, has no conflicts. Mass., on the other hand, has plenty. Paris wooed by Domitia, the mistress of the emperor, fearful to refuse the great woman and fearful to accede (*Rom. Act.*, IV, 2) ; Mathias's and Sophia's struggles against temptation in the *Pict.* ; Vitelli's in the *Ren.*, etc.

[2] See *C. C.*, pp. 17–24, where Less. appears and meditates with his " author " on the rarity of friendship ; then holds conversations with three gallants who proffer friendship, more like those in old parables or the *Gesta Romanorum*, with their balanced and evenly distributed proffers and evasions, than those of a drama. And when he meets the true friend, the tense interest, urgent dissuasion of Cleremond, (*P. L.*, 131) is here but faintly echoed ; the more contemplative interest, however, of the irony of his situation — " miserably blest " — remains.

[3] Except Shirley.   [4] See Koeppel.

him [1]) is made more clear and likely by tracing the evolution in this story down from Marston through two plays known as Beaumont and Fletcher's — the *Scornful Lady* and the *Little French Lawyer*, — the one certainly known to Massinger, and the other partly the work of his hand. This development is distinctly toward the Massinger form — that of the woman's "cruelty" and offended modesty — and not toward that of Webster.

The *Scornful Lady*, [2] printed in 1616, and written, as title-pages and critics agree, [3] by both Beaumont and Fletcher, presents, among other matter, the story of an accepted suitor who in public had forced a kiss from his lady, and for that is condemned by her to a long and arduous task. He tries, however, to outwit her ; brings in disguise the report of his own death ; and so elicits a rueful declaration, like Leonora's in the *Parliament of Love*, that were he alive she would marry him. All this furnishes just the essential transition needed from Marston's to Massinger's version [4] ; one, too, that, in view of the early printing of the play and Massinger's extraordinary intimacy with Beaumont and Fletcher's work, [5] must certainly have served him. [6]

And a further transition, not in this case essential, yet interesting as discovering something of the gestation of the fable in Massinger's brain, is furnished in the *Little French Lawyer*. This play, probably to be dated before May, 1622, [7] is, as all critics admit, by both Fletcher and Massinger ; — proved, anyway, to be in the latter's mind when he wrote the *Parliament of Love* by the four proper names [8] borrowed

---

[1] See above, p. 164.

[2] Boyle somewhere observes that the *Sc. L.* and the *P. L.* have points in common.

[3] Dyce, Fleay, Oliphant, and Boyle.— See, too, the *Varior.*, *B. & F.* (Lon. 1904), vol. I, pp. 356-60.

[4] None of these new features in the *Sc. L.* version is to be found in the source from which Mars. drew, the story of the Countess of Celant. — See *P. L.*, pp, 126-7 and 142 b.

[5] A commonplace of criticism. See p. 174. — *Sc. L.* must have been very popular. Few B. & F. plays were printed before the Folio. This was assigned over May 8, 1617, and there are other ed. bearing the date 1625, etc.

[6] It is worthy of note that the complication is in both plays first presented to us in a conversation between the lady and the hero, in which the hero recites to her his misdemeanor (for our benefit, of course, not hers), and justifies himself by his having often kissed her in private, and the lady pronounces the penalty. *Sc. L.*, p. 80, and *P. L.*, pp. 126-7.

[7] Mr. Oliphant (*Engl. Stud.*, XVI, p. 185) says it *must* be so dated, on the basis, I suppose, of the play's not being in Herbert's Office Book, which starts then.

[8] Dinant, Cleremont (spelled Cleremond in *P. L.*), Beauprè, and Lamira. If it should be objected that as the date of the *L. F. L.* is not certain, it might be later than *P. L.* (lic. Nov. 24, 1624), I should be content to retort even with this argument of the borrowing alone. For see the following list of rare names borrowed from B. and F. : Chamont (Shamont), *Nice Valour* (Fleay and Thorndike, 1612-13), Mass.'s

from it for that play. The likeness between it and the *Parliament of Love* is greater on second thought than first; some of the incidents are but differently distributed, or are reversed. The young man, Dinant, engaged to fight as Principal in a duel, receives, like Montrose, Second in the *Parliament of Love*, a commission from his mistress in what nearly concerns her honor,[1] and, unlike Montrose, is deterred by it from fighting by the side of his friend and Second, Cleremont. The latter is thus left in the lurch, to meet single-handed both Principal and Second of the other side. Here, then, as in the *Parliament of Love*, the Second proves a truer friend than the Principal, and the Principal receives as a condition of her favor[2] an unreasonable and outrageous command from his mistress, which he slavishly, against all dictates of conscience, obeys; and while in the *Parliament of Love* the Second, in face of the appointment within two hours to meet his mistress on business which concerns her honor, stands fast for friendship, the Principal here gives way, and goes, on like business, a two-hour errand for her. Thus we see how first the relations of the two types of friend — the friend who gives up friendship for love and the friend who gives up love for friendship[3] — form in Massinger's mind as those of Principal and Second in a duel; and, further, discern the two main forces of the later story fully developed (though yet blent together), — the ruthless command of an imperious woman delivered to the Principal as a condition of her favor, which starts the action, and the mere conflicting command (or appointment), delivered to the Second, in business which concerns her honor, which tends to hinder the action and is a measure of the friendship[4] of the Second.

Unnat. Com. (Fleay, c. 1621), and *P. L.* (1624); Vitelli, *Love's Cure* (Dyce, 1608–12; Thorndike, 1606), and Mass.'s *Renegado* (lic. Apr., 1624); Malfort, *Lovers' Prog.* (lic. Dec., 1623), and Mass.'s *Unnat. Com.*; Ascanio, *Sp. Cur.* (1622), *Double Marr.* (1620?), *Triumph of Love* (1608?), and Mass.'s *Bashful Lover* (lic. 1636); Calista, *Lovers' Prog.*, and *P. L.* (Beauprè's disguise). This last point fixes the backward limit of the last-named play.   [1] *L. F. L.*, p. 416 b, and *P. L.*, 131 a.

[2] *L. F. L.*, 416 b. Lamira is guarded, and does not promise absolutely.

[3] The parallel is, of course, not perfect. Cleremont, the Second in the *L. F. L.*, has no struggle with love.

[4] In the *P. L.* the *ruthless command* (to kill the dearest friend) comes to Cleremond from Lamira, his mistress, and the *conflicting appointment* (to meet in two hours on what concerns her honor) to Montrose, the Second, from his mistress: in the *L. F. L.* the only command given is that of Lamira to the Principal, Dinant, having these features of the ruthless command — the peremptory order to do something to injure a friend (leave Cleremont in the lurch), to a suitor, as a condition of favor; and these of the conflicting appointment — that it comes not as causing the duel but as conflicting with it, and that it concerns her own honor or reputation. In Web. the conflicting appointment is represented only by the consideration, urged upon Bonvile, that he is on his wedding eve, and by the sudden appearance of Annabel in the midst of their conference.

Equally important to the development is the presence here of details —
some of them those that appear also in Webster, — as furnishing
more definite and tangible, though less essential, links. Cleremont,
the name of the Principal in the *Parliament of Love*, is that of the
Second in the *Little French Lawyer*; the scene, as in the *Parliament
of Love*, is in Paris, and the duel a few miles out; and the Second here
must fight as well as the Principal,[1] and congratulates himself on his
side being first on the field,[2] just as in the *Parliament of Love* and in
Webster.

The tracing of this evolution down from Marston is of itself, to my
mind, argument. It explains completely the rise of the fable in
Massinger's mind without help from Webster, and could not possibly
be wrested to explain such in Webster except with Massinger coming
in between. In the *Scornful Lady*, indeed, we are yet on neutral
territory. But while the play may have been known to Webster, it
serves to explain nothing in him: it *must* have been known to Massinger. After that, in the *Little French Lawyer*, we are on Massinger's own ground, a play in which he had a hand, or which, as
certainly as black is black and white is white, was known to him; and
from here the course of the stream runs straight toward his *Parliament of Love*. Here, in the *Little French Lawyer*, arise all the
remaining important features of the *Parliament of Love* version, as
well as many of the more striking details : — the friend who proves
more lover than friend and the friend who proves more friend than
lover, in the relation of Principal and Second in a duel ; the ruthless
command of an imperious woman, and the mere conflicting command ;
the details of proper names, fighting of Seconds, joy at being first
on the field, and the rest. The stream runs straight, and we have no
need of Webster. Indeed, Webster's version coming between (if we
can conceive it there), with its confused and wavering motivation,
sophisticated handling, and clumsy adaptation, could never have
helped, and would only have hindered, the natural culmination, of the
development in Massinger's brain, the brilliant version of the *Parliament of Love*. And, on the other hand, Webster's version as branch-
ing off from the *Little French Lawyer* and attaining independently
results so identical with Massinger's, is still more inconceivable.
Before examining the *Little French Lawyer* we thought the two versions so like as necessarily to be related in the way of cause and
effect [3] ; and we must think so still. The elements of the story to be
found in the *Little French Lawyer* are enough, since we have proof
that they were in Massinger's mind, to lead up to the outcome

---

[1] *L. F. L.*, 416-18. Cf. above, p. 163.   [2] *L. F. L.*, 416 a.   [3] See above, pp. 163, 165.

in his *Parliament of Love ;* but that they, still colorless and scattered
as they are, should in a *second* mind, Webster's or any man's, — even
had we proof that they had reached it, — lead independently to an
outcome so similar, is beyond belief.

We may conclude without much hesitation, then, as we gather up
in mind all the evidence here presented, that Webster borrowed the
story of cruelty and offended modesty from Massinger, and bound it
up, without appropriate change, with the old Marstonian, or for that
matter, world-old, motive of jealous love.[1]

II. THE INFLUENCE OF FLETCHER AND MASSINGER.

With such brevity as the limits of this work impose I wish to treat
of a subject hitherto never broached, the influence on Webster, in his
last plays, of Fletcher and Massinger. Such influence of the reigning
fashion we have already noted at this very day in the veteran Chapman[2] ; such Mr. Thorndike and others have shown at an earlier day in
Shakspere ; it need not, therefore, surprise us, or pain us, if found in
one who, though he thought worthily and seriously of his art, could
have thought no more worthily and seriously than they. Rather, it
should seem to us only natural. Since the day of *Westward Ho* and
Northward Ho Webster had done no work in comedy, and then he
was under Dekker's thumb. As now, twenty years after, without a
bent for any special style, he turned his hand to comedy, how should
he write but in the dominant style of the day, that of the court poets,
Fletcher and Massinger[3] ?

---

[1] I have devoted so much space to attain this result, remember, in order not only to
ascertain the source but also to settle the date. See Chap. I, p. 34. Confirmation of
such date (after Nov., 1624) is furnished by a comparison with the *D. L. C.* (1621-23),
which at several points is touched by *C. C.* but never by *P. L.* It, too, contains two
duels (the second not as in *C. C.* merely intended) between two young men,
about a woman ; Calais sands (p. 103) are mentioned as a duelling-ground ; one
of the duellists has his will made and sent to the bride (*D. L. C.*, 48 ; *C. C.*, 54) ; there
is warning given not to fight (*D. L. C.*, 27 ; *C. C.*, 93) ; an intentionally obscure letter
is sent by the woman to her lover (*D. L. C.*, 107 ; *C. C.*, 13) ; the question of wearing
a privy coat and the honorableness of it arises in very similar fashion just before the
fight (see above, p. 38). Even at this last point the *C. C.* comes in contact with *P. L.:*

    The defence I mean is the justice of my cause ;

    . . . .

    What confidence thou wearest in a bad cause !   *C. C.*, 47.

    See how weak an ill cause is !   *P. L.*, 135.

Of itself such evidence proves nothing, but it is incidental confirmation that in the
meantime the *P. L.* has intervened.   [2] See App. II.

[3] This seems likelier still if we acknowledge B. & F. influence even in the sec.
Period. See p. 151.

To *tragi-comedy*, I should say, for such are Webster's two plays, and the type of Fletcher and Massinger he followed. In this case it is a modification of the dramatic romance of Beaumont and Fletcher, defined so accurately by Mr Thorndike,[1] and is represented by such later plays as the *Little French Lawyer*, the *Lovers' Progress*, the *Fair Maid of the Inn*, the *Bondman*, the *Renegado*, and others. These, like the earlier romances, are ingenious, artistic puzzles in plot, things of suspense and mystery, which — often against fact and human nature — hold the interest to the end.[2] Like them, they deal with foreign rather than English life, gentlemen and ladies[3] or their dependants, no low life (except the idyllic, sylvan, or pastoral), and marvelous, often fabulous, complications. Like them, they present conventional types of character within a definite and narrow range, and make them use practically one and the same language. Like them, their plots are invented far more than borrowed, are thoroughly made over for dramatic needs, and cover not years and decades in the action nor the map of Europe in scene, as did the old-style plays before Beaumont and Fletcher, but days or even hours, and one district or city. Like them again, and unlike the old plays, they do not deal with one central tragic passion and issue in a uniform tone : there is no one unmistakable hero, but several ; the sentimental love-story is made not the relief of the tragic action but the core of it ; and so the same action runs, with constant variety, now deep and tragic, now light and sentimental. Both regard stage-effectiveness. They strive after movement and "business," after intensity of situations rather than coherency and firmness of plot, and after a pleasant variety of sensations, even at the expense of naturalness in resolutions, of truth of character, and of dignity and nobility of tone.

----

[1] For brevity's sake, I must refer once for all to his *Influence of B. & F. on Shak.*, Chap. VII, ' The Romances.' Practically all I say of the romances of B. & F. I draw from him, except where they are discussed as *differing* from the later plays. Although the later plays, too, are romantic enough, I shall for convenience sake use the word *romances* as applying only to the plays Mr. Thorndike considers, *M. Tr., Phil., Thier. & Theod., K. N. K., Cup. Rev.*, and *Four Plays in One*, the only plays, indeed, in which B. (apart from his own plays, *Woman-Hater* and *Knight of the Burning Pestle*) can have had much share.

[2] Esp. in the lively dénouement, taken notice of by Professors Wendell and Thorndike. This is conspicuous in *D. L. C., C. C.*, and, by Virginius's relentings and Icilius's cure for them, even in *A. & V.*, though in all cases without the B. & F. ingenuity. Comp. the vicissitudes of the action in the dénouement of Chapman's *Alphonsus* at this time (see App. II). Contr. close of *Byron* and *Bussy*, mere declamation.

[3] This much in common ; but in the romances they are courtiers and the scene is a court, while (see *infra*) in Flet. (as in Web.) they become more and more ladies and gentlemen.

In other ways they are unlike. They lack the distinctively Beaumontesque features, — the high tragic note, the hearty, floundering fun, or the bent for the mock-heroic and burlesque; the keen dramatic sympathy which made separate situations more vivid and absorbing than any out of Shakspere; Beaumont's irony, pathos, tender idyllic or chivalrous sentiment, and stately rhythm. But the root of the matter is that they lack Beaumont's, the early Elizabethan, fidelity to morals and to art. Their whole end is to entertain and surprise. In a measure and way unknown even to Beaumont, character is made subservient to plot and plot to situations. In the romances, the characters, psychologically considered, remained fairly consistent; or when they were not, the break was not made much of, but smoothed over.[1] And, morally considered, they remained consistent throughout the play: the hero and villain of the beginning were hero and villain at the end. Quite otherwise with the plays of Fletcher and Massinger. In these the souls of men labor under all sorts of "sudden alterations" and eclipses, disguises and dissemblings, conversions and relapses, and they wax and wane in goodness, are murderers or saints, within the moment. They are but puppets, and utter the lively, eloquent, unreal speeches (with no need of pathos or irony), and do the startling things, that the plot demands.[2] Consequently, the old characterization by description, as extravagantly good or extravagantly bad, together with the contrasts involved, falls away[3]; all are good or bad as the scene changes, as the kaleidoscope turns; and thus puzzle of character is added to puzzle of plot. Even the construction sticks full of insincerity, of false reports, false auguries, and mock events — unexpected, impossible turns, — to fetch a telling situation, and of such a measure of dramatic injustice as rewards and saves all the good and forgives all the bad. Partly as a result of this dramatic method, partly as the expression of the authors' own views and those of the day, there prevails a great and general insensibility to the reality of morals. Monstrous and flagitious things are intended, even done, for the situation's sake, and no one is troubled. Credit and reputation, the name of a thing and not the thing, the deed and not the motive, are what count. Pure women are conceived by themselves and by others only as standing on the brink of impurity, and

---

[1] See below, p. 180.

[2] Nowhere is all this so frankly confessed as at the end of *Corinth*, p. 46 b, Euphanes's second speech, in which he admits the whole present sc. to be nothing but dramatic hoax and humbug.

[3] See Thorndike as to this in the B. & F. romances, p. 120. The women in *M. Tr.*, *Phil.*, etc., are described, then represented as very good, or very bad, and a contrast is thus established between pure and sensual love.

chances are coolly taken on the outcome ; and when they have fallen,
on the other hand, it is only a brief matter of conversion and repentance to make all straight again. And courtesy is turned to hardness
and grossness. Beaumont's Arethusas, Aspatias, and Spaconias give
place to Fletcher's and Massinger's foul-mouthed prudes and viragos ;
the chivalry of Amintor and Philaster to the glittering conventionalities of Fletcher's Lisander [1] and Massinger's Vitelli. [2] Purity, then,
nerve, veracity, and simplicity have everywhere sadly waned, and that
delicacy and chivalrousness of feeling under which in Beaumont's
work vice itself lost half its evil by losing all its grossness, has faded
away like a mist.

——We have spoken of Fletcher's later work and Massinger's work
as if they were one, and for our purposes it is convenient. Of
Massinger too little a body of independent work has come down to
us, and that little generally too late or uncertain in date, and, anyway,
too deeply impregnated with the influence of his great compeer, to
warrant his claim to be Webster's sole sponsor. On the contrary, not
only is there almost no point in Webster's art at which Massinger's
influence can be shown where Fletcher has not been before him, but
also there are many points, such as the comic aspects of the *Cure for
a Cuckold*, where Webster seems to touch Fletcher alone. Indeed,
the type of the *Cure for a Cuckold* (that play which borrows so largely
from the plot of a play of Massinger's) and, in less degree, of the
Devil's Law-Case, bears decisively the stamp of Fletcher. In the
doing away with the political element which was part and parcel of
the older romances — intrigues, usurpations, conspiracies, and rebel-
lions ; — in the laying of the scene in gentlemen's families instead of
at court, and in modern Spain, France, or England instead of in the
realms of fancy [3]; in the depicting of the gallants and belles
of the day, with all the local color and contemporary allusions
impossible in the romantic, pseudo-classical atmosphere of a Lycia or
Sicilia, or in the age of '' gods '' and goddesses [4]; and in the general

---

[1] In the *Lovers' Prog*.   [2] In the *Renegado*.

[3] This is characteristic of Fletcher, esp. in the latest plays. Instead of '' Lycia ''
and '' Pannonia '' or an equally fanciful, unhistorical '' Corinth,'' — Valladolid,
Segovia, Paris, Candia. Eng., however, seems to be reserved for pure comedy, as in
Wit without Money, *Night Walker*, though *Mons. Thomas* at least is an instance of
Fletcher's laying the scene of a tragi-comedy there. Cf. *C. C.*, — Besides in the plays
cited here, the scene is laid in French or Spanish gentlemen's families in such plays
as *Fair Maid*, *Pilg.*, *Love's Pilg.*, *Noble Gent.*, *Love's Cure*, etc.

[4] This appears, of course, much more in the pure comedies — *Wild Goose*, *Wit
without Mon*. — but nevertheless in *Mons. Thomas*, and, in a Spanish or French garb,
but still with plenty of direct and indirect satire of '' England,'' in *Elder Bro.*,

lowering of the tragic tone, — the *Devil's Law-Case* and the *Cure for a Cuckold* are like the *Parliament of Love*, indeed, and the late *Guardian*,[1] but still more like the much earlier plays of Fletcher, the *Lovers' Progress*, the *Maid in the Mill*, or the *Spanish Curate*.[2] Of direct borrowing from Fletcher, moreover, there is, though no proof as with Massinger, yet some indication. Archas in the *Loyal Subject* may have been, as we shall see, the model for Virginius. ——

Quite such are Webster's two tragi-comedies, especially the *Cure for a Cuckold*. They, too, as never before in Webster, are puzzles in plot and character. They, too, depict ladies and gentlemen, and unfold marvelous events and complications. They, too, present lay-figures instead of fresh, original characters. They, too, seek stage-effectiveness, and at a like cost in truth of character and circumstance. But all this must be viewed piece by piece.

THE SUBSTANCE OF THE FABLE.

In mere material the *Devil's Law-Case* and the *Cure for a Cuckold* have much in common with these later plays of Fletcher's and Massinger's. They present a love-story developed tragically but ending happily. They deal with strange, improbable complications, more like those of a fairy-tale than of a drama, but offering always, in their extremes, situations of telling power or chances for striking dramatic reversals. Such in Webster are the stabbing that cures a man, the unheard-of law-case,[3] the command of the beautiful woman to her lover to kill his dearest friend,[4] the story of Rochfield the honest thief, all of which have not only a general but a particular likeness to situations in Fletcher and Massinger. Here, too, certain stock incidents and scenes of the Fletcherian comedy recur: sea-fights,[5] woodland scenes in which helpless women meet woodmen, outlaws,

---

L. F. L., etc. The romances have instead much false heathen atmosphere, appeals to the "gods," and Venus and Cupid actually on the stage.

[1] Acted Oct. 31, 1633.

[2] Given only as examples: there are plenty of others, as *L. F. L.*, the dates of which are not decisively to be settled. — The *Sp. Cur.* dates 1622, the others 1623.

[3] See above, p. 154 f, the analogues of these in Fletcher.

[4] See the command of Olinda to her suitors, *Lovers' Prog.*, I, 2, and others below, p. 191.

[5] Narrated in *C. C.* as having just occurred, pp. 56–7. In Flet. they occur repeatedly, as in *Beg. Bush*, pp. 223–4, narrated ; *Doub. Marr.*, II, 104–5, and *K. Malta*, 131, on the boards. They are of a piece with Flet., who is full of wrecks, sea-adventures and pirates, as well as sailors and sea-captains, outlaws, amazons, and martial maids. See *Sea-Voy.*, *Cus. Count.*, *Martial Maid*, etc. Cf. Mass.'s *Very Woman*, *Ren.*, etc.

or robbers,[1] trials and law-cases,[2] trial by combat,[3] and, above all, duels.[4] All this is very different material from any hitherto treated by Webster, whether in the citizen comedies or in the revenge tragedies : not one of these incidents or situations (except the bare law-case) resembles any in them.

CONSTRUCTION.

But the construction is the main subject of imitation. The plot in both Beaumont and the later court-drama, as we have seen, is a fascinating, moving puzzle. Complications forming, complications resolving, or rather seeming to resolve, but running immediately into new, — how will it all end ? we ask. For the method is that of mystery and surprise. Conclusions are not foregone, intrigues are not confessed and expounded before they are executed, motives are but darkly hinted at, and disguises and concealed identity are often left as impervious to the spectator as to the characters on the boards. Issues, moreover, are not abruptly and simply decided ; they waver and librate tantalizingly before they settle.

To Webster this method of keeping one's counsel, or of keeping issues agitating, was hitherto unknown. The schemes and intrigues of the citizen-plays and the revenge-plays are blabbed out beforehand [5] : there is no diversion or suspense (except somewhat in the dénouement of *Malfi*) in the executing of them, and disguises are always betrayed to the audience from the beginning. Not so with his later plays. The trial in the *Law-Case*, for instance, is a great technical advance over that in the *White Devil;* the intent of the plaintiff is but darkly hinted at, and revealed only in open court, and the identity of the judge with the co-respondent is kept back for a climax to the whole.

---

[1] *C. C.*, pp. 27-30. This is old: it appears in *Two Gent. of Ver.* and *Cymbeline*. But it becomes one of the stock situations in the very romantic romances of B. & F., with their pastoral or sylvan scenes ; appears in *Phil.* (hence in *Cym.*, see Thorn.), and so often in later plays of Flet., as *L. F. L.*, IV, 5, and V, *Pilg.*, *Beg. Bush*, V, 1.

[2] Appear repeatedly in Flet. and Mass.

[3] End of *D. L. C. — K. Malta*, pp. 136-7 ; *Love's Cure*, end.

[4] One occurs in each play, *D. L. C.* and *C. C.*, besides the trial by combat at the end of *D. L. C.* and the duel threatened at the end of *C. C.*, p. 93. — *Lovers' Prog.*, pp. 643, 650 ; *Hon. Man's Fort.*, p. 487 ; *Beg. Bush*, 216 ; *L. F. L.*, p. 415 ; Mass. *Unnat. Com.*; etc. ; as well as a lot of duels threatened but hindered, and single combats like duels, only lacking the preliminary formal challenge, as in *M. Tr.*, *Love's Pilg.*, *Eld. Bro.*, *Love's Cure*, etc. — There is always a fight impending ; nothing furnishes so much of the business as the clatter and flash of swords. " Draws," " offers to stab himself," occur time and again in every play.

[5] *I. e.*, when there are any. Web. generally so neglects motivation (see above, p. 92), that simply nothing is said. Once, however, in connection with the dénouement of *Mal.* mentioned above, Bosola only hints at his plan, in the Fletcherian " something I will do." *V. Mal.*, p. 252.

176

And in the *Cure for a Cuckold* the emotion of suspense, hitherto almost unknown in Webster, appears in Lessingham's expectation of Clare's reply, in the search for a friend, and at the disclosure of his purpose on the field.[1] In both plays the heroes, or rather villains, hint darkly at the project in hand, almost in the stereotyped "something I will do"[2] of Fletcher and Massinger.

But Fletcher (he more than Massinger) often chose to neglect mystery and to abbreviate suspense, in order to gain effects of surprise,— vivacity of movement or intensity of situation. His characters do abrupt, inconsistent things,[3] — I mean, not that violence

---

[1] The consideration of the stage-effectiveness of individual situations in W.'s last comedies would, if there were space for it, furnish of itself sufficient proof of W.'s indebtedness to at least the first great masters at that, B. & F. There is nothing in Web. so skilfully contrived for the stage as the suspense of Lessingham's waiting for Clare's reply, under fire of the gallants' chatter and raillery, and the still greater suspense of Lessingham's meeting with Bonvile while on his fatal search for a friend. The latter sc., though by no means equal to Mass.'s version so far as regards the subjective qualities, the presentation of the contention of motives in the seeker, of desire to meet his mistress and headlong devotion in the friend, is (for a marvel) superior to it in objective quality, in mere stagecraft. There is the sharp reversal of Bonvile's impetuous entry, "Why how now *friend ?*" just when Lessingham had averred "there 's no such thing beneath the moon," and that specially well-timed entry of Annabel, Bonvile's bride, just when she is in both their minds, with its purely suggested pathos and struggle of emotions (*C. C.*, pp. 23–4). "Dover ?" cries Bonvile, as she goes out. What an opportunity for an actor! Cf. with this examples cited below, p. 186, for the stagecraft of Flet. in comic situations. See both Mass. and Flet. *passim* for tragic ones : esp. the suspense of Ordella's meeting with Thierry veiled (*Thier. & Theod.*, IV, 1) ; 4th sc. of Act III in *Lovers' Prog.*, with the well-timed, pathetic, and yet thrilling entries of Cleander, the injured husband, together with the many other sensations (voices, pistol shot, etc.) ; the sensational entry of Alberto and Cesario in *Fair Maid*, V, 3 ; the arrival of the challenge in *Lovers' Prog.*, II, 1, with its purely suggested emotions ; or such business and stagecraft as in *Fatal Dowry*, IV, 4, where Rochfort is robed, chaired, and blindfolded, to judge between his daughter and son-in-law.

[2] The set phrase, with variations such as "something I will say," etc., and generally with the addition, "but what it is I know not," in which the villain or the jealous hero darkly intimates his plot. It occurs repeatedly in Mass. ; and in doubtful partnership plays Boyle (*Eng. Stud.*, IX, 238) holds that its occurrence at such a juncture in the plot (at least in the case of a jealous hero) indicates his hand. On the lips of others than jealous heroes, however, it occurs in plays which Boyle himself assigns entirely to Flet.,— *Woman's Prize* (p. 213) and *Island Prin.* (pp. 240, 242), as also in *Lovers' Prog.* (p. 648), *K. Malta* (p. 133), and its equivalent in *Captain* (p. 635). The originator of it, then, is surely Flet., not Mass.—" I will do somewhat," etc., *C. C.*, 72 ; "I am full of thoughts, strange ones, but they 're no good ones," *D. L. C.*, 49. Cf. *D. L. C.*, p. 73.

[3] *I. e.*, things that break entirely with the person's former trend of conduct. Any fine cavils of psychology are, of course, out of the question here, for, whether in Flet. or in Beau., the characters are rather acting figures. Nor are distinctly comic, "humorous" characters to be considered. See below.

to character, so common in Elizabethan plays, to bring about a happy
dénouement, but ruptures in the middle of the action : — do with a
whole heart what they have just said they would not do [1]; attack their
friends and defend their enemies [2]; reject a lustful woman's advances
and then as warmly woo them [3]; win a coveted honor at every hazard
only to renounce it [4]; burst suddenly into love and as suddenly and
unreasonably into jealousy [5]; even deliberately renounce virtue or
vice (as the case may be) on the spot. [6] These unnatural, unexplained
changes (or *turns*, as we may conveniently call them) prove later on
to have been either pretended — mere dissembling and lying [7] — or
(the distinction is often hard to draw) final and genuine : in all cases
they are at first, and often continue to be, unjustifiable surprises and
cheats. [8] Nor are turns of plot lacking (here the surprise is in the

---

[1] *Lover's Prog.*, p. 643 b, where Lisander tells Lidian he cannot help him, Lidian
makes all he can out of that situation, grows very desperate, and starts to fight
again, whereupon Lisander does interfere.

[2] *Sp. Cur.*, p. 182, when Don Jamie takes Violante's part, and seizes his friends.
Cf. Martia's conduct in *Doub. Marr.*, p. 107 ; and Miranda's visit to Mount., which
ends in his fighting *against* his sweetheart, *K. Malta*, II, 3, 5; *Hon. Man's Fort.*,
p. 482, Dubois's hiring out against his friend.

[3] Mass. *Pict.*, III, 5, and IV, 1 ; Matthias and Honoria.

[4] *Candy*, p. 371, Antinous's surprising demand ; *Lovers' Prog.*, p. 660, Clarange's
renunciation of Olinda (cf. p. 657, where he claims her vehemently). Cf. also *Cus.
Count.*, p. 131, Guiomar's sensational relenting after her relentlessness.

[5] Of this there is no end in Flet. and Mass. The sudden falling in love is not so
significant — that is commoner in lit. generally and is to be found in Beau. (*K. N. K.*,
Tigranes) ; but such headlong plunges from love into jealousy as Demetrius's,
Gomera's, or, above all, Theodosius's, are peculiar to them. (*Hum. Lieut.*, IV, 8;
Malta, III, 2 ; *Emp. East*, IV, 5.)

[6] I do not count the repentances and confessions of the finale, which are but too
common. — See *Wife Month*, IV, 3, p. 583, ''Come home again, my frighted faith
my virtue,'' etc. ; *Valent.*, V, 3, where Maximus in one speech turns villain ; *False
One*, IV, 3, end, Septimius's backsliding ; *Pict.*, III, 6, end, ''Chastity, Thou only
art a name, and I renounce thee!'' — See, too, many conversions, suddenly and
mechanically brought about : that of Lelia, the strumpet, in the *Captain*, of Quisara
in *Isl. Prin.* (V, 2), of Donusa in the *Ren.*, and of Athenais in *Emp. East*.

[7] So, in example quoted in note 6 above from *Wife Month*, it is hard to decide
whether she had been only dissembling ; so, in *Lovers' Prog.*, it is hard to decide
whether C. had the intention of giving Olinda up at the beginning of his game.

[8] Most of the turns must be interpreted as dissemblings, — tricks to try one, etc.,—
but practised without warning to the spectator. Such are *K. Malta*, II, 3, Miranda
(cf. II, 5) ; III, 4, Mir. persuading Lucinda ; *Faith Fr.*, II, 1, Tit. scolding Ruf. ; II,
2, Armanus suing for Philadelphia's love ; *Valent.*, V, 6 f, Eudoxia acceding to
Maximus's suit ; *Wom. Pleased*, III, 1, Belvidere siding with her mother ; *Beg. Bush*,
I, 2, Wolfort's repentance ; IV, 4, Hubert dissembling with Hemp. ; *L. F. L.*, V, 1,
Dinant's threatening Lamira ; *Wife Month*, I, 1, Evanthe triumphing over Maria ;
Hon. Man's Fort., I, 3, Montague persuading the Duchess ; II, 2, Dubois ; III, 3,
Lamira's roughness with Mont. ; V, 3, where it appears that all Charlotte's wooing

outcome instead of the beginning), false reports[1] which affect the action, bloody, oracular commands to be fulfilled by the aid of sophistry[2] or startling tricks of logic and word-play,[3] false foreshadowings or auguries which bear both actor and spectator in hand,[4] and mock events of signal importance like death, stabbing, or shooting.[5] The nature and purpose of these is like that of the turns of character : both sorts are unjustifiable surprises and cheats played upon the spectator, both are made to add — beyond the condition of things in Beaumont and Fletcher — to the stir on the stage, to the number and piquancy of situations.

—— Even in the romances there is the germ of this. Beaumont (or Beaumont and Fletcher if you please) seeks sensations and does violence to character, but he plays no hoaxes and effects no disappointing

was as a proxy ; *Mons. Thom.*, III, 1, Cellide's changes with Francisco ; *Love's Pilg.*, where dissembling abounds ; most of the instances cited above, etc., Mass. : *P. L.*, III, 3, Bellisant yielding to Clar., etc. But many of these dissemblings are so sudden, so complete and perfect that they might just as well pass for the real thing, a "sudden alteration." Of this last there are some unmistakable instances : *Doub. Marr.*, III, 3, where Virolet, hitherto infatuated with his new love, now that he has won her abruptly rejects her ; see p. 178, above, note 4, Guiomar ; note 1, Lisander, etc. See *Pict.*, IV, 1, Honoria's change, and IV, 1 and 4, Matthias's ; *Bash. Lov.*, IV, 1, Lorenzo's " Stay, I feel A sudden alteration " ; ref. in note 2 above.— Of the same general dramatic effect, though without the abrupt break in character, are the frequent unjustified shiftings of the persons of the drama from the one side to the other, from the good to the bad. See esp. in *Fair Maid* the changes of Baptista : in I, 3, he commands his son in indignation to beg Alberto's pardon at any cost ; in II, 3, he is going to revenge his son's wrongs on Alberto, his son Cesario, and his whole family ; in III, 2, at close of the trial, he and his son suddenly vow constant friendship with Cesario and ' make a scene ' ; in the next scene and thereafter, without any explanation, he and his son are again at enmity with Alberto and Cesario. And see in *Isl. Prin.* how we are led, by the praises of her at every hand and by her demeanor at her first appearance, to think Quisara a blameless character, and find her shortly instigating a murder.

[1] See *Lov. Prog.*, II, 4, report of death of duellists ; IV, 4, of Clarange's death ; *K. Malta*, IV, 1, of Oriana's death ; *Cus. Count.*, II, 4, of Duarte's death *Emp. of East*, V, 2—of Paulinus's death.— All of these deceive the spectator as well as the persons of the drama ; *that* is to be understood in all this discussion.

[2] See *Fair Maid*, II, 1, p. 362, Alberto's command, which seems inevitable, but which Cesario wrests.

[3] See *Maid Mill*, IV, 2, Bellides's challenge — to be friends ; *ib.*, p. 598, Bustopha's tricks.

[4] *Sea-Voy.*, V, 4, the sensational altar and horrid music portending death ; *Ren.*, V, 3, p. 120.

[5] *K. Malta*, III, 2, and IV, 2, Oriana's ; *Mad Lover*, V, 4, Polydore's ; *P. L.*, V, 1, Montrose's ; not to mention comedies like *Woman's Prize* and *Night-Walker*. In some cases, as this last, the deception is intended by the person himself, and the turn of plot becomes one of character. *Hon. Man. Fort.*, IV, 2, pp. 492, 493, the mock stabbing and shooting.

179

surprises.[1] The effect sought in the later *turns* is the sharp dramatic reversal, and nothing is commoner in Beaumont than reversals; but his are fair and square — reversals brought about by manipulation of plot, cunning, but plain as day, — not by wrenches of character and foul play with the audience. If Philaster is minded to be temperate and just, that moment he must, of all things, set eyes on Bellario bending over Arethusa: a storm follows; there is a reversal and sensation, but by straightforward means.[2] Or his characters do extreme and sudden things, — draw, challenge, offer to kill themselves, or hurl a person into prison before any reason appears.[3] Or, where there is a mystery to disclose, they vouchsafe for a time only laconic, thrilling enigmas and paradoxes.[4] But there always *is* a reason, a disclosure, and it is not long withheld. The bark of Philaster and Arbaces may be worse than their bite — their fury greater than their disclosures, — but the one is not an empty shock of surprise nor the other a gullery. They serve to rouse, and appease, suspense. There are, indeed, some downright breaches done to character in the romances — incredible reconciliations or conversions. But they are few; they are not for this particular situation's sake but for plot; and they are not thrown into relief, but justified (as far as may be) or glozed over. Instances are Thierry's being led, through Brunhalt's lie, to condone the death of Theodoret, his brother, at her hand, that she may continue her intrigue[5]; the smoothing-over of the enmity between Philaster and the king, to lead to the happy dénouement[6] just at hand; and Melantius's bullying of Evadne into contrition and vengeance (which has even been admired for its psychology),

---

[1] The mock stabbing and shooting above, however (p. 118, note 2), is in the *Hon. Man's Fort.*, a play in which Beau. is held to have some share.

[2] *Phil.*, IV, 3. — Of such sharp, but justifiable, reversals there is plenty, of course, in the later plays of Flet. and Mass. See a striking one in *Pict.*, IV, 1, where Matthias looks at the picture. But, though not unknown to Shak. (*R. & J.*, V, 1), they are to Web. up to this Period. See Bonvile's entry at the moment of Lessingham's despair, *C. C.*, 21, and below, the comic reversals, p. 185. They are further evidence of at least a B. & F. influence, if not of the Fletcherian alone.

[3] Often, indeed, the reason is clear at the start, and the rash activity only makes a natural complication to solve, when swords are bare. So *M. Tr.*, III, 2, p. 14 a. But often (as in this very sc., pp. 14 a and b, Amintor) the character insists on action first, explanation afterward: here, only after seven speeches do we learn the motive. Cf. Arbaces's wild, enigmatic deportment on laying eyes on Panthea, *K. N. K.*, III, 1. — There is nothing of this sort, of course, in the older drama, as Shak.

[4] See Evadne's cold, thrusting speeches in *M. Tr.*, II, 1; Arethusa's tantalizing coyness, *Phil.*, I, 2; Gobrias's disclosures, *K. N. K.*, V, 4.

[5] *Thier. & Theod.*, p. 417. Very discordant with Thierry's kindliness toward his brother. See p. 409 b, etc.

[6] *Phil.*, V, 3, end.

to make way for the very telling situations which ensue.[1] So, too, with the few dissemblings and deceits practised : they are purely for construction and plot's sake, and are either announced to the spectator at the time or are of themselves perfectly apparent.[2] Of real breaches in character, then, Beaumont and Fletcher make, when they perpetrate them, no sensational capital, —but only (in a fair way) of manœuvers of "business" and dialogue, by way of attaining effects of suspense [3].——

Of this clap-trap of Fletcher's Webster has plenty. He has perhaps even some of the Beaumontesque sensations. Bonvile turns the tables well enough by suddenly defying Lessingham, though he has a poor reason to give for it and he gives it rather promptly [4]; but breaches done to character are here not glozed over, nor are dissemblings intimated to the audience, nor are there any tantalizing, enigmatical disclosures. Webster has felt the touch of Fletcher. As deceptive to both actor and spectator, and as sensational, as any of Fletcher's, are Bonvile's dissembling with Clare and Jolenta's with Romelio [5]; and, though he has no deliberate, formal renunciations of good or evil, those of his turns which are made in all sincerity, such as Clare's rejoicing at Bonvile's death [6] or Jolenta's transference of affection to Ercole,[7] are almost as abrupt and unnatural.[8] And there are tricks of construction, besides. There are ambiguous commands and

---

[1] *M. Tr.*, IV, 1.

[2] *Phil.*, p. 36, Dion's lie ; p. 44, Arethusa's ; *Thier. & Theod.*, p. 420, Martell's ; p. 409 b, Thierry's roughness ; *Cup. Rev.*, pp. 386-7, Leucippus's ; *Thier. & Theod.*, p. 417, Brunhalt's, where, though not explicitly avowed, all is plain to the spectator.

[3] What is said of the work of B. & F. means, as always in this discussion, only the romances (see above, p. 172). Purely comic work, of course, though of so early a date and so certainly Beaumont's as the *Woman Hater* and *Burning Pestle*, cannot be considered ; for there, in the midst of "humorous" and comic extravagance, we must expect starts and inconsistencies. And to include any of the other, later plays in which Beau. may have had a share, —the *K. of Malta*, the *Hon. Man. Fort.*, the *Captain*, and the rest,—with all their problems of date and authorship to settle, would in a work of these limits be impossible. At any rate, my contention is only that Web. imitated the *later*, the Fletcherian type. Now in the later partnership plays, as all will admit, Flet. had the main share, and they belong in all particulars to the type as I have sketched it. The romances, on the other hand, are dominated by Beau.

[4] *C. C.*, p. 48.   [5] *C. C.*, p. 75 ; *D. L. C.*, 62-3.

[6] *C. C.*, 70. She had just lamented it ; and has no reason for the change.

[7] *D. L. C.*, 65. One may *suppose* that Jolenta changes out of jealousy.

[8] Others are : *D. L. C.*, 118, Romelio's longing for the churchman, etc., after his cynical, boorish rejection of him on pp. 115, 116 ; *A. & V.*, 153, Virg.'s sudden turn against his soldiers ; 201, his stabbing without a word of warning and with a play on words ; *C. C.*, 69, Clare's wheeling about ; 70, "Why now sir, I do love you," etc. ; 75-6, Clare's hate ; 72, Bonvile's hate or jealousy.

messages,[1] with various juggling interpretations. There are tricks played with words and logic,[2] and even purely dramatic complications[3] solved by them. There is one false report of a hero's death, made merely for the sensation, and a dirge and sinister forebodings for a man who comes off hale and hearty.[4] The whole round, then, of Fletcher's sensational artifices is represented in Webster's last three plays.[5]

Of such tricks and clap-trap there is practically nothing in Webster's previous work. True, there is a deceptive, wretched sophism tossed back by Lodovico at Giovanni,[6] and there are sensations like Camilla's rushing at Flamineo sword in hand and Flamineo's later pretense at dying.[7] But no more; and even these, as we were disposed to think, are traces of the incipient influence[8] of Beaumont and Fletcher.

THE COMIC ELEMENT.

As we should be led by the preceding investigation to expect, the comic element of this class of tragi-comedy inheres in the Action. It lies, not in the conception of human character, but in the play of dialogue, the business and by-play, the incidents and situations. There

---

[1] Jolenta's message to Ercole, probably designed to mislead and so bring about this good situation, *D. L. C.*, 107–8 ; Clare's ambiguous command, interpreted so differently by herself and the young men. See above, p 165.

[2] *C. C.*, 47, privy coat; 48–9, interpretation of command and play on the notion "dead friend " ; 87, wounded ; 89, give ground ; *A. & V.*, 132, Appius's play on the word "banish " ; 207, Virg.'s "surrender " ; *D. L. C.*, 107, "begot by her brother," in conformity to her promise, p. 65.

[3] *C. C.*, 49, 87, 89. [4] *D. L. C.*, 114–15.

[5] It must be observed, however, that some of the abruptness in these plays is not new, is due only to that crabbedness and dearth of rhetoric, and to that neglect of motivation, we noted in the revenge-plays. Flamineo kills his brother without wasting words (*W. D.*, p. 108) : this, too, is a sensation and surprise. But mark that with Virginius there is a technical advance. Flamineo when last on the stage had quarreled with and challenged his brother ; he now rushes in and slays him. Virg. remains throughout on the stage ; speaks often, utters a long last farewell, and never hints directly or aside what he is about to do : the slaying comes, though a shocking surprise, as a fine stage-climax. Another point : most of the turns in these late plays of Web. lack such climactic effect. Of Flet. and Mass., on the other hand, it is a characteristic ; it is their way of redeeming the loss in suspense and mystery which the surprise method entails. Clarange's generosity comes as the striking close to a rather extended, evidently selfish, intrigue ; so with Antinous's in *Candy* (see above, p. 178, note 4) ; so with Virolet's rejection of Martia in *Doub. Marr.*, Guiomar's marrying Rutilio in *Cust. Count.*, etc., etc. Compared with such construction, Web.'s use of turns, as in *C. C.*, 69–71, is decidedly jerky, inartistic. Yet we remember that just now, in the suspense of the law-case and of the meeting of Lessingham with Bonvile, he was learning his first lessons in the subtle grouping of events.

[6] *W. D.*, 142. "*Lod. By thine.* " etc.

[7] *W. D.*, 109, 134–5. [8] See above, p. 118.

is little humor, much wit, and — thanks to the abundant business, the varied, rapid complications and resolutions, the turns, quirks, and tricks of construction — a great number of comic doings and changes. This sort of comedy is practically Fletcher's creation ; it is not to be found, at any rate, in Beaumont. Beaumont's (and Shakspere's, too), had been a comedy of character, of humor ; and whenever the comedy was shifted into the business or construction proper, it turned out little less than buffoonery, horse-play, or mere imitation of the ancients. The dramaturgic sense had not yet been sufficiently developed and refined to invent comic incident much more subtle than cudgellings of cowards and blind-man's-buff tricks, or to bring about those swift, significant combinations, reversals, and diversions which make the light and airy comedy of Fletcher.[1] Not that this is the whole of Fletcher's comic sphere. He has plenty of comic characterization, too, — for instance, those freaks of comic extravagance so characteristic of him, the combative non-combatant Lawyer La Writ, the brave coward the Humourous Lieutenant, as well as the steady "humors" of the coward, the angry man, or the fussy man, — and he reinstated the old-fashioned fool and clown. But even in these it is interesting to discover, on analysis, how much of the comic effect is really expressed by the situations, the incidents, and the suggested business : how La Writ or Galoshio in order to be laughable must be pictured by the reader on the stage,[2] and how often their speeches are funny because pat or surprising,[3] and, detached, are nowise so significant or enjoyable as Falstaff's or Dogberry's are. Indeed, the treatment of the clown in Fletcher's hands measures better than anything else the great change comedy undergoes in his hands : the clown (or fool) is no longer episodic, as all Shakspere's are, but has a real place among the dramatis personæ and in the plot,[4] and, for comic effect, he depends no longer upon mere talk, but upon his doings on the stage in specific situations, — falling from a ladder at a pistol-

---

[1] See for all this the *Woman Hater, Knight of the Burning Pestle*, the poltroons and braggarts Bessus, Protaldy, Pharamond in the romances, and the rough treatment they undergo. (I do not mean to imply that Flet. had no hand in the comedy of characters just mentioned ; it is enough, for my purposes, that this sort of thing hardly appears in the later plays.)

[2] See *L. F. L.*, II, 1 and 2 ; *Nice Val.*, III, 1 and 2.

[3] The patness of a remark like the 3 Gent.'s, *Pilg.*, III, 6, p. 605, as in the madhouse the visitor Pedro, the Pilgrim, hearing and seeing Alinda, cries, " O my soul ! " — " What fit's this? The Pilgrim's off the hooks too ! " : or surprises such as Bustopha's (*Maid Mill*, IV, 2, p. 598 a) in the startling pauses to his tale.

[4] As appears especially in the Fool's appearing as fool, not merely with master or mistress, but with any of the characters. See, on this and the whole subject, Eckhardt, *Lust. Person*, 295 f.

shot unwounded, kicking a still more cowardly master, lugging in the heavy dinner, scared to death in the forest, or struggling in vain to extricate himself from his rôle in the antimasque when it comes to a matter of reality.[1] But comic effect is with Fletcher not the business of any one character, whether freak or fool : it is almost purely objective, a matter of complication and resolution, a comic *surprise*. It may be a sudden turning of the tables on the hero or his enemies, or a bugaboo scare put to flight, or a death from which one rises and takes to his legs, or a sudden discovery of a disguise or dissipation of an illusion.[2] Action, then, stage-fitness, deft use and manipulation of specially histrionic and scenic (rather than poetic) means, distinguish the Fletcherian comic art.

Of this sort of thing there had hitherto been nothing in Webster[3] : the *Devil's Law-Case* and the *Cure for a Cuckold* show the only examples. In the former play the comedy (what there is in that sour and sombre play) is still somewhat one of character, as in the remarks of the lawyer's clerk, Sanitonella, and of the waiting-woman. But the sudden changes in point of view wrought upon the surgeons, and at another time upon Contilupo, by the glitter of gold,[4] are, though well-worn motives, examples of objective, acting comedy, and the sensational disclosure in the law-case (to the delight of his scapegrace son, and to the discomfiture of the woman and her party) of the exemplary judge himself as the putative co-respondent, is, technically at least, altogether in the spirit of Fletcher. For not only are there comic instances in Fletcher of the efficaciousness of gold with men's memories or opinions (most notable of which is that delightful one in the *Spanish Curate*[5]), and abundant sensational disclosures of identity or discoveries of disguise just at the critical moment, where they solve the complication,[6] but (what is more important) the comic effect is in both cases produced in the same way as the Fletcherian, — by stage-craft rather than by characterization, by quick and deft change in the one case, by mystery, suspense, and skillful clapping together of incongruities in the climax, in the other.

---

[1] Soto in *Wom. Pleased*, I, 3 ; Galoshio in *Nice Val.*, III, 2 ; Shorthose in *Wit without Money*, IV, 5 ; Boor in *Beg. Bush*, V, 1 ; Bustopha in *Maid Mill*, II, 2.

[2] See the examples below, p. 186.

[3] The citizen plays, as we have seen, are thoroughly Dekker's ; and the comic effect in them depends on humor of character, tricks pre-announced, boisterous business like the trouncing of the Bawd and locking up of Bellamont, not on deft, vivacious handling of the action. — In the subsequent discussion, the *D. L. C.*, though itself influenced by Flet., has to stand, in default of any purely Websterian comedy, as a standard to measure the Flet. influence in the later *C. C.*

[4] *D. L. C.*, pp. 58, 78.   [5] II, 1, Leandro with Lopez and Diego.

[6] *Wom. Pleased*, V, 2, Claudio's ; *Cus. Count.*, V, 5, Duarte's, etc.

It is only in the *Cure for a Cuckold*, however, that the Fletcherian comic art comes fully into play. While the young tyro Rochfield — the "honest thief" — is trying gently to disengage Annabel's bracelets from her arms, she draws his sword.[1] Here there is hardly any humor of character; the comic effect (enhanced, indeed, by such considerations as that of the appropriateness of the slip in a young gentleman committing his first theft upon a handsome young woman) lies in the sudden, laughable reversal, and in the lively business and by-play involved. The same is to be said of a later scene, at Annabel's house. When Rochfield hesitates to accept the gold, she calls her father and friends, who had just gone out. He thinks, and we think, she is about to divulge his attempt at robbery : she only begs them to welcome her friend.[2] Here again the fun lies all in the action — the momentarily serious complication, quickly, happily resolved — and in the chance given for lively, amusing acting on the part of the arch Annabel, concerned old father, and shaking thief. It is just such a situation as one of Fletcher's — now serious, now comic : it has the true light and graceful stage-fun, which is but suggested in the printed page and lacks any specially human character or meaning. Both situations, indeed, may have been borrowed from him : in the *Elder Brother*[3] there is a disarming and a comic turning of the tables, and in the *Spanish Curate*[4] there is a similar, harmless scare given a suitor when Amaranta calls her husband.

But a matter of borrowing is of less importance : the main thing is, that the spirit of Fletcher, the great comic poet, is fallen on Webster, the great tragic poet, — the gift for comedy in incident and situation. For, that this is true these last instances in the *Cure for a Cuckola* seem to me to prove. The sourness, the grimness, the Marstonian tone, is gone ; something of the deftness and gaiety of Fletcher — the exuberance and hilarity of fancy were too much for Webster — has come. In the *Devil's Law-Case* the comic success of the author was perhaps greater in the character portrayed — the humorous disgust of the lawyer's clerk,

> Uds foot, we are spoiled :
> Why my client's proved an honest woman,[5] —

than in the stage sensation just then attained : in the *Cure for a Cuckold* it is all in the situations, in his stagecraft. So with Fletcher in

---

[1] *C. C.*, 29.
[2] *C. C.*, 41-2. Web. characteristically repeats this motive. See p. 40, Annabel and Rochfort.
[3] IV, 3. Cf. *Rule a Wife*, V, 4, Estifania showing a pistol.
[4] III, 4. The situation and the handling are practically identical.
[5] *D. L. C.*, 98.

dozens of situations : as when Lurcher suddenly presents his astonished mistress to his astonished friend Wildbrain [1] ; or when, equally astonished, Cleremont meets his terror of a bedfellow face to face [2] ; or when destitute Valentine bursts upon the gaze of his censors in fresh finery [3] ; or when the shrew-tamer, at being mourned by his mate for his life, not his death, rises groaning from the bier [4] ; or when Oldcraft overreaches himself in the artfulness of his presenting Sir Gregory [5] ; or when Bustopha struggles in vain to make it clear that the play is over and real life begun. [6] Here is the same delight in abstract and impersonal comedy, as we might call it, — the comedy of incident and situation, — and the same quick alternation of the comical with the serious.

CHARACTERS.

The characters are Fletcherian. They belong to Fletcher's conventionalized types of ladies, gentlemen, and gallants, — the slavish young lover as hero, the cruel mistress as heroine, the merry old man as uncle or father, and the faithful-faithless friend. [7] So at least in the *Cure for a Cuckold*. In the *Law-Case* there is still attention given to original characterization, as in the scoundrelly, cynical, and melancholy Romelio, the droll lawyer's clerk Sanitonella, and the waiting-woman ; though even here, perhaps, something of the Fletcherian appears in the characters of the young men and women, Contarino and Ercole, Jolenta and Angiolella. Something of it appears, too, in *Appius and Virginia ;* Virginius, as we shall see, is one of Fletcher's blunt and noble soldiers, a replica of Archas [8] : but what other characters are distinct enough to deserve the name are, though conventional enough (as Numitorius, who represents the caution of old age), at the same time stereotyped, colorless, not specially of the stamp of Fletcher.

What are these types (new to Webster every one), as best exemplified in the *Cure for a Cuckold?*

First, there is the hero, a young lover (as always in Fletcher and Massinger, for the Lears, the Macbeths, and even the Othellos, as

---

[1] *Night Walker*, V, 1.
[2] *L. F. L.*, III, 3, p. 426 b.
[3] *Wit without Money*, IV, 1.
[4] *Woman's Prize*, V, 4.
[5] *Wit at Several Weap.*, I, 1, p. 331. Oldcraft introduces Cunningham to his niece as her future husband, then Sir Gregory Fop, to delight her by the contrast. The contrast works in the opposite way ; the niece thinks quite innocently, and to Oldcraft's despair, that it is *now* that her uncle is joking.

[6] *Maid Mill*, II, 2, p. 589. Cf., for quick alternation of comical and serious, Bustopha's scaring of old Julio, IV, 2, p. 598.

[7] There are a few constantly repeated types in the B. & F. romances (see Thorndike, chap. vii), but these of the Flet. and Mass. tragi-comedies are somewhat different.
[8] See below, p. 192, note.

heroes, have left the stage for good) who slavishly worships and obeys his mistress, and yet, just after he has won her favor, falls into a furious jealousy of her. As loud as were his praises of her and her sex at the beginning, are his railings at the end. He served her then, now he goes about to injure her. He was the hero, now he is almost a villain. Such are Demetrius and Gomera in Fletcher [1]; such, more exactly, Leosthenes, Matthias, Theodosius, and Sforza in Massinger.[2] Such, with less of fury and rhetoric, is Webster's Lessingham.[3]

Then, there is the imperious heroine, scornful and "cruel" it may be, or proud and wayward, who hates a lover on principle, on the one hand, or who will tolerate no jealousy, domination, or rivalry, on the other. Of the one sort is Webster's Clare, of the other his Annabel. Such are the Quisara, Calis, Scornful Lady, and Celia of Fletcher, and the Marcelia, Leonora, Cleora, Honoria, and Almira of Massinger.[4]

Thirdly, there is the merry old man (Woodroff in the *Cure for a Cuckold*), father or uncle of the young folk and much interested in their pleasures, who is equally impetuous in merriment, anger, hospitality, or bounty. He speaks fondly of his own youth, and considers himself youthful still. His manner is blunt and his jokes coarse. Such are Miramont and Dorilaus in Fletcher,[5] and Durazzo and Eubulus in Massinger.[6]

---

[1] *Hum. Lieut.*, IV, 8; *K. Malta*, III, 2.

[2] *Bond.*, IV, 3; *Pict.*, IV, 1; *Emp. East*, IV, 5; *Milan*, III, 3. As in *C. C.*, jealousy is a favorite motive to give a further diversion to the action just at the point where it seemed to be coming to a happy end. Like Less. all of these sorry heroes burst wildly, completely into jealousy as the plot demands (in Leosthenes, indeed, Mass. shows beforehand jealousy of temperament); all curse the sex, and wonder that any should "trust a woman." (*C. C.*, 71.)

[3] Less.'s stronger motive, at p. 71 and thereafter, is not horror at Clare's sin but jealousy of Bonvile. Flet.'s jealous heroes do not, indeed, enter upon a career of base intrigue; their repentance comes soon. But Flet. has quite as many cases of heroes and heroines turning villain. See the princess Quisara in *Isl. Prin.*, who, after all the fuss about her at the start, turns murderess (III, 1); the dastardly changes in Cesario (*Fair Maid*), etc.

[4] Of the scornful sort, who impose cruel or bloody commands like Clare's, are Quisara in *Isl. Prin.*, III, 1, Calis in *Mad Lover*, I, 2, Lady in *Scorn. Lady*, I, 1, Leonora in *P. L.*, II, 2; of the wayward sort, who meet signs of jealousy with an aside, "Ill fit you" (*Hum. Lieut.*, p. 257; *Bond.*, p. 92), and an aggravating demeanor such as Annabel's, are Celia in *Hum. Lieut.*, IV, 8, Cleora in *Bond.*, IV, 3, Marcelia in *Milan*, IV, 3. Of the same stripe as these last are Honoria in *Pict.*, who deliberately set out to conquer the man who praised his wife above her, and Almira in *Very Wom.*, who rejected one suitor with all manner of abuse, and later, when he appeared disguised as a Turkish slave, fell boundlessly in love with him. And *all* these are monsters of caprice or cruelty; though heroines, mere puppets of the plot.

[5] *Eld. Bro., Lovers' Prog., passim.*

[6] *Guardian, Pict., passim.* Eubulus is, however, only a counsellor in the court, not a relative. Flet. has plenty of bluff "merry men" in his plays, as the Master in the *Sea-Voyage*, Norandine in *K. Malta.*

187

Finally, there is the group of the hero's friends (the four gallants Raymond, Eustace, Lionel, and Grover, in the *Cure for a Cuckold*), who take no part in the play, as one may say, for themselves. This is an institution of the Beaumont and Fletcher romances, continued and further developed by Fletcher and Massinger. The persons of the group are generally of the same rank as the hero (when he is not king or prince) — gentlemen, gallants, captains, or, if the scene be at court, courtiers or lords. Under this general designation they are bracketed together as one in the dramatis personae [1] ; — a matter not without significance, for they enter together, go out together, often talk together alone. They are always named (not numbered, as First Lord, Second Gentleman), and often have in themselves some noticeable individuality ; but in their sympathies, their moral bias, they are one. They are the chorus of the play. They explain the opening situation, give an inkling of the character of the persons of the drama, or describe them, and sympathize with, sometimes help, the hero. But their activity is a minor one — the running of errands, the raising of insurrections off the stage, the furnishing of information to the characters and the audience. Nothing happens to them, they neither marry nor die. They serve these merely functional ends, and, by their lively conversation, their banter and gossip, furnish atmosphere and background to the drama. As used in the *Cure for a Cuckold*, such a group is something new in Webster : Roderigo and Grisolan in *Malfi*, and Antonelli and Gasparo in the *White Devil*, are not friends of leading characters, but dependants ; and the part they fill is purely mechanical, "supernumerary." In Fletcher it is common, and it is to be found in Massinger. [2]

---

[1] This of itself determines nothing : groups of the sort we speak of are always bracketed, but so are the true heroes (or scoundrels) in *P. L.*

[2] Most often, the group is made up of three. It often has at the beginning to give the audience the key to the remarkable situation on which the play is based, as in *Cup. Rev.*, I, 1, Dorialus, Agenor, and Nisus before the entry of the principal persons (cf. *C. C.*, I, 1, p. 12) ; or to describe the bent and bias of the characters, as in *Phil.*, I, 1, Dion, Cleremont, and Thrasilene, after entry of King, Pharamond, etc. This description of the *moral* character of the persons of the drama falls away decidedly in the later plays (see above, p. 173) ; yet in *Wife Month* there is an instance.— A list of these groups follows : *Sp. Cur.* — Angelo, Milanes, and Arsenio ; *Coxcomb* — Uberto, Pedro, Silvio, "three merry Gentlemen, Friends to Ricardo " ; *Maid in Mill* — Gostanzo, Geraldo, Philippo, "three Gentlemen, Friends to Julio " ; *Cup. Rev.* and *Phil.*, see above ; *Mad Lover* — Eumenes, Polybius, and Pelius, "three Captains " ; *Pilg.* — Curio, Seberto, "friends to Alphonso " ; *Wife Month* — Camillo, Cleanthes, Menallo, "three honest Court Lords " ; *Corinth* — Neanthes Sosicles, Eraton (but they sympathize with and help the villain prince). Mass.'s *Guardian* — Camillo, Lentulo, Donato, "three Neapolitan gentlemen."

Nor is Fletcher's or Massinger's influence lacking in Webster's style and metre; yet (as with Shakspere in his Beaumont and Fletcher period [1]) less markedly than in characterization and plot, — in a vaguer, and often negative, way. Under it Webster loses in this Period his wealth of figure and reflection and his 'frequency of sentence,' which had clogged the action, and takes on something of the jejuneness and colorlessness of Massinger. But while he loses he some ways gains. He gets rid of the old crabbedness and obscurity, of the old bouts at baiting and abuse, [2] and cultivates Massinger's perspicuous eloquence and declamatory ring. The eloquent, tender peal of Lessingham's speech to Bonvile

> O my friend,
> The noblest ever man had! etc. [3]

and of Virginius's last farewell, [4] the ease of transition and variety of movement of the first dialogue between Clare and Lessingham, [5] are like nothing else in Webster, and are echoes of Fletcher and Massinger. Yet, though new in Webster, they are his own; and though they echo the masters of the day, they show none of their special tricks and mannerisms. Webster follows the lead of the dramatic rhetoricians of his day after his own fashion.

The same is to be said of his metre. Webster does not cultivate the two-word feminine ending and end-stopt line [6] of Fletcher, any more than did Shakspere before him, or the weak ending and run-on line [7] of Massinger: he follows these poets only in the general way of avoiding prose and rime, [8] and of smoothing off his verse. He has least

---

[1] See Thorn., *Inf.*, *B. & F.*, pp. 142–5. — Perhaps in the matter of easier dramatic sentence-form (for the old oratorical one), in increase of colloquialisms, parentheses, feminine endings, but hardly in more.

[2] To be found in every play of Webster's unaided work but the *C. C.* See p. 141.

[3] *C. C.*, p. 45.

[4] *D. L. C.*, pp. 200–1.

[5] *C. C.*, 9–11. Cf. with this conversations of somewhat similar theme and manner in Mass.'s *Very Wom.*, I, 1, pp. 336–7; Flet.'s *Fair Maid*, I, 1, pp. 356–7. There is the same urbane manner, and easy flow and transition. Contr. *D. L. C.*, III, 3, where the rough rhythm, the abrupt, crabbed speech and retort of *Malfi* yet persist.

[6] Flet. has 40 % fem. endings, 20 % enjambement (Schipper, II, p. 320 f); acc. to Boyle (*Eng. Stud.*, V, 87), 50–80 % fem. endings. By two-word fem. endings, I mean such as *told you*, etc. See Schipper for an account of this in Flet.

[7] Of run-on lines, Mass. has seldom less than 30 %, of light and weak endings, 5–7 %, of fem. endings generally 40 %. — Boyle, *ib.*

[8] There is *no* prose in Flet.'s *Rule a Wife, Hum. Lieut., Mad Lover, Loyal Sub.* — Schipper, II, 324, 329. Even letters are often in verse, as in *Lovers' Prog., Maid Mill* (*Works*, II, pp. 583, 641) — Dagegen haben Mass. und Flet. in ihren spätern Dramen keine prosa, Boyle in Gelbke's *Engl. Bühne*, I, p. 31.

rime, least prose, least superfluous syllables and epical cesuras, in his latest plays [1] ; — that is all tables and figures will show. And yet

[1] No account of Web.'s development can be complete without some examination of his metre, but, as still more important matters have had to be excluded (see pref.), I have touched on it (as here and above, p. 113) only to illustrate purely literary matters. Moreover, a detailed investigation of it is already at hand, that of Meiners (Halle, 1893), which, though it is not even in a mechanical way satisfactory, labors for the most part only under difficulties which obstruct and invalidate any metrical research at this day. He uses an unedited, very uncertain text, much of which (as in *Malfi*), though printed by Hazlitt as verse, deserves (as by Vaughan) to be printed as prose ; he has no canons at all to guide him in the counting of the total number of lines (short lines of dialogue, which may or may not be combinable into whole lines), against which the percentages are to be reckoned ; nor has he any good canons for distinguishing run-on from end-stopt lines. As to these last, indeed (those of the St. Petersburg Shakspere Circle, *Eng. Stud.*, III, 473 f), Dr. Meiners does much worse than to follow them, and arrives at such remarkable figures for enjambement in the *W. D.* as .85%, in *Mal.*, 1.7%, etc. ; but this is the sort of thing that will continue to occur and make investigations in Eng. metre almost worthless to any other than the investigator himself, until the rules given by the St. P. Circle — a step in the right direcion — have been amplified and modified to suit our needs. (See the strictures of G. König, *Shakspere's Vers.*, only he goes to the other extreme, and will have no rules.)

I give a table below which shows W.'s development in the important metrical phenomena. The figures are my own, except when followed by an M. (Meiners), and are founded in each case on the examination of from 500 to 700 ll. (short ll. counted only when reconstructible into long ll., except when *within* the bounds of a speech of 5 accent verse), according to the size of scenes and acts.

	run-on ll.	l. and weak end.	ep. cesura.	extra syll. excl. ep. ces.	fem. end.	ratio of two-word to total fem.	rime.
W. D. . .	36.28%	.32% M.	2.88% M.	18.6%	31.4% M.	10.84%	4.5 %
Mal. . .	49.95%	.95% M.	5. % M.	35.5%	32.6% M.	20. %	2.1 %
D. L. C. .	35.8 %	.76% M.	5.5 % M.	29.8%	32.6% M.	15.75%	1.03%
A. &. V.	28.76%	.53% M.	1.5 % M.	11.8%	27.1% M.	13.13%	5.6 %
C. C. . .	28.88%	1.56%	1.4 %	10.9%	19.5%	14.76%	1.17%

Prose. Most in *Mal.*, least in *C. C.* (Web.'s part of course ; Rowley's is nearly all prose) ; next to the least in *A. & V.* — Meiners (p. 38) says *A. & V.* has least, but he ignores *C. C.* altogether (*v. infra*) ; and the fact is that *A. & V.* has solid prose in the clown and serving-men scenes, while Web.'s *C. C.* has no prose passage beyond two lines in extent.

Cf. Meiners's table. All the figures for the *C. C.* I have had to add, for he considers the play doubtful ; his figures for run-on ll. mean nothing to me ; and his figures for rime I have reduced by eliminating the " weak " (unaccented) rime (*sick* and

190

there can be no doubt that it was the new, potent influence of the day, that of Fletcher and Massinger, which turned Webster's earlier asperity into verse so mellow as the first dialogue in the *Cure for a Cuckold* or that on the sands of Calais.

MORALS.

Finally, Webster shows the baneful influence of the day — that of Fletcher and Massinger — in morals. Even in that sort of morals we immediately think of when the word is used in connection with literature, Webster once in the *Cure for a Cuckold* [1] sinks lower — nearer to Fletcher and Massinger — than at any other time. But this increased pruriency is only one phase of a deeper evil. The root of the matter is, that there is grown up in Fletcher and Massinger out of the life of the day (on the one hand) an indifference, as I have said, a purblindness to moral relations of any sort, except as the proprieties, the expediencies; and within their art (on the other hand), the baneful convention of the subservience of character to plot. [2] This latter, purely dramatic, esthetic, immorality appears, for instance, in "bloody" commands such as that of Leonora in the *Parliament of Love*, or of the Duchess in *Women Pleased*, or of Quisara in the *Island Princess*, or of Alberto in the *Fair Maid of the Inn:* for neither Fletcher nor Massinger nor anybody in their Caroline audience approved of such things except as making situations in dramas. The real, *ethical* immorality (if I may use the expression) appears more unmistakably in what is not essential to plot, — in the view, constantly avowed or implied in these plays, that virtue is but credit and reputation, that any woman (and of course any man) may be persuaded, that one may talk and think as he pleases and yet be virtuous and the hero.

The two influences react and shade into each other indistinguishably : what concerns us is the results. Moral forces are employed by Fletcher and Massinger, moral standards are observed, only when it suits the author's plan ; and then, in an empty, frivolous way. Crimes and criminal intents, conversions and repentances, are freely, irresponsibly used — like pigments — to vary and enliven the action. One

---

physic, forego me and *pity*, etc.), most of which in Web. (though not in Chapman) is purely accidental and unnoticeable.

The remarkable increase in rime in *A. & V.* may be due to the number of saws and apothegms (in which most of it occurs), or may be due to the example of Heywood in *Lucrece*. (See Sect. III, below.) But H. rimes very differently.

[1] *C. C.*, 74. It is the grosser in that it is conversation held between some of the best characters.

[2] Both sorts appear, of course, in the romances, but (see above, pp. 172–4, 179–80) in less gross form.

man may kill another and never bother to repent,[1] or repent in five minutes and pass for righteous.[2] Heroes rage in hypocritical fury against women whom they not even suspect of doing worse than they themselves[3]; heroines who have committed adultery at heart are complacently pure.[4] And all are treated with no justice. The bad generally end by repenting and saving their skins, and — what is worse — the good by pardoning.

The same words may be used of Webster's morality in this Period. In the earlier Period, as we have seen, it was he that infused a higher morality and a truer dramatic justice into the old, convention-ridden revenge-play. Now he weakens and conforms. Of the two heroines, Jolenta, out of jealousy of her mother, consents to own Romelio's bastard child as her own, and Clare commands her lover to commit murder and rejoices when she learns he has done so; and the hero, Lessingham, undertakes to kill his dearest friend, and, when saved that, tries to destroy his happiness. As for the outcome, Lessingham and Clare perfunctorily repent; Leonora, too, repents, — she who had tried to marry her daughter off to one she hated in order to keep her daughter's lover for herself, and revenged herself on her son by going to the lengths of perjury and robbery; — Romelio, though a villain of the deepest dye, has only to restore stolen property and marry; and Virginius, the child-slayer, relents toward the lustful tyrant when he has him in his power, and thinks on second trial he would do better. What a fall for the stern justicer of human error — of the folly of Antonio and the Duchess, of the crimes of Bosola and the Arragonian brethren, — thus to be playing with it as in a puppet-show![5]

---

[1] Silvio in *Wom. Pleased*, I, 3, who thinks he has killed his friend Claudio, and never bothers about it afterward.

[2] The atrocious Lelia's indignant complacence: *Captain*, V, 5, p. 644, "I have a heart as pure as any woman's."

[3] See Matthias in *Pict.*, IV, 1, in the midst of his futile intrigue with Honoria.

[4] Honoria and Sophia in *Pict.*; Calista in *Lovers' Prog.*

[5] Some remaining points of similarity between W.'s plays and Flet.'s. In *D. L. C.*: analogues of the incident of Romelio's stabbing, cited above, pp. 154-5; Romelio's appearing in the garb of a Jewish doctor before Contarino's surgeons with the pretense of a remedy, strikingly like a scene in Mass.'s *Milan* (*D. L. C.*, pp. 53-6; *Milan*, V, 2, p. 72); Leonora's vying with her daughter for Contarino's favor, like Antigonus's with his son, in *Hum. Lieut.*; false report of the death of the hero after a duel like one in *Lovers' Prog.*, II, 4; trial by combat as dénouement, like that in *K. of Malta* and *Love's Cure*; Jolenta's revealing herself to her lover in masque-like verse at close of play, like Belvedere's in *Wom. Pleased*; etc. In *A. & V.*: likeness between the rough, honest general Virginius, who brings a false report of good treatment at hands of the authorities to the mutinying army, and toward it is relentless, and the general, Archas, in the *Loy. Sub.*, who does likewise, and, besides, is once at point of slaying his son (*A. & V.*, 151-6; *Loy. Sub.*, IV, 7; cf. V, 6 and 7);

But he does not all descend; it is only the esthetic immorality that he accepts. Dramatic injustice, and violent, irresponsible treatment of character — dissemblings, starts, conversions, relapses — he adopts as bound up inextricably with the Fletcherian style. Not so the supererogatory evil — the obscene prudery and polite obscenity, the shallow deference to ideals and frivolous cynicism, dashed from the lips of Fletcher's and Massinger's characters. Webster's speak foully, but straightforwardly; they do not cant. They forego the glittering phrases of chivalry; they have no word to say of "lawful pleasures" and "temperate flames"[1]; they neither plume themselves on their virtue, nor canvass it in themselves or another; they drop no hint of conceiving chastity and honor in mere terms of credit, reputation, or hearsay. Such lengths, fortunately, were yet beyond Webster; his truckling to Favor would not carry him so far. In the *Devil's Law-Case* he yet keeps much of his tragic dignity; his Romelio meditates like his Bosola[2]; and if there be a greater measure of cynicism and less of melancholy now in his irony, as he speaks of the heralds[3] laughing in their black raiment, or makes the waiting-woman, who has grown old together with her mistress 'talking nothing and doing less,' confess that they have spent their life

> in that which least concerns life,
> Only in putting on our clothes,[4]

that is only natural now as he joins company with frivolous Fletcher and the court players. And in the *Cure for a Cuckold*, where he is more than ever a Fletcherian, he remonstrates faintly still: he has lost his old notions, he has taken up their colorless, conventional ones, but he eschews their specious ones.

III. THE INFLUENCE OF SHAKSPERE AND HEYWOOD ON *APPIUS AND VIRGINIA*.

SHAKSPERE.

The influence of Fletcher and Massinger was not the only one of this Period: Webster conformed with the present, but he reverenced the past; and with as much academic research as that with which he

---

introduction of sentimental ideas into prehistoric Rome, use of Marcus beyond authority as go-between (cf. Rufinus), like *Faithful Friends*. In *C. C.*: romantic story of a sea-fight told in *Beg. Bush*, IV, 3 (cf. *C. C.*, 56–7), and the merry old man's impetuous anger against the impugner of his daughter's honor (*Lov. Prog.*, IV, 3, p. 653, and *C. C.*, 88–9). In none of the above cases can W.'s indebtedness be proved: they serve only to show the general closeness of relation between his work at this time and the fashionable Fletcherian drama.

[1] These and their equivalents common in Flet., above all in Mass.
[2] See *D. L. C.*, 47–8 and 114–15. [3] *D. L. C.*, 47. [4] *D. L. C.*, 74.

collected material for the fable of *Appius and Virginia*, he studied the early Roman plays for technique. In particular, those of Shakspere. The folio of 1623, there is every reason (as we shall see) to believe, had appeared, and made *Julius Cæsar* and *Coriolanus* for the first time accessible in print. Diffident and timid in this his first attempt, Webster learned from these most famous models a technique, and a knack of dealing with Roman conditions, new to him but now old-fashioned.

The most striking piece of imitation and borrowing is the mutiny-scene. There is no such thing in his authorities; but Webster, as all his searching and delving shows, was gravelled for matter to fill out his five acts, and hit upon this in that other drama of early Rome, *Coriolanus*.[1] In the case of *Appius and Virginia* it is soldiers mutinying in camp[2]; in *Coriolanus* it is citizens within the walls: both mutiny on account of famine. The soldiers rail against their superiors for their luxury and usury, above all against Virginius; the citizens, on quite the same score, against the patricians, above all Coriolanus. In the one case, Minutius enters to mollify them, and fails; in the other, Menenius. Last, in both cases, comes the man they hate, the man they have vowed to kill, who cows them. The conduct of the dialogue, moreover, is in both cases the same: — there are no names, but *First Citizen*, *Second Citizen*, and *All* or *Omnes;* and the First Citizen is in both cases a rude, loud-mouthed fellow who does the lion's share of the talking.[3]

Never before had Webster tried to deal with masses of people,— mobs, mutinies, armies, or the like,—but in this play three times over ![4] Surely this is through the influence of Shakspere, for he, above all other Elizabethan dramatists, whether in his Roman or in his other histories, abounds in them. Number, indeed, proves little as against method and spirit; but it is just in this last that Webster follows him closest. He has taken over the spirit that prevails in the treatment of Jack Cade and his Kentishmen, and of the stinking, filthy, brutal mobs in *Julius Cæsar* and *Coriolanus*, though in the very teeth of Livy. Some excuse there was for painting the People black, with a high-flying patrician of Coriolanus's stamp on one's hands for hero: but with the tyrant Appius for villain there could be none. Evidently, it is the awe of Shakspere's name that has led

---

[1] *Cor.*, I, 1. [2] *A. & V.*, II, 2.
[3] There is another mutiny by which Web. may have been influenced, that in Flet.'s *Bon.*, II, 1, p. 52. This is a mutiny of soldiers, at which brother-officers intercede for the repentant soldiers, as Minutius does with Virginius. No other points in common. And another in *Loy. Sub.*, V, 6, see above, p. 192. [4] II, 2; IV, 2; V, 2

Webster thus to play history false. The Sabine question, constitutional rights, the cravings for freedom and the grievances of the Roman People never get voiced; and Valerius and Horatius, the champions of liberty, sink away into names and supernumerary nothingness. Instead, the People appear as the "Roman fry," the "rabble," against the fickle favor of which even Appius, now no Patrician but an upstart [1] demagogue, has cause to rail. Appius, after all, is made to meet his end like a "Roman gentleman," in intended contrast [2] with his servant, who is bred from the base "rabble." Icilius, according to Livy very forward in the cause of the People, scorns it. Virginius, pointing to a lineage of eight hundred years, scouts a parvenu like Appius, whom the heralds have known but these eight months. [3] And the "Roman fry" itself is made, like Shakspere's, cruel and fickle, boastful and cowardly, childishly, ludicrously ignorant. [4] How, then, should Webster, who never before gave sign of specially aristocratic bent, have come to stray at this one point so far from his authority, if not under the stress of some such great example?

Another scene from Shakspere is the military parley. [5] This is old, goes back at least as far as *Jeronimo*, and had been so long out of style that Webster would hardly have been prompted to use it now for the first time, were it not for its occurrence, twice [6] over, in a great Roman play such as *Julius Cæsar*. One of these takes place between the opposing armies, the other between the friendly armies of Brutus and Cassius: either might serve as a model. Here, as in Webster, the two armies march on the stage; the order to "stand" is given; and the leaders step forth as representatives of either side to rail at each other. In the parley between Brutus and Cassius, moreover, it is angry friends that meet, and there is no final fling of defiance; — a situation more nearly like that in Webster.

Still another sort of scene appears here for the first time, and under the influence of Shakspere. The Advocate scene just before the arrival of Virginius and his army, and the serving-men scene just before the trial of Virginia, in both of which information is given as to what has

---

[1] P. 158, "a petty lawyer t' other day," 199.

[2] *A. & V.*, 222 and 223. It is made very explicit. [3] P. 199.

[4] That Web. had Shak.'s Roman citizens in mind appears from echoes like: *Min.* You wrong one of the honorablest commanders. *Omnes.* Honorable commander! Cf. the retort to Antony's words, *J. C.*, III, 2, 158: *Fourth Citizen.* They were traitors: honorable men! Another, perhaps, is the "hydra-headed multitude," p. 217. Outside of W. it is a common expression, this and its variants "many-headed beast," etc., to be found in Flet., Chap., and Mass.; but probably in no play but *Coriolanus* does it appear thrice: III, 1, 93; II, 3, 18; IV, 1, 1-2.

[5] *A. & V.*, V, 2. [6] *J. C.*, IV, 2, 30 f. and sc. 3; V, 1, 20 f.

happened, fears and expectations are uttered as to what will happen, and only subordinate characters take part, are both of a type to be found in Shakspere,[1] especially in his Roman plays. Besides, the situation of the guilty Advocate, fearfully expecting the arrival of Virginius and his army and preparing an address to him, has a *material* likeness to that of Sicinius and Brutus expecting Coriolanus and the Volscian army,[2] on the one hand, and to that of Artemidorus, or of the Soothsayer, ready to address Cæsar on his arrival, on the other.[3]

And in style *Appius and Virginia* echoes here and there that larger utterance of the Shaksperean Roman plays, particularly that of *Julius Cæsar*. Virginius's words as he contemplates the fall of Appius remind us involuntarily, not only in cast of phrase but in melody and accent, of Antony's over Cæsar :

> Uncertain fate ! but yesterday his breath
> Aw'd Rome, and his least torvèd frown was death.[4]

Another has much the same high accent,

> let the sword and slaughter
> Chase the gowned senate through the streets of Rome,
> To double-dye their robes in scarlet[5] ;

and still another,

> To that giant,
> The high Colossus that bestrides us all,[6]

is too exact an echo to be mistaken. There is, moreover, a heightened and grandiose key to utterance like

> Let him come thrill his partisan
> Against this breast, that through a large wide wound
> My mighty soul might rush out of this prison,
> To fly more freely to yon crystal palace,
> Where honor sits enthronis'd.[7]

> Come, you birds of death,
> And fill your greedy crops with human flesh ;
> Then to the city fly, disgorge it there
> Before the Senate, and from thence arise
> A plague to choke all Rome.[8]

---

[1] *Cor.*, IV, 3, a Roman and a Volsce ; (*J. C.*, II, 3 and 4, Artemidorus, Soothsayer); *Lear*, III, 1 ; *Mac.*, II, 4.

[2] *Cor.*, V, 1 and 4.   [3] *J. C.*, II, 3 and 4.

[4] *A. & V.*, 219. Cf. *J. C.*, III, 2, 123,

> But yesterday the word of Cæsar might
> Have stood against the world.

Cf. *J. C.*, III, 1, 148 f.

[5] *A. & V.*, p. 141.   [7] *A. & V.*, p. 205.

[6] *A. & V.*, p. 168 ; *J. C.*, I, 2, 134–6. Pointed out by Dyce.   [8] *A. & V.*, p. 151.

> O Rome, th' art grown a most unnatural mother,
> To those have held thee by the golden locks
> From sinking into ruin ! [1]

that is unlike anything else in Webster, from *Wyatt* to the *Cure for a Cuckold*, and goes back to the day of that heaven-aspiring speech and apostrophe which Beaumont and Fletcher ridiculed in the *Knight of the Burning Pestle*, the day of Shakspere's Hotspur, Cassius, and Cæsar.

Now this indebtedness [2] — in language, technique, and inspiring spirit — to *Julius Cæsar* and *Coriolanus* is so various and minute as to indicate the use of the printed page. These plays first appeared in the Folio of 1623. Such a date for *Appius and Virginia* would be in complete accord with the notable omission of it in Webster's list of his independent plays, given in the epistle dedicatory to the *Law-Case*, sometime between 1620 and the summer of 1622. [3]

HEYWOOD.

In *Appius and Virginia*, a tragedy of ancient, legendary Rome, there is a clown, an English one though with Latin name, [4] little

---

[1] *A. & V.*, 150. Note esp. the apostrophes and direct addresses here cited — things elsewhere almost unknown in Web. — particularly those to " Rome " and the " gods " ; and the fondness for personifying Rome — " fair Rome," etc. — and for harping on this word and on " gods " in any connection. These words seem to have a fascination, and are laid on thick for "local color." All this appears abundantly in Shak.'s Roman plays, and not in the later, romantic Roman play, full of the sentiment of latter-day chivalry, as fashioned by B. & F. and Mass. Addresses, apostrophes, and personifications of " Rome " — *A. & V.*: 140, 141, 144, 147, 150, 157, 158, 167, 167, 223. Shak.: (I cite only more striking cases). *Cor.*, I, 9, 20 ; II, 1, 179 ; III, 1, 291 ; III, 3, 110 ; IV, 5, 136 ; *J. C.*, I, 2, 151 ; II, 1, 56 ; II, 2, 87 ; V, 3, 100 ; *Tit. And.*, I, 1, 69 ; I, 1, 70 ; etc., etc. See in Web. and Shak. esp. " great Rome," " ungrateful Rome," Rome as mother, etc. In *A. & V.*, the word " Rome " occurs 48 times, and " gods " 42 times ; and see the endless lists of these words in Bartlett — for *Cor.* (Rome 89 times and gods 48), *J. C.*, and *Tit. And.* In B. & F.'s *Faith. Friends* (to take an example) there is no case of address to Rome or personification of her, and the word itself occurs only 24 times ; and " gods " is largely superseded, after Jonson's more knowing method, by Jove, Mars, Hercules, and the rest.

[2] For completeness sake let me add other points of possible indebtedness to Shak.: Virg.'s farewell to his daughter, pp. 200–1, and Lucius's words to his son in *Tit. And.*, V, 3, 160-170 ; "jewels more worth than all her tribe," *A. & V.*, 197, and *Othello*, V, 2, 347, " cast a pearl away, Richer than all his tribe." (This last in Dyce.)

[3] We may count as circumstantial evidence in favor of this the mention (twice over in II, 1) of a Lady Calphurnia. Such a name is not to be found in all Livy, Painter, Dionysius, or the *Pecorone*, and is probably to be attributed to W.'s recent reading of *Jul. Cæs.* It may not be superfluous to add that the word is spelt as in the Folio (Berlin and Chatsworth copies) *Calphurnia* (cf. Ital. *Calfornia*), not *Calpurnia*, the true Latin form, used in North's *Plutarch* throughout (in all ed. at least up to 1603). Yet it is to be noted that the orig. Q. of *A. & V.* (Brit. Mus.) prints *Calpharina* — a blunder, prob., in which only the small, obscure letters are affected.

[4] Corbulo. A Corbulo, Roman general, died 67 A. D.

accommodated to his classical surroundings. *Any* anachronism need not startle one in an Elizabethan drama ; but the fact is, Roman plays were handled rather charily, and aside from Webster's, only one has such a thing as a clown, Heywood's *Rape of Lucrece*.[1] Our minds refuse to conceive Webster as intending, single-handed, an innovation of such magnitude. Heywood's play deals with a story which immediately comes to mind — as was actually the case with Webster at the close, with Giovanni Fiorentino, and with Livy himself — so soon as that of Virginia is mentioned ; it appeared in 1608, and still held the stage (the same stage, too, as Webster's play) in 1639[2]; and Heywood himself, as appears from Webster's collaboration with him, his praise of him in his preface to the *White Devil*, and his verses on his *Apology for Actors*,[3] was his friend. It would be nothing strange, then, to find that Webster, who, for the devising of his fable, leaned always so heavily on authority and precedent, had borrowed this matter from him.

In both cases the clown is servant to the heroine, and he appears in like situations. He is sent by his mistress on errands,[4] is taken to task by her for ogling at her maid (and that in the latter's presence),[5] and is left to chatter with other servants alone.[6] He jokes about his mistress's misfortune,[7] about the sinners in the suburbs,[8] and, being a Roman, out of the Latin grammar.[9] And the comic side of both is the same. It lies all in the speeches — the clown plays no pranks and suffers no mishaps ; — and it has an episodic, random, and anachronistic character. It is all jest and repartee, puns, quibbles, and catches, and those neither clever nor new ; and the drift of it all, whenever it gets beyond words, is satire on London life and manners.[10] It is good-humored, moreover, naive, and dirty. Clearly, then, Webster in the making of his Roman clown had an eye on Heywood's.

---

[1] There is one, indeed, in Lodge's archaic *Wounds of Civil War*, pub. 1594, and at this same period there probably were others. And in Flet.'s *Prophetess* there is a Fool — a different thing,— but not in any respect like Corbulo.

[2] It is in Beeston's list of 1639, where *A. & V.* is mentioned. See above, p. 33. Both, then, belonged to the Cockpit.

[3] Prefixed to the first ed., 1612.

[4] *Luc.*, II, 1 ; IV, 6 ; *A. & V.*, 145, 175.

[5] *Luc.*, II, 4 ; *A. & V.*, 172. In the latter case, however, there is no scolding.

[6] *Luc.*, IV, 2 ; *A. & V.*, 186-9.

[7] *Luc.*, IV, 6, p. 401 f ; *A. & V.*, 188. Eckhardt, *Lust. Person*, p. 433, also notices this, and asserts that Web. drew from Hey.

[8] *Luc.*, II, 1, p. 350 ; *A. & V.*, 173.

[9] *Luc.*, II, 4, p. 364 ; *A. & V.*, 145.

[10] Both in the Clown's talk, p. 173, and the Lictors', p. 171, W. shows this anachronistic bent : " book of common prayer," " banquerouts," " French fly " and " French rheum," lawyers in term-time and their practices. Cf. *Luc.*, pp. 349-50, 365, 373, 374, 376, where there are even Dutch songs.

And where Webster's clown does not resemble the clown in *Lucrece*, he resembles this or that of Heywood's eighteen others.[1] Nearly all of these are servants, who speak in prose, are good-natured, lively, not specially clever, given to punning, and to twisting and confounding words. Those in *Challenge for Beauty* and the *Golden Age* (like Corbulo again) are fitted out with the paraphernalia of Euphuism — parisonic antitheses and parallelisms of the true *not only — but also* and *though — yet* stamp, paronomasia, repetition,[2] alliteration[3] above all, with here and there a touch of extravagance that implies burlesque.[3] And one in *Fortune by Land and Sea* is, like Corbulo, lugubriously sympathetic, and, as well as the one in *Love's Mistress*, facetiously condescending toward his fellow servants.[4]

This sort of clown was now old-fashioned. We have already learned how different Fletcher's — the height of the fashion — was; and (aside from what we then learned) he was not naive, not lugubrious, not much given to punning and to playing with words, not Euphuistic at all, and he spoke in verse not prose.[5] Webster's clown is arrayed in the garb of Speed, or of Dromio of Syracuse, or of John Lyly's merry Servants[6]; and he is furnished with a stock of Joe

---

[1] See Eckhardt for an account of Hey.'s clowns, index sub *Hey*.

[2] Examples: *Works*, Vol. V, p. 64: III, p. 10; *A. & V.*, pp. 186–9, etc. "Parison" is used by Landmann and Child for the precise balancing of words within balanced or antithesized clauses or sentences. See for this and the other matters as essentials of Euphuism, Mr. C. G. Child's excellent *Lyly and Euphuism*, Erlangen, 1894, p. 52 f.

[3] This appears from alliteration so extravagant as that in *Fort. by Land and Sea* (Vol. VI, p. 383), *Love's Mistr.* (Vol. V, p. 113), or from paronamasia so elaborate as that in *Chall. Beauty* (Vol. V, p. 64) — "Danger I find but little in that face, and 't is able to outface the best face," etc., and in *A. & V.*, 187 — " service," " serve," etc. ; or from Web.'s parody of Euphuism, *A. & V.*, 172–3 — "There is a certain fish that, as the learned divulge, is called a shark," etc. Cf., too, the evidently ludicrous effect intended by Flet. and Mass. in their extraordinary use of alliteration, *without*, any Euphuistic concomitants. (See Eckhardt, p. 365).—The simple and frank delight that men took in the devices of Euphuism in its day of honor is quite gone.

[4] *Works*, VI, pp. 383, 406; V, pp. 112–13. Cf. *A. & V.*, 186–9. They use antitheses, oratorical questions, and alliteration, as well.

[5] There are rare exceptions, as in *Fair Maid of the West*.

[6] Corbulo shows a greater variety of Euphuism than any of Hey.'s clowns, perhaps than all of them. Indeed, he has Euphuism of *Euphues*, such as less often appears in Lyly's plays, and never in the mouths of his servants — comparisons from fictitious botany and zoölogy ("poor camomile," *Hen. IV!*) introduced by the elaborate "there is in Africa," etc.; trains of balanced examples, or metaphors, from the world of "stones, stars, plants, fishes, flies" (*A. & V.*, 172, 187); and, at the same time, some of the tricks of the Lyly Servant sc. (imitated also by Shak.) such as the conundrum (what am I?), the inventory of his mistress's points (*A. & V.*, 172), discussion of their masters, etc. See *A. & V.*, 186–9.

Millers such as Fletcher and the Court would never have stomached.[1]
So, though in less degree, with some of Heywood's clowns[2]; and I
see no way so likely for Webster to have come at these old fashions as
through the example of the creator of the clown in *Lucrece*.[3]

IV. MACHIAVELLISM AND MARLOWE.

After Euphuism, after Shakspere and Heywood, we need not be
surprised at Marlowe and Machiavellism. Machiavellism appears in
the two villains of the Period, Romelio and Appius. These are alike,
and different from any other villains in Webster; and it is in
Machiavellism that much of this likeness (and difference) lies.

They are egoists through and through, without an altruistic
instinct, and are fired with what for Webster is a new motive — ambition.[4] Their policy is the old one of the lion and the fox, but above
all the fox.[5] Not afraid to strike, they prefer, like true Machiavels,
to deal by dissembling, hypocrisy, and craft. They use men like
nails to drive out one another.[6] They boast of their achievements and
smile at their skill. Not that either of them is a " bottle-nosed knave "
or " wall-eyed slave " like Barabas or Aaron : they have something of
the address and finesse that go with a gentleman ; they are sleek,
Caroline versions of the rough, hirsute Elizabethan type. But the
type, at any rate, is the same, as we have yet to learn from their
maxims and from their conduct and utterances in typical situations.

---

[1] Many of the old jokes recur, indeed, in Flet. (as, for that matter, today), but
newly, ingeniously phrased. Here, unchanged, are the old quibbles and puns, —
base and treble, woodcocks, mutton, caper, heir (air), and son (sun) — that go back
at least to the day of Lyly.

[2] This is not to say that Hey.'s clowns are without any of the qualities of the
fashionable type. The active, unepisodic part many of them play, as in *Fair Maid
of the West, Love's Mist.*, for example, shows the contrary.

[3] *Chall. Beauty* and *Love's Mist.* contain Euphuism, as we have seen, and the
latter shows some definite indebtedness to Lyly's comedies, as in the clown's love
for Amaryllis (Eckhardt, p. 421, who points this out), and, I would add, in the matter of introducing into the play King Midas, old Grk. myth. material, and the
clown's comical superciliousness with the swains (cf. *L. M.*, Hey. *Works*, vol. V, pp.
112–13, and Lyly's *Mydas*, I, 2 ; II, 2). Both plays were published in 1636, and it may
be that they were affected directly by the collection of Lyly's Court Plays, published
in 1632. For *A. & V.*, too, this date may be the backward limit.

[4] Previous villains were all revengers, or, like Flam., unambitious tool-villains.

[5] See Meyer's *Machiavelli and Eng. Drama*, p. 12, for this celebrated maxim of
Machiavellism, and basis for the Elizabethan characterization of Machiavellians.
So long as I speak of the character of Machiavellians in general I am indebted to
this book. — The words Machiavel and Machiavellian I use in this discussion only
in the sense of the false, Elizabethan Machiavellism, not the Machiavellism of
Machiavelli.

[6] A common maxim.

These last let us compare together, marking at the same time shreds
and remnants of antiquated, conventional phrase.[1]

1. Appius, on various occasions, presents a full complement of
Machiavellian maxims,—of biding one's time, of fraud and dissembling, of using one ill to cure another :

> Appius, be circumspect, and be not rash
> In blood, as th' art in lust : be murderous still ;
> But when thou strik'st, with unseen weapons kill.   *A. & V.*, 163.
>
> We should smile smoothest where our hate's most deep,
> And when our spleen's broad waking, seem to sleep.
> . . . .
> Great men should strike but once, and then strike sure.   *A. & V.*, 164.
>
> . . . one ill must cure another.   *A. & V.*, 186.

Citations for comparison are almost superfluous ; I give but a few :

> *Bar.*[2] . . . Nothing violent,
> Oft have I heard tell, can be permanent.   *Malta*, I, 1, 132–3.
>
> *Glou.* Why, I can smile, and murder whiles I smile.
>   *3 Hen. VI*, III, 2, 182.
>
> *Lorenzo.* Thus must we practise to prevent mishap,
> And thus one ill another must expulse.   *Sp. Tr.*, III, 2, 106.
>
> *Guise.* For this I wake when others think I sleep
> . . . .
> For this, this head, this heart, this hand, and sword,
> Contrives, imagines, and fully executes,
> Matters of import aimèd at by many,
> Yet understood by none.   *Mass. Paris*, sc. II, 47–54.

2. True Machiavel that he is, Appius warns and prompts himself
in his part. Very striking in this connection is the survival of the
old-fashioned addressing oneself by name [3]:

> *App.* Appius, be circumspect, etc.   (See preced. par.)
>
> *Guise.* Now, Guise, begin those deep-engender'd thoughts.
>   *Mass. Paris*, sc. II, 32.
> Then, Guise,
> Since thou hast all the cards within thy hands,   *Ib.*, sc. II, 88.
>
> *Bar.* And, Barabas, now search this secret out.   *Malta*, I, 1, 177.
>
> *Yorke.* Now Yorke, bethink thyself and rouse thee up.
>   *Contention*, p. 168.

---

[1] Dr. Meyer sees no Machiavellism in these plays—only some insignificant matters in the *W. D.* But Dr. Meyer and I are concerned with two different matters :
he only with traces of Machiavelli's name and personality, his maxims and the
pseudo-Machiavellian maxims of Gentillet ; I, with the characterization, the ways
and doings, of Machiavels as portrayed in the Eng. drama.

[2] I can not here take space to show how all these personages — Barabas, Rich. III,
Lorenzo, Eleazar (*Lust's Dom.*), Piero, Guise, etc. — are Machiavellians. The reader
may consult Meyer.

[3] Not to be found elsewhere in Web., except, indeed, in old-fashioned *Wyatt*,
pp. 36, 48, 54.

3.   As his victim goes out, Appius throws off the cloak of dissimulation, and utters a threat [1]:

> Go to thy death, thy life is doom'd and cast.   *A. & V.*, 163.

So :

> *Charles.* Come, mother,
> Let us go to honour this solemnity.
> *Q. Mother.* Which I'll dissolve with blood and cruelty.
>   *Mass. Paris*, sc. I, 24–6.

> *Bar.* I'll pay thee with a vengeance, Ithamore.   *Malta*, III, 4. 114.

> *Eleazar.* Do, and be damned : Zarack and Balthazar,
> Dog them at the heels.   *Lust's Dominion*, p. 127.

4.   The Machiavellian brushes aside a difficulty or a scruple, cheer-
ful, ruthless devil that he is, with a *tut* or *tush* [2] :

> *App.* Tush, any fault
> Or shadow of a crime will be sufficient
> For his committing.[3]   *A. & V.*, 185.

> *Aaron.* Tut! Lucius, this was but a deed of charity
> To that which thou shalt hear of me anon.   *Tit. And.*, V, 1, 89.

> *Aaron.* Tut! I have done a thousand dreadful things
> As willingly as one would kill a fly.   *Ib.*, V, 1, 141.

> *Gloucester.* Tut, I can smile, and murder when I smile,
> I crie content, to that which grieves me most.   *True Trag. York*, p. 64.

> *Glou.* Tut! were it farther off, I'll pluck it down.[4] *3 Hen. VI*, III, 2, 195.

> *Bar.* Tush!
> As good dissemble what thou never means't,
> As first mean truth and then dissemble it.   *Malta*, I, 2, 290.

> *Q. Mother.* Tush, man, let me alone with him
> . . . .
> Tush, all shall die unless I have my will.   *Mass. Paris*, sc. XIV, 61.

> *Northumberland.* Have we not the king and council's hands unto it?
> Tut, we stand high in men's opinion
> And the world's broad eye.[5]   *Wyatt*, p. 6.

5.   The main thing, however, is this Machiavel's having attached to
himself a henchman, Marcus, who, like Ithamore in *Malta* and Buckingham in *Richard III*, does his rough work, admires his "policy,"
and exchanges crude endearments with him.

---

[1] This, of course, is not necessarily to be connected with the Machiavel: it is
merely something old-fashioned that belongs to them as to other villains of their
day, and is new in W.

[2] This word is to be found only once elsewhere in Web.'s own work — in *C. C.*, p. 21.

[3] *I. e.*, to put off on his shoulders.

[4] *I. e.*, the crown.

[5] North. starts, we remember, as a Machiavel. — See above, p. 46.

a. The henchman admires, or is called upon to admire, his policy :

> *Marcus.* Excellent, excellent lapwing,
> There 's other stuff clos'd in that subtle breast.   *A. & V.,* 133.
>
> Let me adore your divine policy.   *A. & V.,* 185.
>
> *App.* How dost thou like my cunning ?
> .   .   .   .
>   laugh, my trusty Marcus ;
> I am enforc'd to my ambition.   *A. & V.,* 131.
>
> *Bar.* Now tell me Ithamore, how likst thou this?
> .   .   .   .
> *Ith.* O master, that I might have a hand in this!   *Malta,* II, 3, 368–71.
>
> *Ith.* O mistress, ha! ha! ha!
> *Abig.* Why, what ailst thou?
> *Ith.* O my master !
> *Abig.* Ha !
> .   .   .   .
> *Ith.* O, my master has the bravest policy.   *Malta,* III, 3, 5–12.
>
> *Bar.* . . . say, will not this be brave?
> *Fern.* O excellent!   *Malta,* V, 5, 41–2.
>
> *Guise.* Now Madam, how like you our lusty Admiral?
> *Q. Mo.* Believe me, Guise, he becomes the place so well
> That I could long ere this have wished him there.
>   *Mass. Paris.,* sc. XI, 14–16.
>
> *Piero.* Ha, Strotzo, is 't not rare?   *Ant. Rev.,* I, 1, 74.
>
> *Lorenzo.* How likes Prince Balthazar this stratageme?
>   *Sp. Tr.,* II, 1, 110.

b. Endearments :

> *App.* O my trusty Claudius !
> *Mar.* My dear lord, etc.   *A. & V.,* 185.
>
> *Bar.* O, Ithamore, come near :
> Come near, my love : come near, thy master's life,
> My trusty servant, etc.
> *Ith.* Why, I 'll do anything for your dear sake.   *Malta,* III, 4.

and similar blandishments in the *Massacre at Paris,* between the
Guise and Queen Mother, II, 2, and III, 2; in the *Malcontent,* IV, 1,
ll. 215–17; in *Hoffman,* between the villain-hero and his accomplice, Lorrick, ll. 615, 683; in *Richard III,* between Gloucester and
Buckingham, II, 2, 151 f.

6. Laughter at success in their deviltry, on the part of either
Machiavel or henchman. See examples quoted above from *Appius
and Virginia* and *Malta,* and the following :

> *Eleazar.* Farewell my lords ; meet there ; ha, ha, ha !
>   *Lust's Dom.,* p. 187.
>
> *Piero.* He [Pandulpho] grieves ; laugh, Strotzo, laugh.
>   *Ant. Rev.,* II, 2, 130.

and compare the familiar passage in *Titus Andronicus,* V, 1, 110–20,
where Aaron gloats and laughs ; and *Lust's Dominion,* p. 188, etc.

7. Finally, the Machiavel and his henchman play a hypocritical hoax together. In *Appius and Virginia* there are three cases — the faint refusal of office at the beginning and the two sham trials.[1] The one resembles Gloucester's hypocritical refusal of the crown urged upon him by Buckingham, in *Richard III*, III, 5 and 7, and Mortimer's of the Protectorship, in *Edward II*, V, 4; and the others (though far more adroit), similar 'policies' in *Malta* (IV, 3, for instance, where he and Ithamore make one friar believe he has killed the other), and in *Antonio's Revenge*,[2] as where Piero and Strotzo play their uncouth game. This, again, is new in Webster.

All this has been about Appius, our thesaurus of illustration being Marlowe, the great dramatist of Machiavellism. A word now about Romelio, less as a Machiavel than simply as showing traces of reminiscences from Marlowe, more especially from the *Jew of Malta*. A Machiavel ruthless and crafty as Barabas we have already seen him to be. No more than the Jew does he hesitate to play the lion, to stab Contarino for his money, when the time comes for that; but like him he prefers the fox — intriguing, disguising, dissembling. Like all Machiavellians, he delights in pitting one man against another, as his sister against his mother; and he has even the Machiavellian's infidelity. But, more than all that, he stands directly under the shadow of the burly Jew. Romelio, too, is a man of untold wealth; he, too, loves it and boasts of it; and his words, as he does so, are unmistakably a reminiscence of the first scene of *Malta*:

> I 'll give the king of Spain
> Ten thousand ducats yearly, and discharge
> My yearly custom. The Hollanders scarce trade
> More generally than I : my factors' wives
> Wear chaperons of velvet, and my scriveners,
> Merely through my employment, grow so rich,
> They build their palaces and belvederes
> With musical water-works.
> . . . .
> *Pros.* I pray, sir, what do you think
> Of Signior Baptisto's estate?
> *Ro.* A mere beggar:
> He 's worth some fifty thousand ducats.
> *Pros.* Is not that well?
> *Ro.* How, well! for a man to be melted to snow water,
> With toiling in the world from three-and-twenty
> Till three score, for poor fifty thousand ducats!
> . . . .
> Faith, and for silver,
> Should I not send it packing to th' East Indies,
> We should have a glut on 't.   *D. L. C.*, 9, 10.

---

[1] After the second trial A. shows no more Machiavellism. He is a "Roman gentleman" in the prison-scene.   [2] I, 2, and IV, 1.

Here is a like extravagant fancy — the same contempt for silver, the same sweating oneself to death, and the same use of customs to measure to our imagination the immeasurable total treasure assessed. Again, when Romelio enters the distinctively Machiavellian situation of recounting his career of villainy,[1] he seems directly to refer to Barabas:

> for slight villainies,
> As to coin money, corrupt ladies' honours,
> Betray a town to th' Turk, or make a bonfire
> A' th' Christian Navy, I could settle to 't.   *D. L. C.*, p. 53.

Add to this a line of Appius's, charged with Marlowesque hyperbole, — a figure which calm Webster never uses, —

> Had I as many hands
> As had Briareus, I 'd extend them all
> To catch this office[2];

and the sum of the evidence of phrase and characterization seems to point, as I think, unmistakably, in the case of the *Law-Case* as in that of *Appius and Virginia*, to Webster's consorting in this Period with the great dramatist of Machiavellism, Marlowe.

The Guise.

In the epistle dedicatory of the *Devil's Law-Case*, we remember, Webster mentions, among other of his plays, one now lost; and follows this order — chronological in part at least — *White Devil, Malfi, Guise*. This *Guise* must certainly have been written out of a full knowledge of the *Massacre at Paris* (which play, we know, went also by that title), if, indeed, it was not merely a recast of that archaic, Machiavellian play. If, now, we should hold the order to be *altogether* chronological, and the *Guise* to follow *Malfi* and precede the *Law-Case*, then we should have a rational explanation of the sudden appearance, in this last Period, of Machiavellism and Marlowe. A place is needed for the *Guise*, and here is the place to hand. If *not*, we may let the *Guise* still shift for itself, and have recourse, as before with the reminiscences from Shakspere and Lyly, to Webster's senile sterility and his eclectic, academic tendencies. But an explanation for two facts is better, and more satisfying, than one for one.

---

[1] Rom. does so, however, only in his imagination. See Barabas's and Aaron's recitals, *Malta*, II, 3, 177 f, and *Tit. And.*, V, 1, 127-144.
[2] Cf.   Had I as many souls as there be stars,
          I 'd give them all for Mephistophilis. *Faustus*, sc. III, ll. 104-5.
and cf. the scores of hyperboles (also under *Vergleich*), as tabulated in O. Fischer's *Zur Charakteristik der Dramen Marlowe's*, München, 1889.

V. THE PERIOD AS A WHOLE.

The great facts of this third Period are Webster's break with the style of his prime, his yielding to other influences — to the fashion of the day, on the one hand, and to bygone fashions, Academic models, on the other, — and the abeyance of creative power. In the second Period Webster gave more than he took; now he takes more than he gives. This is not what we expect of a great poet in his last Period. We expect him not altogether to lose the utterance he achieved in his prime; we expect the changes in him not all to come from without. But Webster is thus only the child of his age. The profession he followed was a craft, too thoroughly popular, too un*literary* and uncritical, and too much the handmaiden of the hour, to be what we nowadays conceive as art; and in his decline he followed it only as the greatest of his day, and the greatest name of his day, — Shakspere and Chapman — followed it in theirs. Yet, in one way, Webster realizes more nearly than these (though still not untrue to his later, Caroline Age) what we expect of a poet in his decline. He grows Academic, eclectic: like Massinger and Shirley he cons the new folios[1] and multiplying quartos, and, though in a more senile, slavish, and wholesale way, he resuscitates outworn motives and mannerisms.

The main influence is that of Fletcher and Massinger. It appears in all three plays of the Period; it furnishes matter, pervades the whole technique and spirit, and chokes out the old Marstonian (not to say Websterian) art. From Massinger, as we have seen, is taken the main-plot of the *Cure for a Cuckold;* on Fletcher is modelled many a single situation; and from Fletcher, or Fletcher and Massinger both, are drawn the conventionalized types of character. Fletcherian, moreover, are scene of action, methods of construction, conception of the relation of character to plot and of plot to morals, and the comic spirit. And before the glare of Fletcher's genius Webster's own pales and shrinks away. There is rapidly less and less, and finally, in the *Cure for a Cuckold*, none, of his old baiting, fabling, and meditating; of his crabbed and sententious utterance, sombre imagery, and melodramatic setting and machinery; of his strong grasp on truth of character and morals, stern dealing of justice, and tragic gloom[2]; even of what might seem his more personal qualities — his pathos, irony, and humor. The author of *Vittoria Corombona* and the *Duchess of Malfi,*

---

[1] Of Shak., 1623; of Jonson, 1616-31; of Mars., 1633. In 12mo, six plays of Lyly's, 1632.

[2] *I. e.,* to mention those few elements of the revenge-period which do in some measure occur in *D. L. C.* or *A. & V.*

who might stand alone, forsakes himself to follow after the reveller, Fletcher.

It would be a sign of the remarkable wholeheartedness with which Webster followed Fletcher, if we were to take it that it was from him that Webster now learned the practice of contriving his plots. This is not unlikely; such a practice, at all events, is a note of his Fletcherian Period. In the *White Devil* and *Malfi* Webster takes his plot from history or his Italian novel in the old-fashioned way, quite whole. In these later plays he weaves together strange strands, like the tale from Goulart and the tale from *Lust's Dominion*, in the *Devil's Law-Case*, with many a strand of his own spinning. Such is the case above all in the *Law-Case*, and even in the *Cure for a Cuckold*, where he does some wholesale borrowing, and in the *Appius and Virginia*, where by the nature of things he must more or less follow his authorities. To be sure, Webster is not a good hand at it, and does no honor to his defter, more resourceful master. Patching and plastering as best he may, he has much ado to make the plot of the *Law-Case* hold together; and with the motivation of the *Cure for a Cuckold* he has got into a sad muddle.[1] Invention and construction are not his forte. But whether it be Fletcher or merely himself that is to blame, the undertaking was a pretty mettlesome and valorous one at these years.

Of the old-fashioned models to which Webster reverts in this Period, some, as Heywood and Shakspere, he imitated deliberately; others, as Marlowe and other undetermined Machiavellian and Euphuistical writers, half unconsciously, it may be, through reminiscence of early days. Both sorts of imitation may be explained, as we please, as arising out of senile abeyance of creative power, out of the present accessibility of the texts of earlier masters and the rising critical interest in them, or out of embarrassment in the making of *Appius and Virginia* (in which this imitation is most evident) — a Roman play. This last is not improbable, for in this same play, as we have seen, Webster was hard put to it for material, and for it ransacked the histories as much as he did old Roman plays for hints in technique and form. However we explain it, eclectic and academic tendencies must

---

[1] As to this last, see above, p. 165 f. As for *D. L. C.*: See the inexplicable conduct of Sanitonella, Crispiano's clerk, who for no reason becomes Leonora's nefarious agent, and no longer seems acquainted with his master, nor he with him (II, 1, and IV, 1 and 2); the plastering on p. 51, where Ercole explains why he should announce his death, and how he can at the same time avoid damaging Contarino; the utterly unreasonable prank of Romelio, locking up his mother and the Friar when they try to save him (p. 115), in order to make a complication, and his equally unreasonable change of heart (p. 118), to solve it. Cf. Marcus's absurd scheme to bring Virginia to terms by scantling her father's pay (*A. & V.*), Icilius's quarrel (p. 213).

be recognized as not new and foreign to one who, even in the Period of his prime, showed fruits from the careful, discriminating study of many and various dramatists, and who, even then, was evidently, notoriously, a slow, laborious worker.[1]

The breach we have noticed between this third, or Fletcherian, Period and the foregoing, or revenge, Period, however, is nothing to that between the first, or apprenticeship, Period and both following ones. In the latter case there is no connecting link of phrase or incident of technique or spirit[2]; in the former there is all of this. Phrases from the revenge plays are echoed in the Fletcherian Period in some number[2]; here and there a fragment of plot and characterization reappears[3]; and in the *Law-Case* and *Appius and Virginia* there is fabling,[4] baiting,[5] and aphorizing,[6] deeds of blood and subtle, poetic villains. The *Law-Case*, indeed, really fills the place our date assigns to it — of transition. It alone of these last plays retains something of the old, keen phrase and charnel-house imagery,[7] vestiges of the uncanny stage-properties, and a malcontent villain, meditating (in rime too) like Bosola.[8] And that more worldly, cynical irony we have noticed in this play, now not of the soul as a lark in a cage, but of heralds laughing in their black raiment, of ladies spending their own lives and their waiting-women's putting on clothes, and of Romelio brushing aside the question of death, is possibly, we have seen, Webster's own mood as he turns from the gloom and reality of *Malfi* to the comedy of Fletcher.

CONCLUSION.

We have now followed Webster from the beginning to the end. We were with him in his Dekkerian Period and found him altogether another Dekker, or else a characterless, colorless hack. We were with him in his Revenge Period, and here, at his zenith, found him at almost all points an imitator, at many a wholesale borrower. We were with him in his Fletcherian Period, and found him forsaking his old methods and point of view, even the style that seems to the casual

---

[1] See the preface to *W. D.;* and the piecing together of sentences from the *Arcadia* in *Mal.*   [2] See above, pp. 80–2.

[3] Three law-cases, in *W. D.*, III, 3; *D. L. C.*, IV, 3; and *A. & V.*, IV, 1, each conducted by a foolish, pettifogging lawyer; Isabella, Cornelia, and Leonora, all lying to save husband or son, *W. D.*, 39–41, 109–10, *D. L. C.* 101; the woman 'taking an inventory' at an interview with her lover, *Mal.*, 173, and *D. L. C.*, 25. See, further, those cited in connection with *C. C.*, p. 38 f.   [4] See above, pp. 38–40.

[5] *D. L. C.*, 33–5, 43–6, 85; at the law-cases in both *D. L. C.* and *A. & V.*, and in *A. & V.*, 213–15.   [6] It abounds in *A. &. V.*

[7] *D. L. C.*, 47–8, 79, 114–15. In the *A. & V.* there is nothing but what is stereotyped and mediocre. The only gloomy image in *C. C.* is at p. 46.

[8] *D. L. C.*, 47–8, 57. Cf. above, p. 133.

reader so individual, to follow after Fletcher and others, till, in what is probably his last play, the *Cure for a Cuckold*, there is nothing but insignificant tricks and phrases left to show he is Webster still.

In following this development, in determining the periods of it, we have kept the standpoint of influence; and here is our justification. No one ever owed influence more. Marlowe, Marston, Dekker, Jonson, Beaumont are recognizable in all their work; and, in spite of their habit of collaboration, Fletcher and Massinger. So even with the "myriad-minded" one: *Titus Andronicus* and *Richard III* are not Marlowe, nor *Henry VIII* and the *Winter's Tale* Beaumont and Fletcher. Infinitely receptive and impressionable, Shakspere was nevertheless not imitative, but creative; and by ceaseless creation he preserved his identity. And, without study of Webster as a whole, one would expect the same of him — the 'terrible Webster' of the *White Devil* and *Malfi* — so individual, conscious, and haughty in his art. But, as we have seen, it is not so. No one so strong ever leaned harder on the staff of tradition; no one ever looked about him more narrowly for material or studied more closely others' methods. The truth may be, that he had no spring of invention welling within him: that he had profound insight, subtle taste, and a zeal to toil, but that he had not that within him which of itself would change and make new — make his own — all that he touched. His works are few, follow at long intervals, and show the marks of the file; the materials in them he culled from afar, often left unchanged, or used again and again, but what determined his choice, or his change, was less some inner necessity than the model he, as a student, then held before him, the influence he then obeyed. These changed; and Webster's work — laborious, discriminating, artistic, but not spontaneous — changed with them.

APPENDIX I.

For two reasons, as we have already seen, it is important to ascertain the date of Tourneur's *Atheist's Tragedy* ; — that is, in order to determine the value of the references to it in the *White Devil*, as tending to fix the date of the latter, and in order to furnish a solid basis for the history of the development of the revenge type traced in Chapter III.[1] There we took the composition of the two plays, *Revenger's Tragedy* and *Atheist's Tragedy*, to be in the order of their registering and publishing, and in either case close to those dates — 1607 and 1611.[2] Messrs. Churton Collins and Fleay, on the other hand, and most scholars who have turned their attention to the subject, have inverted the order of the plays, and so have removed the dates of composition somewhat from those of the registering and publishing.

Surely on insufficient basis. Collins, who was the first to do this, and was followed by Symonds and Ward,[3] based his assumption on the purely subjective ground of internal evidence. He found the *Ath. Tr.* a rawer, more immature work of art, and inferred that it belonged to the author's raw and immature years. Such vague, purely esthetic, *a priori*, argument is not here to be considered[4]; anyway, the major premise of the example before us is not sound. Many " mature " works of genius are early, and are followed by the comparatively crude and immature. What childish blood-and-thunder in the *Massacre of Paris*, after *Tamburlaine* and *Faustus*! What trifling in *Cymbeline* or *Pericles* or the *Winter's Tale* after *Lear* and *Hamlet*! What trash in the way of railroad and ladies' stories after the *Recessional* and *Without Benefit of Clergy*! But, as I said, this absolute point of view is simply not to be taken : we have to consider sources and influences, and to comprehend this esthetic crudity as a stage in the author's development. Accordingly,[5] in the *Rev. Tr.* Tourneur appears to be working under the tutelage and guidance of an established and elaborated tradition ; in the *Ath. Tr.*, to be breaking with it : and the crudity and immaturity, as is often the case, is largely the effect produced by a break with tradition in a daring, single-handed experiment. In the one case, he carries forward to their limits motives handed down to him — revenge, ghosts, physical horrors, and portents, etc., — and he profits by the past. In the other, he tries to go his own gait, revolts against the old bloodthirstiness and yet retains the old machinery, and thrusts into the midst of the old forms and scheme of plot startling ideas and utterances, and ludicrously inappropriate incidents, of his own. Immature, then, the *Ath. Tr.* may from the esthetic standpoint be ; but only in the sense of being revolutionary and experimental, not in the sense of green and youthful.

Of a different sort (though to my mind likewise untenable) is the judgment of Mr. Fleay, accepted by Mr. Thorndike. He finds the references to the siege of Ostend to be proof that the play was written contemporaneously, even before the

---

[1] See p. 111 f.

[2] The *Rev. Tr.*, reg. Oct. 7, 1607, pub. the same year ; *Ath. Tr.*, Sept. 14, 1611, pub. the same year (Arber).

[3] Ward, III, p. 69 ; Collins's *Tour.*, vol. I, p. xxxviii.

[4] See an example of it confuted at end of App. II.

[5] See above, pp. 105–13, and esp. p. 113.

siege had ended (1604). In II, 1, Borachio, as a pretended eye-witness, reports events at the opening of the sluices, which took place some time before the end, — Jan. 7, 1602,[1] as Mr. Thorndike adds. Hence, Mr. Thorndike infers, the play must have been written not later than 1603 and not earlier than 1602. The latter half of this induction is certainly flawless : the former, almost as certainly, not.

For, this long report of the siege and battle at Ostend, forming as it does an integral part of the plot and original plan, is evidence very different from passing allusions such as those in *Westward Ho* to Ostend or that in the *Law-Case* to Amboyna. These latter are legitimate evidence as to date : — unconnected, unpremeditated allusions, that are unthinkable except as contemporaneous, as starting up into the author's mind out of the environment in which he is writing, only for the joke's or the news' sake. But in our play Ostend is part and parcel of the story, and finds a place there rather to serve a functional need, as providing a convenient battle or disaster in which Charlemont might be reported to have fallen. To this end, Tourneur chose, with a veritable Elizabethan instinct for realism, simply the nearest and most interesting to Englishmen, though Zutphen would have done as well. And he describes it, not as something now on everybody's lips, not pertly and allusively, nor with an abundance of newspaper detail, but in strains of colorless and elaborate poetry such as might have been effused over Agincourt or Hastings. There is not a vestige of evidence in the reference to Ostend, then, that Tourneur is writing *Ath. Tr.* before 1603, or, for that matter, for a score of years after.

There is some evidence, on the other hand, for our very justifiable presumption that the dates of the registering and printing of the plays represent pretty nearly the dates of composition. For not only is it improbable that Tourneur should have written the *Ath. Tr.*, half emancipated as it is from the revenge conventions,— from bloodthirstiness, infernal and supernal machinery, and the Marstonian close plot of intrigue in the style of the *Malc.*,—with its evident revolt against *revenge* and its parody of it, and then have written a play absolutely in the spirit of the old tradition ; it is improbable from so definite and simple a point of view as that of metre. The metrical technique of the *Ath. Tr.* is as much in sympathy with the progress of a later day as is the purely dramatic. At the latter point the play shows, as we have already seen, the influence of Shakspere's later tragedies ; and, very naturally, it shows also some of the metrical tendencies of these plays — hardly influence from them — as regards rejection of rime (triplets and couplets) and adoption of run-on lines and light and weak endings. The *Rev. Tr.*, on the other hand, here as everywhere following the lead of Marston,[2] has, as our table below indicates,[3] abundant couplets and triplets, few run-on lines, and very few light and weak endings. Now, all this, especially abundance of light and weak endings, is a pretty certain test of late work. For, though conservative features like rime and end-stopt lines may be found even increasingly in a dramatist's later work, as rime

---

[1] Thorndike, *Hamlet*, etc., p. 136.

[2] It is impossible to go into the matter here, but there can be no doubt that the metre of *Rev. Tr.* is the more old-fashioned metre of Marston. Let me cite briefly the following, to be compared with the table below. Abundance of rime (*A. & M.*, 7.68%, *Ant. Rev.*, 10.01%, *Soph.*, 15%) ; the same riming methods, — triplets, couplets separated by one unrimed line, riming of separate speeches, riming of lines of very unequal length, genuine weak (schwach) rime. For these facts, so far as Marston is concerned, see Von Scholten, *Metrische, Untersuch. über M.*, Halle, 1886. For Marston's lack of l. and w. endings see Schipper, II, p. 333 f. The reading of a few pp. of *What You Will* or the *Fawn* will show how T. caught M.'s lilting movement.   [3] See below, p. 212.

in Marston and end-stopt lines in Fletcher, there is no case known (or probable) of the innovations, light and weak endings, giving way, at this time when they were just coming in,[1] to strong endings and end-stopt lines. That Tourneur himself, at least, was no such case, the verse of his elegies tends to show. The traditions and uses of elegiac and dramatic verse are, I know, generally so different that not much can be argued from the one to the other; yet, this, being, like the dramatic, five foot iambic in couplets, seems to offer no unfair comparison. At all events, *A Greife on the Death of Prince Henrie*, London, 1613, exhibits in the matter of run-on lines and light and weak endings exactly the same advance over the *Funerall Poeme upon the Death of Sir Francis Vere*, 1609,[2] as the *Ath. Tr.* (if it follows) does over the *Rev. Tr.* Now since the course of metrical development as thus shown in the case of Tourneur's elegies, is just that of the Elizabethan drama generally, it seems nowise likely that in the case of Tourneur's dramas it should have been reversed.[3]

There is good ground, then, to justify our natural presumption that the dates of registering represent approximately the dates of composition. But suppose, for one instant, Messrs. Collins and Fleay right, and the *Rev. Tr.* to follow the *Ath. Tr.* We then have, because of allusions to *Lear* and Marston's *Fawn*,[4] to crowd the only

[1] *I. e.*, 1603-7: *Macbeth* (1603-10), *Lear* (1606) have light end. but very few weak end.; *Ant. & Cleo.* (reg. May, 1608), 1. e. 2.53%, w. e. 1.00%; *Pericles* (pub. 1609), 1. e. 2.78%, w. e. 1.39%.—Ingram.

[2] The dates of publishing indicate very accurately the date of composition. For Sir Francis Vere died Aug. 28, 1608, and Prince Henry Nov. 6, 1612.

[3] Table showing the increase of run-on lines and of light and weak endings in both plays (1607-1611) and elegies (1609-1613); showing, further, the decrease in rime (couplets and triplets) in the plays:

	no. of ll.	run-on	1. & w. end.	triplets	couplets
Rev. Tr. . . .	460	105/20.2%	1 only	4	49/10.6%
Ath. Tr. . . .	402	152/37.7%	30/7.4 %	—	12/ 2.9%
Vere	617	257/41.6%	12/1.94%	—	—
Henrie	141	71/50.3%	7/4.96%	—	—

The number of lines taken in the plays is in both cases the whole first act. In the case of the elegies, the whole poem. In the matter of run-on lines I have tried to count according to a uniform principle, adopting the St. Petersburg rules with necessary modifications: for the light and weak endings I have adopted the St. Petersburg rules unreservedly. The elegies are in size so unequal that the comparison as to so rare phenomena as light and weak endings is hardly fair; yet observe that in the first 7 pages of *Vere* (a no. of ll. equal to all *Henrie*) there is but *one* such ending.

[4] The allusion to the *Fawn* (1606, cf. p. 107) lies in the character and name of Dondolo, the fool in the *Rev. Tr.* It is hardly to be doubted, since the name is not to be found elsewhere (so far as I can discover) in the Eliz. drama, and everywhere else (*v. supra*) Tour. borrows from Mars. The echoes in the *Ath. Tr.* from *Lear* (see above p. 112, note) are almost equally certain, for D'Amville, like Lear, is mad. Shak. seems about this time (1611) to have been making a name for his mad-scenes (cf. Web.'s unmistakable imitation of them, *supra* p. 142); moreover, the idea D'Amville expresses seems too original for Tour. *Lear* was first acted the last of 1606 (St. Stephen's day), before the king.

two plays Tourneur has left us into the year 1607 and before October 7th. Plays so different in spirit and ethics, in metre and rhythm! The *Rev. Tr.*, moreover (the later, according to our momentary supposition), containing no allusions to any of the greatest plays of Shakspere, just now appearing, or indeed to any of his,[1] and emulating the style of old-fashioned Marston, and the *Ath. Tr.*, the earlier, containing references to *Hamlet*, *Lear*, and *Othello* and emulating Shakspere's art. The improbability of our supposition — of Collins's and Fleay's theory — is too great.

APPENDIX II.

Influence of Fletcher on Chapman.

The influence of the later poets appears unmistakably in Chapman's *Alphonsus* and *Revenge for Honor*, not to mention *The Ball*, written in partnership with Shirley. The very lively series of turns to the dénouement of *Alphonsus* (last sc.) is not like the old Chapman, or the old Tragedy of Blood, but Fletcher; the trick of Abilqualit's telling Tarifa aside what he disavows so soon as the latter blurts it out before the others, is exactly copied from the trick of Melantius on Calianax in the *Maid's Tragedy* (*Rev. Hon.*, IV, 1, p. 437, and *M. Tr.*, IV, 2, pp. 19, 20), as well as the funny, yet not heartless, comment of the comic personage upon the death of the hero, at the end (Selinthus and Calianax). The dramatis personæ, with their stock types, show Fletcher still more: especially such as Selinthus, the "honest, merry court lord," p. 428; Osman, the captain, p. 441; Mura, a "rough lord," p. 416; — all being such types as Melantius in the *M. Tr.*, Leontius (" a brave, old, merry soldier ") in the *Hum. Lieut.*, Fabritio (" a merry soldier ") in *Captain*, Chilax (" an old, merry soldier ") in *Mad Lover*, and the " three honest court lords " in *Wife Month*. Space forbids expatiation, but there is no question that our "noble poet," as Dekker and Webster call him (see Chap. II), is here leaving his old, " Senecal " vein of *Bussy* and *Byron* for the new-fangled airs of the Jacobean court-poets.

Indeed, I think there is absolute proof that this *Rev. Hon.* is deeply indebted to one play of Beaumont and Fletcher's, *Cup. Rev.* Aside from the above points:

1. A young prince (Leucippus — Abilqualit) lyingly denies before his father, the king, what would stain the name of the sensual woman he loves (Bacha-Caropia), though prompted to acknowledge the truth by his rough soldier-friend (Ismenus Tarifa). *Cup. Rev.*, 387; *Rev. Hon.*, 437. (Sit. derived orig. from the *Arcadia*.)

2. The pretense urged by the prince's enemy (Timantus-Abrahen) that the prince had plotted against the king's life. *Cup. Rev.*, 398; *Rev. Hon.*, 438.

3. The popular uprising which frees the prince. *Cup. Rev.*, 400. In *Rev. Hon.*, two, — one to free him from punishment, and one later to set him on the throne.

4. The king, his father, dies suddenly; in *Rev. Hon.*, by poison, as is probably the case in *Cup. Rev.* (it is not clear).

5. The prince stabbed by craft, in either case at the very close of the play, by the sensual woman whose honor he had defended.

6. In his last words the prince, Hamlet-like, names his rough soldier-friend (Tarifa-Ismenus) heir and successor.

7. At the close, there is similar Machiavellian cursing on the part of the villain (Bacha-Abrahen) when in the throes of death.

---

[1] Mr. Collins adduces some parallels in his preface and notes, but none that indicate at all clearly direct contact with Shak.

8. The rough soldier-friend Tarifa is a striking imitation of Ismenus, especially in his attitude toward the conflicting interests of the woman (cf. Dion's ruthlessness toward Arethusa for Philaster's sake, III, 1, p. 36, and Melantius's toward his sister Evadne for Amintor's, and cf. Leontius in *Hum. Lieut.*, IV, 4, p. 254 b). Osman, also, another captain and friend, is like Ismenus in this respect, uses similar language of ladies in general and of this one in particular, *Rev. Hon.*, 441 b, *Cup. Rev.*, 402 b, etc.

9. The contrast and antagonism presented between the point of view of court-lords and warriors : Timantus and Ismenus, *Cup. Rev.*, 391, 396, Selinthus and the two — Osman and Gaselles, — *Rev. Hon.*, 416–17.

10. Fletcherian two-word feminine endings in some number, interesting and lively conduct of plot, a Beaumont and Fletcher levity even at tragic moments (Selinthus, *Rev. Hon.*, p. 447 ; *Cup. Rev.*, II, 5, etc.).[1]

---

[1] This fixes the date more narrowly. *Rev. Hon.* was first reg. Nov. 29, 1653 ; *Cup. Rev.* was acted Jan. 5, 1612 (first pub. 1615) ; so 1612 is the backward limit. This quashes the conjecture of Köppel — *der wohl noch jugendliche Dramatiker* (*Ch. M. F.*, p. 73), and p. 79 still stronger, *Mir machen Rev. Hon. und Alphonsus mit ihrer Häufung von Gräueln, ihrem Gemetzel einen entschieden jugendlichen Eindruck.* Another example of the fruits of that judging of an author's work separately, according to preconceived notions of the crudity of youthful work and without regard for the influences and traditions which have presided over the making of it. (Cf. App. I as to Collins on the *Ath. Tr.*) Perhaps, however, he is only following Mr. Fleay (II, 311), who attributes *Alphonsus* to George Peele, and finds a reference to it in the *Taming of the Shrew !* (Induction, l. 5 ; as if " Richard Conqueror ", which Fleay interprets as " Richard, Earl of Cornwall," were anything but a Partingtonism like " Arthur's bosom " : Richard Crookback — William the Conqueror.)

ERRATA AND ADDENDA.

Page 17, line 14, for *Edward* read *Everard*.

Page 18, line 6 from foot, for *Hæc* read *hæc*.

Page 19, "an abrupt cry." Prof. Kittredge is of the opinion that it was, in both cases, a cry taken from life. Cf. "a rescue!" In that event the support of the testimony of the *Ath. Tr.* to the date of *W. D.*, of which we have little need, falls away.

Pages 21, 22. Prof. Kittredge doubts whether Webster may not have drawn this Latin independently from Martial (XIII, 2 ; X, 2) and Virgil. The last — "Flectere si nequeo" — he assures me was a common saw. But as for the quotations from Martial, the use of them in prefaces, — which, in the case of Jonson's at least, Webster was now studying — and the similar use, word for word, of the "non norunt," at the very end of the preface, seem to me evidence not to be slighted. Moreover, in the case of the sixteen-word quotation from Martial, XIII, 2, Webster uses only what Dekker quotes, although the latter is not quoting the Epigram consecutively ; and in the case of the "non norunt" Webster uses the phrase quite as Dekker does, — of the immortality of great writing, not, as Martial himself, of the perpetuity of paper and ink. "Calumny may wound my name, but not kill my labours ; proude of which, my care is the lesse, because I can as proudly boast with the poet, that *Non norunt hæc monumenta mori.*" This seems decisive : Webster may also have had recourse to Martial himself, but it was Dekker that suggested him.

Page 24, line 1, for *or* read *and*.

Page 47, line 4, read *historical*.

Page 78, line 20, read *City*.

Page 94, line 2, delete *at the end*.

Page 94, line 16, delete comma after *Revenger's Tragedy*.

Page 96, line 3, for *is* read *are*.

Page 105, line 3, for *was* read *were*.

Page 105, line 17, put the comma after *as*.

Page 121, line 18, for *owls* read *owl's*.

Page 124, line 2, delete the comma.

INDEX OF PLAYS AND PLAYWRIGHTS.

THE index is not complete, is intended only to supplement the table of contents and the frequent captions of the text. Single plays of which the author is known are listed only when occurring isolatedly or when something important or definite — as the date — is at issue. In other cases see under the author. *n* stands for note.

DATE DUE